The Proper Lady and the Woman Writer

WOMEN IN CULTURE
AND
SOCIETY
A Series Edited by
Catharine R. Stimpson

THE
PROPER LADY
AND THE
WOMAN WRITER

Ideology as Style in
the Works of
Mary Wollstonecraft, Mary Shelley,
and Jane Austen

MARY POOVEY

THE UNIVERSITY OF CHICAGO PRESS

Chicago and London

The University of Chicago Press, Chicago 60637
The University of Chicago Press, Ltd., London

© 1984 by The University of Chicago
All rights reserved. Published 1984
Paperback edition 1985
Printed in the United States of America
94 93 92 91 90 89 88 87 86 85   6 5 4 3 2

Library of Congress Cataloging in Publication Data
Poovey, Mary.
    The proper lady and the woman writer.

    (Women in culture and society)
    Bibliography: p. 269
    Includes index.
    1. English literature—19th century—History and
criticism.   2. English literature—Women authors—
History and criticism.   3. Women in literature.
4. Sex role in literature.   5. Social ethics in literature.   6. Wollstonecraft, Mary, 1759-1797—Political and
social views.   7. Shelley, Mary Wollstonecraft, 1797-
1851—Political and social views.   8. Austen, Jane,
1775-1817—Political and social views.   I. Title.
II. Series.
PR469.W65P66   1984   823'.7'09352042   83-3664
ISBN 0-226-67527-0 (cloth)   0-226-67528-9 (paper)

Contents

Foreword

THE SERIES "WOMEN IN CULTURE AND SOCIETY" embodies a belief: the study of women entails the most spacious, yet subtle, reconstruction of our understanding of gender, culture, and society. This intellectual renewal must alter patterns of thought and institutions of knowledge. *The Proper Lady and The Woman Writer* represents such work at its most sophisticated, exacting, and persuasive.

Mary Poovey has selected three English women writers for study: Mary Wollstonecraft; Mary Shelley, her daughter; and Jane Austen, who was twenty-two years old in 1797, the year in which Mary Shelley was born, and in which Mary Wollstonecraft died in childbirth. She explores their social, psychological, and linguistic relations with that evolving, but stable, figure from bourgeois ideology—the Proper Lady. Demanding that women be decorous and domestic, the Proper Lady possessed sufficient cultural authority to suffocate a woman's desire to write, even desire itself. The woman who wanted to write could obey the Proper Lady and inhibit her creative and imaginative impulses, or, more aggressively, she could engage in strategies of resistance, from accommodation to subversion. What she could not do was to flee the Proper Lady's shadows.

Valuable though it would be, *The Proper Lady and the Woman Writer* is more than the narrative of such a process. For Poovey has the flexibility and amplitude to unite "feminist criticism . . . with a variety of critical methods." She aligns "those methods on a single conceptual axis" (p. xviii). Precise yet supple, she uses and fuses an analysis of feminine and masculine roles, that combination of sexual difference and stratification; psychoanalytic theories about sexual longing, sexual fears, and the cunning byways of sublimation; a sharp awareness of social class; and sensitivity to literary convention. She documents how much a historical period, in general, defines a writer's rhetoric, and how much, in particular, a period's theory of gender does genre.

Finally, Poovey finely recognizes the interplay of ideology, self, and style, to her "the lived experience of cultural values." Partly because

vii

of the figure of the Proper Lady, bourgeois men and women have had dissimilar roles in this drama. Illuminating them, Poovey enhances our sense of history and of ideology, that construct of history that, like Frankenstein's creature, becomes a historical force.

CATHARINE R. STIMPSON

Preface

IN 1676 THE REVEREND JOSEPH GLANVILL identified the origin of contemporary moral and political chaos by means of categories based explicitly on gender. "Now this is the present unhappy state of Man," he lamented:

> our *lower* powers are gotten *uppermost*. . . . The *Woman* in us still prosecutes a deceipt like *that* begun in the Garden; and we are wedded to an *Eve,* as fatal as the Mother of our Miseries. The *Deceiver* soon found this soft place in *Adam,* and Innocency it self did not secure him from *this* way of seduction: We now scarce see any thing but through our passions, that are wholly blind, and incapable.[1]

A century and a half later another writer, sensing another crisis, once more invoked gender in his response. "The hope of society is in woman!" Edwin Hood exulted. "The hope of the age is in woman! On her depends mainly the righting of wrongs, the correcting of sins, and the success of all missions."[2] From metaphorical agent of damnation to literal agent of salvation. How, in the course of the eighteenth century, did woman accomplish this dizzying ascent to the Victorian pedestal? Or, more plausibly, how was the transformation, which was really not an ascent, effected by the culture of which she was a part? And how did the transformation, with all its intermediate stages, affect the way real women conceived of themselves, wrote about themselves, expressed themselves? Indeed, given these two positions and these two roles, how could real women express themselves at all, since self-expression, as the Western emphasis on "self" implies, requires at least the assumption of autonomy and the power to participate in culture as an initiating subject? For if eighteenth-century English fiction is arguably gynocentric, eighteenth- and early nineteenth-century English society was emphatically not. Not only was the fundamental bourgeois personality male, as Margaret George has argued,[3] but the organizational principles of bourgeois society were unabashedly made by men for men. From the laws of strict entail, which awarded the entire patriarchal estate to the eldest son, to the Matrimonial Act of 1770, which prosecuted as witches "all women . . . that shall . . . impose upon, seduce, and betray into matrimony any of His Majesty's subjects by means of scent, paints, . . . false hair, . . . high-heeled shoes, or bolstered hips,"[4] women were legally "cyphers," prohibited from political and economic activity except through the agency of a legal "subject," man.

The late seventeenth-century "Mother of our Miseries" and the mid-nineteenth-century "hope of the age" are not really so far apart as they might initially seem. The latter can even be seen as the triumphant sublimation of the sexual anxiety that generated the former, with Woman in each case the object—as passive and as secondary as that term suggests—of the desiring, dreading subject, Man. Both stereotypes, in fact, rigidly confined real women to prescribed roles; as a daughter, a wife, a mother, a widow, as a virgin or a whore, every woman was defined by relationship—explicitly to a man, implicitly to sexuality itself. The initial purpose of this book is to trace the continuities of this idea of Woman within the evolution of images from Glanvill to Hood and to explore the function these images served in eighteenth- and early nineteenth-century society. The ideal of feminine behavior that emerged quite early in the secular literature of the eighteenth century assumed, by the end of the century, the status of female "nature," and it culminated, in the nineteenth century, in the paradigm of the Angel of the House. We will want to see the ways in which this "Angel," or "Proper Lady," accommodated the "blind, and incapable" passions Glanvill castigated, how much authority she might have had, and the paradoxes inherent in the epithet "proper."[5]

The primary purpose of this book, however, is to look beyond these images of woman to examine the shadow the Proper Lady casts across the careers of some of the women who became professional authors despite the strictures of propriety. The struggle each of these women waged to create a professional identity was in large measure defined by the social and psychological force of this idea of proper— or innate—femininity. Because gender roles are part of familial, political, social, and economic relationships, the terms in which femininity is publicly formulated dictates, in large measure, the way femaleness is subjectively experienced. As early as 1788 the French philosopher Condorcet made this remark on the personal dimension of such cultural "constraint": "A species of constraint put upon the strength and the mind of women by public opinion as to what custom deems acceptable, from childhood on, and especially at that point where genius begins to unfold, must harm [women's] progress in every sphere."[6] In the chapters that follow, I will examine some of the ways

[Handwritten margin notes: "legal + social male bias?"; "woman as object"; "role based on rel'ships w/ man"; "feminine ideal (again w/ relation to + from persp of men)"; "gender roles owned off social formation + female subjective experience"]

in which unfolding "genius" was restrained in the works of Mary
Wollstonecraft, Mary Shelley, and Jane Austen, but I will also point
out some of the ways in which genius made itself comfortable in the
presence of the Proper Lady. Many of the works I discuss betray their
author's unmistakable inhibition or hesitation before the cultural
definition of femininity, but others reveal considerable ability to
expand stereotypical images of the female self and even to turn those
images into sources of strength. For to say that women were legally
or economically marginal or even that they were characteristically
relegated to the object term of cultural grammar is not to say that
they were denied all forms of power. Indeed, even the fear that
echoes from Glanvill's reference to Eve alludes to a power that is both
felt and feared. But perhaps more powerful strategies for living and
for art were derived from what Mary Wollstonecraft called the "negative virtues" of "patience, docility, good-humour, and flexibility." As
we will see, such strategies of indirection and accommodation could
enable women to make their presence felt in bourgeois society, and
in some cases they even facilitated the creation of an expressive self
within the behavior of the self-effacing Proper Lady.

The evidence I have used in chapter 1 to delineate the Proper Lady
comes primarily from conduct books, popular magazines, novels, and
women's memoirs or diaries. Although I have consulted conduct
material written by clerics, such as James Fordyce, I have not relied
heavily on religious material as such because even nominally devout
women like Hester Thrale insisted that clergymen tended to espouse
an unapproachable ideal of virtue. Thrale blames even the popular
William Law, whom she calls "delicate," for "failing to define Luxury
or Temperance" in relevant terms and thus for leaving his readers
"uninform'd whether any thing but Acorns & Water are allowable to
people of strict Virtue."[7] In the absence of convents in eighteenth-
century England, Law's notion that the "higher degrees of perfection" must be sought "in a virgin state of life"[8] was hardly practical,
and his injunctions against finery in dress and the acquisition of
feminine "accomplishments" were unlikely to help any young girl (or
her parents) compete in what had become a highly competitive marriage market. Most of the conduct books I refer to advocate both
religious principles and practice, and some even copiously cite Scripture for authority; but, in general, conduct books present a popularized, and sometimes frankly secularized, version of the ideas more
rigorously set out in sermons. Eighteenth-century conduct books and
periodicals tend, as we will see, not to emphasize original sin or to
insist on strict denial; instead, moralists sought to adjust and adopt
Christian ideals to the exigencies of their increasingly competitive
society. The ideals disseminated by conduct books and periodicals

also cut across both denominational lines and the infinitesimal strata
of the "middling classes" and helped, I think, make women of different
beliefs and slightly different social positions more nearly of one faith
and one class than their fathers or brothers were.

Except for Richardson's *Clarissa,* which Dr. Johnson described as a
veritable conduct book, an enduring reference "for the busy, the
aged, and the studious,"[9] I have also avoided relying heavily on men's
literary portraits of women. Although I certainly agree with Sandra
M. Gilbert and Susan Gubar that men's dramatizations of women
provided a compelling and frequently distorting mirror in which
women sought their own images, I am not persuaded that these
masculine stereotypes of female nature were always interpreted in
the same way by women or that women writers responded primarily
to literary images of females rather than to the implicit value system
that governed not just aesthetic self-expression but their every social
act.[10] Particularly in chapters 3, 4, and 6, I do discuss some of the
influences literary conventions had on these writers' works, but I am
really more concerned with the tendency of women authors to use
(or succumb to) expectations generated by such genres as sentimental
novels, lyric poetry, or romances than with their responses to the
female characters depicted in them. Implicit in my argument is the
assumption that these genres, the expectations they capitalized on,
and the literary stereotypes they employed were all informed by
priorities and preconceptions in bourgeois ideology itself. Men's literary presentations of women certainly provide particularly accessible
and well-defined versions of some of these cultural preconceptions;
but, as the anonymous author of *The Ladies Library* suggests, precisely
because these images were more accessible, they were easier to reject
than the more subtle, and more coercive, norms that lay behind
them. This woman scorns the female characters depicted by Otway,
Milton, and Dryden because, she says, such authors charge that
women "are made up of Affectation, Coquettry, Falshood, Disguise,
Treachery, Wantonness and Perfidiousness." But perhaps, she continues, "it is the Business of ingenious debauch'd Men, who regard us
only as such, to give us those Ideas of our selves, that we may become
their more easie Prey." Instead of these images, this woman turns to
"more solid Authors" for guides; she will model herself, she says,
after those who provide ideals, rather than acknowledge herself con-
victed by those who levy "scandalous Intimations against my very
Nature."[11]

Even though the tone and implicit assumptions of conduct material
change during the period covered in chapter 1, the general goal of
all conduct material was to provide such emulatable models as this
writer desired—models for acceptable behavior, legitimate values,

and even permissible thoughts. Thus the first connection between this conduct material and the individual texts examined in the next six chapters of this book is an implicitly causal link between the values and ideals society allotted to women and three women's imaginative—or symbolic—responses to this education. But conduct books and periodicals tell us more than what young girls growing up in this society might have been likely to read or hear about what they were or ought to be. For, as examples of the public discourse of middle-class society, these works themselves reproduce the system of values—the ideology—of this society. And it is in this sense that conduct material has its second, and more important, connection to the narratives of Wollstonecraft, Shelley, and Austen. These three writers not only explicitly discuss propriety in their works; implicitly, in both their works and their life choices, they also replicate the tensions, paradoxes, and contradictions that we see in the conduct material. Two of my basic assumptions in this book are, first, that all social (and even psychological) gestures are symbolic responses to "real" experiences and, second, that every individual develops, in the course of his or her life, a relatively unified, identifiable style of social, psychological, and conceptual behavior.[12] My third basic assumption is that social experiences—and therefore the responses symbolized as style—are informed at every level by ideology. Therefore, "style," understood in the largest sense of this term, represents ideology as it has been internalized and articulated by an individual. These assumptions have enabled me to understand some of the complex ways that ideology influences an individual's life—how, for example, values are internalized so as to delimit the way in which one conceptualizes "happiness," "success," or "femininity," or how one's solutions to aesthetic problems may be subtly guided by the cultural weight given to such modes of interaction as confrontation or imitation. The phrase "ideology as style" suggests the lived experience of cultural values, and it reminds us that all imaginative activity is part of that experience. Thus, in the chapters that follow, I treat all of the works I interpret as narratives that, simply by virtue of their position within society and history, necessarily participate in the representation and evolution of ideology. For this reason, all of these texts—whether conduct books, travelogues, political tracts, or novels—help to "explain" each other. For this reason, too, my readings of individual narratives often open onto more general interpretations of the cultural ideology that informs them.

It is important to keep in mind two facts about my use of the word "ideology." The first is that I do not use the term simply to mean "false consciousness." Although the prevailing system of values at any given historical moment inevitably serves to protect the interests of a powerful class or social group, it does not necessarily follow that simply identifying the social function of ideology will enable one to escape or even to challenge it. Ideology, as I use the term, governs not just political and economic relations but social relations and even psychological stresses as well.[13] Ideology, in other words, is virtually inescapable; for, simply by living together, men and women establish priorities among their needs and desires and generate explanations that ratify these priorities by making them seem "natural." In this respect, despite its inevitable kinship with power, ideology *enables* ideas and actions; it *delimits* responses, not just in the sense of establishing boundaries but in terms of defining territories.

The second critical feature of my use of this concept is that ideology is never static. For the purposes of analysis it has often been necessary for me to describe this "system" or "set" of values as if it were a rigid "structure" or "configuration." But in actual history, dramatic and imperceptible changes at every level of society mean that ideology is always developing. As ideology evolves, its internal dynamics may change, its implications for a particular group may alter, or its inherent tensions may be exposed in what is generally perceived as a crisis of values. Indeed, such critical moments offer an especially illuminating perspective on the internal dynamics of ideology; for when history brings the antagonistic positions within ideology into prominence, individual texts articulate the contradictions between these polarities more clearly, either unself-consciously or in explicit challenges to society's values.

By its very nature, ideology always contains contradictions, precisely because it "explains" or "naturalizes" the discrepancies that inevitably characterize lived experience. At the level of everyday life, these contradictions may exist between the placating promises formulated by a ruling group and the actual material rewards the majority has access to. But this political example is only an extreme version of a more general principle. For contradictions also exist between the real (and often obscure) configurations of power and the ways in which individuals subjectively experience and explain their own social position; or, more generally still, contradictions exist between the ideal and eternal life the imagination projects and the diminished reality that the earth's limited resources and human mortality allow. The contradictions that appear in literary texts both reproduce these tensions and represent their authors' attempts to resolve them imaginatively.[14] In any imaginative work, these contradictions may appear at the level of content or form; they may emerge in the discrepancy between an author's explicit aesthetic program and the emotional affect the text generates, or they may show up simply as significant inconsistencies within an individual character or convention. We should remember that, just as lived experience is delimited by ideology, so too is artistic creation. Thus, on the one hand, even successful symbolic resolutions do not by themselves materially affect the social inconsistencies that made such resolutions necessary in the first place. On the other hand, imaginative responses to social experience *can* actively contribute to the evolution of ideology. And, in a sense particularly relevant to this book, the mere representation of ideology (whether conscious or not) can sometimes expose its implicit contradictions and thus lay the groundwork for outrage and eventual change. In this regard, the very act of a woman writing during a period in which self-assertion was considered "unladylike" exposes the contradictions inherent in propriety: just as the inhibitions visible in her writing constitute a record of her historical oppression, so the work itself proclaims her momentary, possibly unconscious, but effective, defiance.[15]

The period during which Mary Wollstonecraft, Mary Shelley, and Jane Austen wrote constitutes just such a critical phase in the history of bourgeois ideology and thus provides a particularly revealing perspective upon the way in which lived and imaginative experiences are informed by ideological contradictions. This was the period in which the French Revolution represented a dramatic symbol of social and economic changes that seemed to threaten England as well. As such, it provoked both explicit challenges to the political inequality inherent in English patriarchal society and adamant defenses of the whole system. And once Mary Wollstonecraft and others made the issue of sexual equality a part of this political and ethical debate, other women were encouraged to a new self-consciousness about (and, more often than not, a more conscious defense of) the social hierarchy that had seemed for so long a part of nature itself. But the French Revolution was only the most dramatic challenge to traditional English society and its ideology. The real antagonists to this way of life were already invisibly at work in the form of economic developments and within the very ideology of capitalist individualism. As a consequence of these forces, the social order based on patronage gradually gave way, between the 1790s and the 1830s, to the practices and pressures of individualism. As competition and confrontation replaced the old paternalistic alliances of responsibilities and dependences, women in particular found their position becoming increasingly anomalous; for in some very practical ways women had always been protected by the values and allegiances of paternalism, and now, as exemplars of paternalistic virtues, they were being asked to preserve the remnants of the old society within the private sphere of the home. In doing this, however, early nineteenth-century women epitomized within their own "virtues" one of the fundamental contradictions of bourgeois ideology. For both their idealized helplessness and the domestic life they kept separate from the marketplace were increasingly at odds with the competitive spirit that was rapidly transforming every other sector of English society.

I have chosen to focus on these three writers because each of them represents a significant, and significantly different, response to this period of social and ideological turmoil. Mary Wollstonecraft's contribution is perhaps most obvious in this regard, for in her *Vindication of the Rights of Woman* she identified many of the ideological contradictions responsible for women's political, social, and psychological dependence. But from her career taken as a whole we see that even achieving such a level of insight did not necessarily make ideology transparent to Wollstonecraft or advance her, to use her own words, "before the improvement of the age." For as long as an individual's self-definition—the terms in which he or she conceptualizes and evaluates behavior—is derived primarily from the values implicit in the culture he or she wishes to change, the solutions the imagination generates will be governed, on some level, by these values. Thus we discover in Wollstonecraft's work what pieces of ideological baggage even this self-consciously political woman simply could not leave behind.

Mary Shelley's artistic career represents virtually the opposite response to an even more contradictory version of this ideological configuration. In a very real sense, Wollstonecraft, who died giving birth to her daughter, is more important as one facet of Mary Shelley's "situation" than as her biological mother. For Wollstonecraft's example of courage and independence, which was reiterated and rendered even more immediate by Percy Shelley, symbolized one compelling model of behavior for the young Mary Godwin. But this model was always at odds with the ideal of feminine propriety that was endorsed at nearly every level of early nineteenth-century society and that was reinforced, in Mary Shelley's case, by her father's conservative principles. The course of Mary Shelley's career traces the confrontation of these two ideological extremes; and the stages by which she dissociates herself from the more radical position provide an example of the kinds of psychological and imaginative accommodations that eventually bolstered the Victorian ideal of woman as the Angel of a man's house. But the fact that even Shelley's most conservative novels retain traces of the aggression that distinguishes *Frankenstein* suggests that even the most orthodox propriety could not wholly silence female desire. Indeed, as we will see in our examination of Shelley's *Falkner,* propriety effectively facilitated the articulation of female desire, even though it disguised impermissible emotions by displacing them and making their expression indirect.

To most readers, Jane Austen will seem the anomalous figure in
this trio, for her life was not so flamboyant as those of Wollstonecraft
and Shelley, her concerns were not so explicitly political or melodramatic, and her six novels—according to most readers at least—are
not so deeply riven by interesting (but debilitating) contradictions. But
placing Jane Austen in this company does two things. In the first
place, it reminds us that Austen's novels are also symbolic responses
to the ideological situation to which the other two writers more
obviously reacted, and in doing this it enables us to see Austen's
famous decorum and reserve as facets of this woman's complex
relationship to the values of her society. In the second place, it allows
us to see how some of the aesthetic dilemmas that inhibited Wollstonecraft and Shelley in such different ways were "solved" by a
contemporary woman writer. Jane Austen's position within the ideology of propriety effectively places her "between" Wollstonecraft and
Shelley, for she was neither as outspokenly critical as the first nor as
ostentatiously self-effacing as the second. This order is also consistent
with chronology; however, I have chosen to discuss Jane Austen last,
for if her attitude toward propriety initially situates her "between"
Wollstonecraft and Shelley, her aesthetic solutions to the dilemmas
shared by all three effectively take her work "beyond" Mary Shelley's
last novels. Through her irony and skillful manipulation of point of
view, Jane Austen developed artistic strategies that "resolved"—at
least at the level of art—some of the most debilitating ideological
contradictions of this period of chaotic change.

For each of these writers, I have chosen to discuss only works that
constitute significant stages in their personal and literary development. Thus I have not dealt extensively with either of Wollstonecraft's first two works because she self-consciously gave birth to her
"professional" persona only when she moved to London to write for
Joseph Johnson. I have omitted analyses of several of Shelley's minor
novels, her short stories, and her late nonfiction because these works,
for the most part, simply elaborate phases of her career already (and
more complexly) set out in other works. Finally, I have not interpreted at any length all of Austen's juvenilia or *Northanger Abbey,
Emma, The Watsons,* or *Sanditon* because despite interesting variations,
the aesthetic solutions she achieved in her other novels adequately
represent her artistic accomplishment.

One other feature of this book needs to be explained. In general
my design in each literary interpretation has been to move from
contradictions evident in the text to the ideological tensions behind
or implicit in them, but within this general design the exact methodologies I use vary slightly from author to author. This variation is in
part dictated by the different kinds of evidence available for each

author. Numerous letters have preserved Mary Wollstonecraft's responses to her social situation, and Mary Shelley's journal and letters provide a private supplement to the public record of her life, but the calculated editing Cassandra Austen performed on her sister's personal papers has left us with only a sampling of letters—a miscellany that may be more misleading than otherwise. On the other hand, Jane Austen produced six novels that are still widely read and available, but Mary Shelley wrote only one work that is still frequently reprinted. Mary Wollstonecraft's works are beginning to find a new audience, but even her apologists often suggest that this has as much to do with her political insights as with the aesthetic quality of her writing. In keeping with such facts of literary history, I have been able to incorporate into my analyses more of the private writings of Wollstonecraft and Shelley and even the facts of their lives than I have been able to do with Austen.

This discrepancy is regrettable, but it is not, I think, ruinous to the book as a whole; for the range of methodologies I use in this book has another implicit rationale as well. Essentially, I want to show how feminist criticism not only makes itself at home with a variety of critical methods but also aligns those methods on a single conceptual axis. As chapters 3 and 7 most clearly demonstrate, rhetorical analysis, when placed in the context of a woman's social situation, leads naturally to ideological analysis; and, as my chapters on Mary Shelley suggest, when propriety is understood as fulfilling or frustrating psychological needs as well as social requirements, then psychoanalytic categories can be applied to help illuminate the dynamics of an individual imaginative work or even an entire career. If sufficient evidence (and space) were available, each of the interpretive paradigms I use here could be applied to each of the works; the result would be a series of mutually supportive explanations of each text, which, taken together, would help define the author's "situation" as well as the individual text. Feminist criticism implicitly argues for such an expansion of interpretive perspectives; for in taking as one of its primary assumptions the fact that a woman's sexuality materially affects her economic, political, cultural, psychological, and imaginative position within society, feminism argues for recognizing the connections among all the spheres of an individual's behavior.

In her essay "Women and Fiction," Virginia Woolf argues for a similar "elasticity" in our analyses of women writers. "In dealing with women as writers," Woolf says, "as much elasticity as possible is desirable; it is necessary to leave oneself room to deal with other things besides their work, so much has that work been influenced by conditions that have nothing whatever to do with art."[16] I would amend Woolf's statement only by generalizing it: men and women

alike are inevitably "influenced by conditions that have nothing whatever to do with art." Or, perhaps better still, I would say that even
conditions that seem to have "nothing whatever to do with art"
always do have everything to do with it, even though their precise
"influence" may be difficult to identify and even though every facet
of art is, as we all know, complexly and apparently confoundingly
overdetermined. To that I would add that only by expanding our
interpretive perspectives, only by seeing imaginative creation in relation to social and psychological behavior and conditions, will we
begin to grasp the complex relationship between the ways we are
socially and psychologically constituted, between what we are taught
to be and what we feel we are, between what we do and what we
dream.

influence of ideology is inevitable

Acknowledgments

In the course of writing this book I have come to appreciate more deeply the meaning of these twin truisms: that no idea springs fully formed from a single mind and that no achievement is purely the product of individual will, effort, or desire. The debts I have incurred in the past few years are numerous; my gratitude is even greater.

For the financial support that enabled me to research and complete this project, I would like to thank the National Endowment for the Humanities, Swarthmore College, and Yale University. For reading and advising me on various parts of the manuscript, I am grateful to Philip Weinstein, Lee Devin, Leo Damrosch, Martin Price, Ronald Paulson, and the members of Constantia. I would like to thank Sarah Lawrence for helping me to prepare the manuscript. I also owe thanks to Margaret Homans, with whom I am always in dialogue and from whom I always learn. And finally, I would like to express a measure of my appreciation and affection for my friend Pat Spacks and my husband Charles Russell, both of whom have constantly encouraged me, challenged me, and helped keep this book alive.

Though they have since been heavily revised, several chapters of this book have appeared in earlier publications. Part of chapter 3 was published as "Mary Wollstonecraft: The Gender of Genres in Late Eighteenth-Century England" in the Winter 1982 issue of the journal *Novel: A Forum on Fiction*. Chapter 4 appeared as "My Hideous Progeny: Mary Shelley and the Feminization of Romanticism" in the *Proceedings of the Modern Language Association*, vol. 95 (1980), pp. 332–47. One section of chapter 5 appeared as "Fathers and Daughters: The Trauma of Growing Up Female" in *Men by Women*, edited by Janet Todd (New York: Holmes & Meier, 1981), pp. 39–58 (*Men by Women* is vol. 2 [n.s.] in the journal series *Women and Literature*, published by Holmes & Meier). Finally, part of chapter 7 appeared as "*Persuasion* and the Promises of Love" in *The Representation of Women in Fiction:*

Selected Papers from the English Institute, edited by Carolyn G. Heilbrun and Margaret R. Higonnet (Baltimore: John Hopkins University Press, 1983), pp. 152–79. All of this material is used here by permission of the publishers.

The Proper Lady and the Woman Writer

1

The Proper Lady

BY THE END of the eighteenth century the Proper Lady was a familiar household companion. Her presence was comforting and salutary, for her desires bent gracefully to her master's will. Such was the nature of things, Thomas Gisborne confidently assumed.

> Providence, designing from the beginning that the manner of life to be adopted by women should in many respects ultimately depend, not so much on their own deliberate choice, as on the determination, or at least on the interest and convenience, of the parent, of the husband, or of some other near connection; has implanted in them a remarkable tendency to conform to the wishes and example of those for whom they feel a warmth of regard, and even of all those with whom they are in familiar habits of intercourse.[1]

A century earlier a Dorsetshire clergyman had described a similar image of feminine propriety, but he seems to have felt less certain that his female listeners would automatically exhibit a "remarkable tendency to conform," for the "should" in his statement hints at depths of female desire that Gisborne denies. Speaking of the bride who presumably stands before him, this clergyman says, "God had also fully indicated her function when he deliberately created her for the Profit and Comfort of man. A good wife should be like a Mirrour which hath no image of its own, but receives its stamp from the face that looks into it." A woman must not only obey her husband, he continued, but must bring "unto him the very Desires of the Heart to be regulated by him so far, that it should not be lawful for her to will or desire what she liked, but only what her husband should approve and allow."[2]

This vision of tractable female desire was not *simply* a masculine fantasy. In the last decade of the seventeenth century an early champion of women formulated a similar portrait of feminine propriety. Mary Astell proposed her female seminary in part to shelter heiresses "till a convenient Match be offer'd by her Friends. . . . Modesty requiring that a Woman should not love before Marriage, but only make choice of one whom she can love hereafter; She who has none but innocent affections, being easily able to fix them where Duty requires."[3] Presumably, "innocent affections" are nonassertive affections; innocent desire responds rather than initiates. Like Gisborne, Astell describes women as having only a mediate relation to sexual desire. Desire, in effect, centers on and returns to a woman; it does not originate in her emotions, her imagination, or her body. Yet, like her Dorsetshire contemporary, Astell suggests that there *are* reservoirs of female passions restrained by propriety if not by natural law: a woman must, after all, be governed by modesty, for she does have the capacity to "love hereafter."

Both Astell and the Dorsetshire clergyman imply that women must internalize what Gisborne, a century later, assumes to be a female characteristic: a "remarkable tendency" to defer desire. But all three of these writers accept the fact that self-effacement, if not natural, is at least proper for women, and all three therefore think that women's behavior must significantly differ from that of men, who express their own wishes, make their own choices, and imprint their images on the receptive glass. Because this image of woman and the double standard to which it is related are so deeply interwoven into the fabric of eighteenth and nineteenth-century culture, I think it is important to examine not only the complexities of the paradigm but also its social function. Because she was a prominent figure in the apparently seamless web of culture, the Proper Lady was difficult for contemporaries to challenge, and at times it is difficult even for us to distinguish her from the real women who lived in her shadow. But by looking at the anxieties this image initially assuaged and the function it continued to serve, we can begin to understand both why the ideal of feminine propriety had such monolithic power and how it affected the middle-class girls who grew into women during these decades.

One of the most popular seventeenth-century contributions to the "woman question" provides a place to begin. In his *Araignment of Lewde, Idle, Froward, and vnconstant women* (1617), the misogynous Joseph Swetnam loosed this tirade:

> Eagles eate no men till they are dead but women deuour them aliue, for a woman will pick thy pocket & empty thy purse, laugh in thy face and cutt thy throat, they are vngratefull, periured, full of fraud, flouting and decit, vnconstant, waspish, toyish, light, sullen, proude, discurteous, and cruell.[4]

Swetnam suggests at least two reasons for fearing women with active, assertive desires. Cursed with a leering, apparently insatiable appetite, women are unabashedly promiscuous—"vnconstant . . . discurteous, and cruell"—and, what is more, they lust after the money that is the very lifeblood of man; they "deuour" him by emptying his

purse and yielding no commensurate return. The first of these fears
bears a lineage at least as old as the composition of the Book of
Genesis, although Saint Paul's analogy between woman and the flesh
is no doubt the pertinent scriptural authority here. At root, the
persistent fear of female sexuality may well be an incarnation of
men's more general recognition of the limitations of the human
condition. As Jane Austen has Anne Elliot remark, men have had the
advantage of telling the story; the result is that women have typically
been cast as the inscrutable Other, as agents of the incapacities that
beset us all. Because sexual desire momentarily undermines self-
control, women are voracious; because the future is uncertain, they
are inconstant; because life is full of contradictions, women are irra-
tional; because mortality perpetually mocks the will, women are
vampires, heralds of death and decay. Swetnam's second fear has
equally profound psychological and material facets, both of which
were given a special edge during the seventeenth and eighteenth
centuries. For with the gradual intensification of capitalism and the
transformation of the basic middle-class economic unit from the cooperative household to the individual competitive man, woman seemed
to pose a threat to a man's upward mobility or even to the preservation of his current position. As consumers rather than contributors
to the household economy, women might almost literally "deuour"
a man's wealth.

During this period, then, it is no surprise that these two anxieties
dovetailed in the worry that, as a "flouting" and "vnconstant" partner, a woman's craven appetite could jeopardize the hold on immortality her husband had through his land. Especially for Protestant
members of the rising middle classes, property was the visible sign
of a man's inner worth. And, for everyone, property was the source
of present income, the measure of social prestige, the basis of political
power, and the legacy that carried a man's name beyond his grave.
As Harold Perkin has pointed out, the importance of property during
this period superseded its cash yield or value.

> The social prestige and power over one's neighbours which were annexed to
> property . . . added prizes of a psychologically more satisfying kind to those
> of mere acquisition. . . . The pursuit of wealth *was* the pursuit of social status,
> not merely for oneself but for one's family.[5]

Because of the complex economic and psychological roles of property, a woman could, by one act of infidelity, imperil both a man's
present security and his dynastic ambitions.[6] So profound were such
anxieties that philosophers like Samuel Johnson and Jean-Jacques
Rousseau depicted the threat women represented as a challenge to
the social order itself. "Consider," Johnson advised Boswell, "of what

importance to society the chastity of women is. Upon that all the property in the world depends. We hang a thief for stealing a sheep; but the unchastity of a woman transfers sheep, and farm and all, from the right owner."[7] Rousseau is even more severe:

> No doubt every breach of faith is wrong, and every faithless husband . . . is cruel and unjust; but the faithless wife is worse; . . . when she gives her husband children who are not his own, she is false both to him and them, her crime is not infidelity but treason. . . . Can any position be more wretched than that of the unhappy father who, when he clasps his child to his breast, is haunted by the suspicion that this is the child of another, the badge of his own dishonour, a thief who is robbing his own children of their inheritance. Under such circumstances the family is little more than a group of secret enemies, armed against each other by a guilty woman.[8]

Throughout this period, then, the dual function the ideal of feminine propriety served was, implicitly if not explicitly, to harness the appetites men feared and associated with women to their own more reliable masculine wills and then, by extension, to protect the property upon which the destiny of both individuals and an entire society depended. The suspicion that women were more profligate than men never wholly disappears during this period, nor does the desire that women continue to accept—and even arouse—men's sexual appetites. But in the interest of social and personal security, it was crucial that women act upon, and even experience, their own sexuality only in mediate terms. The fact that references to the dual function I have identified reappear throughout this period but are increasingly subordinated to other, more idealizing descriptions of women's nature and role attests to the success with which compensations for these anxieties and interests were simply assimilated into definitions of "nature." By the end of the eighteenth century, in fact, "female" and "feminine" were understood by virtually all men and women to be synonomous. Before I turn to an examination of the image of propriety itself, it is important to trace some of the factors that helped to naturalize femininity and, in doing so, helped to formulate the stereotype with which most women compared or identified themselves.

Institutions of Social Control:
Religion, Middle-Class Morality, and Property
Arrangements

In the seventeenth and eighteenth centuries the legal status of women remained as it had been defined under Roman law. The law of "coverture" decreed that "the very being or legal existence of the woman is suspended during the marriage, or at least is incorporated and consolidated into that of the husband: under whose wing, protection and cover, she performs everything."[9] In Tudor England women had managed to bend the rigidity of this law through their economic activity in domestic industry and even, as widows, in retail trade,[10] but under the Stuarts women apparently increasingly conformed to the more narrowly defined model of a dutiful wife, "incorporated and consolidated" into their husbands' interests, emotionally and economically as well as legally. Among the many factors that helped to delimit women's situation in this way, two in particular solicit our attention. The first is the ascendance of Puritan and then Evangelical principles during these centuries; the second is the rise to prominence of the middle classes. Each of these developments is important because of the complex way it tended to formulate female nature in a way that would accommodate female energy.

The Puritans' contribution to the definition of woman's situation is particularly significant precisely because of its complexity. On the one hand, Puritan clergymen helped promote their goal of spiritual and social reformation by emphasizing the importance of the family as a unit of religious and social discipline. By stressing the benefits of family life and the priesthood of all believers, Puritans gave women an importance Protestantism did not and even introduced the possibility of complete religious equality for the sexes.[11] Moreover, the Puritans' celebration of family life led them to deplore adultery by either party as a threat to the conjugal bond. On the other hand, because the Puritans rigidly emphasized the patriarchal family organization ratified by Scripture, their doctrines tended, in practice, to restrict women's activity to narrowly defined domestic duties. More important, as Keith Thomas and Christopher Hill have argued, the Puritan reign did not challenge the connection between women's chastity and men's property and thus did not fundamentally alter the function played by propriety. "Thy virginity is not all thine to dispose of," Daniel Rogers warned a young woman: "in part it's thy parents', father hath a stroke in it, mother another, and kindred a third." "Men have a property in their wives and daughters," Gilbert Burnet flatly asserted.[12] In effect, then, Puritan theology helped institutionalize the contradictions inherent in women's situation: by emphasizing the spiritual importance of the family unit, Puritanism simultaneously reinforced the injunctions against the free expression of female desires *and* provided women a role that seemed constructive rather than destructive. The fact that women did not really acquire the equality that Puritan doctrines seemed logically to promise appeared to most women insignificant beside the acquisition of their new spiritual and socially meaningful role. This was true in part because Puritan theology helped to institutionalize these contradictions by making competition legitimate for women, thus increasing their investment in the dominant capitalist value system. According to Puritan doctrine, women could emulate men's economic competition in "feminine," nonmaterialistic terms. For example, Mary Astell could promise her readers that the assiduous practice of propriety "wou'd help you to surpass the Men as much in Vertue and Ingenuity, as you do in Beauty, that you may not only be as lovely, but as wise as Angels."[13]

The influence of the Puritans' principles outlived their brief political reign. One of their legacies, the elevated and spiritually significant position of the home, reinforced women's social importance when separation between the home and the workplace became the middle-class rule rather than the exception. So completely was their spiritual office fused with their superintendence of family integrity that, by the early decades of the eighteenth century, women could even take pride in sacrificing their sexual desires for this "higher" cause. The anonymous author of *The Ladies Library,* for example, acknowledged that "the *Preservation* of Families from any *Mixture*" constituted "the Root and the Excuse" for a double standard, but she went on to argue that "this *Injustice*" had ample compensation: "if in this the *Sex* lies under any *Disadvantage,* it is more than recompensed by having the *Honour* of *Families* in their keeping."[14] By the second half of the eighteenth century, women, like men, were apt to interpret the double standard not as a sign of men's distrust but as proof of their own moral superiority. "Every appearance of vice in a woman is sometimes (something?) more disgusting than in a man," Clara Reeve cheerfully argued; "which I think is a presumption that woman was intended to be a more perfect creature than man."[15]

The idealization of female nature that is evident in Reeve's statement was further facilitated by the rapid spread of Evangelicalism after 1740, for the Evangelicals not only generalized to society as a whole the virtues the Puritans had associated with the domestic sphere; they also provided women with practical opportunities for exercising their influence outside their own homes. The reforming zeal of the Evangelical sects focused on both spiritual reformation and social improvement. The first goal was furthered by the tendency of some sects to channel the disruptive energies of the laboring classes into religious "enthusiasm"—to make religion itself "a thing of sensation and passion," as Robert Southey phrased it.[16] It was also furthered by hard work and seriousness, for all of the Evangelical sects (and they appealed to the middle as well as the lower classes) regarded these as the chief means of earning—and proving—spiritual salvation. In fact, the promulgation of such virtues as self-discipline, temperance, and cleanliness was one of the primary means of achieving the second Evangelical goal. And, because charitable work simply extended women's domestic activities into the neighborhood surrounding the home, this reform movement was one in which women could legitimately participate. Ministering to the poor, disseminating religious pamphlets, and teaching morality and decency in Sunday schools and religious associations were essentially selfless activities, requiring no "masculine" skills and devoted to celebrating the Holy Spirit rather than his humble agent. Indeed, in one sense women might be considered the primary beneficiaries of the reform movement, for such work gave both married and unmarried women a constructive vehicle for their talents and, in return, a heightened sense of their ability and self-worth. "Formerly there seemed to be nothing useful in which they could naturally be busy," Hannah More said of her hard-working middle-class peers, "but now they may always find an object in attending the poor."[17]

Through the activities of such reformers as Hannah More and William Wilberforce, the religious ideals of the Evangelicals rapidly gained influence during the last decades of the century. This was true at least partly because these ideals helped reinforce the social hierarchy, which was threatened by the increasingly restive lower classes.[18] In 1795, in the midst of rampant inflation brought on by the war with France, Parliament voted *not* to fix minimum wages to alleviate the distress of the poor; after this, it became clear that the old paternalistic system of reciprocal duties and responsibilities was giving way to a laissez-faire economy and the creation of an antagonistic class society.[19] Only the principles of Christian morality given to the lower classes by the Evangelicals seemed capable of containing the potential disruptiveness of this transformation. If the poor embraced Evangelicalism largely to gain spiritual salvation, their economic and political governors adopted Evangelical practices (if not always their doctrines) at least partly as a means of controlling labor and improving the conditions and the productivity of their workers. As an astute *Blackwood's* commentator observed in 1830, morality had the power to enforce even blatant inequality:

> The first great distinction which so early takes place, into the holders of property and those who are born to labour, must appear from the beginning to establish a natural warfare between the rights of one part of the community and the cravings of another. Yet moral institution is found sufficiently powerful, while it has power, to keep down this hostility, and to maintain the order of society; but take morality away, and there is no human power of avail to guard against the boundless depredation that is let loose upon it.[20]

As we will see, during the last decade of the eighteenth century women were increasingly assigned a central role in maintaining this "moral institution." Their connection with the traditional hierarchy and values of patriarchal society thus remained strong even as they extended their influence beyond their "proper sphere," the nuclear family.

IN ADDITION TO, and as a part of, these religious and social develop-ments, the eighteenth century witnessed the political and economic triumph of the English middle classes. This development simulta-neously enhanced women's position and gave female nature a more strict—if idealized—definition. The duties a woman fulfilled in the home directly supported capitalist values. For example, the sympa-thetic, nonjudgmental affection the ideal wife offered her husband helped offset the frustrations and strains a man suffered in his work-place and thus both contributed to the rewards associated with work and helped a man renew his energies for another day's labors. As a discussion of "Female Character" in 1828 points out, in a marketplace economy, characterized by division of labor, women perform a serv-ice no one else provides:

> The world is dead to sympathy. Man is too much occupied in the pursuit of wealth or fame, to lend a willing ear, or a consoling voice, to the complaints or the afflictions of disappointed hope, and blighted expectation. But there is an ear, which is open to the sorrows of man; there is a voice, whose sweetest accents are the accents of comfort and consolation. The vine that clings to the oak for shelter and protection, and supports itself by its mantling embrace, in it [sic] turn affords support, when age has destroyded [sic] the strength, or the lightning has shivered the body of the tree. So woman, who naturally leans upon man for succor, in her turn supports him in adversity, when the cares and troubles of life threaten to bear him down, or the mortifications of disap-pointed ambition prey upon his spirits.[21]

In addition to providing this kind of comfort in the home, a woman also taught her children a morality centered on discipline and self-control; in doing so, she helped promote the values necessary to another generation of successful competitors.[22] Given these impor-tant practical and spiritual responsibilities, most women probably found a large measure of personal satisfaction in their daily occupa-tions, and, since their energies were consistently channeled into these socially constructive activities, their desires no doubt did begin to seem—even to them—more or less commensurate with their duties.

But women contributed to the rise of the middle classes in a yet more material way; as a consequence, the way their role was formu-lated was further affected by their position within England's econo-my. First of all, as literal bearers of their husbands' or their fathers' wealth, they were visible indices of a man's position in his quest for social prestige. Even more concretely, the conspicuous consumption practiced by middle- and upper-class women helped stimulate Eng-land's domestic market and thus helped fill the coffers of the manufacturing and trading classes. But, perhaps most important, women were crucial pawns in the struggle for landed wealth, upon which both political power and social prestige ultimately depended. Marriages between aristocratic (but often encumbered) land and merchant money enabled the older titled families to maintain or even extend their estates and, simultaneously, permitted the middle classes to improve or establish their families. Because such marriages sent middle-class daughters into the families of the upper classes, this practice helped to infuse bourgeois values into the less-restrained aristocratic "high life." As both representatives and guarantors of property, then, women became objects of men's aspirations and ambitions—a position that implicitly demanded that women desire to *be* nothing but men's property.

In his discussion of Pope's *Rape of the Lock,* Louis A. Landa has identified some of the complexities of the position women held as consumers and thus as indirect contributors to England's national wealth and self-esteem. On the one hand, a woman like Pope's Belinda was, "as a consumer, the embodiment of luxury, whose ambiance is defined by the mere mention of such objects as Indian gems, Arabian perfume, ivory combs, a fluttering fan, diamond pendants in her ears, a sparkling cross, a new brocade, and the hoop petticoat, [and, as such, she] was . . . recognizably the final point in a vast nexus of enterprises, a vast commercial expansion which stirred the imagination of Englishmen to dwell on thoughts of greatness and magnificence." On the other hand, Belinda's penchant for what Defoe called "Foreign Trifles" could be seen as a threat to the market for such English products as cotton.[23] Thus women could be viewed either as stimuli to trade or, in the mood of mercantile conservatism, as potential threats to domestic industry. Still, no matter how they were described, women were consumers par excellence,[24] and, as such, they actually helped set a pattern of expenditure among the middle classes that rivaled that of their social betters. And because taxation fell most heavily on landowners, standards of expenditure set by the increasingly affluent manufacturing classes ultimately contributed to making marriage between these social groups more attractive to the cash-starved aristocracy. Thus, through a series of economic associations, women as consumers indirectly helped defuse potential class rivalry or even conflict. However, as we will see, a woman who was part of an impoverished but landed family might very well perceive the competition posed by wealthy tradesmen's daughters as cause for genuine alarm, both for herself and for the solidarity of her class.

Women's role in helping bond the wealth of the middle classes to the political power of the landed families is crucial to any understanding of eighteenth-century society. For the landed families, the goal was to protect family estates against attrition through debts or taxation. For families of the middle classes, the immediate goal was to acquire land, and the eventual goal—as such novels as *Clarissa* or *Camilla* suggest—was to establish the family name as "one of England's first." Essentially, all of these goals were facilitated by the practice of strict settlement, a legal provision developed in the middle of the seventeenth century to ensure that the family estate would descend intact to the eldest son of each generation. Under the principles of strict settlement, each man was only the life-tenant of the family estates. Generally, the essential articles governing property were settled on the eldest son's marriage: the amount of his maintenance, his wife's jointure (an annual income that would provide for her in the event of her husband's death), and the form and amount of portion that the younger children of the marriage would receive. The marriage articles also generally empowered the father and his newly married eldest son to raise capital sums against the estate for their respective wives and for the younger children's portions, but the life-tenant was prohibited from selling or mortgaging any part of the estate for any other purpose than to raise the money promised for portions.[25] Thus the practice of strict settlement reinforced the primacy of families over individuals, helped landed families keep their estates (and their power) intact, and encouraged the aspiring middle classes to attain status through marriage rather than simply through personal industry.

H. J. Habakkuk estimates that in the mid-eighteenth century approximately half the land in England was governed by strict settlement.[26] For women of established or aspiring families this meant, first of all, a strict reinforcement of the rule of chastity, since, as we have seen, a bastard could completely undermine dynastic ambitions. Second, the prevalence of strict settlement in a period of growing capital wealth resulted in an increased competition in the marriage market for eldest sons of landed families.

In the mid-seventeenth century, Habakkuk explains, a representative ratio between a bride's dowry and the jointure her husband settled upon her was £660 to £100. By the early eighteenth century, however, the common ratio was £1,000 to £100,[27] and, by the end of the century, a woman like Mary Ann Radcliffe might lament these "modern days, when women endow their husbands, and, with large portions, frequently purchase a very heavy bondage."[28] In other words, throughout the course of the eighteenth century, husbands were becoming more expensive, or, to reverse the formula, women were becoming less valuable. This trend resulted from a combination of factors. On the one hand, the growing capital wealth of families whose income did not depend on land enabled them to endow their daughters more generously, thus driving up the rate of portions landowners were required to settle on their daughters. On the other hand, a decrease in the number of eligible bachelors among the landowners made competitive bargaining increasingly necessary.[29]

The greater size of portions meant, of course, that daughters were an increasing drain on a family's capital wealth, a fact that could lead expectant sons to begrudge their "encumbering" sisters. James Harlowe's bitterness toward Clarissa, for example, is rooted in part in his vested interest in the family's estates: "a man who has sons brings up chickens for his own table," James sneers, "whereas daughters are chickens brought up for the tables of other men."[30] Such insinuations undoubtedly placed pressure on young girls to acquiesce in their parents' demands, perhaps even to simulate affection for a man who could enhance the family's status. The disproportionate number of socially and economically suitable bachelors also meant that a woman had less choice as to her future husband; the complaisance of male suitors, who took their success for granted, is a commonplace of eighteenth-century novels, as is the sad circumstance of uncourted daughters. Even the woman who subordinated pragmatic concerns to genuine affection, who married an adoring man despite an inadequate portion, might continue to dread later accusations of fraud or feel guilty long into the marriage; Hester Thrale, for example, always lamented bringing her husband less dowry than he expected, despite his apparent unconcern.[31]

The overall effect of these conditions was to perpetuate among the middle and upper classes the attitude that women were counters to be used in negotiating rather than individuals deserving of choice. Habakkuk contends that the first half of the eighteenth century witnessed "an increasing subordination of marriage to the increase of landed wealth, at the expense of other motives for marriage," and, as corroboration, he quotes Sir William Temple (1750):

> These contracts would never be made, but by men's avarice, and greediness of portions with the people they marry, which is grown among us to that degree, as to surmount and extinguish all other regards or desires: so that our marriages are made, just like other common bargains and sales, by the mere consideration of interest or gain, without any love or esteem, of birth or of beauty itself, which ought to be the true ingredients of all happy compositions of this kind.[32]

The very fact that Temple laments this practice reveals, of course, that it was not universally accepted. But despite the fact that considerable evidence suggests a decline in arranged marriages toward the end of the century,[33] informal safeguards continued to enforce the importance of economic considerations. Throughout the century, for example, conduct books, diaries, and novels reiterate the lesson that children—especially daughters—should obey their parents' will in this most critical of all decisions. Works as diverse as Bernard Mandeville's *The Virgin Unmask'd,* Sarah Pennington's *An Unfortunate Mother's Advice,* and Hannah More's *Strictures on the Education of Daughters* all insist that, although parents owe consideration to the preferences of their children, "no demerit in a parent can absolve a child from that duty which has the double sanction both of God and Nature."[34] Moreover, marriage settlements and financial negotiations continued to play an important role in all but the most romantic of novels. By the end of the eighteenth century, negotiating a marriage solely according to financial considerations was explicitly denounced as scandalous,[35] but personal memoirs, such as those of Sarah Pennington, Hester Thrale, or Mary Ann Radcliffe, reveal that the economics of marriage were still sometimes the paramount concern. And novels such as Fanny Burney's *Cecilia* or *Camilla* and Ann Radcliffe's *Mysteries of Udolpho* suggest that, no matter how many "companionate" marriages might occur, women still sufficiently feared being reduced to economic counters to fantasize its horrors. After all, as Clarissa Harlowe knew, the price of acquiescence could be disastrously high:

> To be given up to a strange man; to be ingrafted into a strange family; to give up her very name, as a mark of her becoming his absolute and dependent property; to be obliged to prefer this strange man, to father, mother—to everybody: and his humours to all her own—or to contend perhaps, in breach of a vowed duty, for every innocent instance of free-will. . . . Surely, sir, a young creature ought not to be obliged to make all these sacrifices but for such a man as she can love. [*Clarissa,* 1:153]

By the end of the eighteenth century, then, the qualities that a century earlier had been described as necessary defenses against women's appetites were increasingly considered to be "natural" female traits, invaluable to society as a whole. In the seventeenth century even champions of women felt it necessary to admit that most women "live as if they were all Body,"[36] but, by the last decades of the eighteenth century, even to refer to the body was considered "unladylike." In 1782, for example, Hester Thrale shocked her female companions by reading aloud a passage from the *Spectator*; as she reports, "even the Maid who was dressing my Hair, burst out o' laughing at the Idea of *a Lady* saying her Stomach ach'd, or that something stuck between her Teeth."[37] By 1803 Miss Hatfield could describe women as if they were more nearly spiritual presences than physical beings:

> To their smiles, the festive scene owes its heightened zest; to their soft attentions, the pining hour of langour and of drooping melancholy, its relief.—Their

fortitude and tenderness sustain them, not only in a patient, but willing endurance of all the tedious cares and watchings of a sickchamber.

   These are among the virtues that actuate the female sex; from the aggregate
use of which, they become raised into characters of exemplary piety.[38]

Because their contributions to society were rewarded both by men's
grateful approval and by a sense of their own worth, women had a
clear investment in accepting the naturalization of the feminine ideal.
But as women accepted a definition of "female nature" that was
derived from a social role, they found it increasingly difficult to
acknowledge or to integrate into their self-perceptions desires that
did not support this stereotype. And, by the same token, they found
it increasingly difficult to recognize that the stereotype was prescrip-
tion, not description, and thus to renounce it. But all kinds of writing
by women of this period suggest that, even though women may not
consciously have acknowledged their own impermissible desires, energies not sanctioned by propriety did exist. Although they celebrated their proper, feminine nature, women found ways to express the
energies that were not satisfied or silenced by fulfilling the role of an
altogether proper lady.

The Paradoxes of Propriety

   The definition of female nature that emerged by the end of the
eighteenth century both reinforced and formalized the complex social
role that actual women played during this period. But because bourgeois society simultaneously depended on and perpetuated a paradoxical formulation of female sexuality, the late eighteenth-century
equation of "female" and "feminine" is characterized at every level
by paradoxes and contradictions. The first of many such complexities
is evident in the fact that, even though late eighteenth-century moralists described femininity as innate, they also insisted that feminine
virtues needed constant cultivation. During the eighteenth century,
in fact, an entire body of literature emerged that was devoted exclusively to this cultivation. Instructions about proper conduct appeared
in the numerous periodicals addressed specifically to women,[39] in
more general essay-periodicals like the *Spectator,* and in ladies' conduct books. This last genre, which consisted of works composed by
both men and women, was directed primarily to the middle classes
and was intended to educate young girls (and their mothers) in the
behavior considered "proper," then "natural," for a "lady." Conduct
material of all kinds increased in volume and popularity after the
1740s, in keeping with the increased emphasis on domestic education
and the growing number of middle-class women readers.

Letters from readers, published in these periodicals, suggest (since their authenticity cannot be guaranteed) that women did look to this material as a guide to their own conduct. These readers frequently provided examples from their own lives to prove the justice of a moral precept (often, interestingly enough, by their having violated it), and sometimes they even asked that a principle be made more strict so as to be more definitive. This conduct material is instructive, not only because it probably served a prescriptive function for mothers and daughters, but also because, as products of the everyday discourse of eighteenth-century propriety, the essays are themselves expressions of the implicit values of their culture. Indeed, in many respects this conduct material provides the best access both to the way in which this culture defined female nature and to the ways in which a woman of this period would have experienced the social and psychological dimensions of ideology. For in reproducing the ideological configuration that protected bourgeois society, both the hierarchy of values and the rhetorical strategies contained in these works provided real women with the terms by which they conceptualized and interpreted their own behavior and desires.

If we compare, for example, equivalent issues from two companion periodicals, some of the culture's unspoken attitudes toward women immediately emerge.[40] In January, 1793, both the *Lady's Magazine,* which dominated its market from 1770 to 1830, and the *Gentleman's Magazine,* the most popular monthly periodical of the last half of the century, opened the new year with a statement of purpose and a response to the trial and death of France's Louis XVI. The editor of the *Gentleman's Magazine* greeted his readers with a direct allusion to the dangerous events in France:

> Europe since the period when it was overrun by the Goths and the Vandals, has never experienced more alarm and danger than at the present moment— Religion, Manners, Literature, and the Arts, are all equally menaced by a foe, whose characteristic is a compound of impetuosity, ignorance and crime. To resist and counteract these machinations, has been the honest and unremitting endeavour of the *Gentleman's Magazine* and ever will be so, as long as our Political and Religious Constitution shall require our indefatigable support.[41]

The editor of the *Lady's Magazine* begins on a different note:

> The utility of Miscellanies of this kind [ladies' periodicals], for the promoting of knowledge and the liberal arts, need not be insisted on. . . . In the *Lady's Magazine,* which has now been favoured with the public approbation for three and twenty years, the interest of morality and religion have constantly been especially attended to.[42]

Each periodical is affirming its commitment to established English values, but where the *Gentleman's Magazine* explicitly warns its readers of a political and cultural menace, the *Lady's Magazine* presents a reassuring picture of stability and continuity. The form in which the statements are cast also reflects this difference: the *Gentleman's Magazine* boldly claims to offer a specific response to a specific historical situation ("to resist and counteract these machinations . . . as long as . . ."), but the *Lady's Magazine* formulates its purpose in a subordinate phrase and as an ongoing activity ("for the promoting . . . constantly been . . . attended to"). Finally, the *Gentleman's Magazine* appeals to its readers' reason and convictions and invites each individual to judge the merit of its enterprise, but the *Lady's Magazine* couches its appeal in terms not of personal conviction but of established standards—"morality and religion"—and collective, "public," opinion.

The terms in which news of the terrifying events in France are reported also bear out this difference. In the January issue of the *Gentleman's Magazine* the cumulative effect of the "Foreign Intelligence" section supports the author's claim that all Europe is "at the present moment" in a state of "alarm and danger." We learn of the death vote taken for the king in Paris, antiagitator actions in Poland, Jacobin arms-smuggling into Bilbao, and, in Ireland, a riot and the successful plundering of munitions by "banditti" (p. 81). In the February issue of the *Lady's Magazine,* on the other hand, the death of the king is reported but no such general alarm is raised. The editors do describe anti-Gallic military preparations in Spain, Austria, Sardinia, Germany, and Russia, but no French victories are reported, the French Republic is depicted as being impoverished by "the rapacity of the French contractors," and the French troops are described as inadequately clothed because of "the negligence of the commissaries" (p. 107). The *Lady's Magazine* also tends to draw reassuring conclusions for its readers. The article on naval preparations, for example, comments that "it is not difficult to prognosticate that, in case of war, the French will be unable to contend with Great Britain for the dominion of the ocean" (p. 107).

The *Gentleman's Magazine* reports the execution of Louis XVI in a normal entry in the part of the news section entitled "Historical Chronicle." The *Lady's Magazine,* on the other hand, which rarely reports any political events, places its account first among its entries and accompanies it with a full-page engraving of the king. That the *Lady's Magazine* is especially interested in the appearance of the king is borne out by this detailed description, which has no equivalent in the *Gentleman's Magazine*: "His hair was dressed in curls, his beard shaved; he wore a clean shirt and stock, a white waistcoat, black florentine silk breeches, black silk stockings, and his shoes were tied with black silk strings" (p. 8). This information is not given to help the magazine's readers form individual opinions about the political events. Rather, because the editors recognize that "public attention will probably be turned for some time to this tragical event" (p. 5), such details are designed to provide the substance for polite conversations.

We can infer from these differences that men were typically given an assortment of facts (all thirty-eight points of the proposed Alien Act, for example, as well as transcriptions of parliamentary proceedings) and were expected to formulate from them personal judgments, and that women, on the contrary, were encouraged to accept conclusions offered by an authoritative voice and to be more interested in the appearances of events than in their causes or political significance. Men, expected to take an active political—if not military—role in England's defense, were aroused by the specter of an alarming foe; women, expected to keep the domestic circle free of such anxieties, were given a picture of national strength and an incompetent enemy. The appeal to men is explicit and direct because the assumption is that men's passions as well as their reason are subject to individual consciousness and control. The appeal to women, on the other hand, is indirect; it is couched in sensual rather than intellectual terms and is supported by numerous references to "public opinion," by moral stories, and by other "entertaining instruction." The implicit assumption is that women's quick passions will be more effectively engaged by such formulations than by either less overt moralizing or more direct reporting of facts.

Such thematic and rhetorical "cultivation" was considered necessary in part because what most moralists described as the most fundamental female characteristic—a woman's emotional responsiveness—was regarded as a profoundly ambivalent trait. This "amiableness of disposition," which was thought to form the basis of a woman's benevolence, her "sprightliness of imagination," and her "sensibility of heart," is, if properly governed, productive of the greatest personal and social good: the domestic harmony and social charm celebrated by numerous moralists. But if, by chance or oversight, this female receptivity is exposed to internal or external temptations, it can rapidly degenerate into sexual appetite, which seventeenth-century writers explicitly feared. Eighteenth-century moralists formulated this complexity in various ways. Some, for example, described female passions as external forces that occasionally overwhelm a woman's essentially "feminine" nature: "the agents of nature are often at work in apparently open disobedience to her laws . . .; if the agitations of passion . . . have hurried their unhappy victim from the paths of rectitude and principle . . . , it would be weakness, not wisdom, to infer that such were the characteristics of the species."[43] Others, like Adam Smith, viewed susceptibility as the inevitable inverse of feminine virtue. "Humanity," according to Smith, "is the virtue of a woman, generosity [is the virtue] of a man."

> Humanity consists merely in the exquisite fellow-feeling which the spectator entertains with the sentiments of the persons principally concerned, so as to grieve for their sufferings, to resent their injuries, and to rejoice at their good fortune. The most humane actions require no self-denial, no self-command, no great exertion of the sense of propriety. They consist only in doing what this exquisite sympathy would of its own accord prompt us to do.[44]

The implication of Smith's definition is that because women do not habitually practice self-denial their "natural receptivity" is dangerously alive to all kinds of stimuli. But whether moralists describe women's passions as inexplicable eruptions of disobedient nature or as the logical extension of female sympathy, all definitions of female virtue allude to—and try to control—sexuality. Far from dismissing the specter of female sexuality, in fact, the late eighteenth-century ideal of feminine propriety simply transmutes it into its opposite. The result of this inversion is the fundamental paradox that pervades all discussions of women: at the heart of the explicit description of "feminine," Angelic women, superior to all physical appetite, resides the "female" sexuality that was automatically assumed to be the defining characteristic of female nature.

The persistence of the assumption that women are fundamentally sexual can be seen in nearly all examples and at nearly every level of the conduct material. Early in the century the phrases used to describe female nature are transparent euphemisms for sexual appetite. Such writers as Daniel Defoe, Bernard Mandeville, and Jonathan Swift, for example, did not let their readers forget that fear of women's "frailty" lay behind the "custom, which we miscall modesty." "Inclination, which we prettily call love," Defoe acknowledged, exchanging one euphemism for another, "does sometimes move a little too visibly in the sex, and frailty often follows."[45] Several decades later Dr. Johnson was still alluding to sexuality when he remarked that, "Nature has given women so much power, that the law has wisely given them little."[46] The anonymous female author of *The Polite Lady* was even more explicit than her male peers: women's passions, she acknowledged, "are much more keen and violent than those of the other sex, or, which is the same thing, we are less capable to check and restrain them."[47]

More subtle reminders appear throughout the century as explicit allusions to female sexuality gave way to more idealizing descriptions of femininity. Most of the activities that moral essayists consistently described as "unladylike" or "unnatural" were the ones that might jeopardize conjugal fidelity: frequenting the theater or masquerades, coquetting, or dressing provocatively or immodestly. All attacks on female "appetite" were also, implicitly, defenses of female chastity. These appetites were legion; and, as numerous commentators revealed, the underlying assumption was that, once indulged, any appetite would become voracious and lead eventually to the most dangerous desire of all. Thus moralists warn against gambling, overeating, or drinking too much ("She who is first a prostitute to Wine, will soon be to Lust also"),[48] and even against reading novels ("The appetite becomes too keen to be denied . . .; the contents of the circulating library, are devoured with indiscriminate and insatiable avidity. Hence the mind is secretly corrupted").[49] For Hannah More, one particularly prevalent incarnation of female appetite is vanity. As the following passage reveals, what looks like simply an uncontrollable appetite for praise has more ominous repercussions. More is warning men against choosing a wife at a public assembly:

> If a man select a picture for himself from among all its exhibited competitors, and bring it to his own house, the picture being passive, he is able to *fix* it there: while the wife, picked up at a public place, and accustomed to incessant display, will not, it is probable, when brought home stick so quietly to the spot where he fixes her; but will escape to the exhibition-room again, and continue to be displayed at every subsequent exhibition, just as if she were not become private property, and had never been definitively disposed of.[50]

A woman who is not "private property" is implicitly available for public use, a fact on which More does not have to elaborate.

Throughout the conduct material the litany against female appetite goes on: A woman whose beauty has once been praised will crave more public applause, and a female wit "lives on flattery as its daily bread."[51] Even the obsessive cultivation of virtue—as Clarissa Harlowe learned—can be a form of "intemperance," an indulgence of the appetite for notice. Thomas Gisborne ratified this assumption when he lamented the ends to which indulging female appetite could lead: to "unsteadiness of mind; to fondness of novelty; to habits of frivolousness, and trifling employment; . . . to an unreasonable regard for wit and shining accomplishments; . . . to sudden excesses; [to] unmerited attachments."[52] And the author of *The Polite Lady* makes the connection between self-indulgence and sexual profligacy even clearer when she explains that indulging *any* desire is finally

> an enemy to this virtue of chastity. For, it not only inflames the blood, and raises the passions; but, at the same time, darkens and clouds the mind, and renders it less capable to resist and regulate the inferior appetites. It debases and corrupts the heart: it gives us too strong a relish for the pleasures of sense, and too great a disgust for those of a rational nature.[53]

Immediately behind such warnings is, as I have suggested, the desire to secure both men's property and their peace of mind. When these moralists offer explanations, however, they are more likely to allude to the order of the universe than to the well-being of an estate or an individual. According to the author of *The Ladies Library,* for example, unrestrained appetite

> is the Spring and Original of infinite Confusions; the grand Incendiary, which puts Kingdoms, Churches and Families in Combustion; a Contradiction, not only to the Word, but to the Works of God; a kind of anticreative Power, which reduces things to the Chaos from whence God drew them. . . . So especially the Female Sex, whose Passions being naturally the more impetuous, ought to be the most strictly guarded, and kept under the severe Discipline of Reason; for where 'tis otherwise, where a Woman has no Guide but her Will, and her Will is nothing but her Humour, the Event is sure to be fatal to herself; and often to others also.[54]

Given the voraciousness that female desire was assumed to have, the surest safeguard against overindulgence was not to allow or admit to appetites of any kind. Thus women were encouraged to display no vanity, no passion, no assertive "self" at all. In keeping with this design, even genuinely talented women were urged to avoid all be-havior that would call attention to themselves: " 'Tis the duty of a young lady to talk with an air of diffidence, as if she proposed what she said, rather with a view to receive information herself, than to inform and instruct the company"; a woman "should be carefully instructed that her talents are only a means to a still higher attain-ment, and that she is not to rest in them as an end; that merely to exercise them as instruments for the acquisition of fame and the promoting of pleasure, is subversive of her delicacy as a woman"; a woman, in fact, should "think it [her] greatest commendation not to be talked of one way or other."[55]

All of this self-effacing behavior was included in the general catego-ry of "modesty." But even modesty perpetuates the paradoxical formulation of female sexuality. For a modest demeanor served not only to assure the world that a woman's appetites were under con-trol; it also indicated that female sexuality was still assertive enough to *require* control. That is, even as modesty was proclaimed to be the most reliable guardian of a woman's chastity—and hence the exter-nal sign of her internal integrity—it was also declared to be an advertisement for—and hence an attraction to—her sexuality.[56] This paradox appears in nearly every eighteenth-century discussion of modesty. The anonymous author of *The Ladies Library,* for example, assures her readers that, properly displayed, modesty constitutes an infallible protection against men's "most impudent Attack":

> For 'tis certain a modest Countenance gives a Check to Lust; there is something
> awful, as if there was something divine in it; and with all the Simplicity of
> Innocence, it has a commanding Power that restrains the Fury of Desire. Such
> an Authority there is in Virtue, that where 'tis eminent, 'tis apt to controul all
> loose Appetites, and he must not only be lustful but sacrilegious who attempts
> to violate such a Sanctuary.[57]

Yet the same author declares modesty to be a woman's most effective
lure: "An innocent Modesty, a native Simplicity of Look, eclipse all
the glaring Splendors of Art and Dress" (1: 117). Modesty is provocation; it whets the lover's appetite; it suspends both partners momentarily in the delicious foreplay of anticipation:

> Mankind esteems those things most which are at a distance; whereas an easy
> and cheap Compliance begets Contempt. While Women govern themselves by
> the exact Rule of Prudence, their Lustre is like the Meridian Sun in its Bright-
> ness, which, tho' less approachable, is counted more glorious. . . . If Women
> affect Finery and Comeliness to render themselves agreeable only, let them
> know, they are never so comely and fine, as when they are cloathed in Virgin
> Modesty; never so amiable as when they are adorn'd with the Beauties of
> Innocence and Virtue. [1:129]

Because the glory of its eventual conqueror is directly proportion-
ate to the resistance modesty poses, its efficacy is directly proportion-
ate to its conspicuousness. Richard Allestree, from whom the author
of *The Ladies Library* derives much of her imagery, organization, and
language, more fully describes the paradoxical nature of modesty.
Like the "Meridian Sun," modesty "eclipse [s the] glaring Splendour"
of ostentatious art. But

> if boldness be to be read in her Face, it blots all the lines of beauty, is like a
> cloud over the Sun, intercepts the view of all that was otherwise Amiable, and
> renders it's [*sic*] blackness the more observable, by being plac'd near somewhat
> that was apt to attract the eyes.[58]

In this metaphor, woman is the object of man's attention. Yet, like
the sun, her modesty cannot be directly seen; it is know by the light
it reflects, light that hints at its radiant center but that brings into
sharp relief only the man who pursues, then obtains this hidden prize.
Modesty announces purity in a virgin, promises fidelity in a wife, and
thus will continue to be a reflection of her husband's power. "Boldness," on the other hand, calls attention to the woman herself ("inter-
cepts the view"), instead of reflecting a man's gaze *through* the woman
back to himself. ("All that was otherwise Amiable" here suggests not
only the modest woman but also the man aggrandized by her con-
sent.) The woman as desiring subject is "blackness," a cultural void,
a negative that comes into view only when it interferes with the ideal
woman, who cannot be seen at all.

The paradox of modesty—and the paradox of female sexuality it simultaneously concealed and revealed—necessarily established the terms in which real women both consciously conceptualized and evaluated their own behavior and even unconsciously experienced their own gender. For the fact that this definition was reinforced by nearly every bourgeois institution and social experience meant that to define oneself by some other category than the paradox of sexuality/chastity was to move wholly outside of social definition, to risk being designated a "monster." Indeed, even to define oneself explicitly in terms of sexuality was to exclude oneself from the gender to which female anatomy theoretically relegated a woman. The least departure from modesty, as Richard Allestree unequivocally explained, is "a proportaionable [sic] receding from Woman-hood," and "the total abandoning it ranks them among Brutes."[59] More practically, a woman's social position depended completely on her obedience to men's will, and it was partly for this reason that women tended to embrace chastity as "the greatest glory and ornament of our sex," even though chastity might mean self-denial and even though its loss might affect her husband and his property more than the woman herself (barring, of course, an unwanted pregnancy).

The importance women assigned to chastity is aptly conveyed by the lament from one woman to another that, "this lost, every thing that is dear and valuable to a woman, is lost along with it; the peace of her own mind, the love of her friends, the esteem of the world, the enjoyment of present pleasure, and all hopes of future happiness."[60] But it is also important to recognize that there were positive incentives for a woman to accept the equation between "female" and "feminine." Indeed, if any principle that advances the interests of one group at the expense of another is to operate effectively as ideology, it must at the very least provide psychological rewards for those who are ruled as well as practical benefits for those whose rulership it supports. A woman might well consider chastity her "greatest glory and ornament" because to do so enhanced her social value and promised her the eventual gratification of the very desires that modesty was supposed to deny. In other words, because the code of modesty was paradoxical in its very configuration it allowed for both indirect expressions of desire and the promise of rewards both immediate and deferred.

But despite incentives and rewards, this ideology, from the perspective of a woman's lived experience, presented at least two critical problems. Equating chastity with value not only required a woman to suppress or sublimate her sexual and emotional appetites; it also required her to signal her virtue by a physical intactness that is by definition invisible. In reality she could display her chastity only indirectly or—even more precisely—negatively: by *not* speaking, by *not* betraying the least consciousness of her essential sexuality. Modesty was one form of indirect display; an expressive "countenance" was another. "Modesty," according to Dr. Gregory, "will naturally dispose you to be rather silent in company. . . . [But] one may take a share in conversation without uttering a syllable. The expression in the countenance shews it, and never escapes an observing eye."[61] Hannah More also describes such communicative but decorous silence: "an inviolable and marked attention may shew, that a woman is pleased with a subject, and an illuminated countenance may prove that she understands it, almost as unequivocally as language itself."[62] Such "unequivocal" silence is theoretically communicative, of course, only as long as the external sign of the countenance is assumed to bear a perfect, indeed automatic, relationship to the interior self: Nature has "marked the genuine feelings of modesty with a look and manner . . . correspondent and expressive."[63] As long as one postulates such a correspondence, the silence of the Proper Lady can presumably be read like an open book; she is (or should be) quite simply what she seems to be.[64]

The assumption that one can interpret a woman's subjective feelings by visible, objective signs—her "look and manner"—has an even more embracing, but equally delimiting, counterpart: the notion that one can interpret a woman's essence by her context—by her reputation or her "situation." The cultural importance granted to reputation is reflected in the consistency with which eighteenth-century novelists dwell on this subject. Anna Howe's advice to Clarissa to marry Lovelace even after the rape is one of the most memorable of these references, if only because here reputation seems so thoroughly beside the point.[65] For eighteenth-century heroines, "situation" is still another piece of the equivocal cultural code. "Situation," as we learn from Burney's *Evelina,* can refer not simply to a woman's position in society (to her *father's* position more precisely, or, as in Evelina's case, to her lack of an acknowledged father and hence to her lack of a determinate, protective social position); it can even refer to her immediate physical surroundings. When Evelina wanders lost through the dark footpaths of Vauxhall, every man who sees her assumes she is a prostitute; and when she is forced to take tea in the Branghtons' parlor, visitors immediately conclude that she is one of their kind. In order for such an ambiguous system of values to remain intelligible, everyone must assume that all external signs are organic expressions of the hidden essence. Just as how you look must designate what you are, so where you are must invariably tell who you are.[66]

But the paradoxical formulation of female sexuality, upon which all these values are based, means that this correspondence does *not* necessarily exist. Just as a woman's modest demeanor actually disguises her essential sexuality, so a woman's situation, her reputation, or her countenance could dramatically *mis*represent her character. This possibility obviously poses a threat to men, but, as the examples of *Clarissa* and *Evelina* suggest, it also threatens women. So numerous—and so frightening—were the possibilities that the code of propriety would distort or repress genuine feelings that catastrophes of this sort constitute a staple of many of the best novels of the period. The works of Fanny Burney provide one such vision of what these values must have looked like from within. In *Camilla* the heroine is repeatedly thwarted because she cannot openly declare her love for Edgar Mandlebert. Struggling desperately to master the conventions of female indirection, Camilla tries to maneuver Mandlebert into taking the initiative by flirting with his rival, Sir Sedley Clarendel. But, unfortunately, Camilla's boldness alienates Edgar, and, when she tries to retreat from Sir Sedley, her modesty arouses the unwanted suitor all the more. Unwittingly, Camilla has twice misjudged the message her behavior conveys and thus has twice exposed herself to misinterpretation. Her efforts to clarify her true feelings to Sir Sedley only inaugurate further misunderstanding, for in her desire to speak to Clarendel alone Edgar sees only the stereotype of a woman making an open declaration—presumably, of her love.

Burney's first novel, *Evelina,* explores another discomforting facet of propriety. Unlike Camilla, who knows but cannot speak her heart, Evelina has been so thoroughly protected by her guardian that she has never felt—much less learned to understand—genuine desire. Evelina's predicament is a perfect example of a phenomenon that Mary Wollstonecraft explores: the fact that a woman's situation, far from being either an accurate index of her heart or even simply a misrepresentation of her actual position, can actually help constitute the responses it seems to represent. Situation—and the behavior it requires—can actually *make* a woman into a Proper Lady, or, as in Evelina's case, it can unnaturally prolong her childhood. Situations do eventually educate Evelina: in London, she gradually discovers how to interpret the language of social intercourse and even the clamors of her passion. But this cannot occur until her ignorance, fostered by her initial protected situation, is finally dispelled. So apt is unconsciousness as a trope for Evelina's persistent innocence that her one decisive, spontaneous action—saving Mr. Macartney from suicide—immediately causes her to faint.

Evelina's innocence is, of course, her primary attraction in the eyes of the worldly Lord Orville. But because her innocence is predicated on ignorance, Evelina experiences both embarrassment and helplessness in London's high society. Pursued by the leering Sir Clement Willoughby through London's treacherous amusements, Evelina suffers the consequences of living in—without understanding—the paradoxes of propriety. As a proper young lady she is theoretically ignorant of sexuality, but as a fully developed young woman she clearly *is* a sexual being. When she blushes, she unwittingly signals not only her modesty but also her consciousness of her innocence. This consciousness is exactly what Willoughby wants to see, for it introduces the possibility that the girl will recognize—if not respond to—his advances. The dilemma for Evelina is that, in a knowing world, a woman can*not* be truly innocent, for she will always unintentionally betray the sexuality that virtue exists to protect. The only guaranteed protection is to avoid the adult world altogether, as Evelina's guardian said she should. The moralist, Dr. Gregory, explains this impasse of virtue explicitly:

> A virtuous girl often hears very indelicate things with a countenance no wise embarrassed, because in truth she does not understand them. Yet this is, most ungenerously, ascribed to that command of features, and that ready presence of mind, which you are thought to possess in a degree far beyond us; or, by still more malignant observers, it is ascribed to hardened effrontery.
>
> Sometimes a girl laughs with all the simplicity of unsuspecting innocence, for no other reason but being infected with other people's laughing: she is then believed to know more than she should do.—If she does happen to understand an improper thing, she suffers a very complicated distress: she feels her modesty hurt in the most sensible manner, and at the same time is ashamed of appearing conscious of the injury.[67]

A woman is not to betray knowledge of sexuality (or even, in compromising circumstances, the absence of knowledge, which may be read as knowledge disguised) because knowledge denotes experience and hence potential, if not actual, corruption. "She that listens to any wanton discourse," Allestree declares, "has violated her ears; she that speaks any, her tongue; every immodest glance vitiates her eye, and every the lightest act of dalliance, leaves something of stain and sullage behind it."[68] Yet a woman cannot convince anyone that she is completely without sexual desire, either. As Clarissa Harlowe discovers, even a mother will not believe that a girl is altogether free of desire; if she will not allow her affection to be directed by her parents, the Harlowes assume, a young girl must already be "prepossessed" by love for another man.[69]

Another paradox evident in eighteenth-century discussions of women constituted a further, less consciously identifiable, dilemma for real women trying to formulate and interpret their own behavior. By now it is a commonplace that eighteenth-century England witnessed the rise of individualism; it was part and parcel of the consolidation of bourgeois values that we have already examined. During the eighteenth century, philosophers, following John Locke, generally stressed the importance of applying reason to empirical observations in order to reach truths that everyone could acquire. Individualism also governed political theory, economic principles and practice, and even, under the influence of Protestantism, religious beliefs. And, especially during the second half of the century, individualism acquired a concrete form in the scientific achievements that rapidly began to transform society. Individual effort became the mark of past accomplishments and the guarantor of future success; this was the era of the "self-made man," when aristocratic privilege could finally be challenged on a wide scale by individuals possessed of talent, opportunity, and the capacity for hard work.

Middle-class women were no doubt familiar with the values and even the rhetoric of individualism; even if they had never heard of Joseph Priestley, Josiah Wedgwood, or John Locke, they mouthed the truisms of this doctrine every time they read their children *Goody Two-Shoes* or taught them the benefits of self-discipline.[70] In fact, the very translation of sexual control into "duty" is perfectly in keeping with the tenets of individualism: a woman's social contribution was, in essence, self-control, just as her primary antagonist was herself. "If women guard against themselves," the aphorism assured, "they may bid defiance to all the arts of men."[71] Yet despite their obvious incorporation into the ideology of individualism, middle-class women were not encouraged to think of themselves as part of this nation of individuals. Because of the need to protect their virtue, they were advised to acquire knowledge only indirectly—by reading history, perhaps, or by talking to an older female friend. As the author of *The Polite Lady* advised her readers, "the knowledge, learning, wisdom, and experience of your friend will, in effect, become your own; because you may always use them with the same freedom as if they were your own property."[72] Women were also urged to think of themselves collectively—not as a political unit, or as beings possessed of individual talents, capacities, or rights, but simply in terms of the universals of what Richardson's Lovelace called "the sex, the sex."

As we will see more clearly in the works of Mary Wollstonecraft and Jane Austen, this paradox could prove significant for women in a variety of ways. Women of the aspiring trading classes, like Mary Wollstonecraft, unconsciously adopted the values of individualism; they therefore tended to imagine that social change comes from individual effort—their own as well as men's. Yet because they were women they actually had neither the political nor economic power necessary to contribute to social change. Moreover, because ambitious women of this class tended automatically to identify themselves with other aggressive, upwardly mobile individuals and not with women as a group, they often ignored the common problems women shared; thus they worked against establishing the solidarity that would eventually prove necessary to political reform. On the other hand, women of the landed gentry and professional classes, like Jane Austen, tended to occupy an even more complex position within the ideology of individualism. In keeping with the basically feudal habits of their class, women of this social group could easily interpret the individualistic ambition of the tradesmen and Dissenters as a challenge posed to the traditional values of their fathers and brothers. But in keeping with the rhetoric of progress everywhere evident in their culture, they, too, could most easily envision the defense of their class in terms of individual moral efforts. Thus Jane Austen unintentionally echoes the values of individualism when she assigns to individual women the task of correcting the moral wrongs of an entire class if not of society as a whole. However, her heroines' limited accomplishments and the fairytale quality of her novels' conclusions suggest that Austen senses, at some level, the futility of this "solution."

Given these paradoxes at the heart of eighteenth- and early nineteenth-century values, nearly every moralist felt compelled to forestall frustration by celebrating the virtue of endurance and the rewards of self-denial. "*Bear* and *forbear*," is Clarissa's private litany. For the unfortunate Sarah Pennington the example of Griselda implicitly governs the advice she gives her cherished daughters. Having inherited a private fortune from a doting relative, as Clarissa did, the real-life Sarah Pennington unintentionally aroused her husband's anger. Despite the fact that she had previously obeyed his every command, Pennington accused his wife of adultery and drove her out of his house and away from her children. From her solitary retreat, Sarah Pennington was forced to communicate with her daughters by public letter; with remarkable forbearance, she advises them to protect above all else their future husbands' "Repose." Even his infidelity should be ignored, she argues, or, better yet, left undiscovered: "the fewer Faults you discover in your Partner, the better; never search after what it will give you no Pleasure to find; never desire to hear what you will not like to be told."[73]

Despite all these explicit and implicit strictures on their self-conceptions and self-expression, eighteenth-century women *did* find ways to communicate and even satisfy their desires. The important thing to notice, however, is that the forms that female self-expression typically assumed are characterized by indirection. For, as we have already begun to see, the code of propriety did accommodate women's desires, but only as long as the expression of those desires conformed to the paradoxical configuration inherent in the code itself: self-assertion had to look like something other than what it was. Women's "accomplishments," for instance, were one legitimate vehicle for the indirect indulgence of vanity. Piano-playing, singing, dancing, fine needlework, and painting were only thinly disguised opportunities for the display of personal charms; and the fierce competition this display often promoted was, like Mary Astell's "Vertue and Ingenuity," an acceptable version of men's professional competitiveness. As long as it was strictly confined to certain arenas and ultimately obedient to men's will, women were also allowed to exercise considerable personal—if indirect—power. Before she married, a young girl possessed the power of what moralists called "her Negative": the right to resist or even reject the proposal of a suitor. In exchange for relinquishing this right, a woman acquired what moralists considered her greatest power: the power of influence. Especially in the first decades of the nineteenth century, moralists waxed eloquent on the beneficent effects of woman's simple presence. Here is Miss Hatfield in 1803:

> As the benign properties of the solar rays dissipate and dispel gross vapours in the material world, so does the presence of women operate in the intellectual. Over the mind of a good and sensible man her power is gentle and prevailing; his councils are assisted by her prudence; the rude vicissitudes of fortune are softened by her sensibility and friendship.[74]

In 1810, Reynald Morryson explained to readers of the *Gentleman's Magazine* that, because "modesty is [the] native grace" of women,

> they must immediately inspire humility and gentleness in others; as they are accustomed to diffidence, they teach the blessing of liberality and a charitable judgment: their sympathy must add a charm to benevolence; and their cheerfulness, which never exceeds decorum, is the assurance of innocent pleasures, and the shame of all that is intemperate.[75]

The most effective operation of a woman's influence, however, centers in the home. It is as a mother, the moralists agreed, that a woman exercises her highest capacity for "power." As Hannah More declaimed:

> The great object to which you who are, or may be mothers, are more especially called, is the education of your children. If we are responsible for the use of influence in the case of those over whom we have no definite right; in the case of our children we are responsible for the exercise of acknowledged *power*: a power wide in its extent, indefinite in its effects, and inestimable in its importance. On YOU, depend in no small degree the principles of the whole rising generation. . . . And, remember, the dignity of the work to which you are called, is no less than that of preserving the ark of the Lord.[76]

Abigail Mott, writing in 1825, is equally adamant: "Let every mother consider herself as an instrument in the hand of a kind Providence to provide its realization," she proclaimed.

> Let her reflect how much the proper education of one single family may eventually contribute towards it. And that while the fruits of her labour are a rich compensation of peace, virtue and contentment, which may descend through generations yet unborn, she will herself enjoy a suitable and perma-nent reward.[77]

Like the effects, the rewards of this activity are deferred; indeed, they are as oblique as the effort—which is really no effort at all—with which women act in society. Simply by being what late eighteenth-century moralists believed they were, women could enjoy praises never bestowed on their wanton alter egos. And, as vehicles for exercising their influence were gradually institutionalized in the form of charitable and religious organizations, women could even actively participate in socially constructive work without seeming to assert themselves at all. By the end of the century, participation in such indirect activity was probably automatic for most women. Almost everything in their education and culture conspired to make such behavior seem not only proper but natural.

The French Revolution and the English Response

Even though the paradigm of femininity had come to dominate the experience of most middle-class Englishwomen by the last half of the eighteenth century, the Proper Lady did not fully evolve into the etherealized Angel of the House until the last decade of the century. Ironically, the evolution was completed largely in response to the very process by which the equation between female and feminine was finally explicitly questioned. On the one hand, the French Revolution, with its accompanying economic, political, and ideological ferment, posed a direct threat to the principle of subordination, of which feminine propriety was a part, and thus brought the issue of "women's rights" to the attention of men and women alike. On the other hand, this same social and political turmoil generated a conservative back-lash that eventually buried this issue altogether. The ultimate effect of the revolutionary decades was to intensify the paradoxes already inherent in propriety: discussions of the inequality of women's posi-tion and the complexity of female "nature" almost completely disap-peared from polite discourse even as the actual contradictions between women's real needs and the increasingly idealized image of feminini-ty were being exaggerated. As a consequence, the women who grew up during these decades, or who immediately inherited their ideologi-cal legacy, experienced a particularly intense version of the contradic-tions we have been examining.

The 1790s in England—the period Hester Thrale characterized as one of "Famine & Insurrection"[78]—witnessed numerous "rational" discussions of women's nature and position. These inquiries, both polemical and novelistic, included, in addition to Wollstonecraft's famous tract, Walter Bage's *Man as He Is* (1792), Thomas Holcroft's *Anna St. Ives* (1792), Mary Hays's *Memoirs of Emma Courtney* (1796), and William Godwin's *Enquiry Concerning Political Justice* (1793). But these radical investigations of the "perfectibility" of human nature general-ly give us less insight into the everyday preoccupations of the majori-ty of Englishmen and women than do the more conservative defenses of England's traditional order. One of the most interesting glimpses of the anxieties precipitated by the French Revolution is provided by Laetitia Hawkins's *Letters on the Female Mind* (1793). Begun as a re-sponse to Helen Williams's more radical *Letters from France,* the two volumes of *Letters on the Female Mind* were composed between Sep-tember 1792 and January 1793, a period inaugurated by the deterio-ration of the optimistic premises of the French reforms and culminating in the beheading of Louis XVI. Although Hawkins's initial goal is to prove that women's minds are naturally unsuited to politics, the crisis abroad rapidly catapults her into the very heart of political disquisi-tion. And in the course of her mounting anxiety, Hawkins reveals the specifics of her persistent fears.

Initially, Hawkins's concern is for society in general. Lamenting the current "want of subordination," she contrasts the old, reassuring social order with what she considers to be a terrifying new chaos:

> Subordination taught us all that we had places, and that others had rights, and as it was a necessity not confined to the peasantry, the yeomanry, or even to the gentry, but subsisting in all the several gradations of rank, it was thought neither hardship nor disgrace. There was a *quid pro quo* for every man; there was a station provided for every member of a community. . . . But now that no man will be any man's *servant,* and every Miss considers her father's nominal purse as a passport and introduction to all the refinements of those in a higher class, it is most painfully difficult to find occupations for young men, or to satisfy the thirsty vanity of young women.[79]

As she continues, it becomes clear that what Hawkins primarily fears is not the economic chaos of a democratic society but rather the simple difficulty of distinguishing rank—and therefore character—in a society where everyone can dress the same—where, in other words, the social signs have come loose from the "reality" of class. The social fabric now seems to her impenetrable; manners no longer seem to protect her at all. "I feel it impossible," she mourns, "with any degree of comfort, or even security, to walk in London, unprotected by a gentleman. The levelling principle has rendered all persons, making an appearance at all above the common rank, obnoxious to the most galling abuse, and often to personal insult" (2:166).

Hawkins's general concern for society is ultimately centered in what must have been a widespread issue for women: fear for her own safety and for her ability to interpret and thus negotiate social conventions. Similarly, her scorn of women's rights is anchored in her dread that, in gaining equality, women like herself will lose all power. Talk of "equal rights, the abjectness of submission, the duty of every one to think for themselves" (1:80–81), is threatening "the national female character," she fears. And fueling this talk is the unprincipled doctrine of sentimentality:

> The dominion allowed to the passions under the specious name of sentiment, has, to the grief of all serious persons, dreadfully shaken the foundation of all moral virtue: the more noisy but equally insidious clamour for universal liberty, will be the fatal blow to this lovely fabric; for I do not scruple to assert, that by diminishing the respect formerly paid to authority, the national female character is endangered. She who is taught the merit of resistance is taught to be obstinate; she who has early imbibed an aversion towards the kingly character, will easily be persuaded to consider her husband as an unauthorized tyrant, and fancying she has reason on her side, if he is not very easy to live with, she will applaud the spirit that turns inconvenience into misery. [1:105–6]

Hawkins cannot imagine a revision of the family unit so complete that patriarchy would be unacceptible—even though she knows that it sometimes entails "inconvenience." The family is the nexus of a woman's power, and to jeopardize that institution is to threaten her very sense of self. Thus she fears that the rights of women will culminate in divorce and promiscuity (soon women will "chuse their *protector,* as men do their rulers; to-day William, to-morrow John" [1:87]) and lead to insurrection in the home. Her scenario of domestic chaos indicates how relentlessly her anxieties emanate from her own situation:

> Man disdains to be shackled by custom: woman is confessed his equal: to cultivate the understanding is surely not only the most innocent, but the most laudable of all pursuits. Let me read; Nurse, take Mary away. No, replies nurse, I have learnt that we are all equal; to be confined to a place or employment is slavery . . . take care of Mary yourself.—I will not be taken care of, cries Miss Mary; to be guarded is to be a prisoner, &c. &c. Query, who now is the slave? [1:85]

The answer, clearly, is woman. Repudiated by man,[80] defied by the servants, denounced by her children, she is deprived of the only power of which she was secure: the power of influence in the home.

Hawkins, finally, rejects the possibility of equal rights because, not having been educated to consider political issues, she dreads incurring the responsibility for making decisions: "The wider our path, the more difficult is it to walk a right line" (2:190). She cherishes the freedom woman's limited lot affords her: freedom "from all the perplexities of human interests . . . all the danger of becoming guilty through vice or error . . . from all the fatigue of intense thought . . . from all the ten thousand miseries of power" (2:193–94). She cherishes the security of the protected home: "The whole world might be at war, and yet not the rumor of it reach the ear of an Englishwoman—empires might be lost, and states overthrown, and still she might pursue the peaceful occupations of her home; and her natural lord might change his governor at pleasure, and she feel neither change nor hardship" (2:194).

It is in the light of such wishful ideals and in the shadow of such immediate, personal fears that Hannah More called on her countrywomen "to come forward with a patriotism at once firm and feminine for the general good!"[81] "I would call on them to come forward, and contribute their full and fair proportion towards the saving of their country," More declared.

> But I would call on them to come forward, without departing from the refinement of their character, without derogating from the dignity of their rank, without blemishing the delicacy of their sex: I would call them to the best and most appropriate exertion of their power, to raise the depressed tone of public morals, to awaken the drowsy spirit of religious principle, and to re-animate the dormant powers of active piety. [1:4–5]

More is calling on women to support the traditional system of English values through an even more emphatic performance of their traditional offices; they are to continue to act indirectly: through the influence that radiates outward from the home. Now, however, this role is considered to be not merely supportive of national security but essential to it. As superintendents of "religious principle" and exemplars of "public morals," women now have the opportunity to inaugurate a spirit of reform that will arouse "the dormant powers of active piety" and thus make women saviors of all that is valuable in England. Through their association with spiritual values, women were to ascend the Victorian pedestal. For, as Arthur Young believed, the dissemination of Christian values could protect the imperiled hierarchy of society. "The true Christian will never be a leveller," he proclaimed hopefully in 1798. "He who worships God in spirit and in truth will love the government and laws which protect him without asking by whom they are administered."[82] In order to lead this crusade of religious reform, women would, of course, have to renounce the possibility of equal rights; but this, according to More, was an insignificant sacrifice, for "the Christian hope more than reconciles Christian women to these petty privations, by substituting a nobler prize for their ambition, 'the prize of the high calling of God in Christ Jesus.'"[83]

In her *Strictures on the Modern System of Female Education,* Hannah More echoes nearly every one of Hawkins's fears. She says that "the phrenzy of accomplishments" will confound social distinctions (1:64), that talk of the rights of men will culminate in absurd "descants on the *rights of children*" (2:38), that political powerlessness protects women from "the responsibility attached to such privileges" (2:38). But More's work is particularly interesting because in it she reveals that she is aware that there are contradictions between the normative images of what women *ought* to be and the real facts of what women are. More does entreat her readers to follow the role that "providence" has set for them, but she cannot deny that talk of natural rights and universal equality has encouraged some women to act on desires that the code of propriety explicitly denied (and implicitly controlled). "Is it not . . . more wise as well as more honourable," she cajoles her readers, "to move contentedly in the plain path which Providence has obviously marked out to the sex . . . rather than to stray awkwardly, unbecomingly, and unsuccessfully, in a forbidden road?" (2:23). Evidently More had come to the conclusion that, to deter women's aspirations to achieve equality, threats of failure might serve better than talk about impropriety. More reinforces her case with the grim reminder that, no matter what "ought" to be, social stability needs—and thus demands—sacrifices. Women *must* learn early to curb their natural appetites:

> An early habitual restraint is peculiarly important to the future character and happiness of women. They should when very young be inured to contradiction. . . . They should be led to distrust their own judgment; they should learn not to murmur at expostulation; but should be accustomed to expect and endure opposition. It is a lesson with which the world will not fail to furnish them. . . . It is of the last importance to their happiness in life that they should early acquire a submissive temper and a forbearing spirit. [1:152–53]

The importance of woman's social contribution was, however, soon proved by the general triumph of the reforms that Evangelicalism helped to sponsor; and, as the immediate social turmoil of the revolutionary decades subsided, women were again more frequently applauded for their moral virtues than reprimanded for their wayward appetites. Rapidly, women's position was consolidated. As embodiments of the pure ideals of the middle classes, they were celebrated during the nineteenth century for their superiority to all earthly desires. Depicted as a being completely without sexual desire and delicate to the point of frailty, urged not only to be dependent but to cultivate and display that dependence, the Victorian Angel of the House was to be absolutely free from all corrupting knowledge of the material—and materialistic—world. In her proper sphere, of course, she reigned as queen, for she was held to be an accessible image of God's most sacred mystery: the miracle of one who, like Christ, finds supreme self-fulfillment in absolute self-denial. In his celebration of this woman, John Ruskin described her as

> enduringly, incorruptibly good; instinctively, infallibly wise—wise, not for self-development, but for self-renunciation: wise, not that she may set herself above her husband, but that she may never fail from his side: wise, not with the narrowness of insolent and loveless pride, but with the passionate gentleness of an infinitely variable, because infinitely applicable, modesty of service—the true changefulness of woman.[84]

As we will see in the case of Mary Shelley, this image could exert annihilating pressure—or provide an avenue for escape. The process we have been examining culminated in a radically simplified stereotype of femininity that branded as "monstrous" any unconventional attempt to explore, develop, or express the female self, and, while it granted women considerable influence in society, this image effectively inhibited many women's ability to understand, much less to satisfy, their own desires or needs. Taught to emulate the "natural ideal," young women either repressed or sublimated other inclinations. What autonomy a woman earned was often purchased at the cost of either social ostracism or personal denial of inadmissible aspects of herself.

The Situation of Women Writers

The importance of this image for women writers must be obvious. Not only was marriage virtually the only respectable "occupation" for women (and both learning and writing were frequently seen as threats to domestic duty), but writing catapulted women directly into the public arena, where attention must be fought for, where explicit competition reigned. Samuel Johnson's description of the writer as pugilist suggests the extent to which the literary market was a man's domain: "he that writes may be considered as a kind of general challenger, whom every one has a right to attack; since he quits the common rank of life, steps forward beyond the lists, and offers his merit to the publick judgment. To commence author is to claim praise, and no man can justly aspire to honour, but at the hazard of disgrace."[85]

Woman's knowledge, according to Hannah More, "is not often like the learning of men, to be reproduced in some literary composition, nor ever in any learned profession; but it is to come out in conduct . . . ; her talents are only a means to a still higher attainment . . . ; merely to exercise them as instruments for the acquisition of fame and the promoting of pleasure, is subversive of her delicacy as a woman."[86] Writing for publication, in other words, jeopardizes modesty, that critical keystone of feminine propriety; for it not only "hazard[s] . . . disgrace" but cultivates and calls attention to the woman as subject, as initiator of direct action, as a person deserving of notice for her own sake. Taken to its logical extreme, to write is to assume the initiative of creator, to imitate *the* Creator; and, as Sandra Gilbert and Susan Gubar have pointed out, it is to usurp the male instrument of power, the phallus that the pen may symbolize.[87]

Still, there were ways in which women could get around these barriers, and by the end of the eighteenth century there was a burgeoning tradition of women writers, especially in prose fiction.[88] In 1773 the *Monthly Review* reported that the prose fiction "branch of the literary *trade*" was "almost engrossed by the Ladies"—a sentiment that was repeated in 1790.[89] Once more, indirection anchored the accomplishment: one could write without *personally* seeking *public* notice. In fact, as Robert Halsband has pointed out, the tradition of late eighteenth-century women writers developed from two groups that emerged earlier in the century: respectable women who wrote primarily for their own or their friends' amusement, and the faintly or frankly disreputable women who published for profit.[90] In the second category were Susannah Centlivre, Eliza Haywood, Mary Delariviere Manley, and Aphra Behn. In the first, much larger, group, the leading figure was Lady Mary Wortley Montagu. Montagu's attitude toward writing was clearly in keeping with her aristocratic station; she considered writing "demeaning if done for publication, and disgraceful if for profit": "The Greatest Virtue, Justice, and the most distinguishing prerogative of Mankind, writing, when duly executed do Honor to Human nature, but when degenerated into Trades are the most contemptible ways of getting Bread."[91] Yet Montagu confessed herself "haunted . . . by the Daemon of Poesie," and, if her writing is any indication, she was also haunted by the demon of need for public recognition. Montagu resolved the dilemma between her principles and her ambition in two ways. In the first place, she allowed her unpublished writing to be circulated privately among her social peers, thus earning admiration without contending for applause; in the second place, she published political or critical writing anonymously.[92] Both practices were widespread throughout the century (although during the 1790s anonymous publication decreased somewhat); both allowed women an indirect, disguised entrance into the competitive arena of literary creation.

At least three factors helped to open literature up to women during the course of the century. First, the rapid demise of literary patronage after 1740 meant that a woman *could* publish anonymously, without having either to solicit the interest of a patron (nearly all of whom would have been male) or even to acknowledge her own sex. The practice of having a father, brother, or husband negotiate with a publisher was common for a young woman writer, as the examples of Fanny Burney, Mary Shelley, and Jane Austen suggest. Second, the informal society of the Bluestockings provided a model for the literary women, as well as a specific place and opportunity for women of late eighteenth-century London to meet and discuss literary interests. Although Hannah More claimed that the society met "for the sole purpose of conversation," its members' interests and accomplishments extended considerably beyond the art of polite discourse. Elizabeth Carter, for example, read Latin, Greek, Hebrew, French, Italian, Spanish, German, Portuguese, and Arabic, published her first poem at seventeen, made £1,000 by the subscription publication of her translation of Epictetus, and saw her collected poems go into three editions. Such "Blues" as Elizabeth Montagu, Emily Boscawen, Hester Chapone, and Hannah More were significant because they preserved their unimpeachable reputations *and* published for profit and public esteem. Thus they helped elevate what had been genteel amateurism into an acceptable professional career.[93]

The activity of women writers was also enhanced by a third factor, the eighteenth century's embrace of philosophical empiricism and the accompanying interest in and emphasis on individual feelings. As we will see in the case of Mary Wollstonecraft, "sentimentalism" proved an ambiguous attraction to women writers, but, despite some qualifications, it is important to remember that feeling was one significant theater of experience that could not be completely denied to women. Excluded from learned argument—indeed, from an entire tradition of intellectual achievement—because they were not taught Latin or Greek, women could nevertheless write of their own feelings and from their own imaginations, especially when "expression" replaced intellectual substance as the primary criterion of quality. In 1789 Mrs. Thrale noted the new fashion in literature with qualified approval:

> In Cowley's Day nothing was hunted for but new & fine Thoughts, & hang the Expression . . .—and at present if all the Epithets are compounded, & the Periods elegantly arranged, it appears that all Meaning is needless, and Thought superfluous. . . . This fashion makes well for us Women however, as Learning no longer forms any part of the Entertainment expected from Poetry—Ladies have therefore as good a Chance as People regularly bred to Science in Times when *fire-eyed Fancy* is said to be the only requisite of a Popular Poet.[94]

Mrs. Thrale somewhat exaggerates the democracy of the Muse, if for no other reason than that "*fire-eyed Fancy*" was still harnessed to personal experience, a realm severely circumscribed for women. Yet the novel of sensibility, developing along the patterns established by

Richardson, provided women with a genre apparently tailor-made for their experience, confined as it was to domestic concerns and affairs of the heart. Even critics of excessive sentimentalism, such as Hannah More, agreed that women were "naturally" suited to this species of composition. "In almost all that comes under the description of polite letters," More explains, "in all that captivates by imagery or warms by just and affecting sentiment, women are excellent. . . . They are acute observers, and accurate judges of life and manners, as far as their own sphere of observation extends; but they describe a smaller circle."[95]

But it is also important to remember that, although women found in the sentimental novel a subject and even a genre, these works frequently simply ratified the ideal we have been discussing; thus they called attention primarily to women's weaknesses and helped to drive further underground the aggressive, perhaps sexual, energies that men feared in women. The "tradition" of women's fiction that developed during the eighteenth century was undeniably important, but its importance must be seen as qualified and limited. First, women writers often simply embraced the social role that women as a group had generally internalized. For the most part, women writers were scrupulous about fulfilling the office of educator, and, as a consequence, their novels often echo conduct books almost verbatim, stressing self-control and self-denial to the exclusion of psychological complexity and attributing almost all initiative to the evil characters rather than to the heroines. Second, far from encouraging women to come to conscious terms with their social position, sentimental fiction often provided them with compensatory gratifications, ideal rewards, and ideal revenges,[96] all of which discouraged them from seeking material changes in their actual position. As we will see in the cases of Wollstonecraft and Shelley, the impulse to compensate imaginatively for the comparative poverty of their professional opportunities could tempt a woman not only into pure wish-fulfillment but also into taking up a vocabulary and set of values that automatically undermined even conscious efforts to analyze the realities of her situation. One of the most persistent dilemmas of the woman writer during this period proved to be the problem of controlling her own attraction to ideal compensations, along with the difficulty of subordinating to her aesthetic design the powerful feelings that generated this attraction in the first place. Not surprisingly, we will often see the complexities of their position within ideology most clearly at the moments these writers dramatize the eruptions of female feeling.

The "tradition" that developed in the eighteenth century was also impeded by continuing social resistance. Women who wanted to publish continued to encounter—or fear—the persistent prejudice against learned ladies; Hester Thrale suspected, for example, that most men would "prefer the Delicacy of the Queen of Love to all the Intelligence of Minerva."[97] And, even if they were willing to hazard frowns, women faced the more practical difficulty of finding the time and the quiet that writers need. "I . . . charge all my Neglect," Mrs. Thrale sighed, "to my young ones Account, and feel myself at this moment very miserable that I have at last, after being married four-teen Years and bringing eleven Children, leisure to write."[98] After the manuscript was completed, women were often subjected to mistreat-ment by male booksellers or publishers,[99] and, perhaps even more debilitating, they were treated with condescension by the critics. The kind of critical indulgence male reviewers accorded women served to keep them in their proper place more effectively than even the most hostile criticism would have; it flattered the more tractable women into complaisance and humiliated the more discerning. Women were praised for their "quickness of apprehension," "delicate taste," and for not presuming to "strong judgment." Even the critical vocabulary applied to women's writings calls for special interpretation; to say that a lady's novel is "in the main correctly written" is to praise grammar and spelling rather than ideas.[100] Such treatment persuaded Hannah More that, for a women, to write at all was to court mortificat-ion:

> But there is one *human* consideration which would perhaps more effectually tend to damp in an aspiring woman the ardours of literary vanity . . . than any which she will derive from motives of humility, or propriety, or religion; which is, that in the judgment passed on her performances, she will have to encounter the mortifying circumstance of having her sex always taken into account, and her highest exertions will probably be received with the qualified approbation, *that it is really extraordinary for a woman.* Men of learning, who are naturally apt to estimate works in proportion as they appear to be the result of art, study, and institution, are apt to consider even the happier performances of the other sex as the spontaneous productions of a fruitful but shallow soil; and to give them the same sort of praise which we bestow on certain sallads [*sic*], which often draw from us a sort of wondering commendation; not indeed as being worth much in themselves, but because by the lightness of the earth, and a happy knack of the gardener, these indifferent cresses spring up in a night, and therefore one is ready to wonder they are no worse.[101]

No doubt partly to escape this humiliation, More published all except the last four of her works anonymously even though her work was instantly recognizable to all her readers. Women who did publish under their own names almost always sought to justify their efforts as financially necessary—preferably, to the support of a family (Sarah Emma Spencer's *Memoirs of the Miss Holmsbys* was "written by the bedside of a sick husband, who has no other support than what my writing will produce"); as thoroughly didactic (Ann Radcliffe claimed in *The Mysteries of Udolpho* that the efforts of her "weak hand" were justified because the novel taught the mourner to endure sorrow); or as absolutely commonplace (Laetitia Hawkins prided herself in having made only casual observations "on some topics that force themselves on every one's notice"). Welcoming the concession they felt had been granted them, most eighteenth-century women writers at least paid lip service to the notion that they were intellectually inferior to men. Most women contented themselves with what More called their "shadowy claim to a few unreal acres of Parnassian territory."[102] Few ventured into the forbidden territory of political disquisition, metaphysics, or theological speculation, and, when a stalwart woman like Mary Wollstonecraft did so, the outrage of men and women alike was sufficient to wither her less courageous sisters. For the most part, literature remained for women "an ornament, or an amusement, not a duty or profession"; for, as Jane West continued, "when it is pursued with such avidity as to withdraw us from the especial purposes of our creation, it becomes a crime."[103]

In 1835 the novelist Catherine Maria Sedgwick noted in her diary that her "author existence" was "accidental, extraneous & independent of my inner self."[104] In 1831 another woman, Mary Shelley, described a similar split in her "self." In preparing a preface for the revised edition of *Frankenstein,* Shelley shrank from "bringing [her]self forward in print." But she justified describing the origin of the novel by its distance from her real "personal" self: "as it will be confined to such topics as have connection with my authorship alone, I can scarcely accuse myself of a personal intrusion."[105] This phenomenon, which is only one more manifestation of the indirection, or double consciousness, that we have already seen in women's social behavior, characterizes a remarkable number of women writers in the eighteenth and early nineteenth centuries. Women who wrote or achieved recognition in other "masculine" arenas frequently seemed unconscious of their accomplishment or, perhaps more accurately, thought of themselves in terms that simply did not fully acknowledge what they were doing. Even though they competed for readers and wielded power as energetically as men, these women explicitly rejected the entrepreneurial values that men used in describing such activities. They thought of themselves as textbook Proper Ladies even as they boldly crossed the borders of that limited domain.

Many such women have already spoken on these pages. Outside the realm of imaginative literature, we recall Mary Wortley Montagu, whose comment that a woman should "conceal whatever Learning she attains" is sharply undercut by her mastery of Latin, German, Turkish, Spanish, and Greek and by her own publications;[106] Hester

Lynch Thrale Piozzi, who, despite her genteel education, successfully righted her husband's business after his ineptness had threatened bankruptcy, and who defied the outrage of her own daughters, after Thrale's death, and married her beloved Piozzi; and Hannah More, whose prodigious literary production was matched by the energy with which she and her fragile sisters introduced Sunday schools and social improvements into the district of Cheddar.[107] Within the domain of literature, nearly every woman who wrote was able to internalize a self-conception at least temporarily at odds with the norm we have been examining, and the legacy of this period is a repertoire of the strategies that enabled women either to conceive of themselves in two apparently incompatible ways or to express themselves in a code capable of being read in two ways: as acquiescence to the norm and as departure from it.[108] It is important to recognize that the prevalence of these strategies does not always mean that women writers were conscious of the restrictions they faced or that they deliberately struggled to transcend them. Rather, these strategies must be seen as these women's *interpretations* of the restrictions, as "readings" of contemporary propriety that facilitated everyday life and ultimately, often obliquely, sought to reconcile desire and satisfaction, conventional manners and genuine self-expression.

Perhaps the most significant strategy for survival was simply the act of writing. In an article on female autobiography, Patricia Meyer Spacks has described the complexities of women's writing about themselves and the same observations hold true for eighteenth-century women purportedly writing about something or someone else; for in all of these works the struggle to *be* a self takes place simultaneously with the effort to *express* the self.[109] According to Spacks, women are able, through writing, to master their life-experience in at least two ways: they can avoid reality, as many eighteenth-century novelists did, by means of fantasy; or they can mine their limited sphere for the wealth of concrete details that enable them to master experience. As we have seen in the case of Fanny Burney, women can even turn the frustrations of their social position into the rich stuff of comedy or high drama.[110] By objectifying the details of ordinary behavior, then, women can transform even passivity, self-denial, and resignation into a kind of heroism.

At the same time, however, writing also affords a more obvious protection for the woman taught to efface her aspiring self. Not only does anonymous publication enable her to send a disguised emissary into the same society she frequents (as Fanny Burney did with *Evelina*), but the objective text itself serves as a more general mediator between self and public. To write is to earn attention without directly claiming it; sometimes the text can even serve as a surrogate in the activity one would "personally" never undertake. Such, for example, is the case of Laetitia Hawkins, whose *Letters on the Female Mind* explicitly asserts that women are constitutionally unsuited to address political issues, issues she is "proud to own it above [her] powers to discuss." Yet, apparently without a sense of contradiction, Hawkins uses these letters to air her views on the entire range of contemporary political questions, from the legitimacy of the French monarchy to the advantages of the slave trade, from the social importance of the aristocracy to the superfluousness of poor relief. Similarly, Mary Ann Radcliffe, whose *Memoirs* chronicle a life of hardship and humiliation, explicitly refuses to blame her husband, whose profligacy squandered her considerable inheritance. She will, she claims, not accuse anyone but "fate": "seeing it was my fate, and not able to find out a remedy, I remained passive and silent, (however acute might be my feelings,) still leaving to time, that leveller of human events, to do justice in my cause."[111] Yet Radcliffe's *Memoirs* itself accuses the wastrel husband; along with the explicitly polemical *Female Advocate,* published in the same volume, the *Memoirs* speaks more eloquently, more effectively, than any personal vindication could have done.

In addition to the act of writing itself, women created opportunities for self-expression through strategies of indirection, obliqueness, and doubling that were the imaginative counterparts of the paradoxical behavior they were encouraged to cultivate in everyday life. Significantly, Hannah More identified the habit of intellectual indirection as characteristically feminine. To her, it was a "natural" rather than a learned response, but her observations are nevertheless revealing.

> The female too, wanting steadiness in her intellectual pursuits, is perpetually turned aside by her characteristic tastes and feelings. Woman in the career of genius, is the Atalanta, who will risk losing the race by running out of her road to pick up the golden apple; while her male competitor, without, perhaps, possessing greater natural strength or swiftness, will more certainly attain his object, by direct pursuit, by being less exposed to the seductions of extraneous beauty, and will win the race by despising the bait. [*Strictures,* 2:28–29]

More's version of the maxim that women are naturally more responsive is here translated through the masculine value system of competition, with the finish line signaling the victor and "steadiness" and "direct pursuit" being more effective than "tastes" and "feelings." Yet More inadvertently acknowledges that there might be another system of values at work here too, that the woman, "perhaps, possessing greater natural strength [and] swiftness," might have won had she not found the "extraneous beauty" more appealing than finishing first. If we apply More's paradigm and the alternate hierarchies of values it contains to the novels of, for instance, Fanny Burney, we can see that Burney's characteristic deferral of the inevitable happy ending enables her to accomplish something different from an architecturally balanced, efficiently resolved plot.[112] In each of Burney's works the heroines relatively rapidly reveal their own desires, but inhibiting factors—whether innocence, as in the heroines of *Evelina* and *Camilla,* or a suitor's pride, as in *Cecilia,* or entangling circumstances, as in *The Wanderer*—continue to frustrate satisfactory resolutions during much of the course of what are often very long novels. This plot structure duplicates for the reader the claustrophobic situation of the heroine in society. Forbidden by convention to declare their desires, the heroines must struggle, often ineffectually, to communicate by indirection or even deceit, and the interest of the plot lies in the nuances of frustration and achievement that mark their efforts. Surprisingly little in the way of dramatic events happens in these novels; like Richardson, Burney deals in "sentiment" and emotional accommodation rather than confrontation and triumph.[113]

The introduction of Samuel Richardson into the discussion reminds us, of course, that these strategies are not unique to women. Eighteenth-century male writers could certainly employ them as effectively as women—often more effectively, in fact, because men were able to perceive the significance of restriction more easily than the women whose lives duplicated this restriction. Yet these strategies were *characteristically* feminine, not in the sense that they were "natural" to women, as More suggested, but in the sense that they characterized women's learned or internalized responses to the objective female social situation, which was founded on the prerogatives of bourgeois society and imposed by propriety. Thus, although a second strategy was used perhaps even more frequently by male eighteenth-century authors than by women, it so precisely articulated women's characteristic situation that it was to become one of the distinguishing features of novels written by nineteenth-century women.[114] Both Richardson and Defoe effectively use the technique of "doubling" their female characters, pairing, for example, the resigned, angelic Clarissa with the intractable Anna Howe (or, for that matter, with the demonic Mrs. Sinclair),[115] or the wealthy Roxana with her obedient maid Amy.[116] Eighteenth-century women authors, from Eliza Haywood to Maria Edgeworth, used this technique, for it provided an opportunity not only to dramatize the negative counterparts of the heroine's perfect qualities but also to play at different roles, to explore, often through the characters of servants or lower-class women, direct actions forbidden to the more proper lady. Among the writers I discuss, the most accomplished mistress of this strategy is Jane Austen. Her paired

heroines rarely allow the apparent polarities of sense and sensibility
or pride and prejudice a simple resolution; between these antinomies
there is no easy choice but rather myriads of possible combinations,
each understood in terms of costs and benefits, sacrifices and opportunities.

Many of these strategies constitute what Gilbert and Gubar, revising Harold Bloom, have called feminine "swerves" from masculine
genres or from the stereotypes of women men have popularized.
Parody, the deconstruction and reconstruction of female literary types,
the perfection of "surface designs" that "conceal or obscure deeper,
less acceptable (and less socially acceptable) levels of meaning" are
other such strategies that Gilbert and Gubar describe as at least
implicitly involving a challenge to the authority of male writers.[117] We
will see the presence of just such an overt contest in the works of
Mary Wollstonecraft, and, especially in her polemical tracts, the
"swerve" from masculine authorities provokes both debilitating self-
consciousness and creative revisionist maneuvers. But confrontation
is not the only profitable way of formulating women's relationship
to their literary fathers or their cultural inheritance. Just as frequently
as they explicitly swerve from or confront authorities, women embrace or accommodate themselves to the conflicting tendencies established by their position within cultural values. In this sense, which is
more in keeping with the model of female psychological maturation
proposed by feminists such as Nancy Chodorow and Juliet Mitchell,[118]
parody can be seen as the expression of a desire to retain *both* the
inherited and the revised genre,[119] and the creation of demonic "mad-
women" can be understood as the articulation of simultaneous, if
contradictory, self-images. A version of doubling that seems particularly consistent with this notion of accommodation is Jane Austen's
multiplication of centers of authority in her novels. In a sense, the
narrative persona is only one half of Austen's voice in each novel,
with the entire action of the plot providing the other half. However,
the alternatives posed by the narrator, on the one hand, and the
action, on the other, are not rigidly differentiated; nor is the degree
of irony implicit in the narrator's comments identifiable if this voice
is detached from its context. Only by participating imaginatively in
the choices that the characters in these novels face can the reader
understand the moral complexities of these societies. Especially in her
last novels, Austen negotiates a complex contract with her readers in
which she makes such participation necessary in order for the reader
to understand and evaluate the action *and* the narrator's comments.
In these novels, moral values saturate the social fabric, and no author-
itaive narrator helps the heroines or the reader to master the ethical
intricacies.

Role-playing is also an important form of accommodation employed by both Mary Wollstonecraft and Mary Shelley. Through the use of thinly disguised autobiographical characters, these writers explore, expand, and sometimes revise their own situations in such a way as to express or repress their own deeply felt desires. These characters can either say or do things their authors have not permitted themselves to say or do, or, as in Shelley's works in particular, they can do things differently as a way of imaginatively revising the past. Retaining explicit autobiographical details seems to enhance the degree of control these women feel over reality; at the same time, it provides a more direct sense of participation in the accomplishments achieved through fiction.

Accommodation is also present in women's gothic novels in the form of enclosed episodes in which the author can explore material otherwise considered unladylike. In the hermetically sealed castle or nunnery, often under the protective tyranny of a man, women like Ann Radcliffe's Emily St. Aubert (*The Mysteries of Udolpho*) are able to exercise ingenuity and express curiosity that would be improper in the outside world.[120] Austen's satirical *Northanger Abbey* contains a similar sequence of enclosed episodes, and the fact that Catherine Morland's perception of the tyrannical General Tilney is in many ways ratified by the outcome of the novel serves to highlight the importance of the imaginative freedom Catherine is momentarily granted. As Gilbert and Gubar have pointed out, the topoi of enclosure or confinement often dominate the imagery and themes as well as the structure of women's literature. "Trapped in so many ways in the architecture—both the houses and the institutions—of patriarchy, women . . . expressed their claustrophobic rage by enacting rebellious escapes."[121]

Another important form of accommodation involves what Spacks calls "acts of incorporation." By such maneuvers, women authors are able to make statements about themselves by directing attention to people or objects around them. As Spacks defines the term, these "acts of incorporation" may be "ironic, loving, aggressive, exploratory"; in them, women make themselves known by foregrounding a relationship of which they are a part.[122] In a sense particularly applicable to the eighteenth century, women come into being by adding something to themselves. In that society a woman was often metaphorically described as a "cypher." Etymologically, this word means "empty" or "a void," and by extension it means "a nonentity"; but a cypher is also, numerically, a zero, and this figure has properties that are almost magical. Like the number that is no number, a woman could increase or decrease the value of other figures (and herself) simply by her relationship to them, and, by calling attention to this relationship, a woman writer could call attention to her contribution and her value without having to confront masculine authority directly—without, that is, transgressing the rules of propriety. Thus, the conclusion of Shelley's *Falkner* emphasizes the reconciliation of two men, but the account of this reconciliation obliquely praises the woman who has made it possible. Similarly, Jane Austen's novels all culminate in marriage, but this relationship serves chiefly to display the heroine's achievement of maturity, not the victory of a man or even the establishment of a family.

The presence of these strategies can signal evasion as well as an expansion of possibilities, for they are as double-edged as the situation they interpret. In the works of the three authors I discuss at length in the following chapters, I demonstrate the equivocal nature of these strategies, show how the complexities of the paradox they replicate could overwhelm aesthetic control, and suggest the kinds of accomplishment they could yield. I examine the artistic career of each writer in the context of the biographical material that is available, for only by placing literary activity and style within the entire range of behavior elicited by a cultural situation can we make sense of an author's personal position within an ideology. Artistic solutions were only part of these women's responses to particular (if typical) situations; their strategies in art served as strategies for living as well, and often we see them encountering and trying to solve the same problems in both domains.

Each woman's work, then—and, when understood in its broadest sense, her style—constitutes a representation of (implicitly, a response to) the ideology we have been examining. Mary Wollstonecraft's political tracts, travelogues, and fiction reveal her difficulties in launching a frontal assault on the values of her society. Not only did she encounter public hostility for her political and personal defiance of conventions; she also became emotionally ensnared by the network of rationales, social functions, and cultural fears by means of which ideology penetrates the social fabric. The inhibitions that beset her, she slowly discovered, were not simply imposed from without; having been internalized, they also operated from within. The career of Wollstonecraft's daughter, Mary Shelley, describes the gradual triumph of the simplified image of femininity in which the eighteenth-century paradigm culminates. Although Shelley's early work shows her "monstrous" desire for autonomy at war with the norm of propriety, her later works primarily reveal the guilt that Shelley came to associate with those adolescent desires. In them the Proper Lady triumphs not as an expression but as an evasion of self. Finally, Jane Austen's career demonstrates the way in which some of the strategies I have been discussing could be used to exploit the paradoxes inherent in the idea of the Proper Lady. Writing from inside the ideology of propriety, Austen gradually perfected a form of irony that enabled her to present her personal values in such a way as to make them seem natural correctives to the restrictions of decorum. Simultaneously part of and apart from her society's values, Jane Austen eventually achieved the freedom necessary not only to identify this ideology but—always tactfully and with ladylike restraint—to criticize the way it shaped and deformed women's desires.

In the literary works of these three women we can see traces of the sexuality so castigated in the late seventeenth century. Chiefly, however, we see the degree to which sexual desire has been successfully harnessed to the family unit and the degree to which it has been sublimated into imaginative efforts or altogether repressed, to be betrayed only by silence and guilt. We can also see the entanglement of love with property, the way that the first subject necessarily introduces the second, and the complex role each plays in female maturation. Most clearly of all, we can see in these women's works the shadow of a demure young woman, with eyes downcast and lips pressed into a faint and silent smile. She is the Proper Lady, guardian and nemesis of the female self.

2

Man's Discourse, Woman's Heart:
Mary Wollstonecraft's Two Vindications

BECAUSE MARY WOLLSTONECRAFT'S analysis of propriety became a rallying point for radicals and conservatives alike, her works
constitute the logical starting point for an examination of the effects
the image of propriety had on women who were also writers. More
surely than any of her female contemporaries, Mary Wollstonecraft
took the first step toward liberating herself from the crippling strictures of feminine propriety: she identified the ideology that assigned
women their social position and cultural definition; she then argued
that it was both unnatural and wrong. Indeed, Wollstonecraft's career
virtually documents the way one woman moved from the status of
unreflecting, passive object to that of a self-conscious, articulate, and
vindicating subject. Yet in the course of recognizing the biases at the
heart of her culture, Wollstonecraft stumbled into another of its
ideological snares. In attempting to delineate—and disengage herself
from—masculine definitions of women, Wollstonecraft found herself
vacillating between denying her female feelings altogether and falling
hostage once more to the very categories she was trying to escape.
   The difficulties Mary Wollstonecraft encountered again and again
in her private life and her literary works all center on the issue of
feeling. In both her life and her art she explicitly raised the questions
that late eighteenth-century intellectuals implicitly posed to the normative definition of woman: if a female's most salient characteristic
is her emotional responsiveness, what role can a woman play in the
society of reason and enlightenment then being proclaimed by the
philosophers? And further, what role does feminine receptivity—
susceptibility—play in the self-determination that the Enlightenment
seemed to promise to every human being? All of the maneuvers that
characterize Wollstonecraft's life and literary texts are attempts to
find provisional solutions to these questions. That none of her efforts
yielded a permanently satisfactory answer attests both to the tenacity
of the ideology she tried to challenge and—largely as a consequence
of this tenacity—to her own failure to take her challenge to its logical,
radical extreme.

The early stage of Wollstonecraft's life and writing is characterized by the persistence of two conflicting desires. On the one hand, she constantly craved the emotional rewards that propriety decreed were every woman's most important birthright: love, gratitude, and a sense of being necessary to someone else's happiness. On the other hand, she was driven by a fierce determination to be independent—free not just from financial debts (though these were pressing and very real) but, more significantly, from feeling itself, from hope—from the emotional demands that were also considered a part of female "nature." Wollstonecraft's ambivalence toward feeling resurfaced in its most troubling form when she tried to cope with the emotions and sexual urges traditionally signified by the euphemism "sentiments." Even in her youth we see examples of this characteristic turmoil. When she was only fourteen, for instance, she reprimanded her best friend, Jane Arden, for slighting her in favor of a new companion. In this letter she explains her "notions of friendship":

> I have formed romantic notions of friendship.—I have been once disappointed:—I think if I am a second time I shall only want some infidelity in a love affair, to qualify me for an old maid, as then I shall have no idea of either of them.—I am a little singular in my thoughts of love and friendship; I must have the first place or none.—I own your behaviour is more according to the opinion of the world, but I would break such narrow bounds.[1]

Clearly, Wollstonecraft wants love more than anything else, but she wants it only on her own terms: "I must have the first place or none." She wants to command love, to dictate its intensity and duration, and in doing so she also wants to claim for herself a position of intellectual preeminence and courage: "I would break such narrow bounds."

Wollstonecraft's desire to dictate the terms of the love she so badly wanted is no doubt a common human impulse. But what is interesting here is the particular relation between her ambivalence toward feeling and her personal and class position. For Mary Wollstonecraft occupied, for much of her life, a precarious social position, and this social uncertainty made personal frustrations both more likely and more painful. When she was born, in 1759, her father, Edward John Wollstonecraft, had every reason to think that he would be able to elevate his family into the landed middle classes. As the eldest son of a well-to-do silk weaver, he had been trained in his father's trade, but in 1763 he moved out of London to become a farmer in Epping; then, after his father's death, in 1765, he purchased a considerable estate in Barking.[2] But the son was not as steady or as provident as his father, and by the end of ten years he had squandered his inheritance, lost his estate, and nearly destroyed his family, not only through financial mismanagement but through drunkenness and a tyrannical temper. Largely because of their rapid social descent and her father's irresponsibility, Mary Wollstonecraft took the audacious step of leaving home at the age of eighteen to go to work as a lady's companion.

Even in her precarious position as a self-supporting workingwoman, Wollstonecraft remained—in some conflicting senses—a child of the middle classes. As we will see in her work *A Vindication of the Rights of Men,* she continued to identify with the middle-class ideal of self-reliance and with the bourgeois aspirations that had impelled her father to leave the silk trade for the more gentlemanly occupation of farming. Two of the most dramatic incidents of Wollstonecraft's young adulthood reflect her remarkable determination and self-assertiveness. In 1784, with what must have been nearly unheard-of audacity, she single-handedly "rescued" her distraught sister Eliza from an unhappy marriage—spiriting her away from her husband and child, then hiding her in London from the wrath and entreaties of the abandoned spouse. Then, late in 1785, Wollstonecraft set off for Lisbon alone—again, a daring action for a young woman—to oversee the lying-in of her beloved friend Fanny Blood. She arrived in the foreign country only to watch her friend die soon after giving birth.

Despite their daring, the domestic character of these actions suggests that Wollstonecraft had also internalized the expectations and self-definition of a typical middle-class Proper Lady. She spent much of her young adulthood seeking the kind of emotional situation that would substitute for the unhappy family relationships she had left behind. Throughout her teens and late twenties she turned to a series of father figures—the Reverend Clare, Dr. Richard Price, and, later, Joseph Johnson—and gathered about her, in addition to her two natural sisters, a flock of surrogate siblings—Jane Arden in her youth, then Fanny Blood and her brother George. In her letters Wollstonecraft repeatedly imagines herself constructing a happy family, playing "mother" to her sisters, Eliza and Everina, and to George Blood and establishing—along with her sisters and Fanny—a self-supporting female establishment with herself as maternal presider.[3] Throughout this period Fanny Blood constituted a sort of feminine ideal for Wollstonecraft; she was docile, refined, and nurturing, and Wollstonecraft spoke of herself as being improved by their close friendship. When Wollstonecraft's mother fell ill in late 1780, Mary went home to nurse her day and night until she died in April 1782. On her deathbed, as Wollstonecraft reconstructed the scene in her last work, *Maria,* Mary's mother bequeathed to her an ongoing domestic responsibility: "My mother . . . solemnly recommended my sisters to my care, and bid me be a mother to them."

Wollstonecraft's personal sense of the unreliability of domestic affections, however, contributed to her need to dictate the terms on which she was willing to assume a traditional woman's role. She seems to have felt that no one ever really loved her enough: not her mother, who Wollstonecraft always believed preferred her older brother; not her sisters, of each of whom she complained to the other; not Jane Arden, who always had some other friend; not even Fanny Blood, whose love for Hugh Skyes obviously aroused Wollstonecraft's jealousy.[4] Her anxiety about the possibility of domestic love led directly, as the early letter to Jane Arden suggested, to an anxiety about the possibility of romantic love: if she could not count on love from her natural or chosen family, she may well have wondered how she could ever rely on a man to voluntarily commit himself to her. Her letters from this period suggest that she felt threatened by her susceptibility to both familial and romantic emotions because such feelings made her vulnerable to the unpredictable, unfathomable emotions of other people, to circumstances beyond her control, to her own emotional volatility—in short, to disappointment. Perhaps in defiance of the disappointment she had come to expect and fear, Wollstonecraft began to speak scornfully of romantic love even before the collapse of Eliza's marriage. As early as 1779, when she was just twenty, she yearned for "a kind of early old age" (*MWL,* p. 69; 17 October 1779), a condition that, by 1782, she prided herself on having attained: "I have already got the wrinkles of old age, and so, like a true woman, rail at what I don't possess" (*MWL,* p. 78; late 1782–early 1783). What she didn't possess, Wollstonecraft decided, was not worth having; after all, marriage—and the feeling on which it was presumably based—constituted a bondage of sorts. "I dont want to be tied to this nasty world," she wrote to Jane Arden in 1782. "It is a happy thing to be a mere blank, and to be able to pursue one's own whims, where they lead, without having a husband and half a hundred children at hand to teaze and controul a poor woman who wishes to be free" (*MWL,* p. 79; 20 October 1782–10 August 1783).

By 1785 Wollstonecraft's determined defense against feeling had reached what was for her the logical extension of this desire "to be free": a professed longing for the only satisfaction she could imagine, death. Especially after Fanny's death, her letters are filled with vows of Christian resignation, an attitude she professed to value because it could wean her from this earthly life and thus liberate her completely from feeling and hope. "My constitution is so impaired," she wrote to George Blood, "I hope I shan't live long—yet I may be a tedious time dying— Well, I am too impatient— The Will of Heaven be done! I will labour to be resigned" (*MWL,* p. 102; 4 February 1786). Like Clarissa longing for her Father's house, Wollstonecraft imagined that death was simply a translation into a more satisfying—because more "substantial"—family: "My thoughts and wishes tend to that land where the God of love will wipe away all tears from our eyes—where sincerity and truth will flourish—and the imagination will not dwell on pleasing illusions—which vanish like dreams when experience forces us to see things as they really are" (*MWL,* p. 119; 9 October 1786).

Throughout her youth the only two emotions Wollstonecraft seems to have felt comfortable with were resignation and pity—the first because, in suppressing personal desire, it shifted the burden of feeling to some more authoritative and hence reliable being; the second because, originating in someone else's need, it enabled her to control the emotional dynamics of the relationship. "I love most people best when they are in adversity," she informed George Blood, "for pity is one of my prevailing passions" (*MWL,* p. 92; 20 July 1785). Although Wollstonecraft obsessively questioned the fidelity of her friends, several passages in her letters suggest that her anxiety about the dependability of others originated in the unpredictability of her own feelings. In order to counter this dreaded volatility, she began early in her life to turn to various mechanisms by which to control her own feelings, at least partially, and to disarm disappointment of its sting. Religion was one such control; reason, or "understanding," was another. "I am often with myself at war," she admitted to George Blood in 1786,

> I cannot always feel alike—my heart sometimes overflows with kindness—and at others seems quite exhausted and incapable of being warmly interested about any one— my regards carried beyond the pitch which wisdom pre-scribes—often throw me into apathy; but though I cannot answer for my feelings—I can promise my understanding will ever approve of you. [*MWL,* p. 110; 6 July 1786]

Wollstonecraft's longing for freedom from emotional vulnerability was intensified by the helplessness and humiliation she associated with her social and economic dependence: "I must be independent and earn my own subsistence," she told George Blood, "or be very uncomfortable" (*MWL,* p. 107; 18 June 1786). During the period from 1778 to 1790, she tried virtually every honorable occupation open to middle-class women. In addition to being a lady's companion, she was a seamstress, a schoolmistress, and, finally, a governess for the daughters of Irish aristocrats, the Kingsboroughs. None of these contractual relationships, of course, satisfied her craving for emotional return. For despite her fierce desire to control her feelings, Wollstonecraft repeatedly learned that her emotions—and even hope—were irrepressible. "I am indeed a sociable creature," she acknowledged to George Blood; "but I must curb my affections which are too apt to run into extremes, and rivet me to earth." "I am really very ill and so low spirited," she sighed to Everina; "my tears flow in torrents almost insensibly— I struggle with myself—but I hope my Heavenly Father will not be extreme to mark my weakness" (*MWL*, p. 108, 18 June 1786; p. 127, 17 November 1786). Wollstonecraft composed this letter to Everina when she was employed in the most extended and most frustrating of her occupations. During her stay in Ireland as a governess, Wollstonecraft's insecurity surfaced in nagging doubts that she was qualified for the job, fears that she was not well-dressed or pretty enough, and a perhaps defensive concern that the children were growing too fond of her. Insecurity, loneliness, and home-sickness were exacerbated by what she felt to be an even more "awkward" social position ("this something betwixt and between," she called it [*MWL*, p. 124; 5 November 1786]). Inferior in status, she consoled herself with the thought that she was superior in "sensibili-ty," in "real refinement."

While living in Ireland, Wollstonecraft found another mechanism that seemed to promise relief from her ever-present emotional volatil-ity. In 1787 she read Rousseau's *Emile,* and the "sensibility and pene-tration" she discovered there helped her to define the distress she had felt for so long. Wollstonecraft's letters from Ireland show an inten-sification of her previously intermittent tendency to dramatize herself as an incarnation of the stereotypical sentimental heroine.[5] It is in this period that her vows of Christian resignation begin to be cast in conventional sentimental language and tropes, and her longing for death gives way to an indulgence of the very feeling she had previous-ly sought to escape. "I am like a *lilly* drooping," she postures in concluding the letter that mentions Rousseau. She then finishes with flourishing allusions to both Gray and Shakespeare, the effect of which is to stylize the misery she no doubt genuinely felt: "Is it not a sad pity that so sweet a flower should waste its sweetness on the *Desart* air, or that the Grave should receive its *untouched* charms. Yours an Old Maid— ' 'Tis true a pity and 'tis pity tis true' " (*MWL*, p. 145; 24 March 1787).

What seems like a relapse into feeling paradoxically serves as a means for gaining some distance—hence control—over her own emotionalism. For although seeing herself as a heroine of sensibility did nothing to alleviate the very real financial problems that contin-ued to plague her, the objectification intrinsic to such self-dramatiza-tion enabled her to conceive of her present emotional turmoil as part of a larger, recognizable characterization. Previously she had sought fulfillment within domestic relationships; now she was able to turn to situations in which characters seemed to have emotions as expan-sive as her own. Imitating Rousseau's rhetoric thus enabled her to express, without wholly succumbing to them, the feelings she had previously tried to repress. The gratification she seems to have received from this indulgence of feeling, however, was actually setting the terms for what would prove to be her final battle with ideology. For even though she was eventually able to recognize that emotional indulgence served not only to sublimate frustrated sexual desire but also to inflame emotion and thus keep her hostage to passion, Wollstonecraft was never really able to renounce the idea of romantic "happiness" that sentimentalism seemed to promise. So enthusiastically did she internalize the values and expectations associated with sentimentalism that she even began to embrace her weakness as the trait that made her most "interesting." Paradoxically, of course, this "distinction" also provided her with the means for surpassing her social superior, Lady Kingsborough:

> I give way to whim—and yet when the most sprightly sallies burst from me the tear frequently trembles in my eye and the long drawn sigh eases my full heart—so my eyes roll in the wild way you have *seen* them. a deadly paleness overspreads my countenance—and yet so weak am I a sudden thought or any *recollected* emotion of tenderness will occasion the most painful suffusion. You know not my dear Girl of what materials, this strange inconsistency [sic] heart of mine, is formed and how alive it is to tenderness and misery. Since I have been here I have turned over severy [sic] pages in the vast volume of human nature, and what is the amount? Vanity and vexation of spirit—and yet I am *tied* to my fellow-creatures by partaking of their weaknesses . . . ; new sympathies and feelings *start* up— I know not myself— "Tis these whims" Mr Ogle tells me, "render me interesting." . . . Lady K. and I are on much better terms than ever we were— To tell the truth she is afraid of me . . . . The defect is in her nature— She is devoid of sensibility . . . . [*MWL,* p. 151; 11 May 1787]

This defensive self-characterization could be effective, however, only so long as the young heroine faced no real emotional or practical demands. Sentimental heroines might help channel the energies of a middle-class girl, blessed with more leisure than responsibilities; but for a young woman forced to support herself, indulging sentiment could be only a temporary strategy. Ultimately Wollstonecraft chafed at the dependence epitomized in her position as governess and exacerbated by her sentimental posture ("I am *tied* to my fellows"). "I long for a little peace and *independence!*" she wrote to Joseph Johnson in September 1787. "Every obligation we receive from our fellow-creatures is a new shackle, takes from our native freedom, and debases the mind, makes us mere earthworms— I am not fond of grovelling!" (*MWL,* p. 159; 13 September 1787).

Soon after reiterating this complaint, Mary Wollstonecraft shed her "earthworm" dependence and moved to London, determined to become what she hyperbolically called "The first of a new genus"—a self-supporting, professional woman writer (*MWL*, p. 164; 7 November 1787). What is most important here is that Wollstonecraft was continuing to cast herself in an identifiable role; only the character has changed. For though she began to characterize herself as a professional writer only after moving to London, her literary career had in fact already begun. By 1788 Johnson had published two books for Wollstonecraft, which epitomize the two poles that thus far had dominated the young woman's emotional struggle. The first, *Thoughts on the Education of Daughters: with Reflections on Female Conduct, in the More Important Duties of Life,* differs only slightly from the conduct books we have already examined. In it Wollstonecraft advocated the ideal principles of self-control and submission that theoretically guaranteed a woman love. The second, *Mary, A Fiction,* is a melodramatic heightening of Wollstonecraft's own love for Fanny Blood, her sense of loss, and the frustrated romantic expectations she had tried to renounce. In it Wollstonecraft herself appears unmistakably as the sentimental heroine she had recently tried to become.

For Mary Wollstonecraft, the role of professional writer initially promised to resolve her emotional dilemma; it seemed to offer both independence and a means by which she could fulfill a woman's traditional responsibilities. Even after she had moved to London, Wollstonecraft clung to her determination to "be useful," especially to her two unprotected sisters. "I wish to be a mother to you both," she assured her younger sister Everina in the same paragraph in which she announced her new persona. But if she initially imagined that her new occupation would not conflict with the woman's traditional "occupations" of alternating self-indulgence and self-denial, she soon began to suspect the opposite. For as her familiarity with the business of writing and her consciousness of herself as a writer increased, she gradually began to believe that in order to escape the belittling stereotypes men had canonized she would have to suppress those "mortal longings" she associated with female emotional desire—and therefore with disappointment. Rapidly Wollstonecraft began to make herself over in the "masculine" image of an intellectual. The immediate reward was a new surge of self-confidence and direction: "I had had a number of draw-backs on my spirits and purse," she exulted in 1789, "but still I cry avaunt despair—and I push forward" (*MWL*, p. 181; 28 February 1789). As she cut her losses, choosing "intellectual pursuits" over their apparently irreconcilable opposite, "domestic comforts" (*MWL*, p. 194; 4 September 1790), she continued to rely on the life of the mind, not only to give her financial independence but to help her quell her annoying, persistent desires. Soon after her momentous move to London, she begged Everina to contribute to her self-transformation "by gathering together all the news you can, with respect to literature." "Study," she explained, had begun to silence her intense longings, to cover over—if not to fill— the aching void that resignation had failed to eliminate:

> Many motives impel me besides sheer love of knowledge, which however has ever been a predominate mover in my little world, it is the only way to destroy the worm that will gnaw the core—and make that being an isolé, whom nature made too susceptible of affections, which stray beyond the bounds, reason prescribes. [*MWL,* p. 173; 22 March 1788]

Study would not finally banish the worm, however, nor would Mary Wollstonecraft rest content to become an "isolé." The tensions that characterized her early life would continue to plague the first efforts of her professional career; but gradually, by subjecting her "affections" to the scrutiny of her "reason," she would begin to understand the origin of the desires that still warred in her heart.

A Vindication of the Rights of Men

Within the group of radical artists, writers, and philosophers who frequented Joseph Johnson's publishing house in St. Paul's Church-yard, Mary Wollstonecraft found reassuring proof that it *was* possible to be a "self-made" man, but she also encountered the more troubling but initially unrecognized problem that to be a "self-made" woman involved altogether different obstacles. As Dissenters, Johnson and most of his friends had had to create careers according to unorthodox designs, doing battle with legal restrictions and educational disadvantages in the process. Such friends as William Blake, the civil servant George Anderson, and the painter John Opie had had to overcome abject poverty as well.[6] Having achieved a measure of security himself, Johnson was determined to help others gain intellectual independence. In helping Wollstonecraft, he failed, as she herself did, to anticipate the full psychological price that would be exacted by her desire for independence. Still, the position he offered her, as reviewer for his new periodical, *The Analytical Review,* provided her with the opportunity to begin in earnest the ambitious project of converting the sentimental heroine into a self-made intellectual.

Wollstonecraft's first work for Johnson consisted mostly of reviewing and translating, but by 1790 she felt sufficiently self-confident to undertake an original, self-sustained composition. Significantly, her first extensive production as a self-supporting professional and self-proclaimed intellectual[7] took the form that most people would have considered the least appropriate for a woman—the political disquisition. Requiring knowledge of government (in which women had no share), analytical ability (of which women theoretically had little), and the ambition to participate directly in contemporary events (of which women were supposed to have none), political disquisition was in every sense a masculine domain. Wollstonecraft's choice of a project, then, signals her determination to transcend the limitations she felt her sex had already imposed on her. In this first expression of her professional self, Wollstonecraft actually aspires to *be* a man, for she suspects that the shortest way to success and equality is to join the cultural myth-makers, to hide what seemed to her a fatal female flaw beneath the mask of male discourse.[8]

Edmund Burke published his *Reflections on the Revolution in France* in November 1790. Purportedly begun as a private letter of advice to "a very young gentleman at Paris," Burke's extended defense of English conservatism was actually a public response—specifically, to a sermon delivered on 4 November 1789, at the Dissenting meeting-house of the Old Jewry, by Dr. Richard Price and, more generally, to the revolutionary events in France: the proclamation of a National Assembly in June of 1789, the fall of the Bastille on 14 July, and the march on Versailles on 5 and 6 October. Burke's condemnation of these events is unqualified. Calling the French Revolution "the most astonishing event . . . in human history," he sees in it a direct threat to English political and social stability. The events in France, he says, herald a challenge not only to the institutions of the monarch and heriditary property but also to all "sentiments, manners, and moral opinions." "The age of chivalry is gone," he laments.

> That of sophisters, oeconomists, and calculators, has succeeded; and the glory of Europe is extinguished for ever. Never, never more, shall we behold that generous loyalty to rank and sex, that proud submission, that dignified obedience, that subordination of the heart, which kept alive, even in servitude itself, the spirit of an exalted freedom. The unbought grace of life, the cheap defence of nations, the nurse of manly sentiment and heroic enterprize is gone! It is gone, that sensibility of principle, that chastity of honour, which felt a stain like a wound, which inspired courage whilst it mitigated ferocity, which ennobled whatever it touched, and under which vice itself lost half its evil, by losing all its grossness.[9]

According to Burke, this system of values depends on acknowledging social hierarchy as both "natural" and "right"; it requires "proud submission" and "dignified obedience." Such values form the basis of the English constitution and thus guarantee the English way of life. Against the "levelling principles" of the French liberals Burke proposes the "natural" order of class society; against the "dust and powder of individuality" he offers the continuity of collective traditions; against the "lust of selfish will" he places the "eternal immutable law in which will and reason are the same"—the principles of religion. To protect the benefits the English system affords them,

Burke challenges all English men and women to denounce the enemy now growing in France and perhaps making ready to invade England's green and prosperous land.

As Burke very well knew, Richard Price was only one of the "enemies" already at work in England. Indeed, Burke's powerful *Reflections* provoked many English liberals to rise to his challenge. Wollstonecraft's *A Vindication of the Rights of Men* (1790) was probably the first of these replies. Her work, written in fewer than thirty days and published anonymously, predates Thomas Paine's more famous *Rights of Man* (1791) by almost eleven months. Wollstonecraft's contribution was immediately praised for its "eager warmth and positiveness";[10] the book was so popular that Johnson issued a second, signed edition by December 1790. But despite the bold, self-confident tone with which the book begins, *The Rights of Men* immediately betrays its writer's inexperience in political disquisition. Wollstonecraft's noisy bravado, in fact, masks her insecurity both about how to present the outrage she felt and how to give her largely subjective responses authority. What we soon discover in the *Rights of Men* are the same tensions that had thus far marked Wollstonecraft's life. On the one hand she unleashes the emotionalism with which she feels most at home; on the other she invokes reason, which she believes to be a necessary control for feeling. Then, on the one hand she claims independence, especially from the roles assigned to women, but on the other she resorts to the characteristically feminine posture of seeking shelter within the protective hierarchy of a paternal order.

The "Advertisement" at the front of the book immediately announces Wollstonecraft's divided attitudes, for it both insists on the authority of feeling and lays claim to a rational authorization for this feeling. This "Advertisement" is both explicitly apologetic and decidedly assertive. In it Wollstonecraft depicts the book as a spontaneous outburst of indignant feeling, "the effusions of the moment," which has been published only at someone else's urging.[11] By this aggressive "apology," Wollstonecraft not only deflects personal responsibility for the book, but, by stressing the volatility of the emotion that inspired it, she also emphasizes the energy, hence the power, of that emotion. Wollstonecraft is also anxious to legitimize the prominent role that feeling plays in the organization of her text. *The Rights of Men* follows the associations of Wollstonecraft's own working mind instead of presenting an orderly analysis of the topics discussed by Burke.[12] The young writer explains this technique as necessary to her subject; alternately, she argues that slavish attention to particulars is unnecessary (p. 7) and that, given Burke's contradictions, such logic is impossible (p. 9). Yet despite her implicit and explicit reliance on the power of her subjective response to Burke, she clearly fears that feeling is not a legitimate authority for political disquisition. In order to bolster what at times becomes a completely subjective response, she therefore repeatedly insists that her position is "obvious," that it is based on the absolute, objectively verifiable truth of God; but although she claims that this truth can be "demonstrated," she in fact invokes "objective" principles only to ennoble her subjective responses. "A few fundamental truths meet the first enquiry of reason," she argues, "and appear as clear to an unwarped mind, as that air and bread are necessary to enable the body to fulfil its vital functions" (p. 37). Her "demonstration" of these self-evident "truths" is no less subjective than Burke's defense of very different truths. But what is interesting about Wollstonecraft's reply to Burke is that the manner in which she turns to the authority of these "fundamental truths" suggests that what she is really battling here is not Burke's argument so much as her own old enemy, feeling.

In *The Rights of Men,* Wollstonecraft subordinates her objections to Burke's political argument to an attack on the hyperbolic rhetoric with which she believes he is deliberately manipulating and confusing his audience.[13] Ironically, she objects both to Burke's *lack* of feeling and to his tendency to get carried away by his argument.

> Words are heaped on words, till the understanding is confused by endeavour-ing to disentangle the sense, and the memory by tracing contradictions . . . ; you have often sacrificed your sincerity to enforce your favourite arguments, and called in your judgment to adjust the arrangement of words that could not convey its dictates. [P. 127]

Wollstonecraft's anger at Burke's acrobatic rhetoric is really only one aspect of what proves to be her most sweeping condemnation: the entire *Reflections,* she charges, contains no reasoned argument at all; it is merely an expression of Burke's obsessive vanity, a noisy appeal for public attention. "I know that a lively imagination renders a man particularly calculated to shine in conversation and in those desultory productions where method is disregarded; and the instantaneous applause which its eloquence extorts is at once a reward and a spur" (p. 3). Once such a "lively imagination" is indulged, she argues, its hunger knows no bounds. Had Burke been born a Frenchman, she claims, he would have found equally ingenious language "to prove that the [English] constitution . . . was not a model sufficiently noble to deserve close adherence" (p. 109).

Wollstonecraft's criticism of Burke sounds remarkably like Hannah More's admonitions against female appetite; thus it should come as no surprise that she also scorns what she calls Burke's "unmanly servility" (p. 50). For what Wollstonecraft focuses on in Burke's political program is his universalization of the attitude of "dignified obedi-

ence" that women are supposed to display. Wollstonecraft despises
the passivity of this posture; from her personal experience, she knows
that "subordination of the heart," far from nourishing a "spirit of . . .
exalted freedom," in fact brings only dependence and pain. Intent
on rejecting this feminine psychological and political model, she substitutes for Burke's feminine paradigm a description of human nature
and society anchored in "masculine" behavior, in confrontation and
conquest.[14]

Wollstonecraft does not consistently work out the psychological
model implicit in *The Vindication of the Rights of Men,* nor does she yet
recognize its relationship to the paradigm of feminine propriety. Yet
because this model, which will become more explicit in *A Vindication
of the Rights of Woman,* provides the basis for both her argument with
Burke and her own burgeoning self-consciousness, I want to reconstruct and set it out here. Like so many other eighteenth- and early
nineteenth-century attempts to explain human behavior, Wollstonecraft's paradigm is at once ethical and psychological, epistemological
and teleological. Neither her terms nor her goals are original; her
primary categories are "reason" and "feeling," and her fundamental
aspiration is to find some resolution between the limitations of temporal existence and the ideal of wholeness and complete fulfillment
for which she cannot help but yearn. What is therefore significant is
the extent to which this schema answers Wollstonecraft's own divided but persistent desires.

According to Wollstonecraft, all individuals—men and women
alike—are motivated primarily by an innate desire for love and respect, a craving for recognition from others that ideally affirms the
individual's absolute autonomy. In her two *Vindications,* she does not
speculate extensively about the source of this intimation of totality—
whether it might originate, for example, in a child's memory of its
mother's love or in the soul's intimation of its essential affiliation with
God.[15] Instead Wollstonecraft focuses on the two possible courses this
fundamental desire might take. As the individual grows up, he or she
either passively accepts what gratifications experience offers and compensates for their inadequacy with intellectual rationalizations and
imaginative fantasies or else actively seeks fulfillment and, through
disappointments and failures, gradually comes to recognize the limitations of the self.

In contrast to the first course, passive acquiescence, which perpetuates in the adult the ignorance and helplessness of the child, the
aggressive search for "higher improvement and higher attainments"
eventually leads to self-consciousness—which is ultimately, of course,
the consciousness of human mortality. This recognition of human
limitations yields abundant recompense, however; for, as Wollstone-

craft describes the process in *The Rights of Woman,* consciousness of one's own inadequacy soon generates sympathy for the weakness of others, and this sympathy in turn generates love and a rational humility: "He feels himself drawn by some cord of love to all his fellow-creatures, for whose follies he is anxious to find every extenuation in their nature—in himself. . . . Humanity thus rises naturally out of humility, and twists the cords of love that in various convolutions entangle the heart."[16]

The frustrations an individual inevitably encounters in everyday life are actually productive of his or her greatest good, for they turn desire away from earthly things toward the only being capable of providing absolute gratification, "the centre of perfection," God. This progression stands behind Wollstonecraft's repeated insistence that all desires are instrumental in the education of reason: "the passions are necessary auxiliaries of reason," "the passions should unfold our reason."[17] For even though temporal objects will inevitably fail to satisfy desire, the very passion that motivates an individual will eventually cultivate the "reasonable" craving for God. This argument reminds us of Wollstonecraft's earlier embrace of religion, but the difference here is that earthly frustrations inspire her not to long for death but to assert herself even more. In *The Rights of Men* she explains that

> A present impulse pushes us forward, and when we discover that the game did not deserve the chace [*sic*], we find that we have gone over much ground, and not only gained many new ideas, but a habit of thinking. The exercise of our faculties is the great end, though not the goal we had in view when we started with such eagerness. [P. 29]

Wollstonecraft's charge against Burke is that he has renounced this more demanding, more rewarding, model of individual maturation out of personal cowardice and habitual self-indulgence. From his need to gratify his own vanity and to avoid confrontation, she argues, he has generalized a model of proper human conduct that idealizes acquiescence and passivity before the "authority" of tradition.

But Wollstonecraft does not limit her condemnation to Burke. Indeed, she realizes that intellectual and psychological submissiveness is the prevalent attitude among men *and* women in a class society. As long as inherited private property and rank rather than personal effort determine an individual's position and value, submissiveness will be the general rule. Thus the poor and the rich alike stand condemned by Wollstonecraft's epithet "vulgar," because both, as "creatures of habit and impulse," accept social subordination as natural. And because individuals will not exert themselves against the tyranny of habit, appetite, or the social system, Wollstonecraft fears that society as a whole can no longer progress. "There is no end to this implicit submission to authority," she complains; "some where it must stop, or we return to barbarism" (p. 23).

Wollestonecraft's attack on self-indulgence and submission is preeminently a bourgeois assault made, in the name of individual effort and proven merit, against aristocratic privilege and passivity.[18] We may speculate that the personal invective that Edmund Burke provoked, not only from Wollstonecraft but from other bourgeois radicals, like Thomas Paine, emanated partly from their sense of class betrayal; that Burke, the defender of the American Revolution, a member of the bourgeoisie himself, could turn so completely against liberal principles inspired others besides Wollstonecraft to accuse him of hypocrisy, special interest, and selling out. But unlike those of most of her fellow liberals, Wollstonecraft's assault also articulates the special frustrations of a woman. For just as the wealthy inherit debilitating "privilege" as their "natural" birthright, so women acquire "privilege" through the education that renders "natural" their dependence on men. Unlike rich men, however, women do not have the self-confidence or the power that might enable them to wrench themselves out of their "benumbed" existence. Women's passivity is reinforced by the same political and economic laws that propriety is meant to legitimize. In at least one passage in *The Rights of Men* Wollstonecraft recognizes that her cause lies not just with the middle-class men who challenge social hierarchy by their powerful ambitions but with women as well. For women are kept in their position of helplessness by just such masculine "authorities" as Edmund Burke—men who have nothing to lose by advocating obedience; men who, fearing their own weakness, try to institutionalize weakness in the challenger they can most easily control, women. Burke's entire notion of virtue—which, for him, is epitomized in women—idealizes weakness, Wollstonecraft complains, and thus discourages real women from the self-exertion necessary to the cultivation of reason. The implication is that women are unwitting victims not only of Burke's own psychological insecurity but, in a larger sense, of the insecurity of all men.

> You may have convinced them [women] that *littleness* and *weakness* are the very essence of beauty; and that the Supreme Being, in giving women beauty in the most supereminent degree, seemed to command them, by the powerful voice of Nature, not to cultivate the moral virtues that might chance to excite respect, and interfere with the pleasing sensations they were created to inspire. Thus confining truth, fortitude, and humanity, within the rigid pale of manly morals, they might justly argue, that to be loved, woman's high end and great distinction! they should "learn to lisp, to totter in their walk, and nick-name God's creatures." Never, they might repeat after you, was any man, much less a

woman, rendered amiable by the force of those exalted qualities, fortitude, justice, wisdom, and truth; and thus forewarned of the sacrifice they must make to those austere, unnatural virtues, they would be authorized to turn all their attention to their persons, systematically neglecting morals to secure beauty. [Pp. 112–13]

The warmth of Wollstonecraft's accusation suggests the extent of her personal investment in this position. Here she is beginning to see both what complicated connections exist between the interests of women and those of the aspiring middle classes and how thoroughly the categories by which women are taught to estimate their worth emerge from the special needs of those who rule. She is beginning, in other words, to identify ideology at work in her society and in herself.

Despite Wollstonecraft's brief insight into the stake that women as a group have in this revolution, she refuses in *The Rights of Men* to identify herself consistently with women or even to be sympathetic to the submissiveness they have been forced to assume. Instead of systematically castigating tyrants, she heaps scorn on those who submit: the women who bow to male virtues, the rich who give in to impulses, the clergy who grovel before patrons, the poor who acquiesce to their landlords. Wollstonecraft does not examine the situations that necessitate such subservience; instead, she rejects the female experience of helplessness and frustration for the defiant bourgeois assertion that one can, in fact, be anything one wants. For Wollstonecraft is explicitly adopting here an attitude and set of values that are implicitly at odds with feminine propriety and hence, with the typical female situation; she is allying herself with the individualistic values of middle-class men and heaping scorn on the posture of helplessness, which she can see only as weakness and personal failure.

In one particularly significant passage, Wollstonecraft reveals that her rejection of the feminine position rests on a recognition that the acquiescence it requires is "dangerous." All "first principles" must be demonstrated, she insists,

and not determined by arbitrary authority and dark traditions, lest a dangerous supineness should take place; for probably, in ceasing to enquire, our reason would remain dormant, and delivered up, without a curb, to every impulse of passion, we might soon lose sight of the clear light which the exercise of our understanding no longer kept alive. [Pp. 37–38]

Wollstonecraft here sounds remarkably like the conduct-book writers, yet she reverses the implications they draw from this "danger." Like them, she describes the betrayal as implicitly sexual; yet, for her, the "dangerous supineness," the vulnerable posture of women, can— and must—be overcome by personal effort. For Wollstonecraft, to remain passive—whether before innate feelings or cultural authority—is to court an absolute loss of control, and, implicitly, it is to deliver oneself up to the threatening force of desire or feeling itself.

Submissiveness to feelings is, of course, what Wollstonecraft had always feared in herself. "Reason" should be the active legislator of passion and thus the defense against vulnerability and pain. But the passage I have just quoted suggests that reason would "remain dormant" were it not for the agitation of another faculty, and this faculty, as Wollstonecraft has already told us, is desire or passion ("the passions are necessary auxiliaries of reason"). Thus we are involved in a particularly vicious circle. Wollstonecraft does not want to abandon passion, for she feels too acutely the energy of her own subjective feelings; but she does not quite trust passion either. Thus she tries to vindicate feeling without capitulating to it. Although she admits, in passing, that passion and reason bear a disconcerting likeness to each other ("knowing, however, the influence of a ruling passion, and how often it assumes the form of reason" [p. 66]), she argues for an authoritative and absolute system of values that will simultaneously distinguish between reason and passion and sanction feeling by making it part of a larger design. Interestingly, in order to vindicate feeling, Wollstonecraft inadvertently assumes the feminine position she has just attacked Burke for supporting; for the order she endorses is the patriarchy of Christianity, and the position she embraces within it is the feminine stance of "proud submission."

Before coming to London, Wollstonecraft's religious practice had been basically Evangelical; as her friendship with Johnson and his circle developed, her Christianity was supplemented by the faith in reason and "clear truths" that she announces in *The Rights of Men*. Even during the period in which she was most subject to their influence, however, Wollstonecraft never exchanged her religious faith for the Dissenter's skepticism, for her particular faith served a crucial function in her developing self-image. For her, the authority of God, which can be "deduced" by reason as well as intuited by the heart, frees dependence of the pain that otherwise threatens the vulnerable suppliant. The "proof" that she offers for this objective authority, however, is finally only her belief—or, more precisely, her own need.

> I bend with awful reverence when I enquire on what my fear is built.—I fear that sublime power, whose motive for creating me must have been wise and good; and I submit to the moral laws which my reason deduces from this view of my dependence on him.—It is not his power that I fear—it is not to an arbitrary will, but to unerring *reason* I submit. . . . This fear of God makes me reverence myself. . . . And this, enlightened self-love . . . forces me to see; and, if I may venture to borrow a prostituted term, to *feel,* that happiness is reflected, and that, in communicating good, my soul receives its noble aliment. [Pp. 78–79]

Wollstonecraft "reverences" herself because she believes herself to be "a faint image" of a reasonable, benevolent God; she believes that her own rationality and benevolence reflect God's image because her "enlightened self-love" makes her feel that this is true. This circular logic is finally anchored in "fear" and "dependence," yet, because God "must" be just, such emotions can cause no pain.

Such need may be one eternal anchor for religious faith, but what is important here is the extent to which Wollstonecraft's religious impulses—now harnessed to the cause of political reform—are another expression of the desires that generated her brief career as a sentimental heroine. The important fact is that, in promising consolation for earthly disappointments, religion sanctions the very feelings that, when directed to other people, always seem to end in pain. "I perceive, but too forcibly, that happiness, literally speaking, dwells not here," she acknowledges, "and that we wander to and fro in a vale of darkness as well as tears" (p. 76).

> When friends are unkind, and the heart has not the prop on which it fondly leaned, where can a tender suffering being fly but to the Searcher of hearts? and, when death has desolated the present scene, and torn from us the friend of our youth . . . when memory heightens former pleasures to contrast our present prospects—there is but one source of comfort within our reach;—and in this sublime solitude the world appears to contain only the Creator and the creature, of whose happiness he is the source. [Pp. 95–96]

What we are seeing here is the extent to which Wollstonecraft's gender affects her investment in orthodox religion. On the one hand, believing that a reasonable paternalistic order exists in the universe enables Wollstonecraft to advocate self-assertion, confrontation, and a perpetual struggle after "higher attainments" *without* transgressing the fundamental posture of submissiveness that a woman was expected to maintain. On the other hand, *because* she is a woman, Wollstonecraft is conceptualizing her religious faith primarily in terms of only one facet of what is basically the Protestant ethic. In other words, she endorses the model of individual effort and hard work intrinsic to the Protestant faith, but, because she has to a certain extent internalized the aspirations, expectations, and self-definition of a woman rather than a man, the work she imagines yields spiritual, not material, rewards; it is, in fact, conceived of in terms of self-denial and triumphant suffering rather than self-assertion in the name of spiritual gain. In a letter written in 1787 Wollstonecraft reveals how important this model of a paternal order that mythologizes suffering is to her developing self-conception:

> The main hinge on which my argument turns is this, refinement genius—and those charming talents which my soul instinctively loves, produce misery in this

world—abundantly more pain than pleasure. Why then do they at all unfold themselves *here?* If useless, would not the Searcher of hearts, the tender Father, have shut them up 'till they could bloom in a more favorable climate; where no keen blasts could blight the opening flower. Besides sensibility renders the path of duty more intricate—and the warfare *much* more severe— Surely *peculiar* wretchedness has something to balance it! . . . I humbly hope, that the ordeal trial answered some end, and that I have not suffered in vain. [*MWL,* p. 150; 16 April 1787]

Wollstonecraft's need for an authority to disarm desire of its potential threat, to promise satisfaction and therefore sanction intense feeling, extends beyond her explicitly religious sentiments. Despite her attack on Burke's subservience, she, too, identifies a temporal authority worthy of "dignified obedience." If Edmund Burke elevates Marie Antoinette to the stature of a maternal guardian of culture, Wollstonecraft answers with her veneration of the paternal religious authority, Dr. Richard Price. "I am not accustomed to look up with vulgar awe," she claims, but she presents Dr. Price as a larger-than-life figure, much like Burke's idealization of the French queen. She concedes almost every objection Burke makes to Price: that he abused the pulpit in delivering a political speech, that his "zeal may have carried him further than sound reason can justify," even that his political theories are "Utopian reveries." Yet her admiration and reverence dwarf these objections. Wollstonecraft's respect for Price originated, no doubt, in the personal, paternal role he played for her during her residence at Newington Green, but, as she describes him in *The Rights of Men* the firsthand knowledge of the man recedes behind an obscuring rhetorical flourish—much like Burke's own. Here is Burke: "I saw her just above the horizon, decorating and cheering the elevated sphere she just began to move in, —glittering like the morning-star, full of life, and splendor, and joy."[19] And here is Wollstonecraft:

> I could almost fancy that I now see this respectable old man, in his pulpit, with hands clasped, and eyes devoutly fixed, praying with all the simple energy of unaffected piety; or, when more erect, inculcating the dignity of virtue, and enforcing the doctrines his life adorns; benevolence animated each feature, and persuasion attuned his accents. [P. 35]

Perhaps Wollstonecraft allows herself such unqualified adoration of Price because, in the way she depicts him, he appears not as a vigorous—and thus potentially disappointing—man but as a stereotypical literary character. She describes him, for instance, as "personified virtue and matured wisdom" (p. 36), "tottering on the verge of the grave" (p. 35), and distinguished by "the grey hairs of virtue" (p. 34). Clearly, this image of Dr. Price represents for Wollstonecraft a "reasonable" and necessary authority for her intellectual aspirations *and* her emotional "effusions." For finally, despite her valorization of self-assertion, what Wollstonecraft really wants is to achieve a new position of dependence within a paternal order of her own choosing.

The paternal authority exercised by God in Wollstonecraft's religious faith and by Dr. Price in her intellectual sphere has a counterpart in her vision of a reformed society. In her utopia an entire army of father figures, both secular and religious, ensures happiness by anticipating every need. The poor, for example, "would be watched over with fatherly solicitude, by the man whose duty and pleasure it was to guard their happiness, and shield from rapacity the beings who, by the sweat of their brow, exalted him above his fellows" (pp. 145–46). As a result, society would return to its prelapsarian—and presexual—harmony.

> A garden more inviting than Eden would then meet the eye, and springs of joy murmur on every side. The clergyman would superintend his own flock, the shepherd would then love the sheep he daily tended; the school might rear its decent head, and the buzzing tribe, let loose to play, impart a portion of their vivacious spirits to the heart that longed to open their minds, and lead them to taste the pleasures of men. Domestic comfort, the civilizing relations of husband, brother, and father, would soften labour, and render life contented.
> [P. 147]

Notice that there is no real equality in this garden. Nor are there, literally, any women. But women's presence is implied in the last sentence. Here, women are the invisible center, the silent beings whose simple existence turns men into "husband, brother, and father" and whose actions epitomize indirection: they "soften" labor without working themselves; they "render life contented" and only presumably enjoy the "domestic comforts" that others' happiness yields. They are, in other words, textbook Proper Ladies.

As numerous critics have noted, in such passages Wollstonecraft resorts to the same "pomp of words" for which she castigates Burke.[20] But her rationale for employing such rhetoric differs significantly from his. Instead of controlling the response of the *audience,* Wollstonecraft's rhetoric helps control *her own* emotions. The rhetoric of the passages in which she invokes God, venerates Price, and imagines Utopia helps to give acceptable form to the passion that threatens to explode both language and logic. "I pause to recollect myself," she gasps, as emotion reaches the limits of language (p. 153), and with the words "but I forbear" she abruptly silences a feeling of indignation (p. 155). Wollstonecraft seems very aware of two dangers: the danger of indulged feelings and the danger of inviting the charge of "feminine hysteria," which might subvert her debut in the form of masculine logic. She wants to express and harness emotion, for she knows the very real power of her own experience and longings. Yet, unsure of how to credit personal feeling, uncomfortable with the physical forms in which her imagination projects its gratifications, she retreats into the masculine literary conventions whose artifice she claims to despise. Reliance on rhetoric is for her a form of indirection that distances her from her own unreliable emotion without sacrificing its force. At the same time, it permits her to project the appearance of masculine assertiveness without having to take personal responsibility for it. Just as Wollstonecraft's invocation of reason is really a transvaluation of feeling, so her masculine persona is really a cover for the feminine position she has all along retained.

At the very beginning of *The Rights of Men,* Wollstonecraft betrays the fact that in this first professional adventure she feels less comfortable in the aggressive posture of Dr. Johnson's pugilist than in the more typically feminine position of spectator in a drawing room, protected by and slightly superior in her aloofness. Here Burke is "the little great man," the "ingenious man," and Wollstonecraft is the "attentive observer."

> Such vanity enlivens social intercourse, and forces the little great man to be always on his guard to secure his throne; and an ingenious man, who is ever on the watch for conquest, will, in his eagerness to exhibit his whole store of knowledge, furnish an attentive observer with some useful information, calcined by fancy and formed by taste. [Pp. 4–5]

Wollstonecraft's other self-dramatizations show a similar desire to avoid direct confrontation, a stance more marked because three times she attributes her reticence to her opponent's reluctance ("it would be something like cowardice to fight with a man who had never exercised the weapons with which his opponent chose to combat" [p. 9; cf. pp. 61, 66]). The tension between the "masculine" posture of direct confrontation and the "feminine" strategy of indirection or persuasion, like the tension between reason and feeling, betrays Wollstonecraft's basic uncertainty about the nature of her voice and its authority. Having not yet fully acknowledged the determinate relationship between any individual and his or her social situation, she has yet to identify either her own natural allies or the origin of her own volatile feelings. Having not yet fully worked out the connection between any individual position and a cultural ideology, she still attacks Burke when she might well focus her discontent on the tradition behind him. Wollstonecraft has simply not found her own place within the ideology that surrounds her, and, as a consequence, she still lacks the self-consciousness and self-confidence truly to be the first of that hybrid "new genus," a self-expressive woman in a chorus of male voices.

A Vindication of the Rights of Woman

In October 1791 Mary Wollstonecraft informed her new friend, William Roscoe, that she had begun sitting for the portrait he had commissioned. "I do not imagine that it will be a very striking likeness," she apologized playfully; "but, if you do not find me in it, I will send you a more faithful sketch—a book that I am now writing, in which *I* myself . . . shall certainly appear, head and heart" (*MWL,* pp. 202–3; 6 October 1791). The "sketch" was *A Vindication of the Rights of Woman* (1792), and, as this letter suggests, Wollstonecraft's second political tract proves that during the preceding year she had progressed considerably in her ability to understand not only political issues but also her own place within them. In discovering that her most natural allies in the debate conducted in *The Rights of Men* were women (and not, as that work suggested, either liberal bourgeois males or the poor), Wollstonecraft was more nearly able to come to terms with the emotionalism that disrupted that argument; in learning to harness her emotion and by recognizing its fellow in the emotionalism of other women, she seems to have begun to perceive that the problem that had always undermined her self-confidence was collective rather than personal.

The first of Wollstonecraft's breakthroughs in *The Rights of Woman* was the insight that individual responses are, first and foremost, responses to situations and that, in a telling way, what made the middle-class woman into a Proper Lady was her "situation." Women, like the rich, are "swallowed up . . . *localized* . . . by the rank they are placed in, by *courtesy.*"

> Women, commonly called Ladies, are not to be contradicted in company, are not allowed to exert any manual strength; and from them the negative virtues only are expected, when any virtues are expected, patience, docility, good-humour, and flexibility; virtues incompatible with any vigorous exertion of intellect.[21]

"Rest on yourself," Wollstonecraft replied to the request for advice from the young author Mary Hays, for special danger awaits the woman writer who, accustomed to "courtesy," can be placated by meaningless praise. "An author, especially a woman, should be cautious lest she too hastily swallows the crude praises which partial friend and polite acquaintance bestow thoughtlessly when the supplicating eye looks for them" (*MWL,* p. 219; 12 November 1792).

Wollstonecraft's second important realization in *The Rights of Woman* was that the attitudes and expectations that perpetuate female weakness are institutionalized by the very texts that purport to be "authorities" and even by the values encoded in language. Women respond to local situations as Proper Ladies because from their childhood on they are instructed to conceive of themselves according to masculine assumptions of what "feminine" behavior is. Thus one major cause of the "barren blooming" that Wollstonecraft discerns in women is "a false system of education, gathered from the books written on this subject by men who, considering females rather as women than human creatures, have been more anxious to make them alluring mistresses than affectionate wives and rational mothers" (p. 7). By teaching women to understand themselves solely by men's judgments, to submit to the restraint of propriety, and to pursue their educations only with regard to man's happiness, these male "authorities"—and the women who echo them—have deprived women of the opportunity for self-exertion and, therefore, of the possibility for self-improvement.

The ideal paradigm of maturation that Wollstonecraft introduced in *The Rights of Men* obviously demands an educational program diametrically opposed to this feminine cultivation of "negative virtues." Her assumption here, which anchors the paradigm, is that all human beings are equal in their fundamental capacity to reason; discriminatory education should thus be eliminated because it is detrimental to the improvement of humanity as a whole. Women, as women, have been denied the "rights of man"; they have lost their legitimate position within the collective noun through an education that has denied them maturity.[22] In order to combat this assumption of essential difference and to break down the behavior that institutionalizes it, Wollstonecraft asserts that women, as a social group, have much in common with other, largely male groups. Her basic strategy is to emphasize the similarities between female behavior and that of other groups: the wealthy (pp. 187, 191), soldiers (p. 23), wits (p. 56), and Dissenters (p. 194). Arguing "from analogy," she then asserts that it is reasonable and morally requisite to teach women to recognize their essential affinities with men. Only then will women perceive the crucial relationship between their private actions and the welfare of society at large (p. 183). Only when women are considered—and consider themselves—human beings rather than sexual objects, only when their education develops rather than suppresses their reason, only when they are granted the legal equality they by nature deserve, will they be able to contribute to the overall improvement of humanity. Wollstonecraft insists that her argument is not based on special interest; because she is intent on effacing all sexual discrimination, she declares herself "disinterested" and claims to speak with the neutral voice of the species, "the firm tone of humanity" (p. 3).

Perceiving her own voice as the generalized, ideal voice of collective humanity relieves Wollstonecraft of much of the insecurity that marked *The Rights of Men*. She claims that her admonitions now have the widest possible base; they transcend the charge of egotism or self-interest, and they derive their authority from the instances of reason that, as she continues to argue, are everywhere evident. This position gives Wollstonecraft the confidence to embark on the course of direct confrontation she advocated but did not pursue in *The Rights of Men*. In *The Rights of Woman* she is finally able to identify and aggressively challenge the "authorities" she holds most responsible for female education: Rousseau, and conduct-book writers like Drs. Gregory and Fordyce.

The root of the wrongs of women, according to Wollstonecraft, is the general acceptance of the idea that women are *essentially* sexual beings—or, as Rousseau phrases it, "a male is only a male now and again, the female is always a female . . . ; everything reminds her of her sex."[23] Wollstonecraft's response to this sexual characterization of women is simply to reverse the charge: not *women,* she argues, but *men* are dominated by their sexual desires; *men's* insatiable appetites are the root of both economic inequality and social injustice. Arguments about women's "natural" inferiority, then, are only men's rationalizations for the superior social position they have unjustifiably seized, and their talk of "natural" female wantonness is merely a cover for the sexual appetite that men both fear and relish in themselves. Rousseau is the "sensualist" Wollstonecraft attacks most systematically for indulging in "voluptuous reveries": "Rousseau declares that a woman should never, for a moment, feel herself independent, that she should be governed by fear to exercise her natural cunning, and made a coquetish slave in order to render her a more alluring object of desire, a *sweeter* companion to man, whenever he chooses to relax himself" (p. 25). Thus Rousseau's "discovery" of the "natural law" governing women, she charges, is simply a creation of his own repressed desire:

> Rousseau respected—almost adored virtue—and yet he allowed himself to love with sensual fondness. His imagination constantly prepared inflammable fewel for his inflammable senses; but, in order to reconcile his respect for self-denial, fortitude, and those heroic virtues, which a mind like his could not coolly admire, he labours to invert the law of nature, and broaches a doctrine pregnant with mischief and derogatory to the character of supreme wisdom. [P. 42]

Rousseau, as a "voluptuous tyrant," simultaneously rationalizes his own sensuality and gratifies it, and, at the same time, he punishes the being who tempts him to this self-indulgence by making her responsible for sexual control. Here Wollstonecraft is very close to perceiving how a set of beliefs can be generated from or adopted because of local needs and psychological imperatives. Moreover, she intuits the dynamics of repression and compensation at work in this production: as forbidden longings are censured, sexual desire erupts in another, more permissible form:

> All Rousseau's errors in reasoning arose from sensibility. . . . When he should have reasoned he became impassioned, and reflection inflamed his imagination instead of enlightening his understanding. Even his virtues also led him further astray; for, born with a warm constitution and lively fancy, nature carried him toward the other sex with such eager fondness, that he soon became lascivious. Had he given way to these desires, the fire would have extinguished itself in a natural manner; but virtue, and a romantic kind of delicacy, made him practise self-denial; yet, when fear, delicacy, or virtue, restrained him, he debauched his imagination, and reflecting on the sensations to which fancy gave force, he traced them in the most glowing colours, and sunk them deep into his soul. [Pp. 90–91]

The imagination, far from being the moral faculty philosophers like Adam Smith described, becomes the agent of vicarious gratification; and when the imagination becomes "debauched" in the name of virtuous self-denial, the artist seduces his reader as he indulges himself: "And thus making us feel whilst dreaming that we reason, erroneous conclusions are left in the mind" (p. 91).

Although Wollstonecraft's most direct attack centers on Rousseau and the conduct-book writers, in footnotes and asides she challenges a much more intimidating cultural "authority"—John Milton.[24] Wollstonecraft knows that Milton's portrayal of Eve's "sweet attractive grace, and docile blind obedience" (p. 19) stands behind Rousseau's Sophie. Milton, she implies, is as much a "sensualist" as Rousseau. He acknowledged that Eve is formed precisely in the image of Adam's innermost desires, made "thy likeness, thy fit help, thy other self, / Thy wish, exactly to thy heart's desires" (*Paradise Lost* 8. 450–51). Wollstonecraft therefore asserts that Eve, as sensuality incarnate, with her "wanton ringlets" and "coy submission" (*PL* 4. 306, 310), her "glowing cheek" and "tresses discompos'd" (*PL* 5. 10), stands as commentary not on woman but on the men from whose imagination she sprang—from Milton's Adam and, before him, from Milton himself. With anger restrained only by her veneration for Milton, Wollstonecraft cites the words the poet placed in Eve's mouth as evidence against him:

> To whom thus Eve with *perfect beauty* adorn'd.
> My Author and Disposer, what thou bidst
> *Unargued* I obey; So God ordains;
> God is *thy law, thou mine*: to know no more
> Is Woman's *happiest* knowledge and her *praise*.
>
> [*PL* 4. 634–38; Wollstonecraft's italics]

It is significant that Wollstonecraft cannot attack Milton directly. Of all the cultural "authorities" she engages, Milton is clearly the most imposing, not only because of his preeminence in the English literary, political, and religious traditions but because of the special veneration accorded to Milton by Johnson's London circle. The fact that she can record her outrage against Milton only by allusions and by italicizing words in a quoted text (as in the passage just quoted) suggests the extent to which she is still reluctant to take her aggression to its logical extreme.

From the disguised but ever-present force of male desire, Woll-stonecraft charges, all the evils that oppress women follow. Kept in a prolonged mental childhood to enhance the "innocence" men find so appealing, women are denied access to the personal experience necessary to the formation of a strong "human character" (p. 114). She clearly sees the paradox inherent in this deprivation: denied all challenging encounters and education, women are actually trapped within experience—the narrow domain of their own personal, *sensual* experience. Consequently incapable of "generalizing ideas, of draw-ing comprehensive conclusions from individual observations" (p. 54), women become obsessed with immediate impressions and gratifica-tions. Because men indulge *their* sensual desires, women, trying to please, become slaves to their own senses and thus hostage to every transient emotion. Far from being the beneficiaries of "sensibility," women are actually the victims of feeling:

> Their senses are inflamed, and their understandings neglected, consequently they become the prey of their senses, delicately termed sensibility, and are blown about by every momentary gust of feeling. . . . Ever restless and anx-ious, their over exercised sensibility not only renders them uncomfortable themselves, but troublesome, to use a soft phrase, to others. All their thoughts turn on things calculated to excite emotion; and feeling, when they should reason, their conduct is unstable, and their opinions are wavering. . . . By fits and starts they are warm in many pursuits; yet this warmth, never concen-trated into perseverance, soon exhausts itself. . . . Miserable indeed, must be that being whose cultivation of mind has only tended to inflame its passions! [Pp. 60–61]

Wollstonecraft cannot deny that women are, for the most part, satisfied with the sensual gratification of male attention. And, because they are, they participate in men's voluptuous designs. By internaliz-ing "false notions of beauty and delicacy" (p. 117), they cultivate that "sexual character" of the mind that actually strengthens their chains. Women embrace their inessentialness; thoughts of men continually occupy their minds; they seek out lovers whose ingratiating manners flatter their self-images; they are content to derive their identities from their relationships to men—as "daughters, wives, and mothers"

(p. 26). No wonder, Wollstonecraft laments, that men accuse women of intellectual superficiality and sensual self-indulgence. Indeed, Pope's maxim that "ev'ry Woman is at heart a Rake" is not only a man's wish-fulfilling projection but a self-fulfilling prophecy as well (p. 117). If women do not always rest content within this masculine fantasy of power and self-indulgence, their violations are at best indirect and surreptitious. Cunning is the resort of the powerless who would not lose the illusion of power, and tyranny over her helpless servants and children serves to vent an oppressed woman's wrath.

So intent is Wollstonecraft to reject the prevalent stereotype of women as *all* sexuality that she comes close to arguing that women have *no* innate sexual desires at all. Repeatedly she implies that female sexuality is only a learned response to *male* sexuality, a strategy unconsciously adopted in order to win the emotional acceptance that women really want. "Men are certainly more under the influence of their appetites than women," she flatly states (p. 137). What seems like sexual desire in women is actually either "sympathy" or disguised vanity:

> The sexual attention of man particularly acts on female sensibility, and this sympathy has been exercised from their youth up. A husband cannot long pay those attentions with the passion necessary to excite lively emotions, and the heart, accustomed to lively emotions, turns to a new lover, or pines in secret, the prey of virtue or prudence. I mean when the heart has really been rendered susceptible, and the taste formed; for I am apt to conclude, from what I have seen in fashionable life, that vanity is oftener fostered than sensibility by the mode of education, and the intercourse between the sexes, which I have reprobated; and that coquetry more frequently proceeds from vanity than from that inconstancy, which overstrained sensibility naturally produces. [P. 65]

Promiscuity and repression surely exist; yet Wollstonecraft is at pains to argue that such responses to sexual agitation are rare and, if the euphemism "*over-strained* sensibility" is significant, unnatural. It should not surprise us that Wollstonecraft goes on to describe an ideal marriage as one without passion ("a master and mistress of a family ought not to continue to love each other with passion" [p. 30]), and she asserts with apparent assurance that women will easily be able to transform sexual desire into the more "serious" and "austere" emotions of friendship (p. 130).

Yet the closer we read Wollstonecraft's *Vindication,* the clearer it becomes that her defensive denial of female sexuality in herself and in women in general is just that—a *defense* against what she feared: desire doomed to repeated frustration. Contrary to her assertions, Wollstonecraft's deepest fear centers not on the voraciousness of male sexual desire but on what she fears is its brevity. Thus, while

she can insist that "in the exercise of their maternal feelings providence has furnished women with a natural substitute for love," this
substitute turns out to be necessary because, inevitably, the "lover
[will become] only a friend" (p. 152). The devoted mother she describes proves to be a "neglected wife," driven to seek from her
children the gratification that her "unhappy marriage" no longer
provides. And the heroism of the self-sacrificing widow, which she
celebrates, turns out to be barren and decidedly equivocal: "Raised
to heroism by misfortunes, she represses the first faint dawning of a
natural inclination, before it ripens into love, and in the bloom of life
forgets her sex. . . . Her children have her love, and her brightest
hopes are beyond the grave, where her imagination often strays" (pp.
50–51).

Such repression is necessary, Wollstonecraft implies, because, far
from being the learned response she asserts it is (and wishes it were),
female sexuality is actually as demanding as male sexuality; perhaps
it is even more urgent. In two remarkable passages Wollstonecraft
betrays the fact that she shares the moralists' anxiety about female
appetite. The first passage begins with an indictment of indecorous
eating habits. Men are the worst offenders on this score, but, she
acknowledges, "some women, particularly French women, have also
lost a sense of decency in this respect; for they will talk very calmly
of an indigestion. It were to be wished that idleness was not allowed
to generate, on the rank soil of wealth, those swarms of summer
insects that feed on putrefaction, we should not then be disgusted by
the sight of such brutal excesses" (p. 137). While Wollstonecraft's
scorn for the idle rich accounts for part of her venom here, her
subsequent association of the "refinement of eating" with "refinements of love" more fully explains her vitriolic language. She goes
on to describe female voluptuaries as "the slaves of casual lust . . .
who are, literally speaking, standing dishes to which every glutton
may have access" (p. 138). Clearly her disgust embraces both sexes
here, for she is indicting sexual desire itself: "The depravity of the
appetite which brings the sexes together," she argues, or "sensual
gust," is dignified only when "the feelings of a parent mingl[e] with
an instinct merely animal" (p. 138).

In a second telling passage, however, Wollstonecraft implies that
female sexuality might even be more voracious—and hence more
blameworthy—than male desire. In a final attempt to denigrate the
appetite she feels increasingly unable to deny, Wollstonecraft argues
that platonic "feeling" provides a gratification that is superior to
sexual pleasure. "What are the cold, or feverish caresses of appetite,"
she asks, "but sin embracing death, compared with the modest overflow-
ings of a pure heart and exalted imagination?" (p. 192). The person-

ification here is Wollstonecraft's final embedded allusion to *Paradise Lost*. The scene to which it refers, in book 2, culminates in Milton's first image of female procreation. Death is the son of Sin by Satan; the incestuous coupling of Sin and Death produces innumerable Hell Hounds, which prey upon their mother in a hideous cycle of painful procreation: "These yelling Monsters," Sin laments,

> hourly conceiv'd
> And hourly born, with sorrow infinite
> To me, for when they list into the womb
> That bred them they return, and howl and gnaw
> My Bowels, thir repast.
>
> [*PL* 2. 796–800]

However, in her allusion to this Miltonic image, Wollstonecraft makes one significant alteration. In *Paradise Lost* the ghastly cycle of birth and death is the result of a rape, which Sin graphically describes to Satan:

> I fled, and cri'd out *Death*;
> Hell trembl'd at the hideous Name, and sigh'd
> From all her Caves, and back resounded *Death*.
> I fled, but he pursu'd (though more, it seems,
> Inflam'd with lust than rage) and swifter far,
> Mee overtook his mother all dismay'd,
> And in embraces forcible and foul
> Ingend'ring with me, of that rape begot
> These yelling Monsters.
>
> [*PL* 2. 787–95]

Wollstonecraft's Sin, however, seems much more obliging; indeed, syntactically, *she* is the aggressor: "sin embracing death." Almost parenthetically, and almost certainly unconsciously, Wollstonecraft betrays her fear that female desire might in fact court man's lascivious and degrading attentions, that the subordinate position women have been given might even be deserved. Until women can transcend their fleshly desires and fleshly forms, they will be hostage to the body—a body that in giving birth originates death, that in demanding physical satisfaction makes itself vulnerable to frustration and pain.

The suspicion Wollstonecraft reveals here that female appetite might be the precipitating cause of women's cultural objectification also helps account for her vehement disgust with female physicality. Abhorring those "nasty, or immodest habits" that girls in boarding school acquire, she goes on to attack, in surprisingly vitriolic language, the "gross degree of familiarity" that "sisters, female intimates, or ladies and their waiting-women" exhibit toward one another (p. 127). She cautions all girls to wash and dress alone, lest they take up "some still more nasty customs, which men never fall into. Secrets

are told—where silence ought to reign; and that regard to cleanliness
. . . is violated in a beastly manner" (p. 128). It is difficult to know
exactly what Wollstonecraft is referring to here; her insistent delicacy
may result from some personal memory or a general revulsion from
eighteenth-century girls' boarding-school conditions.[25] But, whatever
the original offense, it is clear that her disgust involves female bodies
and female desires—and all the ramifications of sexuality that she
does not want to think about here.

For most late eighteenth-century writers, such an attack on female
sexuality would have centered, at some point, on the imagination, for
that faculty was generally understood to be the "*source* of sexual
feeling."[26] Certainly Wollstonecraft's ambivalence about imagination
in *The Rights of Men* leads us to expect this. But here she is careful to
distinguish between imagination, which directs an individual's desire
toward spiritual gratification, and "appetite," which fixes his or her
attention on sensual objects. Essentially, Wollstonecraft is desexualiz-
ing imagination so that she can explain how a substitute gratification
can satisfy sexual desire. Echoing eighteenth-century moralists, she
characterizes imagination in sexual terms (it is a "vigorous" principle,
"panting after" its object in "eager pursuit"); but its ultimate function
is to "absorb every meaner affection and desire" as it leads the
individual toward the happiness that is profoundly "not material" (p.
74). That Wollstonecraft continues to use sexual imagery to describe
this substitute happiness suggests, however, that she is at least dimly
aware that religious consolation *is* a substitute gratification. "True
voluptuousness must proceed from the mind" (p. 192), she argues, but
intellectual "voluptuousness" is an image that proclaims the primacy
of the senses. Wollstonecraft intends to strip the maturation process
completely of its sexual character; but if she succeeds in making the
sexes equal, she fails to eliminate the sexual component that is the
source of her ongoing anxiety.

In her attempt to shore up her character, to control the emotional
energy that threatened to explode her political argument in *The Rights
of Men,* Wollstonecraft has turned her argument outward. The result
is a more perceptive analysis both of ideology and of her own position within it. But while her basic assumption—that women are
primarily reasoning rather than sexual beings—enabled her to create
a self-image sufficiently strong to attack prejudices and practices that
traditionally had wholly silenced women's voices in political discussions, her inability to acknowledge or fully assimilate the profoundly
unreasonable longings of her own emotional or physical being caused
her to weaken the argument she had so effectively begun. For Wollstonecraft does not extend to women the same insight she used in
exploding Rousseau's euphemisms and evasions; that is, she does not

develop the idea that either women's characteristically volatile sensibility or her own scheme for emotional gratification might be a sublimation of sexual energy. In order to sidestep the investigation of sexuality that this insight would necessitate—and the admission of "weakness" it would entail—Wollstonecraft repeatedly turns her argument away from every potentially dangerous acknowledgment that women have sexual or physical needs.

We can see one consequence of this evasion in her own use of euphemisms and circuitous phrasing. Whenever Wollstonecraft approaches a subject that arouses her own volatile emotions, her language becomes both obscure and abstract; she shuns concrete nouns as if they were bodies she is trying to cover over. In fact, she will fully indulge her feeling only when its object is physically absent or unidentified. Even then she uses artificial and abstract rhetoric to generalize her emotion and to idealize the provocative situation. Her celebration of modesty is a particularly clear example of the results her abstractions could produce:

> Modesty! Sacred offspring of sensibility and reason!—true delicacy of mind!—may I unblamed presume to investigate thy nature, and trace to its covert the mild charm, that mellowing each harsh feature of a character, renders what would otherwise only inspire cold admiration—lovely!—Thou that smoothest the wrinkles of wisdom, and softenest the tone of the sublimest virtues till they all melt into humanity;—thou that spreadest the ethereal cloud that, surrounding love, heightens every beauty, it half shades, breathing those coy sweets that steal into the heart, and charm the senses—modulate for me the language of persuasive reason, till I rouse my sex from the flowery bed, on which they supinely sleep life away! [P. 121]

Wollstonecraft's celebration of "mellowing," "smoothing," "melting," and "shading" suggests the extent to which she is attempting to dematerialize her subject. Perhaps an even more revealing text is the one in which she defines "human rapture." Here the emotion is twice removed from its physical object and it is described in poetic clichés notable primarily for their imprecision and immateriality. The "rapture," predictably, is not for the physical person but only for "whatever had touched the person"—the glove or slipper, for example—of "an absent or lost friend":

> A shadowy phantom glides before us, obscuring every other object; yet when the soft cloud is grasped, the form melts into common air, leaving a solitary void, or sweet perfume, stolen from the violet, that memory long holds dear. [P. 124]

Although Wollstonecraft repeatedly professes to admire clarity, this image not only describes obscurity but is itself purposefully vague. Only in such a "fairy ground" of spiritual relationships and in such abstract and impersonal language can she allow herself to imagine intense feeling, for in this immaterial context desire can be neither sexual nor literal nor demanding of satisfaction.

An even more severe consequence of Wollstonecraft's refusal to acknowledge female sexuality is her reluctance to consider women as a group capable of achieving solidarity or taking the initiative for social reform. Because she considers the root of culture's values to be *men's* sexual desire, she continues to portray social reform strictly in terms of individual men's acts of self-denial and self-control. Certainly her understanding of the determinate relationship between the individual and institutional or historical forces is more sophisticated in *The Rights of Woman* than in *The Rights of Men*. In it she explicitly acknowledges, for example, the limited efficacy of individual effort (especially in education; see pp. 21, 157) and the necessity for society-wide changes in legal, political, and employment policies (see pp. 145, 147, 148). But when she calls for change, her summons always encourages an alteration in *individual,* particularly *male,* attitudes. "Let men become more chaste and modest" (p. 11), let the nobility "prefer" the practice of reason (p. 22), let "mankind become more reasonable" (p. 56); only then can social change begin. The terms used may pass as generic nouns and pronouns, but they most frequently designate males. Wollstonecraft is generally *not* challenging women to *act.* When she calls for a "revolution in female manners" (p. 45), for example, she is not advocating a feminist uprising to overthrow manners but rather a general acquiescence in the gradual turning that the word "revolution" was commonly taken to mean in the eighteenth century. Women are simply to wait for this revolution to *be* effected, for their dignity to *be* restored, for their reformation to *be* made necessary. The task is primarily men's, and it involves not confrontation but self-control. Wollstonecraft defers her discussion of legal inequality to the promised second volume (which she never wrote) because, in her scheme, social legislation is less effective than individual self-control. And in *The Rights of Woman,* Wollstonecraft emphasizes independence rather than equality both because she conceives of society as a collection of individual attitudes rather than legal contracts and because she imagines relationships to be fundamentally antagonistic rather than cooperative. The major antagonism, however, is not against an external force but against one's own self—against fear and, especially, against desire. This idea, of course, is actually only a generalization of the behavior traditionally advocated for women; it is the Protestant ethic stripped of its component of personal assertion and material reward.

It is partly because Wollstonecraft so thoroughly distrusts her own sexuality that she rejects a female speaking voice in *The Rights of*

Woman. While occasionally she speaks self-consciously as a woman
("in the name of my sex" [p. 150]), more frequently she distinguishes
between herself and "them" ("I plead for my sex—not for myself"
[p. 3]); "I do not wish them [women] to have power over men; but over
themselves" [p. 62]). At least once she speaks "as man with man," but
even then she aspires not to a masculine voice but to a voice totally
unconscious of sexuality. Here she is adopting Rousseau's definition
of men and simply bringing the definition of women in line with the
implicit asexual ideal. "Men are not always men in the company of
women, nor would women always remember that they are women,
if they were allowed to acquire more understanding" (p. 123, n. 4).
Occasionally she addresses women, but both her formal, self-consciously rhetorical address and her condescension distance her from
her natural allies: "Hapless woman! what can be expected from thee
. . . ?" (p. 97); "O ye foolish women! . . . ignorant ye are in the most
emphatical sense of the word" (p. 180). Wollstonecraft clearly wants
most of all to distinguish herself from all sexual categories so as to
attain a neutral voice. She speaks comfortably "as a philosopher" and
"as a moralist" (p. 34), but in her most cherished self-image she speaks
to her "dear contemporaries" as "a fellow creature," using the "firm
tone of humanity" (pp. 92, 150, 3). She even dramatizes herself as
achieving a stance of almost Miltonic "disinterestedness":

> Let me now as from an eminence survey the world stripped of all its false
> delusive charms. The clear atmosphere enables me to see each object in its true
> point of view, while my heart is still. I am calm as the prospect in a morning
> when the mists, slowly dispersing, silently unveil the beauties of nature, re-
> freshed by rest. [P. 110]

Despite the natural tropes, this description actually characterizes the
speaker; *she* is as "calm as the prospect" cleansed of mists, and *hers*
are the "unveil[ed] . . . beauties." In this ideal, disembodied state,
Wollstonecraft transcends her femaleness—and with it, presumably,
the agitations that make her female heart, now still, cry out.

From her evasions and her aspirations, it seems clear that the price
Wollstonecraft felt her new profession exacted was her female sexuality. This was a price she thought she was more than willing to pay;
for if the ideal writer has no sex, he or she is therefore free from both
the body's limitations and its demands. Adopting this characterization of the writer could theoretically protect Wollstonecraft from the
painful vacillations of feeling she had alternately repressed and indulged during her youth. At the same time, this persona allowed her
a certain amount of social self-confidence, especially in Joseph Johnson's circle, where feminine graces seemed to be irrelevant and such
women as Anna Barbauld were acknowledged as intellectual equals

by being criticized as such. But it also, of course, blinded Wollstone-craft to crucial emotional and physical needs—needs that were in-creasingly demanding attention. That she could mistake her growing passion for Henri Fuseli for a purely "rational desire"—even to the point of proposing, to his wife, that she, Wollstonecraft, should join the Fuseli household—attests to the extent of her self-deception and to the power of the desire she tried to philosophize away. Although it made her famous, *The Rights of Woman* did not provide Wollstone-craft with the "stability of character" to which she aspired. Late in 1792, after Fuseli had rejected her advances, she found herself again painfully self-divided, her "heart" once more at war with her beloved reason. "I am a strange compound of weakness and resolution!" she wrote to Joseph Johnson.

> There is certainly a great defect in my mind—my wayward heart creates its own misery— Why I am made thus I cannot tell; and, till I can form some idea of the whole of my existence, I must be content to weep and dance like a child—long for a toy, and be tired of it as soon as I get it. [*MWL*, p. 221; c. late 1792]

Whether or not Wollstonecraft was correct in deducing a funda-mentally nonsexual human essence is, of course, beside the point, for the tensions in her argument demonstrate that, even in her own terms, she had not resolved the complexities of the issue, either theoretically or practically. Clearly, simply to recognize the structure of sexual oppression and inequality, as Mary Wollstonecraft did, was not sufficient to achieve genuine freedom. Remaining a prisoner of the category she most vehemently tried to reject, she allowed what looked like an externalization of rage to return remorselessly to herself. The frustrations behind the contradictions evident in *The Vindication of the Rights of Woman,* her strongest polemic, would be dispelled only when she found a way to allow the writer and the woman to speak with one voice.

3

Love's Skirmishes and the
Triumph of Ideology

IN ADDITION TO UPENDING the social order of one of the most
esteemed nations in Europe, the French Revolution exploded many
political theories; it even caused some philosophers to wonder whether
there was *any* discernible connection between ideas and real events.
Mary Wollstonecraft was no exception. Having journeyed alone to
France to escape the torments of her passion for Fuseli, she watched
a very dignified king of France ushered under guard through the
streets of Paris. For the first time in her life she found herself unable
to sleep without a lighted candle, and her ideals of human perfectability fell beneath the blade of the guillotine. It was also in Paris,
and in the wake of Fuseli's rejection, that Wollstonecraft buried her
theories about "respectful esteem." Talk about sexuality was more
explicit in revolutionary Paris, divorce laws had been made more
liberal there,[1] and in this atmosphere Wollstonecraft discovered for
herself that the vulnerability she had feared was largely offset by the
"substantial happiness" sexuality seemed to offer. With Gilbert Imlay,
the American entrepreneur, she experienced for the first time the
depths of a passionate, reciprocal exchange of love (a "suffusion," she
fondly describes the physical signs of Imlay's passion), and, as a
consequence, she began to reconsider the role of intense feeling in
improving the human soul. Even Milton was redeemed in the course
of her unself-conscious capitulation to sexual love. "I like to see your
eyes praise me," she wrote to Imlay, "and, Milton insinuates, that,
during such recitals, there are interruptions, not ungrateful to the
heart, when the honey that drops from the lips is not merely words"
(*MWL,* p. 235; mid-1793).

Wollstonecraft's happiness was not long-lived, however. After their
child was born, Imlay's attentions flagged, and he became more
distracted by business and more interested in emotional and sexual
variety than in Wollstonecraft's passionate demands. But even as his
absences lengthened and Wollstonecraft succumbed to agonies of
doubt, frustration, and disappointment, she refused to renounce the

new self-image that had bloomed with this brief love. To complement her characteristic determination ("I do not chuse to be a secondary object," she wrote Imlay, echoing her adolescent demand to Jane Arden [*MWL,* p. 275; 9 January 1795]), she developed from this relationship not only a new acceptance of her own emotionalism but also a new openness to emotional dependence and a resolution not to rest content with theories that denied felt desires of body or heart. Having experienced and acknowledged the complexities of her female self, Wollstonecraft suffered the pain her theories of reason had been designed to defend against. But in the course of her suffering she also began to discover new reservoirs of internal strength, resources that enabled her to express this complex being more fully than ever before, in a voice newly responsive to herself and to the world at large.

Letters Written during a Short Residence in Sweden, Norway, and Denmark

Mary Wollstonecraft began her *Letters Written during a Short Residence in Sweden, Norway, and Denmark* (1796) in order to win financial independence from her lover-turned-employer, Gilbert Imlay. Perceiving Imlay's growing discontent, yet refusing to admit an irrevocable change, Wollstonecraft seems to have imagined that the businessman Imlay would feel less burdened if his unanticipated family were financially self-supporting. The epistolary travelogue she produced did not have the effect of reclaiming Imlay's affection, but it accomplished a great deal for Wollstonecraft. William Godwin, for example, who was unmoved by the "harshness and ruggedness" of the *Rights of Woman,* found in the *Letters* "genius" and "gentleness." "If ever there was a book calculated to make a man in love with its author," he wrote, "this appears to me the book."[2] And Godwin's friend Amelia Alderson (who was later to remark that of all new sights only Wollstonecraft and the Cumberland Lakes did not disappoint her) was equally pleased with the softer tone of Wollstonecraft's latest work. "As soon as I read your Letters from Norway, the cold awe which the philosopher had excited was lost in the tender sympathy call'd forth by the woman."[3]

Godwin and Alderson were responding to the direct, unabashedly autobiographical voice that resounds from the first page of this very personal travelogue. Wollstonecraft openly appeals here to her reader's emotions because for the first time she openly acknowledges the primacy of her own feelings and the power of those feelings to engage and persuade. Immediately, the persona, who is, explicitly, "Mary"—Wollstonecraft herself—grants subjectivity and personal experiences the authority she had previously reserved for the objective "clear truths" of reason.

> In writing these desultory letters, I found I could not avoid being continually the first person—"the little hero of each tale." I tried to correct this fault, if it be one . . . but in proportion as I arranged my thoughts, my letter, I found, became stiff and affected: I, therefore, determined to let my remarks and reflections flow unrestrained, as I perceived that I could not give a just description of what I saw, but by relating the effect different objects had produced on my mind and feelings, whilst the impression was still fresh.[4]

This passage announces both the form and the content of Wollstonecraft's new aesthetic program. "Desultory" is no longer a pejorative term, as it was when she accused Burke of being a "desultory writer" in *The Rights of Men*.[5] Instead, Wollstonecraft is frankly acknowledging the associative organization all her works have employed; but here she is granting it a value she had previously denied. To "arrange" thoughts logically is to sever them from the person who conceives them; thus it is to murder thought, to substitute "stiff," "affected artifice" for vital personality. Wollstonecraft decides to "let [her] remarks and reflections flow unrestrained"—to construct her narrative, that is, according to the associations of her own mind—because she now believes that accuracy is measured by the subject's unfolding response rather than by some fixed, objective standard. Her own feelings also make up the content of her work because she now considers these feelings an integral part of the truths she would convey.

Wollstonecraft's endorsement of feeling here reveals a wholehearted immersion in life that is the direct antithesis of her adolescent religious renunciation. As her narrative progresses, she indicates that, in an almost Keatsian way, she now embraces even the intensity of sorrow as essentially life-affirming: "emotions that trembled on the brink of extacy and agony gave a poignancy to my sensations, which made me feel more alive than usual" (p. 16). Every exuberance of emotion she now sees as the expression of a "purified" heart; and accepting her emotionalism signals her freedom from the warfare against self that masculine authorities dictated. "For years I have endeavoured to calm an impetuous tide," Wollstonecraft comments on her years of repression, "labouring to make my feelings take an orderly course. —It was striving against the stream. —I must love and admire with warmth, or I sink into sadness" (p. 74).

Wollstonecraft advances her brave new vulnerability with an authorial confidence her earlier works never achieved. The frequency of such phrases as "in my opinion," "I am persuaded that," "It seems to me," and "I believe" suggests that she is anxious to take personal responsibility for her speculations instead of grounding them in an objective authority. And whereas her personal involvement was deliberately understated or altogether omitted in her earlier works, here her repeated references to autobiographical experiences ("Much of this I have seen," "I have frequently . . . heard") indicate the ease with which she now embraces the role of an authoritative commentator.

Wollstonecraft's new self-confidence is largely due to the relationship she now emphasizes between herself as a particular subject and humanity in general. As early as 1790, in *The Rights of Men,* she had implied that the development of the individual recapitulated that of civilization, but not until the *Letters* does she make use of this connection to justify self-consciousness and self-expression. Although Wollstonecraft claims that her "favourite subject of contemplation" is "the future improvement of the world" (p. 182), she concentrates instead on the present improvement of a single individual—herself. But while the focus of the travelogue may seem to split in two at the juncture of self-expression and social observation, Wollstonecraft's perceptions actually illuminate the twin phenomena of the individual *and* society. By narrating the progress of her own expanding consciousness, she forecasts the course of social improvement. For, she argues, each nation, like an individual, has a collective "understanding" that evolves organically, "ripening" gradually to fruition (p. 198). Thus what might look like egotism becomes a strategy of instruction and provides a plot for historical narrative as well.

Wollstonecraft significantly alters her earlier assessment of the relative roles of reason and imagination in this model of social and individual maturation. Perhaps because she no longer dreads the vulnerability attendant on feeling, she no longer argues for a defensive self-control that requires the imagination to be shackled to the warden, reason. Instead, in the *Letters,* reason and the imagination play equally important roles in educating the individual. Reason, or "understanding," "enlarge[s] the soul" and gives intimations of personal creative power. Feeling or passion is the individual's (or the infant civilization's) first and most primitive response, but only through the combined actions of reasonable reflection and imaginative projection can this instinctive behavior be refined into a mature, sensitive response. This model of maturation is implicitly—and sometimes explicitly—the subject of Wollstonecraft's meditations in the *Letters.* At the same time, the actions of reason and the imagination provide the organizational principle for each significant episode. Wollstonecraft's initial response to each new situation or natural scene is a spontaneous emotion, but only as she reflects rationally on the scene is this emotion generalized to humanity; by the same token, only as she imaginatively projects herself into the scene does she intuit the power that assures her of her own integrity and worth.

In the *Letters* Wollstonecraft no longer conceives of reason as a Lockean, essentially passive, receiver of objective "clear truths." Rather, she now defines reason's primary function as reflection—not the reflection a mirror might yield but the mediation of an active agent. Reason is an inward-turning faculty that allows the individual to examine his or her own prejudices (p. 31) and to empathize with others as a consequence of heightened self-knowledge. Reason is no longer presented as a superior faculty; it neither can nor should control feeling (pp. 94, 109). Indeed, reason often gives way to emotions or even generates them by reflecting on and cultivating inner potential. Wollstonecraft is able to admire a stately pine tree, for example, even though it departs from canonical aesthetic principles, because

> my very reason obliges me to permit my feelings to be my criterion. Whatever excites emotion has charms for me; though I insist that the cultivation of the mind, by warming, nay almost creating the imagination, produces taste, and an immense variety of sensations and emotions, partaking of the exquisite pleasure inspired by beauty and sublimity. [P. 92]

The imagination is also a faculty that discovers and develops individual potential, but, because its primary impulse is outward, its activity is more dynamic. The imagination, activated by a sensed disproportion between the natural world and the individual's desire, projects thought beyond the confines of the temporal world. The imaginative experience is often provoked by a feeling of temporary confinement or by a reminder of the soul's more prolonged imprisonment in the flesh; Wollstonecraft contemplates a collection of coffins, for example, and is inspired to a vision of the endless procession of humanity (p. 71). Because the imaginative experience originates in intimations of loss, the imaginative leap frequently carries overtones of sadness even into reveries of infinity or freedom. But the action of the imagination is essentially life-affirming, for it simultaneously proves the creative power of the individual and anchors the subject in the external world. Thus when Wollstonecraft speaks of "that tender melancholy which, sublimating the imagination, exalts, rather than depresses the mind" (p. 51), she is invoking the etymology of the word "sublimate": *sublimare,* "to take across a threshold." "Tender melancholy," the intimation of mortality, exalts the mind by refining the imagination or raising it to a new level, an experience that yields new surges of power and teaches the subject to love the object that inspires such feelings.

The sadness that provokes and shadows the imaginative leap is, of course, the recognition of personal limitations. As the paradigm implicit in *The Rights of Men* and *The Rights of Woman* suggested, the growth of self-consciousness always yields this bitter fruit. But an index of Wollstonecraft's maturity here is her new willingness to explore the face of death, to accept the fact of human limitations without automatic recourse to religious consolation. The specific loss that haunts her now is, of course, the loss of her lover, Imlay. But she knows that his absence, like all partings, is essentially "death-like," "a sort of separation of soul," "something torn from ourselves" (p. 176). Such shades of imminent annihilation darken nearly every episode in the *Letters*; for a work that essentially celebrates imaginative power, it is remarkably uninhibited in acknowledging the bondage of life to death. When Wollstonecraft relishes "a thrill of delight," for example, in remembering past joy, the emotion surges out of her recollection of her dead "dear friend," Fanny Blood (p. 59); and when she enters an empty mansion, she imagines that its owners are dead, that the worm "riots unchecked" in their corpses (p. 84). Similarly, though the *Letters* describes a summer's journey, Wollstonecraft's thoughts repeatedly turn to winter, summer's icy sepulcher. Watching the Swedish women wash clothes, for instance, she leaps imaginatively to the crueler season to come, when "their hands, cut by the ice, are cracked and bleeding" (p. 26). At one point her sense of winter so completely overpowers the present that she momentarily forgets her whereabouts. The progression in this passage, from concrete description to imaginative vision, without even a shift in verb tense, demonstrates the progress of the imagination and the way that death provokes it and shadows its flight:

> The clouds caught their hue of the rocks that menaced them. The sun appeared afraid to shine, the birds ceased to sing, and the flowers to bloom. . . . The farm houses, in which only poverty resided, were formed of logs scarcely keeping off the cold and drifting snow; out of them the inhabitants seldom peeped, and the sports or prattling of children was neither seen nor heard. The current of life seemed congealed at the source: all were not frozen; for it was summer, you remember; but every thing appeared so dull, that I waited to see ice, in order to reconcile me to the absence of gaiety. [P. 42]

The perception that initiates this imaginative flight is once more a feeling of loss ("the absence of gaiety") and danger (menacing rocks, an obscured sun). But, even though Wollstonecraft's fear carries over into her vision, the fundamental experience is one of transcendence and power. Responding to the threat sensed in the natural world, the imagination carries the observer out of this setting naturally, without calling attention to its own presence. From direct perception ("the clouds caught"), the mind moves to imaginative projection ("the sun appeared afraid"), then to imaginative "perception" of a fully realized visionary landscape ("the birds ceased to sing, and the flowers to bloom"). Self-consciousness intrudes only after the liberation is accomplished, only after the sensed danger has been replaced by the harmless, "sublimated," vision of winter. Wollstonecraft's willingness to engage herself in life and to trust her imagination even in its confrontations with death has enabled her to experience and drama-tize a more fully realized version of the self-affirmation she tried to describe in the *Rights of Men*.

Imagination has the power to affirm the subject, but Wollstonecraft does not grant it autonomy; for here, more conspicuously than in any of her earlier works, she presents the temporal, natural world as the necessary ground of speculation and the crucial field of experience. Nature is "the nurse of sentiment" (p. 58) that both provokes the imagination and provides the images it then takes up. Because she no longer dreads the physical world (or implicitly, the body), Wollstone-craft no longer rejects the sensual images the imagination presents or the longings it arouses. Although she knows that, in "such an imperfect state of existence," responsiveness to nature is painful, hence dangerous, she also knows that only the emotions excited by the real world test the individual's capacity for love and unfold his or her noblest desires: "an affection for mankind, a passion for an individual, is but the unfolding of that love which embraces all that is great and beautiful" (p. 58).

Nature also controls imaginative reveries; for all its "faery power," the imagination can neither generate its own images nor deny physi-cal reality. In Sweden, for example, Wollstonecraft finds that she cannot escape the smell of decaying herrings, which repeatedly in-trudes upon her reveries (p. 41). The imagination is also incapable of actually reproducing experience; its power is limited to "amuse-ment," to provoking each individual to his or her private imaginative excursions—a fact that makes communication problematic: "We can-not find words to discriminate that individuality [of a mountain pros-pect] so as to enable a stranger to say, this is the face, that the view. We may amuse by setting the imagination to work; but we cannot store the memory with a fact" (pp. 37–38).

Because Wollstonecraft recognizes that all perception is inevitably subjective, she uses natural objects to mediate her relationship with her audience. Even though her "jaundiced eye of melancholy" may color every thought (p. 169), she is able to communicate her emotions because she anchors them in the specific physical settings to which they correspond. Nature serves as a common reference point, a touchstone shared by Wollstonecraft and her audience, even though the readers may never see the landscapes for themselves. And be-cause nature facilitates communication, concrete descriptions also anchor the most important organizational unit in the *Letters*. In a typical episode, Wollstonecraft essentially duplicates the activity of her own mind: she observes a natural object or scene, is inspired to an imaginative or intellectual excursion, and then returns to "the straight road" of observing the natural world.[6] The return is frequently abrupt, however, and Wollstonecraft often accomplishes it only by concluding a letter; for the imagination repeatedly strains away from the natural world or threatens to center obsessively on the self.

Wollstonecraft's journey through the barren splendor of Sweden, Norway, and Denmark is most significantly a journey into the depths of her own complex personality. Several critics have noted the similarities between her *Letters* and Wordsworth's *Prelude,*[7] and perhaps the most interesting point of comparison is in their presentations of self. Wordsworth explicitly but unobtrusively uses his vocation as a poet to organize and justify his autobiographical excursion; to mediate her observations, Wollstonecraft uses what she now sees as the most important aspect of her self—her femaleness. Wollstonecraft introduces her gender less self-consciously here than in the *Rights of Woman*; she simply notes matter-of-factly her acquaintances' surprise that a woman should travel to such unusual places (pp. 10, 54) and ask *"men's questions"* (p. 15). In many respects, Wollstonecraft is *not* like other women (as the comparison with her delicate maid, Marguerite, proves), but she insists that her interests and emotions are quintessentially female. No male observer would consider details about child care or women servants significant; no man would contemplate the dilemma of a daughter with "a mother's fondness and anxiety" (p. 55). Wollstonecraft now realizes that her position as a woman has all along dictated both the nature of her experiences and her responses. Her emotion is a woman's emotion, and her thoughts spring from these depths, not simply from asexual reason. "We reason deeply," she comments, "when we forcibly feel" (p. 160).

Like many Romantic poets, Wollstonecraft is aware of the way her (female) consciousness affects her perception of the landscape and the self she would describe. As in her personal letters from Ireland in 1787, Wollstonecraft speaks here of her own life as a text to be read; she has "turned over in this solitude a new page in the history of [her] own heart" (pp. 90–91). Now, however, she is more conscious both of the subjective power implicit in this self-objectification and of the consequent danger of distortion. The self-conscious Wollstonecraft is, like Wordsworth, an observant I as well as an observing eye; yet she does not want her own interpretation of experience to obscure completely the scenes she wants to convey. Occasionally her solution to this dilemma suggests Wordsworth's "ennobling interchange;" for by humanizing natural objects ("the bones of the world" [p. 42]) and by naturalizing human beings (her child is "sweet as the closing flowers" [p. 16]), she dramatizes a reciprocity between nature and the individu-

al's perception of it. More typically, however, she qualifies her subjective response to experience by couching it in borrowed language.
Because she still questions her ability to "read" nature as authoritatively as male poets have done, the book of nature remains for her
a text to be read through other texts. An allusive, poetic description
of nature seems to her to be simultaneously authoritative and deeply,
personally, felt. Thus, she imaginatively flees an interminable meal
for a more inviting "landscape":

> A never ending, still beginning feast may be bearable, perhaps, when stern
> winter frowns, shaking with chilling aspect his hoary locks; but during a
> summer, sweet as fleeting, let me, my kind strangers, escape sometimes into
> your fir groves, wander on the margin of your beautiful lakes, or climb your
> rocks to view still others in endless perspective; which, piled by more than
> giant's hand, scale the heavens to intercept its rays [an allusion to *Paradise Lost*
> 4. 354–55], or to receive the parting tinge of lingering day—day that, scarcely
> softened into twilight, allows the freshening breeze to wake, and the moon to
> burst forth in all her glory to glide with solemn elegance through the azure
> expanse. [P. 23]

Only when Wollstonecraft describes a scene still uncaptured by
poetic rhetoric does she effectively dramatize her subjective engagement with the object. Few poets have described the woman's sphere—
the details of domestic economy, of housekeeping or cooking in these
remote regions—and few poets have noticed young starfish:

> I was amused by disturbing the innumerable young star fish which floated just
> below the surface: I had never observed them before; for they have not a hard
> shell, like those which I have seen on the sea-shore. They look like thickened
> water, with a white edge; and four purple circles, of different forms, were in
> the middle, over an incredible number of fibres, or white lines. Touching them,
> the cloudy substance would turn or close, first on one side, then on the other,
> very gracefully; but when I took one of them up in the ladle with which I
> heaved the water out of the boat, it appeared only a colourless jelly. [P. 76]

Wollstonecraft's images are not particularly "poetic," but they are
vivid and concrete, and they reveal her curiosity and inquisitiveness.
Her typical relationship to nature suggests more of the eighteenth-
century empiricist's fascination with details than a Wordsworthian
appreciation of imaginative power, but her consciousness of the subjectivity of perception distinguishes her, even in such a passage, from
earlier cataloguers of natural phenomena.

Wollstonecraft's oblique invocation of literary authorities is in fact
the only remaining sign of the insecurity that pervades her earlier
works. In the *Letters* she is much less anxious to anchor her subjective
judgments in external, objective authorities. This is especially obvious
in her presentation of her religious sentiments.[8] The *Letters* is not

without references to God, but Wollstonecraft is now much less orthodox in describing God's order and much more inclined to substitute nontheological phrases like "a mighty whole" (p. 17), "all that is great and beautiful" (p. 58), for more traditional, monotheistic terms. Wollstonecraft also now openly acknowledges the fact that her religious inclinations arise from fear and desire as much as from demonstrable evidence:

> Without hope, what is to sustain life, but the fear of annihilation—the only thing of which I have ever felt a dread—I cannot bear to think of being no more—of losing myself . . . ; it appears to me impossible that I should cease to exist, or that this active, restless spirit, equally alive to joy and sorrow, should only be organized dust. . . . Surely something resides in this heart that is not perishable—and life is more than a dream. [P. 76]

Mitzi Myers, in discussing the *Letters* as a prototype of Romantic autobiography, has pointed out that much of the integrity of Wollstonecraft's persona comes from her particular use of the travelogue form itself. Not only does the travelogue provide a natural organizing principle for the interrelation of observation, speculation, and personal expression, but doubling the actual journey, as Wordsworth was to do, with a metaphoric excursion of self-exploration enables Wollstonecraft to evolve a continuity of personality that encompasses the variety of attitudes, roles, and possibilities the journey evokes. According to Myers, the "circuitous, subjective movement of the mind" constitutes the organizing principle that turns the "discontinuous form" of epistolary travel narrative into "an agent of continuity."[9] Moreover,

> just as . . . the demonstration of the powers of her mind . . . holds the book together formally, so the writing of the book quite literally holds her together, as she discovers her power to overcome fragmentation, the power of the self to create unity and make sense of its multiple roles and painful experiences. To give the book its unity is at the same to assert an identity. The work and the self exist in a reciprocal relationship, the work itself an image of what the self can achieve.[10]

In an important sense, Wollstonecraft's *Letters* enables her to objectify her tumultuous emotions in a form that does not demand an integrated, fully formed persona. In such a form, writing can become an act of self-creation rather than self-assertion, the uninhibited revelation of the *process* of seeking inner equilibrium. Wollstonecraft uses the public nature of the travelogue to control the intensity of personal anguish and direct the focus of her inquiry outward into a finished form; but she uses the epistolary form of her narrative to signify the temporal and personal dimensions of what is effectively an ongoing process. "Her persona is not a congealed and completed self (this is what I am), but the protagonist of a quest still uncompleted at the book's conclusion (who am I, and where am I going)."[11]

Wollstonecraft's *Letters,* as the mirror of a maturing self and self-consciousness, does have a plot of sorts, although the most significant unit of action is not the volume as a whole but the movement from observation to imaginative speculation that I have already described. Taken as a whole, however, the *Letters* details the narrator's passage from an initial state of poised expectation (an emotional as well as a nautical "becalmment"), through a period of energetic exploration, observation, and self-discovery, to a gradual decline into melancholy and anger. The specific motives for these emotional developments are left unspecified in the *Letters,* even though Wollstonecraft provides sufficient hints to communicate the general reason for her anguish. A more complete record of the emotional journey is available, however, in her private letters to Imlay, which were published posthumously by Godwin.[12] These letters provide the implicit but suppressed plot of her travelogue. From them it is clear that Wollstonecraft's spirits were initially kept high by her belief that the separation from her unfaithful lover was to be temporary, a period of decision-making for Imlay and (she convinced herself) an opportunity for him to recognize the value of her fidelity. Despite the obvious pain and sorrow Wollstonecraft continued to feel, her letters to Imlay do not become obsessed by anguish or resentment until August 1795, at which time she received letters from him that revealed the extent of his disaffection—and her delusion.[13] Her pain and anger build in her letters from Gothenburg and Copenhagen, as she struggles to come to terms with Imlay's unworthiness,[14] and, by the time she writes from Hamburg, her lingering hopes have been almost completely extinguished by her rising determination to survive this emotional devastation. "Preparing [her]self for the worst," Wollstonecraft announces to Imlay her plan to provide for their daughter Fanny and, by doing so, she severs the financial tie that she knows he can best understand.[15]

In the *Letters Written . . . in Sweden,* the most perceptible turn in the persona's feelings begins in Letter XXII, which narrates her arrival at Corsoer from Copenhagen. Recognition of the death of her love affair with Imlay surfaces in her acute consciousness of the significance of separation ("always a most melancholy, death-like idea" [p. 176]) and her sensitivity to the transience of all joy (pp. 174–75). She valiantly attempts to achieve some distance from her own sorrow by emphasizing the insignificance of all individuals; but even as she praises "the design of the Deity" in preserving the species, her imagination dwells on individual tragedies rather than "the grand plan of the universe": "Children peep into existence, suffer, and die; men play like moths about a candle, and sink into the flame: war, and 'the thousand ills which flesh is heir to,' mow them down in shoals" (p. 180). As Wollstonecraft's return to London looms closer, her ability to maintain perspective on her own situation diminishes, and her personal pain moves nearer to the center of her narrative. Everywhere in Germany she sees signs of commercial activity, a hated reminder of the villain she believes to be behind the transformation of Imlay's loving countenance into his present "money-getting face." Now she cannot refrain from turning her general castigation of commerce into a personal warning to Imlay, as if hoping that heartfelt pleas in this public form will effect what all her private communications have failed to do. "But you will say that I am growing bitter, perhaps, personal. Ah! shall I whisper to you—that you—yourself, are strangely altered, since you have entered deeply into commerce—more than you are aware of" (p. 187). In Imlay's growing preoccupation with business Wollstonecraft confronts the logical extension of the bourgeois energy she celebrated in the *Rights of Men*; one measure of the change she has undergone is that she now cherishes emotional stability and domestic affection over this restless desire for "improvement." Such exertion she now sees as a kind of selfishness, which actually prevents the individual from self-improvement because it concentrates all interest and desire on the self.

A man ceases to love humanity, and then individuals, as he advances in the chase after wealth; as one clashes with his interest, the other with his pleasures: to business, as it is termed, every thing must give way; nay, is sacrificed; and all the endearing charities of citizen, husband, father, brother, become empty names. [P. 190]

Considering herself a sacrificial lamb not so much to Imlay ("You will rouse yourself, and shake off the vile dust that obscures you," she tenaciously believes) but to the commercial spirit invading society, Wollstonecraft melodramatically casts herself as an unheard Cassandra (p. 190) and as a pathetic, betrayed child (p. 184). Both characterizations verge on self-pity; despite her determination to conquer sorrow and her courageous descent into pain, Wollstonecraft comes very close in these last letters to lapsing into her old role of sentimental sufferer. Only by resolutely turning her attention outward once more, to initiate the confrontation that awaits her, is she able to regain sufficient energy to transform her bitterness into a blessing. Her final letter concludes on a note whose triumph is wrested from sadness.

Adieu! My spirit of observation seems to be fled—and I have been wandering round this dirty place, literally speaking, to kill time; though the thoughts, I would fain fly from, lie too close to my heart to be easily shook off, or even beguiled, by any employment, except that of preparing for my journey to London. —God bless you! [P. 196]

If Wollstonecraft does not achieve sufficient stability of character to weather the storm raging within her it is because she is no longer willing to purchase "philosophical contentment" at the price of felt needs. To a woman demanding emotional and sexual fulfillment as well as respect and intellectual independence, satisfaction did not come easily in the late eighteenth century. Indeed, given the tendency of patriarchal society to estimate a woman's value precisely according to her passivity—to her willingness to be an object of desire rather than a human being with needs, and a symbol of property rather than its possessor—satisfaction on Wollstonecraft's terms was virtually unattainable. Her maturation as a self-made woman was taking her directly into the vortex of this contradiction, and the rapid growth of her self-consciousness during the last years of her life can be seen as a recognition of and response to bourgeois society's pervasive devaluation of her sex. In the *Letters Written . . . in Sweden* the villain Wollstonecraft identifies is still an individual—Imlay—and the lust for wealth she attacks is only the faceless tyrant by whom she hopes to excuse his infidelity. But with the growth of her recognition that her own capacity for emotion could become an aggressive version of the emotionalism other women shared, Wollstonecraft comes face to face with the institutional force that stands behind every individual man. The villain she was to identify in her next work was bourgeois society itself and, more particularly, the institution of marriage. Within marriage, even the potential power of female feeling is twisted back on itself and strangles into silence the woman who tries to tell the world of society's wrongs.

Maria, or the Wrongs of Woman

For most of Mary Wollstonecraft's life her uncommon energy and determination seemed fated to be squandered in false pursuits and on inferior objects. And for a while it appeared that her resolution would make the characteristic female revolution: turning back on her self, she would determine to die. The inconstancy of her American lover twice drove Wollstonecraft to attempt suicide. Imlay himself saved her the first time and then sent her packing off to Sweden to recover her peace of mind. Then, on her return, when she found him still evasive, still indecisive, and had to force her cook to tell her what everyone else already knew—that Imlay had taken another lover— she rowed herself to Putney Bridge, walked in the rain for an hour to soak her skirts, and threw herself in the Thames. Boatmen pulled her from the water, however, and gradually her determination and her strong emotions revived once more.

Wollstonecraft emerged from the Imlay affair still resolute, still fixed on obtaining the happiness and fulfillment she considered the birthright of women as well as men. In the last year and a half of her life she struck up a friendship with William Godwin, fell in love again, and, when she found herself pregnant once more, married the evangelist of reason in order to spare her unborn child from shame. For at least this short period Wollstonecraft relished the joys of motherhood, marriage, *and* intellectual freedom. She found that "a husband is a convenient part of the furniture of a house" (*MWL,* p. 396; 6 June 1797) and that, as she wrote Godwin, "There is such a magic in affection that I have been more gratified by your clasping your hands round my arm, in company, than I could have been by all the admiration in the world, tho' I am a woman—and to mount a step higher in the scale of vanity, an author" (*MWL,* p. 360; 10 November 1796).

Yet, as a woman and an author, Wollstonecraft refused to sacrifice the independence she had earned. "My conduct in life must be directed by my own judgment and moral principles," she explained to the wondering Amelia Alderson; "in short, I still mean to be independent, even to the cultivating sentiments and principles in my children's minds . . . which he [Godwin] disavows" (*MWL,* p. 389; 11 April 1797). To prove their independence, Wollstonecraft and Godwin lived in adjoining houses, visited separately, and kept their ideas at least partly discrete.[16] Wollstonecraft's brief physical and intellectual independence, however, did not guarantee her freedom from her society's system of values. Nor did her brief happiness blind her to the circumstances that continued to cause her pain. If anything, this respite from sorrow honed her anger and her righteous indignation and gave her sufficient self-possession to try once more to turn her wrath upon its proper object. "I am not such a child as I thought myself," she wrote to Godwin (*MWL,* p. 365; 28 November 1796). In her last work she speaks with her newfound woman's voice and from a "full heart," but her message is that the struggle has just begun.

In *Maria, or the Wrongs of Woman* (1798), Wollstonecraft sought to popularize the insights of *The Rights of Woman* by turning to a genre she felt confident women would read: the sentimental novel. But the attempt to fictionalize "the peculiar Wrongs of Woman" afflicted Wollstonecraft—for perhaps the first time in her life—with what seems very like writer's block. She had composed *The Rights of Men* in less than a month and *The Rights of Woman* in six weeks, but she spent a year working on *Maria,* only to leave the manuscript less than a third finished when she died. Godwin's description of its composition reveals that the work induced an insistent anxiety:

> She began it in several forms, which she successively rejected, after they were considerably advanced. She wrote many parts of the work again and again,

and, when she had finished what she intended for the first part, she felt herself
more urgently stimulated to revise and improve what she had written, than
to proceed, with constancy of application, in the parts that were to follow.[17]

Almost any passage from the text of this much belabored first part
reveals that the hesitation that afflicted its creation haunts its prose
as well. Syntax is frequently blurred, narratives are broken off literally in midsentence, and, most problematic of all, the relationship
between the narrative consciousness and that of the heroine is incon-
sistent. All of the hesitations in composition and achievement culminate, in fact, in a conspicuous failure to establish a consistent or
purposeful attitude toward the subject under consideration. Even
though *Maria* is an unfinished novel, then, both the time that Wollstonecraft devoted to it and the problems that characteristically beset
it suggest that she was having as much difficulty with this genre as
she had once had with political disquisition.

The problem was not simply that Wollstonecraft could not construct a successful narrative, for both her first novel, *Mary,* and the
story of Jemima, contained within *Maria,* demonstrate her competence as a storyteller. The problem apparently lay, rather, in the
difficulty she had in reconciling her intended "purpose" with the
genre, which here shapes the "structure" of the work.[18] According to
her sketchy preface, Wollstonecraft's purpose was political, to show
"the peculiar Wrongs of Woman."[19] And her structure, like the structure of what she calls "our best novels," was intended to delineate
"finer sensations" rather than "*stage-effect,*" "passions rather than
manners" (pp. 8, 7). The problem here was not, as it was in *The Rights
of Men,* that Wollstonecraft tried to suppress the emotion she feared
was inappropriate to the genre she had chosen. Instead, the *kind* of
feeling that was appropriate to this genre was precisely the kind that
aborted her political purpose. For the emotionalism that had so long
crippled Wollstonecraft, along with the sentimental "structure" developed to dramatize such "finer sensations," were deeply implicated
in the values—indeed, the very organization—of bourgeois society.
It is Wollstonecraft's recognition of the incompatibility and—equally
to the point—her resistance to this recognition that account for both
the hesitations of composition and the contradictions that mark the
text. In this, her final work, Wollstonecraft identified one aspect of
what she held to be the tyranny of eighteenth-century bourgeois
institutions; yet, because her own values—indeed, her own self-definition—were inextricably bound up with the values of these institutions, she was unable to pursue her revolutionary insights to their
logical conclusion.[20]

Wollstonecraft's dilemma is epitomized by the uncertain perspective of the novel's omniscient narrator. In chapter 4, for example,

which traces Maria's emotional surrender to a fellow inmate, the narrator moves from judgmental observer to unreflecting sympathizer. Maria has been imprisoned in a madhouse so that her avaricious husband can gain control of the independent fortunes of both Maria and their infant daughter. As in *The Rights of Woman,* Maria's "situation" proves critical. At the beginning of the chapter, the narrative voice comments authoritatively on this situation. "Pity," the narrator observes,

> and the forlorn seriousness of adversity, have both been considered as dispositions favourable to love, while satirical writers have attributed the propensity to the relaxing effect of idleness; what chance then had Maria of escaping, when pity, sorrow, and solitude all conspired to soften her mind, and nourish romantic wishes, and, from a natural progress, romantic expectations? [P. 48]

The most pressing question here is the narrator's attitude toward Maria's "romantic expectations." The rhetoric of imprisonment suggests that, at the very least, Wollstonecraft understands such wishes to originate in deprivation and confinement. An adjacent passage, moreover, underscores the insight that "romantic expectations" are actually projections of unanswered desire. "Having had to struggle incessantly with the vices of mankind," the narrator continues,

> Maria's imagination found repose in pourtraying the possible virtues the world might contain. Pygmalion formed an ivory maid, and longed for an informing soul. She, on the contrary, combined all the qualities of a hero's mind, and fate presented a statue in which she might enshrine them. [P. 49]

The "statue" is Maria's fellow prisoner, Henry Darnford, who soon emerges from featureless obscurity to become a vital force in her drama. But the narrator remains curiously ambivalent about the precise nature of his role. Her description of Maria's emotional surrender, for example, culminates in a question that seems to announce the narrator's shrewd awareness that "romantic expectations" often do not correspond to real possibilities. Yet the ambiguous origin of the sentiments expressed in the first part of this passage suggests that the narrator still harbors the hope that such romantic expectations might be fulfilled. As the two lovers embrace, "desire was lost in more ineffable emotions, and to protect her from insult and sorrow—to make her happy, seemed not only the first wish of his heart, but the most noble duty of his life. Such angelic confidence demanded the fidelity of honour; but could he, feeling her in every pulsation, could he ever change, could he be a villain?" (p. 50) Is this question the narrator's ironic reminder of the possible delusion inherent in "romantic expectations"? Or does it represent the narrator's desperate attempt to resist the "ineffable emotions" that already seduce Maria? By the end of this brief chapter the distance between the narrator and

Maria almost wholly disappears; even allowing for ironic overtones, as some modern editors do, the enthusiastic rhetoric of this passage suggests that the narrator shares Maria's "romantic wishes" and perhaps her "romantic aspirations" as well:

> So much of heaven did they enjoy, that paradise bloomed around them; or they, by a powerful spell, had been transported into Armida's garden. Love, the grand enchanter, "lapt them in Elysium," and every sense was harmonized to joy and social extacy. [P. 51]

This chapter is particularly revealing because the progression of the narrator here—from detached, critical observer to emotional participant—recapitulates the movement that constitutes the organization and, theoretically, the target of criticism of the novel. The movement is the "fall" into female sexuality or, more precisely, the fall into the susceptibility to romantic expectations that eighteenth-century culture annexed to female sexuality. The problem here is that the narrator—and, by implication, Wollstonecraft herself—has just fallen victim to the very delusion it is the object of this novel to criticize.

This seduction of the narrator constitutes the third occurrence of this pattern in the novel, and, taking all three together, we begin to glimpse both Wollstonecraft's insight and her dilemma. As if to emphasize the importance of this pattern, the novel opens *in medias res,* precisely at the moment when Maria is about to fall into romantic love for the second time. Just as Maria was initially confined in a loveless, repressed youth, so is she now confined in a madhouse. Just as she was "liberated" then into a loveless marriage, so is she now soon to be "released" into the ambiguous, but decidedly dangerous, embrace of Darnford. And—most tellingly from the perspective of the narrative—the pander in each case is sentimentality or, more precisely, a sentimental story.

In what is chronologically the first fall, the sentimental story involves Maria's uncle. Maria seeks from this uncle the love she does not receive from her parents. In return, he tries to teach her the defense against romantic expectations that he has acquired through disappointment. But the effect of the uncle's story is the reverse of what he had intended, as is clear from Maria's comment: "Endeavouring to prove to me that nothing which deserved the name of love or friendship, existed in the world, he drew such animated pictures of his own feelings ... as imprinted the sentiments strongly on my heart, and animated my imagination" (p. 78). Because Maria has not personally experienced her uncle's disillusionment, she responds as contemporary moralists feared women "naturally" respond to sentimental novels; she is "imprinted" with sentiments as she projects herself, a heroine, into his text. Her imagination, that is, is "animated" or aroused.[21]

In the absence of opportunities for action, the aroused imagination projects desire onto whatever comes its way. Her uncle's sentiments, Maria says, along with the books he lends her, "conspired . . . to make [her] form an ideal picture of life," and the emotional vacuum of her home leads her to project her idealism onto a young neighbor, George Venables. Rather shrewdly, Venables remains silent throughout their courtship, for his attraction lies precisely in the imaginative opportunity he presents. In retrospect, Maria recognizes that what she had thought was love was simply an externalization of her own desire:

> He [George] continued to single me out at the dance, press my hand at parting, and utter expressions of unmeaning passion, to which I gave a meaning naturally suggested by the romantic turn of my thoughts. . . . When he left us, the colouring of my picture became more vivid—Whither did not my imagination lead me? In short, I fancied myself in love—in love with the disinterestedness, fortitude, generosity, dignity, and humanity, with which I had invested the hero I dubbed. [P. 80]

Even Maria's wishful idealism, however, cannot survive the brutal reality of marriage with Venables. Soon after marrying, she discovers that what she had imagined to be his love was actually avarice; he really wanted only the £5,000 Maria's uncle had settled on her as a dowry.

In the madhouse in which Venables eventually has his wife confined, the same pattern again threatens Maria. Despite the fact that she now has personally experienced sorrow, she is once more seduced by sentiment. This time the pander is exclusively textual: first some marginalia written by her unseen fellow prisoner, then one of the books he lends her—Rousseau's *Julie*. Once more the narrator's description suggests that Maria's reading leads to a dangerous kind of projection, which is also a form of artistry. Having just glimpsed the owner of the books through her barred window, Maria gives the unknown "all St. Preux's sentiments and feelings, culled to gratify her own" (p. 38). It comes as no surprise, then, that the seduction of Maria's imagination culminates in her sexual acquiescence to Henry Darnford—that she receives him "as her husband" (p. 138), just as she had earlier received Venables.

What *is* surprising is that the narrator does not underscore the similarity of Maria's two falls. Instead of either a consistent condemnation of Maria's situation—an enforced inactivity that nurtures romantic expectations—or a description of a fully satisfying relationship, we get the narrative ambivalence we have already seen. At the very point at which the narrator should shape the "structure" to her "purpose" so as to enlighten the reader, we find more passages like the following:

> With Darnford she did not taste uninterrupted felicity; there was a volatility in his manner which often distressed her; but love gladdened the scene; besides, he was the most tender, sympathizing creature in the world. A fondness for the sex often gives an *appearance* of humanity to the behaviour of men, who have small pretensions to the reality; and they *seem* to love others, when they are only pursuing their own gratification. Darnford *appeared* ever willing to avail himself of her taste and acquirements. [p. 143; emphasis added]

We know that Venables was one of those men who have only an appearance of humanity, but is Henry Darnford another? Is Darnford going to betray Maria? In most of the endings Wollstonecraft projected for the book, she certainly suggests that he will. The six fragments Godwin printed at the end of *Maria* all imply Darnford's unreliability: in the first and most optimistic, the lovers simply remain separated; in the last, the outcome is more explicit. "Her lover unfaithful," the fragment reads. "Pregnancy—Miscarriage—Suicide" (p. 152). But the bleakness of these projected conclusions is still qualified by the narrator's determined optimism. In describing Maria's love for Darnford, the narrator claims, not very convincingly, to resolve the paradox: "We see what we wish, and make a world of our own," she acknowledges, "and, though reality may sometimes open a door to misery, yet the moments of happiness procured by the imagination, may, without a paradox, be reckoned among the solid comforts of life" (p. 139).

It is as if the narrator here is resisting the implications of the very insight her story dramatizes, as if she would like to retain, for as long as possible, the idealism she has shown to cripple Maria. In order fully to understand the implications of Wollstonecraft's narrative hesitations we need to return to those insights, to see precisely how feminine romanticism blasts female sexuality, and how female sexuality, as Wollstonecraft depicts it, is defined by bourgeois society and by the narratives that inculcate its values.

Mary Wollstonecraft's fundamental insight in *Maria* concerns the way in which female sexuality is defined or interpreted—and, by extension, controlled—by bourgeois institutions. The primary agent of this control is marriage, which is, as Tony Tanner has remarked, the fundamental "mythology of bourgeois society." With its institutionalization of kinship distinctions and alliances, its harnessing of individual sexual desire to the economic unit of the nuclear family, marriage is the basis of "all the models, conscious and unconscious, by which society structures all its operations and transactions."[22] As we have seen, according to bourgeois conventions, female sexuality can be legitimately expressed—indeed, can exist as a positive cultural sign—only within the institution of marriage. For, confined within marriage, female sexuality is deprived of its power both to devour a man sexually and to rob him of his ability to identify his heirs. Wollstonecraft is recognizing here not only the consequences of ideology but also its roots and its institutional guardians. The penetration of her analysis of this ideology is remarkable. She recognizes, for example, that marriage makes women property, "as much a man's property as his horse or his ass," as Maria observes (p. 107). Moreover, by making women the vehicles by which property is transferred from one man to another, from one generation to the next, marriage objectifies women. And, as objects, women lose their rights—even, finally, the right to act upon their own desire: within marriage, as Maria phrases it, the woman is "required to moralize, sentimentalize herself to stone" (p. 102).

Because the kind of economically advantageous marriages that frequently took place in this period often entailed reducing women to symbols of property, depriving them of the status of autonomous individuals, such transactions had to be enforced not only by laws but by a set of values that could make inequality seem "right" and even "natural." In *Maria,* Wollstonecraft elaborates on her recognition that one of this system's most effective agents was propriety, the internalized set of values that encouraged women to sublimate their potentially anarchic desires. As she had already pointed out in *The Rights of Woman,* in her society this system of values was intimately connected with sentimentalism. In *Maria,* Wollstonecraft sees even more clearly sentimentalism's paradoxical nature: its role is both to arouse female sexuality and to control it.[23] In the first of these two functions, exemplified by Maria's adolescence, sentimental stories arouse a young woman's imagination (and, by extension, her potentially promiscuous erotic desire) by engaging her vicariously in thinly disguised sexual exploits. But because the young girl is protected (or confined) by both ignorance and inexperience, the expectations generated by reading romantic stories lead her to project her desire uncritically onto a single man, a "hero," with whom she then seeks to realize her imaginative and sexual desires—ideally, through marriage.

The irony (and tragedy) of this situation is that, as often as not, the desire so aroused exceeds the gratification offered women through marriage. Precisely because one effect of marriage was to limit desire and, more perniciously (especially given the legal and economic restrictions of the eighteenth and nineteenth centuries), to strip women of their status as autonomous subjects, sentimentalism theoretically generated a clash between female desire and male will. For, once imprisoned within marriage, a woman existed in the same state of confinement that characterized her adolescence. Thus the desire could threaten to begin again, to lead a woman to seek fulfillment outside the marriage bed. But the second effect of sentimental novels curtailed this threat. Despite the ominous specters of adultery and seduction in eighteenth-century sentimental novels, the function of such flirtations with transgression was actually to sublimate female desire, to provide vicarious gratification, which compensated for the diminished fulfillment of marriage. One function of sentimental novels, then, was actually to reinforce the institution that the desire they aroused could theoretically have subverted.

This was not, of course, the only or even the most explicit function of sentimentalism. As the etymological kinship suggests, "sentimental" was closely allied with both "sentiments" and "sensibility" and thus implied both an initial physiological sensation and the quality of response that that sensation produced.[24] During most of the eighteenth century, "sentimental" did not carry the pejorative connotations we now often associate with it; instead, it suggested feelings that were not only strong but rational. The values associated with sentimentalism were therefore moral as well as aesthetic, and, especially in the second half of the century, sentimental theories were advanced to support many humane programs—from the liberation of the American colonies and enslaved Negroes to the more humanitarian treatment of the English poor.

But even though Wollstonecraft adamantly supported the humanitarian causes with which sentimentalism was associated during the last decades of the century, she repeatedly voiced grave reservations about the "sensibility" that sentimental novels nourished in women. For the very sensibility that might temper a man's acquisitive materialism could easily simply overwhelm women, who were neither consistently encouraged to discipline feeling by reason nor provided with constructive outlets for their aroused emotions. In *The Rights of Woman,* Wollstonecraft had already lamented the fact that cultivating sensibility makes women "the prey of their senses"; she now knows that the fact that men consider such volatility one of women's most "feminine," hence attractive, qualities indicates the extent to which men are anxious to perpetuate their own power at the expense of women's autonomy.

This recognition of the sentimental ways and means of marital tyranny is the heart of Wollstonecraft's insight in *Maria.* Yet despite the clarity of many of Maria's statements about marriage, the heroine remains ominously attracted to the very sentimentalism that has twice ensnared her. "True sensibility," she calls it, "the sensibility which is the auxiliary of virtue, and the soul of genius, is in society so occupied with the feelings of others, as scarcely to regard its own sensations" (p. 126). Even after the scheming brutality of Venables theoretically opens her eyes to the naïveté of such sentiments, Maria continues to extol the selflessness of "*active* sensibility" and to encourage her infant daughter to perpetuate her own mistakes: "Whilst your own heart is sincere," she writes in the memoirs she intends for her daughter, "always expect to meet one glowing with the same sentiments" (p. 77).

This returns us to the central problem, for what is confusing here is how Wollstonecraft intends her readers to take the character of Maria. Do Maria's repeated lapses into the sentimental jargon that Wollstonecraft denounces constitute an ironic presentation? And, if so, does the irony extend to Maria's insights about marriage? Or is Wollstonecraft herself prey to the same delusive "romantic expectations" that she shows crippling Maria? And, if so, what does this tell us about the tyrannical complicity between marriage and sentimentalism that Wollstonecraft is trying to expose?

The most telling argument for reading the characterization of Maria ironically is Wollstonecraft's juxtaposition of Maria's first-person narrative with another first-person narrative, that of Jemima, Maria's warder in the madhouse. Jemima's story is decidedly *un*sentimental. Her history begins not with romantic expectations but with sexual violation ("My father . . . seduced my mother"), and it details the events of a continuing victimization: Jemima is raped by her master when she is sixteen, and the ensuing pregnancy drives her into the streets. After a self-inflicted abortion, poverty forces Jemima into prostitution. But as a self-sufficient prostitute, Jemima experiences an unorthodox, if momentary, freedom, a freedom that, no matter how qualified, Wollstonecraft says Jemima "values": "my independence," Jemima calls it. Such subversive independence cannot be tolerated, however; night watchmen, jealous of her autonomy, soon drive Jemima to seek refuge in institutionalized prostitution—first in a whorehouse, then in a relationship with a "worn-out votary of voluptuousness." This sexual exploitation marks Jemima's entry into middle-class society: the old man teaches her to read and confines her in a monogamous relationship. Upon her lover's death, Jemima learns the other face of bourgeois security: along with her freedom she has squandered her rights. Left penniless, Jemima is reduced, in rapid order, to being a washerwoman, a thief, and a pauper before she finds employment in the madhouse to which Maria is confined.

As the result of her being persecuted, Jemima has developed both intellectual resolution and emotional resilience. "The treatment that rendered me miserable," she comments, "seemed to sharpen my wits" (p. 53), and with these "sharpened wits" she learns how to survive in this culture: she endures by "despis[ing] and prey[ing] on the society by which she had been oppressed" (p. 31). Despite the fact that she is a victim, Jemima is also a survivor—and potentially a new kind of heroine as well.

For if Jemima's experiences have taught her to despise men, they have not wholly frozen her to a more radical expression of female feeling: Jemima retains the capacity to love—not men, significantly, but women. Jemima's only childhood wish was for a "mother's affec-tion," her only feelings of guilt stem from her having made another woman suffer, and she is quick to respond to Maria's anguish. More-over, Jemima's "feminine emotions" are more resilient than Maria's nurtured, middle-class sensibility. When the two women finally es-cape the madhouse, Jemima goes first; and when they are confronted by a last, menacing male, the terrified Maria throws "her arms round Jemima" and cries, " 'Save me!' " (p. 141). In the most developed of the projected conclusions to the novel, Wollstonecraft has Jemima save Maria once more, this time from an attempted suicide, by restor-ing to Maria her lost daughter and then ushering her into the female world just glimpsed at the end of this version.

Jemima's story—which is a radical, indeed feminist, story—has the potential to call into question both the organizational principles of bourgeois society and the sentimentalism that perpetuates romantic idealism. For the anarchy implicit in Jemima's brief assertion of female sexuality combines with the stark realism of the narrative to explode the assumptions that tie female sexuality to romance and thus to the institutions men traditionally control. But Wollstonecraft does *not* develop the revolutionary implications of Jemima's narra-tive. Instead, her story is quickly, ostentatiously, suppressed. Jemima's history occupies only one of the seventeen completed chapters of Maria, and it is suspended prematurely by an unspecified "indistinct noise" whose only function is to curtail this narrative. The only effect Jemima's narrative has on her auditors (two captives in a madhouse) is to produce in them "the most painful reflections on the present state of society" (not effective actions), and, after their escape, Jemima insists on being Maria's "house-keeper" (not her equal). The abrupt manner in which Jemima's story ends and the thoroughness with which her tough attitude is reabsorbed into Maria's sentimentalism suggest that Wollstonecraft is not willing to consider seriously so radical an alternative to women's oppression. Such a solution would entail renouncing not only the bourgeois institution of marriage but also the romantic expectations that motivate Maria and, we must conclude, the narrator as well.

For despite the strong suggestions that Maria's incorrigible roman-ticism is being presented ironically, despite Wollstonecraft's emphasis on the pernicious effects of sentimentalism, the narrator herself repeatedly lapses back into sentimental jargon and romantic idealism. At such moments the theoretical wisdom of the narrator simply collapses into the longing of the character. These repeated collapses are characteristically marked by Wollstonecraft's insistence on semantic distinctions where substantial differences do not in fact exist. "The real affections of life," she comments in a typical passage, "when they are allowed to burst forth, are buds pregnant with joy and all the sweet emotions of the soul. . . . The substantial happiness, which enlarges and civilizes the mind, may be compared to the pleasure experienced in roving through nature at large, inhaling the sweet gale natural to the clime" (pp. 143–44). In keeping with the renewed faith in physicality she exhibited in the *Letters Written . . . in Sweden,* Wollstonecraft desperately wants happiness to be "substantial," "real," physically possible. But the metaphorical language she uses to depict that happiness in *Maria* ("buds pregnant with joy") calls attention only to the literariness, the patent immateriality, of this ideal. Despite her anxious assertions that such happiness is "substantial" and that the "real affections of life" and "true sensibility" somehow differ from the romantic delusions that twice ensnare Maria, Wollstonecraft actually reveals only that her own ideals are insubstantial—that they are, in fact, part and parcel of the romantic idealism they are meant to transcend.

Repeatedly, then, the narrator falls victim to the same sentimental idealism that cripples Maria. Wollstonecraft continues to cherish the belief that, by fidelity to personal feelings kept pure of the taint of self-interest and the "grossness of sensuality," an individual can express a sensibility "true" in the most idealistic sense of that word. Yet even Wollstonecraft knows that something is wrong. In the crucible of her novel, things just don't work out that way: Darnford's love is "volatile," Maria's happiness is less substantial than the bars of her madhouse cell. And the fiction that Wollstonecraft believed "capable of producing an important effect" repeatedly threatens to lose sight of its political purpose and become just another sentimental novel.

Wollstonecraft seems aware that there is a gap between the realism of her isolated political observations and the idealism of her sentimental paradigms. And, as if searching for an antidote to her own susceptibility, she repeatedly aborts the sentimental structure of *Maria* in order to reassert her political purpose. At virtually every point at which the characters' stories begin to elicit the reader's identification, Wollstonecraft ruptures the narrative either by interjecting nondramatic political commentary, by simply severing the dramatic action, or by ejecting characters from the novel. The hiatuses in the novel are frequent and obtrusive, even in the chapters Godwin describes as finished. Yet, significantly, these ruptures are not expressions of am-

bivalence on Wollstonecraft's part toward sentimental *feeling*. Instead, they constitute one version of a crisis of confidence that we will
see repeated in a much more severe form in Mary Shelley's *Frankenstein*. In order to salvage sentimental feeling, Wollstonecraft reverses
the stance she had taken in *Letters Written . . . in Sweden* and focuses
her criticism on one particular aspect of feeling—the creative, self-
expressive imagination.

Wollstonecraft may well have singled out the imagination because,
according to eighteenth-century psychological theories, it was the
primary faculty of projection: in the gesture of sympathy, the imagination projects the self into another's situation; but in the exercise of
vanity, the imagination simply projects personal desire onto the world
at large. Because this latter tendency is so tied up with the former,
Wollstonecraft remained ambivalent about the imagination; she considered it the "characteristic of genius," on the one hand, but, on the
other, she remained wary of its affinity with sexuality and self-indulgence.[25] Like the conduct-book writers, Wollstonecraft was particularly suspicious of women's imaginative activity, not simply because
women's passions were stronger but because women, lacking both
personal experience and practical outlets for their energy, were especially tempted to project their desires into self-gratifying fictions *instead of* into real situations or real relationships. In her *Letters Written
. . . in Sweden,* perceptions of nature had controlled imaginative excess, but in the madhouse, which is emblematic of women's characteristic situation (both social and emotional), nature, which can only be
glimpsed through the barred windows, seems too wildly luxuriant or
decayed to resist the voracious imagination. In so characterizing female creativity in *Maria,* Wollstonecraft seems to ask how many of
women's imaginings are vain—vain, not only in the sense of self-
centered, but in the root sense of that word, *vanus,* "empty, ineffectual."

Thus Wollstonecraft's ambivalence about feeling focuses most consistently on the very enterprise in which she, as an imaginative artist,
is engaged. This ambivalence about the creative imagination becomes
both a theme of *Maria* and a repeated agitator of the narrative structure. Wollstonecraft is wary of the products of the creative imagination because she fears they will have the effect on readers that
Rousseau's *Julie* has on Maria: by engaging their readers' desire for
immediate gratification, fictions *dis*engage those readers from life; by
eliciting imaginative identification, they feed wishful fantasies instead
of initiating political action. Wollstonecraft breaks off the various
narratives of *Maria* at their most affecting moments at least partly
because she senses that the narrative contract established by the text
is drawing the reader into stories that are patently not true and whose

aesthetic closure would artificially resolve whatever politically effec-tive emotions the stories might arouse.

For the same reasons, Wollstonecraft is also ambivalent about the process of imaginative creation. For women especially, this opportu-nity for self-expression—and for imaginative escape—is particularly tempting, but it is also potentially ineffectual. In the madhouse Maria and Darnford both become artists, but while Darnford's composi-tions are primarily political, Maria becomes a sentimental writer. Her first compositions are "rhapsodies descriptive of the state of her mind" (pp. 30–31), and, as she begins to compose her own history, she finds herself embarked on an escapist, sentimental journey: "She lived again in the revived emotions of youth, and forgot her present in the retrospect of sorrows" (p. 31).

Wollstonecraft shows, however, that this kind of imaginative es-cape is really no escape at all. Maria's art is, in fact, an expression—perhaps even a cause—of her political impotence. The composition and effect of Maria's manuscript are almost a paradigm of female sentimental authorship; the writer is confined in a prison of "dispro-portioned" passion, the intended beneficiary (her absent daughter) is cut off from the purported moral, and the major reader (Darnford) is aroused by the story only to the "transporting" passion with which he soon seduces Maria. Despite Maria's determination to plot a real escape, her schemes produce only this romantic—and escapist—narrative. Her liberation comes only at the instigation of Darnford's male guards, and, outside the madhouse, she remains completely ineffectual. Just as she had earlier been outschemed by the crafty George Venables (who is the novel's consummate artist, with the power to deploy as well as imagine plots), so Maria is now outdone by the obdurate masculine logic of the courts. In the last chapter of the novel, Maria is tried for adultery, but her written defense is as easily disposed of as any mere piece of paper. Wollstonecraft seems to fear that female logic—the argument based on feeling—has no authority among the men who author laws with the patriarchal fiat of their all-powerful Word.

In this final chapter of the novel, Wollstonecraft—through Maria's written defense—attempts one last time to fuse "purpose and struc-ture," to find a form that will betray neither her political insights nor her feeling heart. The preceding sixteen chapters, whether narrated in first or third person, tended to be dramatic narratives and to highlight subjective responses; but in this final chapter Wollstonecraft tries to "restrain [her] fancy," to transcend such unreliable, because escapist, flights of the creative imagination. Here, by summarizing objective events rather than feelings in order to diminish the personal aspect of Maria's history, Wollstonecraft specifies the events that are the universal "Wrongs of Woman."

But Maria's final plea does not transcend the problem of women's ineffectualness. For the heart of the problem is not, as Wollstonecraft supposed, finding the proper form of expression for the feeling heart. Rather, the real problem lies in the very concept of the feeling heart itself. Basically, all that Maria's argument does is to foreground this feeling heart: she justifies her flight from Venables by an appeal to her own subjective judgment and urges the members of the jury to consult their own feelings in deciding her case. Moreover, Maria's defense, for all its insight, simply strives to institutionalize female feeling as a new rationale for the old covenant of marriage. Even as she pleads for freedom from Venables, Maria calls Darnford her "husband" and declares that what she really wants is only a new marriage in which better to fulfill "the duties of a wife and mother" (p. 148). We are not really surprised that Maria's attempt to generalize and institutionalize feeling has no effect on the court, for in her argument Wollstonecraft fails once more to take her own insights to their logical conclusions. Just as she turned from exploring the radical implications of Jemima's narrative, she now stops short of exposing the tyranny of the marriage contract itself. Instead, the defiant Mary Wollstonecraft clings to that bedrock of bourgeois society—the belief in individual feeling—and in doing this her voice hesitates and finally falters into silence.

Wollstonecraft does not develop the hybrid form that might have fused "purpose and structure" largely because she cannot relinquish the individualistic values tied up with sentimental structure itself. But Wollstonecraft's dilemma was not unique. Indeed, it is only one example of a philosophical as well as a social problem that beleaguered men as well as women in the late eighteenth century. For the fundamental desire that makes her retain individualistic values and that informs not only this work but all of her literary productions (and her turbulent life as well) is a longing to identify—or assert—a reliable relationship between phenomenal reality and the intimation of transcendent meaning that the imagination irrepressibly projects. In other words, Wollstonecraft's refusal to abandon the ideal of "true sensibility," even after she had recognized that the romantic expectations endemic to such sensibility were agents of the very institutions she was trying to criticize, reflects her persistent yearning for some connection between spiritual values and real, everyday experience. What might now seem to be an artificial and disconcertingly abstract vocabulary expresses—and attempts to satisfy—this longing. The themes and vocabulary of sentimentalism aspire to depict complete happiness in this world in terms that transcend the materiality, hence the mortality, of the flesh. While producing such imaginative gratification may very well be a continuing goal of imaginative literature, the particular intensity of this longing at the end of the eighteenth century signals the inadequacies of empiricism and rationalism either to fill the imaginative vacuum left by Enlightenment challenges to orthodox religion or to quell the anxieties generated by political and social instability.

Perhaps the two most fundamental problems with sentimentalism's solution to this longing lay in its celebration of immaterial, romantic rewards and in its emphasis on individual feeling. For in a society in which one's value, indeed, one's very definition, depended on class position—or, more visibly, on the rewards of money and, beyond that, property and social prestige—the acquisition of romantic love was at best a private supplement to more public indices of power. And if romantic love was not a supplement to, but a substitute for, material rewards (as it would have been for most women), then its pursuit may well have absorbed energies that under different circumstances might have been channeled toward accomplishing more "real"—because more socially effective—goals. The other half of this problem is that the myth of personal autonomy perpetuated by sentimentalism tended to blind its adherents to the way in which an individual's opportunities and even the forms of "happiness" available are, in some important respects, delimited by one's position within culture. Perceptive, intelligent writers like Mary Wollstonecraft continued to envision social change and personal fulfillment primarily in terms of individual effort, and therefore they did not focus on the systemic constraints exercised by such legal and political institutions as marriage. In practical terms, sentimentalism was no more a lasting solution to the imaginative longings of powerless individuals than it was to the continuing political and social inequalities of the late eighteenth-century class system. But, in providing substitute goals and gratifications, it did help shore up the institutions of power and silence their would-be critics. In this sense, Maria's celebration of the "humanizing affection" of the individual actually constitutes Wollstonecraft's retreat from the insight to which she was so close in *The Rights of Woman*: the recognition that the individual's situation—his or her position within class, gender, economics, and history—really delimits freedom and virtually defines the "self."

No doubt the problem of sentimentalism loomed large for any late eighteenth-century liberal (Rousseau is a case in point), but for women the dilemma was particularly acute. For women had a special investment in sentimentalism. Not only did the "humanizing affections" theoretically natural to women and central to sentimentalism give women an important function in a society increasingly marked by economic competition; sentimentalism was also virtually the only form in which middle-class women were allowed legitimate self-expression. A woman's only "business," as Wollstonecraft recognized in *The Rights of Woman,* was the "business" of the heart; for her, sentiments constituted the only "events."[26] Yet because of women's particular place within their culture, this promise of sentimentalism proved to be delusive. As we have seen, and as Mary Wollstonecraft pointed out, the middle-class code of propriety simultaneously defined women exclusively in terms of their sexuality and demanded that their every public action deny that sexuality. Because women were so defined, they were actively encouraged to envision emotional and even spiritual fulfillment in sensual terms and yet, at the same time, because their sexuality had to be susceptible to the control of marriage, they were enjoined to sublimate, to desexualize their real sexuality in highly euphemistic expressions. Thus, middle-class ideology, and sentimental novels in particular, simultaneously tied women's aspirations to the fatal parabola of physical desire and denied them either a cultural myth of female sexual transcendence or complete appreciation of sexual self-expression. Indeed, given the restrictions placed on the expression of female sexuality in eighteenth-century society, women were encouraged to view their sexuality as a function of *male* initiative, a response to present and future relationships, not as self-expression at all.

The twist given female sexuality by bourgeois values is the heart of darkness Mary Wollstonecraft never identified. Yet it helps explain why sentimentalism was so appealing and so fatal to her as well as to many less-thoughtful women of this period. Mary Wollstonecraft could not renounce "true sensibility" because it was the only form in which her society allowed her to express either her sexuality or her craving for transcendent meaning. Yet retaining that form of expression, those values, and that self-definition prohibited her from disentangling her femaleness from male institutions or control. It also helps explain her self-contradictory presentation of sexuality in *Maria.* For in this novel Wollstonecraft insists—to a degree remarkable for any late eighteenth-century novelist—on the importance of female sexual expression, yet, despite her insistence that sexual fulfillment is not only necessary but possible, every sexual relationship she depicts is dehumanizing and revolting. Sexuality is virtually the only human quality that is described in this novel with any degree of physical detail, and the descriptions—like the one of Venables' "tainted breath, pimpled face, and blood-shot eyes"—suggest grotesqueness, violence, and contamination.

In the course of her adult life, Wollstonecraft was repeatedly crippled by this collusion between sexuality and sentimentality. Her early letters to Imlay reveal the unmistakable pleasure of a woman's first emotionally satisfying and physically stimulating relationship. Yet even as she confesses to a "tenderness for [Imlay's] person," (*MWL*, p. 259; 19 August 1794), Wollstonecraft tries to "purify"—and pro-long—their sexual alliance with what she conceded were "romantic" theories of the imagination (*MWL*, p. 263; 22 September 1794). And, in the end, Imlay's betrayal left Wollstonecraft retreating to these "romantic" theories in an attempt to salvage the ideal of "love" from the ruins of physical satiety.

> The common run of men, I know, with strong health and gross appetites, must have variety to banish *ennui,* because the imagination never lends its magic wand, to convert appetite into love, cemented by according reason.—Ah! my friend, you know not the ineffable delight, the exquisite pleasure, which arises from a unison of affection and desire, when the whole soul and senses are abandoned to a lively imagination, that renders every emotion delicate and rapturous. Yes; these are emotions, over which satiety has no power, and the recollection of which, even disappointment cannot disenchant; but they do not exist without self-denial. These emotions, more or less strong, appear to me to be the distinctive characteristic of genius, the foundation of taste, and of that exquisite relish for the beauties of nature, of which the common herd of eaters and drinkers and *child-begeters,* certainly have no idea. You will smile at an observation that has just occured to me:—I consider those minds as the most strong and original, whose imagination acts as the stimulus to their senses. [*MWL*, p. 291; 12 June 1795]

In this last sentence Wollstonecraft transfers the impetus of sexual attraction to the imagination in order to rob physical stimulation of its inevitably devastating primacy. Such a transfer comes close to "purifying" love of its physical component altogether—or, as Woll-stonecraft formulated it both in Maria's relationship to Darnford and in her own letter to Imlay, "love" is defined precisely as the relation-ship in which a man has "sufficient delicacy of feeling to govern desire" (*MWL*, p. 273; 30 December 1794). Although Imlay's betrayal did not stifle either Wollstonecraft's emotional or sexual desires, her first sexual encounter with William Godwin shows her fears surfacing once more. Ironically, in the light of the profoundly ambiguous role Rousseau had played in her developing self-image, Wollstonecraft alludes to him here. "Consider what has passed as a fever of your imagination," she begs Godwin the morning after their tryst, "and I—will become again a *Solitary Walker*" (*MWL*, p. 337; 17 August 1796).

The problem that plagued Mary Wollstonecraft's final efforts to reconcile her intense female feeling with intellectual independence was simply an extreme version of what was, for women of this period, a general dilemma. Not only were late eighteenth-century moralists virtually unanimous in pointing out the twin appeal and danger of sentimental novels for women readers and writers,[27] but most of the examples we have of this genre reveal many of the same problems as *Maria*. Perhaps, in fact, the only effective way a woman who thought as well as felt could successfully deal with the issue of feeling was to satirize "true sensibility," as Jane Austen did in her juvenilia and in *Northanger Abbey*. The irony Austen was to perfect in her mature works can even be seen as a second and more sophisticated handling of female feeling, for the distance irony affords enables Austen to explore her characters' "romantic expectations"—and delusions—without committing herself definitively to the same desires. Austen's relationship to the values of her society remains protectively opaque; she is implicitly critical in isolated phrases at the same time that her narrative celebration of marriage seems to ratify the central institution of bourgeois culture.

IN 1871, ALMOST SEVENTY-FIVE YEARS after Mary Wollstonecraft's death, a more successful woman writer paid tribute to the resilience of Wollstonecraft's feelings. The words are those of Mary Ann Evans:

> Hopelessness has been to me, all through my life, but especially in painful years of my youth, the chief source of wasted energy with all the consequent bitterness of regret. Remember, it has happened to many to be glad they did not commit suicide, though they once ran for the final leap, or as Mary Wollstonecraft did, wetted their garments well in the rain hoping to sink the better when they plunged. She tells how it occured to her as she was walking in the damp shroud, that she might live to be glad that she had not put an end to herself— and so it turned out. She lived to know some real joys, and death came in time to hinder the joys from being spoiled.[28]

It is significant that Mary Ann Evans/George Eliot generalizes Wollstonecraft's determined death-walk ("wetted their garments well"), then individualizes her second thoughts ("it occured to her"): from the multitude of hopeless, deathbound women, this one woman steps forth, capable of imagining "real joys" even in her "damp shroud." Mary Wollstonecraft was nothing if she was not determined, and, even when it was unfashionable to be so determined or so outspoken, her example stood in for many a more retiring woman's fantasies of self-assertion. Thus women novelists like Maria Edgeworth and Fanny Burney, for whose novels Wollstonecraft provided the requisite monitory figure, also used these Wollstonecraft-characters to voice what may have been their own staunchly denied desires. The words of the numerous Harriet Frekes (*Belinda*, 1801) and Elinor Joddrels (*The Wanderer; or, Female Difficulties*, 1814) of early nineteenth-century novels have such resonance that one cannot help but wonder how their authors heard these voices in their own imaginations—whether there was not a secret thrill of kindred souls.

Yet it is also significant that Mary Ann Evans' tribute to Wollstone-craft fully acknowledges the fragility of her salvaged joy ("death came in time"). Within the legal institutions of late eighteenth-century socie-ty, and under the disapproving frown of the Proper Lady, the achieve-ment of female autonomy was almost invariably short-lived. This is the lesson proved by numerous early nineteenth-century women writers but by none as well, perhaps, as by Wollstonecraft's physical as well as spiritual daughter. Wollstonecraft died eleven days after giving birth to a child who would grow up to bear a name fraught with literary and emotional significance: Mary Wollstonecraft God-win Shelley. Yet for the future Mary Shelley, Wollstonecraft's deter-mination, her anger, and her energy would always stand in silent judgment over her own growing fears. All too well, Mary Shelley was to learn that to defy propriety, as her mother did, required a self-confidence and self-consciousness dearly purchased in bourgeois soci-ety. Not many women could so doggedly, so insistently, celebrate "their own minds" as Mary Wollstonecraft did in this letter from her last summer:

> Those who are bold enough to advance before the age they live in, and to throw off, by the force of their own minds, the prejudices which the maturing reason of the world will in time disavow, must learn to brave censure. We ought not to be too anxious respecting the opinion of others.— I am not fond of vindications.— Those who know me will suppose that I acted from princi-ple.—Nay, as we in general give others credit for worth, in proportion as we possess it—I am easy with regard to the opinions of the *best* part of mankind.— I *rest* on my own. [*MWL*, p. 413; Summer 1797]

4

"My Hideous Progeny"
The Lady and the Monster

IN 1838 MARY SHELLEY entered in her journal the following elaborate defense of her refusal to speak out for liberal political causes:

> In the first place, with regard to "the good cause"—the cause of the advancement of freedom and knowledge, of the rights of women, &c.—I am not a person of opinions. I have said elsewhere that human beings differ greatly in this. Some have a passion for reforming the world; others do not cling to particular opinions. That my parents and Shelley were of the former class, makes me respect it. . . . For myself, I earnestly desire the good and enlightenment of my fellow-creatures, and see all, in the present course, tending to the same, and rejoice; but I am not for violent extremes, which only bring on an injurious reaction. . . . Besides, I feel the counter-arguments too strongly. . . ; besides that, on some topics (especially with regard to my own sex), I am far from making up my mind. I believe we are sent here to educate ourselves, and that self-denial, and disappointment, and self-control, are a part of our education; that it is not by taking away all restraining law that our improvement is to be achieved; and, though many things need great amendment, I can by no means go so far as my friends would have me. When I feel that I can say what will benefit my fellow-creatures, I will speak: not before. . . .
>
> To hang back, as I do, brings a penalty. I was nursed and fed with a love of glory. To be something great and good was the precept given me by my Father: Shelley reiterated it. Alone and poor, I could only be something by joining a party; and there was much in me—the woman's love of looking up, and being guided, and being willing to do anything if any one supported and brought me forward—which would have made me a good partisan. But Shelley died, and I was alone. My Father, from age and domestic circumstances, could not "*me faire valoir.*" My total friendlessness, my horror of pushing, and inability to put myself forward unless led, cherished and supported,—all this has sunk me in a state of loneliness no other human being ever before, I believe, endured—except Robinson Crusoe. . . .
>
> If I write the above, it is that those who love me may hereafter know that I am not all to blame, nor merit the heavy accusations cast on me for not putting myself forward. I *cannot* do that; it is against my nature. As well cast me from a precipice and rail at me for not flying.[1]

Mary Shelley's defense of her political quiescence is really a defense of her character. That character, as she defines it for her future reader, is a remarkable combination of stereotypical feminine reticence and unconventional self-assertion. She aggressively defends her behavior, but she defines her character primarily in negative terms: "I am not a person of opinions," "I am not for violent extremes," "I am far from making up my mind," "I can by no means go so far as my friends would have me." Shelley's one unqualified affirmation about herself is that she accepts the conventional wisdom especially pertinent to female education: life is a school of instructive negation; a woman matures by disciplining and denying herself. And yet, even as she defends her retreat from public notice, the way in which she characterizes her situation and her needs transforms what looks like commonplace helplessness into a posture worthy of dramatic presentation: in her extreme loneliness, Shelley is genuinely remarkable—like no one else, in fact, except the omnicompetent victim-vanquisher, Robinson Crusoe himself.

Mary Shelley's entire literary career is characterized by the two competing impulses we see in this passage. On the one hand, she repeatedly bowed to the conventional prejudice against aggressive women by apologizing for or punishing her self-assertion: she claimed that her writing was always undertaken to please or profit someone else, she dreaded exposing her name or personal feelings to public scrutiny, and she subjected her ambitious characters to pain and loneliness. On the other hand, both in her numerous comments about her profession and by her ongoing literary activity, Mary Shelley demonstrated that imaginative self-expression was for her an important vehicle for proving her worth and, in that sense, for defining herself.

Shelley's characteristic ambivalence with regard to female self-assertion was largely a response to her very particular position within the competing value systems of the turbulent first decades of the nineteenth century. Mary Wollstonecraft Godwin Shelley internalized two conflicting models of behavior that became sharply delineated in the wake of the French Revolution. As the daughter of William Godwin and Mary Wollstonecraft and the lover, then the wife, of Percy Shelley, Mary was always encouraged to live up to the Romantic ideal of the creative artist, to prove herself by means of her pen and her imagination. As she herself put it, she was "Nursed and fed with a love of glory," was given again and again the precept "to be something great." Her stepsister Claire Clairmont described the same pressure in characteristically less qualified terms: "In our family," she wryly remarked, "if you cannot write an epic poem or novel, that by its originality knocks all other novels on the head, you are a despicable creature, not worth acknowledging."[2] This pressure to be "original" and "great" was, however, exerted by a relatively small number of artists and radicals; far more pervasive was what we have already seen to be the increasingly rigid social expectation that a woman should conform to the conventional model of feminine propriety.

For the young Mary Shelley, the collision between what we now call the "Romantic" model of originality and the "Victorian" model of feminine domesticity was particularly dramatic. Not only did the public backlash against Mary Wollstonecraft provoke in her daughter an intense combination of pride and shame, anger and fear, but the social conservatism her father embraced after Wollstonecraft's death became as much a part of the young Mary Godwin's situation as her mother's ambiguous legacy. Moreover, the events of Mary's adolescence made her situation complicated, public, and explosive. Percy Shelley epitomized in many ways the independence and self-confidence that Mary Wollstonecraft had celebrated; indeed, as a man and an aristocrat, he was able to assert those principles and act upon them even more flamboyantly than Wollstonecraft had done. Thus, when Mary Godwin eloped with this outspoken radical, she simultaneously followed her mother's example, alienated her father, and brought her private life to the attention of polite society. The scandal of her life was intensified when, through Percy, she met and, for a time, lived in close physical and intellectual proximity to perhaps the most notorious of all the Romantic rebels, Lord Byron. Because of all of these factors, Mary Shelley not only was forced to respond to the general ideological configuration that pitted a model of acquiescence against whatever aggressive desires a young woman might have; she also had to deal with competing psychological, familial, *and* public claims about who and what she was.

Each of Shelley's novels embodies to a greater or lesser degree her ambivalence about female self-assertion, but what the overall development of her career reveals is the way that a certain kind of literary self-expression could accommodate a woman's unorthodox desires to the paradigm of the Proper Lady. After composing the novels that show most clearly the influence of her mother's self-confidence and Percy Shelley's aesthetics—*Frankenstein* (1818), *Mathilda* (1819), *Valperga* (1823), and *The Last Man* (1826)—Mary Shelley began to use her literary career both to defend her behavior and, more significantly, to so characterize it that it would need no defense; in other words, she sought to make her behavior conform to conventional expectations of what a woman should be. Her last three novels—*Perkin Warbeck* (1830), *Lodore* (1835), and *Falkner* (1837)—demonstrate the refinement of this strategy. Through thinly disguised autobiographical characterizations of herself as a docile, domestic heroine, Mary

Shelley was able, in these novels, both to court the approval of a middle-class, largely female audience and to achieve the personal satisfaction of expressing a self that was "original" only in its exemplary propriety.

Because Mary Shelley conceptualized her relationship to her professional activity slightly differently from the way her mother had, her life and art must be examined from a slightly different critical point of view. For while both Wollstonecraft and Shelley were self-conscious about the professional nature of their mature writing, and while both needed the money that writing produced, Mary Shelley did not consistently use her writing to express either polemical positions or even her own unmediated personal feelings. Mary Wollstonecraft seems to have thought that writing was a vehicle for producing an important public effect even when that entailed exposing personal and psychological complexities that exceeded her interpretive powers. It is as if, by exposing these complexities, Wollstonecraft hoped to work through them to their underlying social and ideological causes. As a consequence, in her works, as in her life, Wollstonecraft herself is the best argument for the political reforms she advocates.[3] By contrast, especially after 1830, Mary Shelley considered writing to be less a vehicle for urging her audience to criticize conventions or even for exploring themselves (or herself, for that matter) than a means of covering over whatever psychological complexities might challenge conventional propriety. Her autobiographical allusions, then, are the extreme opposite of unself-conscious. In these late novels Shelley rigorously compartmentalizes her "self" into a private, domestic Mary and a public author-persona, and the characters who represent the former in the productions of the latter serve primarily to revise the real Mary Shelley's past inadequacies and indiscretions so as to make her conform, in every sense, to the ideal of feminine propriety. Whereas Wollstonecraft's works were largely unself-consciously aggressive—politically and personally—Shelley's late novels are, for the most part, self-consciously defensive. The works of both women can be considered didactic, but the lessons they impart are very different.

Because Shelley's late works serve, in many ways, as strategies both to defend herself against public criticism (or her own censure) and to accommodate her personal desires to the conventional paradigm of propriety, they often strive to domesticate—or even eliminate—her personal and sometimes startlingly aggressive and "unladylike" feelings. Instead of exploring the psychological or situational complexities she introduces in these novels, Shelley often dismisses them altogether by providing simplistic, formulaic answers. The residues of her less orthodox impulses do show up, of course—either in the actions of minor characters or, more consistently, in her personal letters and journal. This subtext of personal feeling, which repeatedly ruptures Wollstonecraft's works, is most often relegated to a completely separate, private domain in Shelley's. The private records thus provide an even more crucial complement to Shelley's published writings than Wollstonecraft's letters did for her works. Indeed, only by viewing Shelley's public persona in the context of her private comments and actions can we fully appreciate the paradigmatic place this very unusual woman occupied in the final triumph of Victorian propriety. For in the tensions between the public Mary Shelley and the private one we can identify both some of the sacrifices a young woman had to make in order to conform to propriety and the stages by which unladylike feelings could be reformulated so as never to exceed a woman's proper, altogether tractable, desires.

MARY SHELLEY'S CHILDHOOD was spent in a turbulent household, presided over by a demanding and uncongenial stepmother, peopled by five children of assorted parentage, and beleaguered by chronic shortages of money.[4] What Shelley was later to characterize as an "excessive & romantic attachment to [her] Father"[5] seems largely to have gone unanswered; in 1812, Godwin described his typical behavior toward Mary as "sententious and authoritative" and claimed that he did not know her very well.[6] The only sustained and reliable domestic affection Mary Shelley seems to have enjoyed came from the William Baxter family, whom she visited in Scotland during 1812 and 1813. So appealing was their domestic harmony that, in the 1831 introduction to the revised *Frankenstein,* Shelley dramatized her sojourn in Scotland in such a way as to cast its happiness retroactively over her entire childhood.[7] In May 1814, on her return from the last of these visits, Mary first met Percy Shelley, the self-proclaimed atheist, political radical, and "heir to £6,000 per annum." Percy, already disenchanted with his first wife, Harriet, responded immediately to what he called the "originality & loveliness of Mary's character." The couple eloped to the Continent on 28 July—even though Mary was only sixteen and Percy was still legally married. They took Claire Clairmont, Mary's stepsister, along with them. His own professed skepticism about the institution of marriage notwithstanding, Godwin's disapproval was immediate, uncompromising, and long-lived. Writing to one of his creditors on 27 August of that summer, Godwin stated that he could "not conceive of an event of more accumulated horror." "Jane [Claire] has been guilty of indiscretion only," Godwin continued, parceling out his wrath; "Mary has been guilty of a crime."[8]

Godwin's censure was to haunt Mary Shelley for much of the rest of her life. But it was merely the first of the clouds that shadowed the young couple's domestic establishment during their early months together. After six weeks in Europe, Percy, Mary, and Claire returned to London on 13 September. There they discovered the extent of Godwin's condemnation (he would not let anyone in the family visit or write them, and, though he continued to pester Percy for money, he did not want to see his name and Percy's on the same check);[9] they also suffered the practical consequences of the debts Percy had contracted against his anticipated inheritance. Intermittently separated from Percy so that he could avoid the bailiffs, Mary felt increasingly isolated and rejected. As she watched her domestic ties dwindle to the single, unsanctioned, alliance with Percy, Mary begged her lover to stand in for the family she seemed to have lost. "Press me to you and hug your own Mary to your heart," she begged him; "perhaps she will one day have a father till then be every thing to me love" (*MSL*, 1:3; 28 October 1814). Even when united with Percy, Mary's domestic troubles continued. Presumably to prove herself an apt pupil of her lover's belief in "Free Love in the abstract," Mary, pregnant at seventeen, at least playfully accepted—if she did not return—the attentions of Percy's close friend Thomas Jefferson Hogg during the last months of 1814 and the beginning of 1815. In February of that year Mary gave birth to her first child—a girl; four days later, she woke to find the baby dead. Thoughts of the dead baby and her uncertain role ("I am no longer a mother now" [*MSL* 1:11; 6 March 1815]) continued to haunt the young woman until she found herself pregnant again, two months later. In January 1816 she gave birth to her second child, William, named after her still unrelenting father. In May of that year, harassed by loneliness, Percy's creditors, and public rumors that Percy was responsible for Claire Clairmont's illegitimate pregnancy, the three left for Europe again, this time to take Claire to Lord Byron, the father of the child she was carrying.

Throughout this period of domestic disruption and sorrow, Mary Shelley was almost continuously engaged in another pursuit: making herself "worthy" of her learned lover and her famous parents. Her carefully catalogued list of the books she read in 1814 reveals an eclectic and voracious taste and includes four works by Mary Wollstonecraft and three by William Godwin. October of that year finds her promising Percy, "I will be a good girl and never vex you any more. I will learn Greek" (*MSL*, 1:3; 28 October 1814), and her even longer reading list for 1815 (which includes all twelve volumes of Gibbon's *Decline and Fall*) indicates that she possessed enough linguistic skill to read "Ovid's Metamorphoses in Latin" (*MSJ*, p. 47). Percy Shelley, of course, actively promoted Mary's intellectual endeavors. Their very first meeting, he explained to Hogg in October 1814, convinced him of her perfectability. "She is gentle, to be convinced

& tender. . . . I do not think that there is an excellence at which
human nature can arrive, that she does not indisputably possess, or
of which her character does not afford manifest intimations. I speak
thus of Mary now—& so intimately are our natures now united, that
I feel whilst I describe her excellencies as if I were an egoist expatiat-
ing upon his own perfections.''[10] Percy's identification with Mary is
especially important, for his desire to perfect an absolute union with
her colored her conception of their relationship. After his death, this
ideal was to prove a mixed blessing, but now it fueled Mary's desire
to improve her own intellectual capacities. In the first year of their
relationship, Percy and Mary shared a journal and read and even
wrote together. Mary's first published work, *History of a Six Weeks Tour,*
was an anonymous account of their "honeymoon" excursion, drawn
from both Percy's letters and her own. Percy was enthusiastic about
examining the "productions of her mind that preceded our intercourse" (*MSJ,* p. 5), and when Mary began a novel (revealingly entitled
Hate), he was ecstatic: "Mary begins 'Hate,' and gives Shelley the
greater pleasure," their mutual journal records (*MSJ,* p. 14).

Numerous critics have commented on Mary Shelley's complicated
relationship with her remarkable literary family.[11] Her brief, secret
courtship with Percy Shelley was largely conducted in St. Pancras'
Churchyard, where Mary took her books to read beside her mother's
grave; she read and reread the works of both her father and her
mother while she was growing up; and her letters to Percy show an
ongoing concern both with his works and with her own. Two less
easily documentable considerations are equally important for the
light they shed on Mary's attitude toward her family of authors. The
first is that much of what she read must have alternately sanctioned
and condemned her adolescent ambition and thus served to enhance
the ambivalence she was to continue to display toward any kind of
personal assertion. Reading Wollstonecraft's *Maria* and *The Rights of
Woman,* Godwin's *Memoirs* of her mother or his *Political Justice,* undoubtedly provided intellectual justification for Mary Shelley's defiance
of social values. Yet, even before Godwin's angry reprisal, she must
have anticipated that polite society, at the very least, would judge her
unusual conduct harshly; for the public response to her mother's
Memoirs, in which Godwin revealed Wollstonecraft's affair with Imlay
and the illigitimacy of her daughter Fanny, had been almost universally abusive, and Mary Godwin had now committed virtually the
same "crime."[12] The second important consideration about Mary
Shelley's relationship to her family is that, at least in retrospect, she
felt extreme pressure to measure up to the standards they set. In her
1831 introduction to *Frankenstein,* Shelley records the expectations
that, more than a decade later, constituted some of her most vivid

memories of her young adulthood. "My husband . . . was from the first, very anxious that I should prove myself worthy of my parentage, and enrol myself on the page of fame. He was for ever inciting me to obtain literary reputation" (*F*, p. 223). This injunction—not only to write but to "obtain literary reputation"—reinforced Shelley's persistent association of writing with an aggressive quest for public notice. Moreover, the expectation she sensed in her most intimate companion and projected onto herself, perhaps from the example of her parents, continued to drive Mary Shelley to develop a self-definition based at least in part on the assertive activity of professional writing.

When she was in Switzerland in the summer of 1816, Mary Shelley's creative energies were finally rerouted from "travelling, and the cares of a family" (*F*, p. 223) to this all-important activity of writing. Living next to Lord Byron, listening to—though not participating in—the conversations of the two poets ("incapacity and timidity always prevented my mingling in the nightly conversations," she said [*MSJ*, p. 184]), and no doubt inspired by Percy's example, Mary Shelley began to compose steadily. After 24 July 1816, her journal frequently contains the important monosyllable, "Write," and the attention Percy devoted to the novel's progress, its revisions, and, eventually, its publication reveals that his support for the project was as enthusiastic as Mary could have wished.[13] But the narrative that Mary Shelley wrote between that "eventful" summer and the following April was less a wholehearted celebration of the imaginative enterprise she had undertaken in order to prove her worth to Percy than a troubled, veiled exploration of the price she had already begun to fear such egotistical self-assertion might exact. *Frankenstein* occupies a particularly important place in Shelley's career, not only because it is by far her most famous work, but because, in 1831, she prepared significant revisions and an important introduction, both of which underscore and elaborate her initial ambivalence. By tracing first the contradictions already present in the 1818 edition and then the revisions she made after Percy's death and her return to England, we can begin to see the roots and progress of Shelley's growing desire to accommodate her adolescent impulses to conventional propriety. Taken together, the two editions of *Frankenstein* provide a case study of the tensions inherent in the confrontation between the expectations Shelley associated, on the one hand, with her mother and Romantic originality and, on the other, with a textbook Proper Lady.

The 1818 *Frankenstein*

Even though they praised the power and stylistic vigor of *Franken-stein,* its first reviewers sharply criticized the anonymous novelist's failure to moralize about the novel's startling, even blasphemous, subject. The reviewer for the *Quarterly Review,* for example, complained that

> Our taste and our judgment alike revolt at this kind of writing, and the greater
> the ability with which it may be executed the worse it is—it inculcates no lesson
> of conduct, manners, or morality; it cannot mend, and will not even amuse its
> readers, unless their taste have been deplorably vitiated—it fatigues the feel-
> ings without interesting the understanding; it gratuitously harasses the heart,
> and only adds to the store, already too great, of painful sensations.[14]

Presumably because it was unthinkable that a woman should refuse to moralize, most critics automatically assumed that the author of *Frankenstein* was a man—no doubt a "follower of Godwin," according to *Blackwood's,* or even Percy Shelley himself, as the *Edinburgh Magazine* surmised.[15] These reviewers, however, were too preoccupied with the explicit unorthodoxy of *Frankenstein's* subject to attend carefully to the undercurrents in it that challenged their opinion. Like her mother and many male Romantics, Mary Shelley had chosen to focus on the theme of Promethean desire, which has implications for both the development of culture and the individual creative act; but when *Frankenstein* is considered alongside contemporary works that display even some degree of confidence in imaginative power, it proves to be more conservative than her first readers realized. Indeed, *Franken-stein* calls into question, not the social conventions that inhibit creativity, but rather the egotism that Mary Shelley associates with the artist's monstrous self-assertion.[16] Like Wollstonecraft and most male Romantics, Shelley discusses desire explicitly within a paradigm of individual maturation: *Franken-stein* is Shelley's version of the process of identity-formation that Wollstonecraft worked out in her two *Vindications.* Keats called this maturation "soul-making," and Wordsworth devoted his longest completed poem to it. In the 1818 text, Shelley's model of maturation begins with a realistic depiction of Lockean psychology; young Victor Frankenstein is a *tabula rasa* whose character is formed by his childhood experiences. The son of loving, protective parents, the companion of affectionate friends, he soon finds the harmony of his childhood violated by what he calls a "predilection" for natural philosophy. Yet even though this "predilection" seems to be innate, Frankenstein locates its origin not in his own disposition but in a single childhood event—the accidental discovery of a volume of Cornelius Agrippa's occult speculations. The "fatal impulse" this volume sparks is then

kindled into passionate enthusiasm by other accidents: Frankenstein's father neglects to explain Agrippa's obsolescence, a discussion
provoked by a lightning bolt undermines his belief in the occult, and
"some accident" prevents him from attending lectures on natural
philosophy. Left with a craving for knowledge but no reliable guide
to direct it, Frankenstein's curiosity is kept within bounds only by the
"mutual affection" of his domestic circle.

In this dramatization of Victor Frankenstein's childhood, Mary
Shelley fuses mechanistic psychological theories of the origin and
development of character with the more organic theories generally
associated with the Romantics. Like most contemporary Lockean
philosophers, she asserts that circumstances activate and direct an
individual's capacity for imaginative activity; the inclination or predilection thus formed then constitutes the basis of identity.[17] But when
Shelley combines this model with the notion (implied by Wollstonecraft's *Letters Written . . . in Sweden* and by the poetry of Wordsworth,
Coleridge, Byron, and Percy Shelley) that an individual's desire, once
aroused, has its own impetus and logic, she comes up with a model
of maturation that contradicts the optimism of both mechanists and
organicists. More in keeping with eighteenth-century moralists than
with either William Godwin or Percy Shelley, Mary Shelley characterizes innate desire not as neutral or benevolent but as quintessentially
egotistical. And, unlike Mary Wollstonecraft, she does not conceive
of imaginative activity as leading through intimations of mortality to
new insight or creativity. Instead, she sees imagination as an appetite
that can and must be regulated—specifically, by the give-and-take of
domestic relationships. If it is aroused but is not controlled by human
society, it will project itself into the natural world, becoming voracious in its search for objects to conquer and consume. This principle,
which draws both mechanistic and organic models under the mantle
of conventional warnings to women, constitutes the major dynamic
of *Frankenstein's* plot. As long as domestic relationships govern an
individual's affections, his or her desire will turn outward as love. But
when the individual loses or leaves the regulating influence of relationship with others, imaginative energy always threatens to turn
back on itself, to "mark" all external objects as its own and to
degenerate into "gloomy and narrow reflections upon self" (*F*, p. 32).

Shelley's exposition of the degeneration of incipient curiosity into
full-fledged egotism begins when Frankenstein leaves his childhood
home for the University of Ingolstadt. At the university he is left to
"form [his] own friends, and be [his] own protector" (p. 40), and, given
this freedom, his imagination is liberated to follow its natural course.
To the young scholar, this energy seems well-directed, for Frankenstein assumes that his ambition to conquer death through science is

fundamentally unselfish. With supreme self-confidence, he "pene-
trate[s] into the recesses of nature" in search of the secret of life. What
he discovers in the "vaults and charnel houses" he visits, however,
is not life but death, the "natural decay and corruption of the human
body." In pursuing his ambition even beyond this grisly sight, Frankenstein proves unequivocally that his "benevolent" scheme actually
acts out the imagination's essential and deadly self-devotion. For
what he really wants is not to serve others but to assert himself.
Indeed, he wants ultimately to defy mortality, to found a "new
species" that would "bless [him] as its creator and source." "No father
could claim the gratitude of his child so completely as I should
deserve their's," he boasts (p. 49).

Frankenstein's particular vision of immortality and the vanity that
it embodies have profound social consequences, both because Frankenstein would deny relationships (and women) any role in the conception of children and because he would reduce all domestic ties to
those that center on and feed his selfish desires. Given the egotism
of his ambition, it comes as no surprise that Frankenstein's love for
his family is the first victim of his growing obsession; "supernatural
enthusiasm" usurps the place of his previous domestic love. "I wished,
as it were, to procrastinate all that related to my feelings of affection
until the great object, which swallowed up every habit of my nature,
should be completed" (p. 50). Frankenstein isolates himself in a "solitary chamber," refuses to write even to his fiancée, Elizabeth, and
grows "insensible to the charms of nature." "I became as timid as a
love-sick girl," he realizes, in retrospect, "and alternate tremor and
passionate ardour took the place of wholesome sensation and regulated ambition" (p. 51).

Despite what the reviewers thought, in her dramatization of the
imaginative quest Mary Shelley is actually more concerned with this
antisocial dimension than with its metaphysical implications. In chapter 5, for example, at the heart of her story, she elaborates the
significance of Frankenstein's self-absorption primarily in terms of his
social relationships. After animating the monster, product and symbol of self-serving desire, Frankenstein falls asleep, only to dream the
true meaning of his accomplishment: having denied domestic relationships by indulging his selfish passions, he has, in effect, murdered
domestic tranquillity.

> I thought I saw Elizabeth, in the bloom of health, walking in the streets of
> Ingolstadt. Delighted and surprised, I embraced her; but as I imprinted the first
> kiss on her lips, they became livid with the hue of death; her features appeared
> to change, and I thought that I held the corpse of my dead mother in my arms;
> a shroud enveloped her form, and I saw the grave-worms crawling in the folds
> of the flannel. [P. 53]

Lover and mother, as the presiding female guardians of Frankenstein's "secluded and domestic" youth, are conflated in this tableau
of the enthusiast's guilt. Only now, when Frankenstein starts from his
sleep to find the misshapen creature hanging over his bed (as he
himself will later hang over Elizabeth's) does he recognize his ambition for what it really is: a monstrous urge, alien and threatening to
all human intercourse.

In effect, animating the monster completes and liberates Frankenstein's egotism, for his indescribable experiment gives explicit and
autonomous form to his ambition and desire. Paradoxically, in this
incident Shelley makes the ego's destructiveness literal by setting in
motion the figurative, symbolic character of the monster. We will see
later the significance of this event for the monster; for Frankenstein,
this moment, which aborts his maturation, has the dual effect of
initiating self-consciousness and, tragically, perfecting his alienation.
Momentarily "restored to life" by his childhood friend Clerval, Frankenstein rejects the "selfish pursuit [that] had cramped and narrowed"
him and returns his feeling to its proper objects, his "beloved friends."
But ironically, the very gesture that disciplines his desire has already
destroyed the possibility of reestablishing relationships with his loved
ones. Liberating the monster allows Frankenstein to see that personal
fulfillment results from self-denial rather than self-assertion, but it
also condemns him to perpetual isolation and, therefore, to permanent incompleteness.

This fatal paradox, the heart of Mary Shelley's waking nightmare,
gives a conventionally "feminine" twist to the argument that individuals mature through imaginative projection, confrontation, and self-
consciousness. In the version of maturation that Wollstonecraft sketched
out in her two *Vindications* and in *Letters Written . . . in Sweden* and that
Wordsworth set out more fully in *The Prelude,* the child's innate
desires, stirred and nurtured by the mother's love, are soon projected
outward toward the natural world. Desire takes this aggressive turn
because in maternal love and in the receptivity this love cultivates
"there exists / A virtue which irradiates and exalts / All objects
through all intercourse of sense" (1805 *Prelude,* book 2, lines 258–60).
As a result of both the child's growing confidence in the beneficence
of the questing imagination and nature's generous response, the child
is able to effect a radical break with the mother without suffering
irretrievable loss.

> No outcast he, bewildered and depressed;
> Along his infant veins are interfused
> The gravitation and the filial bond
> Of Nature that connect him with the world.

>   [*Prelude,* 2. 261–64]

The heightened images of the self cast back from nature then help
the child internalize a sense of autonomous identity and personal
power.

In marked contrast, Mary Shelley distrusts both the imagination
and the natural world. The imagination, as it is depicted in Frankenstein's original transgression, is incapable of projecting an irradiating
virtue, for, in aiding and abetting the ego, the imagination expands
the individual's self-absorption to fill the entire universe, and, as it
does so, it murders everyone in its path. In *Frankenstein,* the monster
simply acts out the implicit content of Frankenstein's desire: just as
Frankenstein figuratively murdered his family, so the monster literally murders Frankenstein's domestic relationships, blighting both the
memory and the hope of domestic harmony with the "black mark"
of its deadly hand. William Frankenstein, Justine Moritz, Henry Clerval, even Elizabeth Lavenza are, as it were, literally *possessed* by this
creature; but, as Frankenstein knows all too well, its victims are by
extension his own: Justine is *his* "unhappy victim" (p. 80); *he* has
murdered Clerval (p. 174); and the creature consummates *his* deadly
desire on "*its* bridal bier" (p. 193).

By the same token, Mary Shelley also distrusts nature, for, far from
curbing the imagination, nature simply encourages imaginative projection. Essentially, Mary Shelley's understanding of nature coincides
with those of Wordsworth, Wollstonecraft, and Percy Shelley. But
where these three trust the imagination to disarm the natural world
of its meaninglessness by projecting human content into it, Mary
Shelley's anxiety about the imagination bleeds into the world it invades.[18] In the inhospitable world most graphically depicted in the
final setting of *Frankenstein,* nature is "terrifically desolate," frigid,
and fatal to human beings and human relationships. These fields of
ice provide a fit home only for the monster, that incarnation of the
imagination's ugly and deadly essence.

Thus Shelley does not depict numerous natural theaters into which
the individual can project his or her growing desire and from which
affirmative echoes will return to hasten the process of maturation.
Instead, she continues to dramatize personal fulfillment strictly in
terms of the child's original domestic harmony, with the absent mother
now replaced by the closest female equivalent: ideally, Elizabeth would
link Frankenstein's maturity to his youth, just as Mrs. Saville should
anchor the mariner Walton. Ideally, in other words, the beloved
object would be sought and found only within the comforting confines
of preexisting domestic relationships. In this model, Shelley therefore
ties the formation of personal identity to self-denial rather than
self-assertion; personal identity for her entails defining oneself in
terms of relationships (not one but many)—not, as Wollstonecraft

and Wordsworth would have it, in terms of self-assertion, confrontation, freedom, and faith in the individualistic imaginative act.[19]

Shelley repeatedly stresses the fatal kinship between the human
imagination, nature, and death by the tropes of natural violence that
describe all kinds of desire. Passion is like nature internalized, as even
Frankenstein knows:

> When I would account to myself for the birth of that passion, which afterwards
> ruled my destiny, I find it arise, like a mountain river, from ignoble and almost
> forgotten sources; but, swelling as it proceeded, it became the torrent which,
> in its course, has swept away all my hopes and joys. [F, p. 32]

Ambition drives Frankenstein "like a hurricane" as he engineers the
monster (p. 49) and, after its liberation, he is a "blasted tree," "utterly
destroyed" by a lightning blast to his soul. Through these metaphoric
associations, Shelley is laying the groundwork for the pattern acted
out by the monster. *Like* forces in the natural world, Frankenstein's
unregulated desire gathers strength until it erupts in the monster's
creation; then the creature actualizes, externalizes, the pattern of
nature—Frankenstein's nature and the natural world, now explicitly
combined—with a power that destroys all society. In other words, the
pattern inherent in the natural world and figuratively ascribed to the
individual becomes, through the monster, Frankenstein's literal "fate"
or "destiny."

The individual's fatal relationship to nature is further complicated
by the egotistical impulse to deny this kinship. In retrospect, Frankenstein knows that the winds will more likely yield a storm than calm,
but in the blindness of his original optimism he believes that nature
is hospitable to humanity, that it offers a Wordsworthian "ennobling
interchange" that consoles and elevates the soul. Still trusting himself
and the natural world, Frankenstein cries out with "something like
joy" to the spirit of the Alps, as if it were a compassionate as well as
a natural parent: "Wandering spirits . . . allow me this faint happiness, or take me, as your companion, away from the joys of life." But
Frankenstein's belief in natural benevolence, like his earlier confidence
in the benevolence of his desire, proves a trick of the wishful imagination. His request is answered by the true spirit of this and every place
untamed by social conventions—the "superhuman," "unearthly" monster. Lulled once more by vanity and desire, Frankenstein recognizes
the character of his bond with nature only when it again stands
incarnate before him.

IN ORDER TO UNDERSTAND why Mary Shelley's first readers did not fully
appreciate what seems, in comparison to Romantic optimism, to be

an unmistakable distrust of the imagination, we must turn to the monster's narrative. For Shelley's decision to divide the novel into a series of first-person narratives instead of employing a single perspective, whether first-person or omniscient, has the effect of qualifying her judgment of egotism. Because she dramatizes in the monster— not in Frankenstein—the psychological consequences of imaginative self-assertion, the reader is encouraged to participate not only in Frankenstein's desire for innate and natural benevolence but also in the agonizing repercussions of this misplaced optimism.

In the monster's narrative, Shelley both recapitulates Frankenstein's story and, ingeniously, completes it. Influenced by external circumstances that arouse, then direct, their desire for knowledge, both beings find that their imaginative quests yield only the terrible realization of an innate grotesqueness. But, unlike Frankenstein, the monster is denied the luxury of an original domestic harmony. The monster is "made" not born, and, as the product of the unnatural coupling of nature and the imagination, it is caught in the vortex of death that will ultimately characterize Frankenstein as well. Moreover, as the product, then the agent of Frankenstein's egotism, the monster is merely a link in the symbolic "series" of Frankenstein's "self-devoted being," not an autonomous member of a natural, organic family.[20] Given a human's nobler aspirations without the accompanying power, the monster struggles futilely to deny both its status as a function of Frankenstein and the starkness of its circumscribed domain; the creature yearns to experience and act upon its own desires and to break free into the realistic frame that Frankenstein occupies. But the monster cannot have independent desires or influence its own destiny because, as the projection of Frankenstein's indulged desire and nature's essence, the creature *is* destiny. Moreover, because the monster's physical form literally embodies its essence, it cannot pretend to be something it is not; it cannot enter the human community it longs to join, and it cannot earn the sympathy it can all too vividly imagine. Paradoxically, the monster is the victim of both the symbolic and the literal. And, as such, it is doubly like a woman in patriarchal society—forced to be a symbol of (and vehicle for) someone else's desire, yet exposed (and exiled) as the deadly essense of passion itself.

For the monster, then, self-consciousness comes with brutal speed, for it depends, not on an act of transgression, but on literal selfperception. An old man's terror, a pool of water, a child's fear, all are nature's mirrors, returning the monster repeatedly to its grotesque self, "a figure hideously deformed and loathsome . . . a monster, a blot upon the earth" (pp. 115–16). When the creature discovers its true origin—not in the literary works it finds and learns to read but

in the records of Frankenstein's private experiments—it can no longer deny the absolute "horror" of its being, the monstrous singularity
of egotism: "the minutest description of my odious and loathsome
person is given, in language which painted your own horrors, and
rendered mine ineffaceable" (p. 126). From this moment on, the
monster's attempts to deny its nature are as futile as they are desperate. In its most elaborate scheme, the creature hides in a womblike
hovel, as if it could be born again into culture by aping the motions
of the family it spies upon. Although the monster tries to disguise its
true nature by confronting only the blind old father, De Lacey's
children return and recognize the creature's "ineffaceable" monstrosity for what it literally is. Their violent reaction, which the monster
interprets as rejection by its "adopted family," at last precipitates the
creature's innate nature; abandoning humanity's "godlike science"—
the language of society it so diligently learned—for its natural tongue—
the nonsignifying "fearful howlings" of beasts—the monster embarks
on its systematic destruction of domestic harmony. The creature
makes one final attempt to form a new society; but when Frankenstein refuses to create a female monster, it is condemned, like its
maker, to a single bond of hatred. After Frankenstein's death, the
monster disappears into the darkness at the novel's end, vowing to
build its own funeral pyre; for it is as immune to human justice as
it was repulsive to human love.

The monster carries with it the guilt and alienation that attend
Frankenstein's self-assertion; yet, because Shelley realistically details
the stages by which the creature is driven to act out its symbolic
nature from *its* point of view, the reader is compelled to identify with
its anguish and frustration. This narrative strategy precisely repro-
duces Mary Shelley's profound ambivalence toward Frankenstein's
creative act; for by separating self-assertion from its consequences,
she is able to dramatize both her conventional judgment of the evils
of egotism and her emotional engagement in the imaginative act.
Indeed, the pathos of the monster's cry suggests that Shelley identified
most strongly with the product (and the victim) of Frankenstein's
transgression: the objectified imagination, helpless and alone.

Although in an important sense, objectifying Frankenstein's imagination in the symbolic form of the monster delimits the range of
connotations the imagination can have (it eliminates, for example, the
possibilities of transcendent power or beneficence), this narrative
strategy allows Shelley to express her ambivalence toward the creative act because a symbol is able to accommodate different, even
contradictory, meanings. It is important to recognize that Shelley is
using symbolism in a quite specific way here, a way that differs
markedly from Percy Shelley's description of symbolism in his pref-

ace to the 1818 *Frankenstein*. In his justification for the central scene, Percy stresses not the ambivalence of the symbol but its comprehensiveness: "However impossible as a physical fact, [this incident] affords a point of view to the imagination for the delineating of human passions more comprehensive and commanding than any which the ordinary relations of existing events can yield" (p. 6). Although we know from the Shelleys' letters and from the surviving manuscript of *Frankenstein* that Percy was instrumental in promoting and even revising the text, Mary did not uncritically or wholeheartedly accept the aesthetic program of which this self-confident use of symbolism was only one part. Instead, she transforms Percy's version of the Romantic aesthetic in such a way as to create for herself a nonassertive, and hence acceptable, voice.

Percy Shelley defended his aesthetic doctrines, as part of his political and religious beliefs, with a conviction Mary later called a "resolution firm to martyrdom."[21] Scornful of public opinion, he maintained that a true poet may be judged only by his legitimate peers, a jury "impaneled by Time from the selectest of the wise of many generations."[22] Society's accusation that an artist is "immoral," he explains in the "Defence of Poetry" (1821), rests on "a misconception of the manner in which poetry acts to produce the moral improvement of man." The audience's relationship to poetry is based not on reason but on the imagination; true poetry does not encourage imitation or judgment but participation. It strengthens the individual's moral sense because it exercises and enlarges the capacity for sympathetic identification, that is, for establishing relationships. Following Plato, Percy declares that the primary reflex of the moral imagination is the outgoing gesture of love.

> The great secret of morals is Love; or a going out of our own nature, and an identification of ourselves with the beautiful which exists in thought, action, or person, not our own. A man, to be greatly good, must imagine intensely and comprehensively; he must put himself in the place of another and of many others; the pains and pleasures of his species must become his own. The great instrument of moral good is the imagination; and poetry administers to the effect by acting upon the cause.[23]

Each of Percy Shelley's aesthetic doctrines comes to rest on this model of the imagination as an innately moral, capacious faculty. Because the imagination, if unrestrained, naturally supersedes relative morals (and in so doing compensates for the inhumaneness of the natural world), the poet should not discipline his or her poetic efforts according to a particular society's conceptions of right and wrong. Because the imagination tends to extend itself, through sympathy, to truth, the poet should simply depict examples of truth, thus drawing the audience into a relationship that simultaneously feeds and stimu-lates humanity's appetite for "thoughts of ever new delight."

This model of the artwork as an arena for relationships is the only aspect of Percy's aesthetics that Mary Shelley adopts without reserva-tion. It seems to have been particularly appealing to her not only because it conforms to Percy's ideal but also because it satisfies socie-ty's conventional definition of proper feminine identity and proper feminine self-assertion. In doing so, it also answered needs and as-suaged fears that seem to have been very pressing for Mary Shelley. As we have seen, she did not agree with Percy that the imagination is inherently moral. By the same token, she seems to have doubted that the abstract controls that Wollstonecraft described in her two *Vindications* and her *Letters Written . . . in Sweden* were capable of governing an individual's desire or disciplining the imagination. The factors that reinforced Shelley's doubts were probably as complicated as the anxieties themselves, but we can surmise that Percy Shelley's outspoken atheism helped undermine Mary's confidence in orthodox religion, that society's denigration of women's reasoning ability weak-ened her trust in that faculty, and that society's judgment and her own conflicting emotions conspired to make her doubt the morality of female feeling. For Mary Shelley, then, the only acceptable or safe arena in which to articulate her feelings, exercise her reason, and act out her unladylike ambition was that of personal relationships. In addition to the aesthetic purpose it serves, the narrative strategy of *Frankenstein* also provides just such a network of relationships. Be-cause of its three-part narrative arrangement, Shelley's readers are drawn into a relationship with even the most monstrous part of the young author; Shelley is able to create her artistic persona through a series of relationships rather than a single act of self-assertion; and she is freed from having to take a single, definitive position on her unladylike subject. In other words, the narrative strategy of *Franken-stein,* like the symbolic presentation of the monster, enables Shelley to express and efface herself at the same time and thus, at least partially, to satisfy her conflicting desires for self-assertion and social acceptance.

Before turning to the 1831 revisions, we need to examine the last of the three narrators of *Frankenstein;* for if the scientist and the monster lure the reader ever deeper into the heart of ambition, Robert Walton, the mariner, reminds us that Frankenstein's abortive enthusiasm is *not* the only possible product of human energy. Wal-ton's epistolary journal literally contains and effectively mediates the voices of the other two narrators, and so he may be said to have the last—if not the definitive—word. Like Henry Clerval and Felix De Lacey, Walton provides an example of the domesticated male, the alternative to Frankenstein's antisocial ambition. But because Walton bears closer affinities to his adopted friend than either Clerval or De Lacey does, his ability to deny his selfish desire and to replace it by concern for others stands as Shelley's most explicit criticism of Frankenstein's imaginative self-indulgence.

Like Frankenstein, Robert Walton is from his youth motivated by an imaginative obsession that scorns a literal-minded, superficial conception of nature. Despite known facts to the contrary, he believes that the North Pole is a "region of beauty and delight" (p. 9), and he longs to "satiate [his] ardent curiosity" by penetrating its secrets. Like Frankenstein's, Walton's ambition masquerades as a benevolent desire to benefit society, although it too is really only the egotist's desire for "glory." In his experiments, Frankenstein transgresses metaphysical boundaries; in his exploration, Walton defies geographical limitations; but for both, indulging desire is actually a transgression against domestic relationships. Walton's only living relative is Margaret Saville, the sister with whom his letters initially connect him; but as his ship sails farther into the icy wastes, his narrative becomes nearly as self-contained as Frankenstein's monologue, and the social gesture of writing letters gradually gives way to the more "self-devoted" habit of keeping a journal—a letter to his own future self.

Despite the similarities, however, Walton's ambition remains only an embryonic version of Frankenstein's murderous egotism, for ultimately he does not allow his obsession to destroy relationships. The crucial difference between them resides in Walton's willingness to deny his desire when it jeopardizes his social responsibilities or his relational identity. Walton constantly thinks of himself in terms of relationships: he is from his childhood an "affectionate brother," and he conceives of maturity as entailing extensions of this regulating influence. The "evil" he laments is not the mortality of the individual (as death was the "most irreparable evil" to Frankenstein) but the insufficiency that characterizes everyone.

> But I have one want which I have never yet been able to satisfy; and the absence of the object of which I now feel as a most severe evil. I have no friend, Margaret: when I am glowing with the enthusiasm of success, there will be none to participate my joy. . . . I desire the company of a man who could sympathize with me; whose eyes would reply to mine. . . . My day dreams are . . . extended and magnificent; but they want (as the painters call it) *keeping*; and I greatly need a friend who would have sense enough not to despise me as romantic, and affection enough for me to endeavour to regulate my mind. [Pp. 13–14]

When his ship rescues the "wretched" Frankenstein from the frozen ocean, Walton immediately begins to "love him as a brother" (p. 22), to thaw his icy silence, to nurse him back to intermittent sympathy and generosity. But by this time Frankenstein's ambition has already shriveled his social passions into hatred and a craving for revenge ("I—I have lost every thing," he cries, "and cannot begin life anew" [p.23]). Only Walton is still capable of redirecting his involuted ambition outward into self-denying love, for he himself has never permitted his desire to escape completely from the regulating influence of social relationships. For example, in an early letter he claimed that his resolution was "as fixed as fate," but in that same letter he assured his sister that his concern for others would always override his ambition (p. 15). And, in the end, of course, Walton capitulates to the pleas of his sailors—his family of the sea—and agrees to return south, to safety and civilization. Walton "kill[s] no albatross"; he realizes that denying his ambition will be painful, even humiliating, but he does not commit the antisocial crime of indulging his egotistic curiosity. Finally, his journal even opens outward again and addresses Margaret Saville directly (p. 206). Walton's letters, as the dominant chain of all the narrations, preserve community despite Frankenstein's destructive self-devotion, for they link him and his correspondents (Mrs. Saville and the reader) in a relationship that Frankenstein can neither enter nor destroy.

The 1831 Revisions

The revisions Mary Shelley prepared for the third edition of *Frankenstein,* which was published as part of Colburn and Bentley's Standard Novels Series in 1831, reveal that during the thirteen-year interval her interests had changed in two significant ways. The most extensive revisions, some of which were outlined soon after Percy's death in 1822,[24] occur in chapters 1, 2, and 5 of Frankenstein's narrative; their primary effects are to idealize the domestic harmony of his childhood and to change the origin—and thus the implications—of his passionate ambition. As a consequence of the first alteration, Frankenstein's imaginative self-assertion becomes a more atrocious "crime"; as a result of the second, he is transformed from a realistic character to a symbol of the Romantic overreacher. Shelley's revisions thus extend her criticism of imaginative indulgence, already present in the 1818 text, and direct it much more pointedly at the blasphemy she now associates with her own adolescent audacity. Yet, paradoxically, even as she heightens the domestic destruction the egotist causes, she actually qualifies his responsibility. For in her new conception of Frankenstein's development she depicts him as the helpless pawn of a predetermined "destiny," a fate that is given, not made. The 1831 Frankenstein seems quintessentially a victim, like the monster, who now more precisely symbolizes what this kind of individual is rather than what he or she allows himself or herself to become. In both the text and her "Author's Introduction," Shelley suggests that such an individual has virtually no control over destiny and that, therefore, he or she is to be pitied rather than condemned.

The alteration almost all critics have noted is Shelley's reformulation of the relationship between Frankenstein and his fiancée Elizabeth. Originally a cousin, Elizabeth becomes a foundling in 1831—no doubt partly to avoid insinuations of incest—but also to emphasize the active benevolence of Frankenstein's mother, who, in adopting the poor orphan, is now elevated to the stature of a "guardian angel." This alteration, however, is only one of a series of changes that idealize the harmony of Frankenstein's childhood home. In this edition, for example, Shelley gives more space to the protectiveness of his parents (pp. 233–34) and to the happiness of his childhood ("My mother's tender caresses, and my father's smile of benevolent pleasure while regarding me, are my first recollections" [p. 234]). Not surprisingly, Elizabeth, as the potential link between Frankenstein's childhood and his mature domesticity, receives the most attention. In 1831 she becomes much more like the Victorian Angel of the House; she is "a being heaven-sent," "a child fairer than pictured cherub" (p. 235). Elizabeth is both Frankenstein's guardian and his charge; explicitly, she embodies the regulating reciprocity of domestic love. "She was the living spirit of love to soften and attract: I might have become sullen in my study, rough through the ardour of my nature, but that she was there to subdue me to a semblance of her own gentleness" (p. 237). By emphasizing Elizabeth's pivotal role in what is now an ideal domestic harmony, Shelley prepares to heighten the devastating social consequences of Frankenstein's imaginative transgression and to further underscore the loss *he* suffers through his willful act.

Despite this idealization of the family, in the 1831 version the seeds of Frankenstein's egotism germinate more rapidly within the home, for Shelley now attributes his fall not primarily to accidents or to his departure but to his own innate "temperature" or character. "Deeply smitten with the thirst for knowledge," Frankenstein is now from his birth set apart from his childhood companions. Unlike the "saintly" Elizabeth or the "noble spirit [ed]" Clerval, Frankenstein has a violent temper and vehement passions. His accidental discovery of Agrippa is now preceded by a description of a more decisive factor, the determining "law in [his] temperature"; it is this innate predilection that turns his imagination "not toward childish pursuits, but to an eager desire to learn . . . the secrets of heaven and earth" (p. 237). In 1831 Shelley retains Frankenstein's suggestion that his father's negligence contributed to his "fatal impulse," but almost every alteration contradicts the implication that circumstances can substantially alter innate character. In 1831 Frankenstein resists modern science not because "some accident" prevents him from attending lectures but because "one of those caprices of the mind" distracts him from scientific speculations. By further emphasizing the moralists' description of the imagination's irrepressible energy, Shelley radically reduces the importance of external circumstances and underscores the inevitability of the overreacher's fall. At the same time, she also pushes what had been a realistic narrative, framing the symbolic story of monstrous egotism, in the direction of allegory.

Shelley graphically dramatizes the "fatality" of Frankenstein's character in terms of a contest.

> Thus strangely are our souls constructed, and by such slight ligaments are we bound to prosperity or ruin. When I look back, it seems to me as if this almost miraculous change of inclination and will was the immediate suggestion of the guardian angel of my life—the last effort made by the spirit of preservation to avert the storm that was even then hanging in the stars, and ready to envelope me. . . . It was a strong effort of the spirit of good; but it was ineffectual. Destiny was too potent, and her immutable laws had decreed my utter and terrible destruction. [P. 239]

Characterizing Frankenstein's psyche as a battleground between the personified "spirit of good" and "destiny" blurs the distinction between personal ambition and external coercion and gives the impression that, in an important sense, Frankenstein is merely the passive victim of powerful forces. This impression is reinforced by other crucial alterations in the 1831 text. When Frankenstein sets out for Ingolstadt, for example, he characterizes himself as being hostage to an irresistible "influence," to which he attributes a relentless intentionality: "Chance—or rather the evil influence, the Angel of Destruction . . . asserted omnipotent sway over me from the moment I turned my reluctant steps from my father's door" (p. 240). This "influence" has its counterpart in Frankenstein's own ambition, but, once more, Shelley personifies its workings so as to make Frankenstein seem a victim:

> Such were the professor's words—rather let me say such the words of fate, enounced to destroy me. As he [M. Waldman] went on, I felt as if my soul were grappling with a palpable enemy; one by one the various keys were touched which formed the mechanism of my being: chord after chord was sounded, and soon my mind was filled with one thought, one conception, one purpose. So much has been done, exclaimed the soul of Frankenstein,—more, far more, will I achieve. . . . I closed not my eyes that night. My internal being was in a state of insurrection and turmoil; I felt that order would thence arise, but I had no power to produce it. [P. 241]

This remarkable passage suggests that one's "soul" can be taken over by an invading enemy, who, having taken up residence within, effectively becomes one's "fate." The "palpable enemy," which we know to be imaginative desire, is no stranger to its chosen victim; but Shelley's repeated use of the passive voice and her depiction of the "soul" as a vessel to be filled, then objectified, makes this "resolution" seem a visitation rather than an act of self-indulgence. Dramatizing the fragmentation of Frankenstein's psyche foreshadows, of course, the literal splitting-off of the monster; but, equally important, it suggests that Frankenstein cannot be held responsible for the "destiny" he is powerless to resist.

In 1831 Shelley also elaborates Frankenstein's misunderstanding of the natural world; but by extending his blindness to the most innocent of all the characters, Elizabeth, Shelley now makes him seem only one victim of nature's treachery. In the revised version of the scene in the Alps, Frankenstein's deception is all the more cruel because nature now specifically invokes memories of his harmonious childhood and even presents the face of his deceased mother: "The very winds whispered in soothing accents, and maternal nature bade me weep no more. . . . The same lulling sounds acted as a lullaby to my too keen sensations. . . . [The forms of nature] gathered around me, and bade me be at peace" (pp. 248–49). But this nature still holds only the monster; and when Frankenstein's trust and betrayal are generalized to Elizabeth, his delusion becomes an inevitable curse of the human condition, not simply a production of his own unleashed imagination. In her revised letter in chapter 6, Elizabeth celebrates nature's benevolent constancy: "The blue lake, and snow-clad mountains, they never change;—and I think our placid home, and our contented hearts are regulated by the same immutable laws" (p. 243). But when Justine is executed, Elizabeth also learns the bitter truth. In this context, her heart-rending speech (". . . misery has come home, and men appear to me as monsters" [p. 88]), retained from the 1818 text, now emphasizes less that Elizabeth is Frankenstein's victim than that all humans are unwitting victims of nature's violence and their own natural frailty.

As one might expect, in 1831 Shelley also alters her portrait of Robert Walton in order to remove the alternative of self-control she now wants to deny to Frankenstein. Walton's victory over egotism becomes less a triumph over his own ambition than the consequence of a mysterious internal revolution. Initially Walton describes himself as a man driven by two conflicting tendencies:

> There is something at work in my soul, which I do not understand. I am practically industrious—pains-taking;—a workman to execute with perseverence and labour:—but besides this, there is a love for the marvellous, a belief

in the marvellous, intertwined in all my projects, which hurries me out of the common pathways of men, even to the wild sea and unvisited regions I am about to explore. [P. 231]

Walton too is a pawn of internal forces, forces which seem to originate from outside him ("there is a love . . . which hurries me"). Thus, although in 1831 Walton's ambition is more pronounced, more like the young Frankenstein's, he is not wholly responsible for his actions. Just as M. Waldman was the external catalyst to precipitate Frankenstein's "destiny," so Frankenstein serves as the critical agent for Walton. Frankenstein's narrative resolves Walton's internal conflict and restores to him the domestic affection that has all along formed the innate "groundwork of [his] character." Walton does not really assert himself or actively choose; rather, true to his character, his original self-denying nature, he allows himself to be acted on by others: to respond to the needs of Frankenstein, then to the sailors in his charge.

Of the three narrations that compose *Frankenstein,* the monster's history receives the least attention in the 1831 revisions—no doubt because Mary Shelley sympathized even more strongly with the guilt and alienation that shadow the egotist's crime. Moreover, by implication, the monster is now the appropriate extension of the curse of the creative artist, not the product of the self-indulged imagination. The monster's grotesqueness and its singularity are still signs of an essential transgression, but its pathetic powerlessness is now a more appropriate counterpart to the helplessness of Frankenstein himself.

WE CAN BEGIN TO UNDERSTAND the significance these changes held for Mary Shelley by examining the introduction she added to the 1831 text. Her primary desire in this introduction is to explain—and justify—the audacity of what now seems to her like blasphemy; she wants to answer, and thus forever silence, the question that, repeatedly asked, insistently raises the ghost of her former self: "How I, then a young girl, came to think of, and to dilate upon, so very hideous an idea?" (p. 222). Even *this* explanation must be justified, however, for Mary Shelley wants most of all to assure her readers that she is no longer the defiant, self-assertive "girl" who once dared to explore ambition and even to seek fame herself without the humility proper to a lady. Now "infinitely indifferent" to literary reputation, Shelley claims to be "very averse to bringing [her]self forward in print." Her commentary is permissible only because she introduces it as coming from and explaining her author-persona, that other self, which is, strictly speaking, not the "personal" Mary Shelley at all: "as it will be confined to such topics as have connection with my authorship alone, I can scarcely accuse myself of a personal intrusion." This splitting of herself into two personae replicates Shelley's narrative strategy of apportioning her sympathies among the various characters in the novel. Just as she did—and did not—identify with the monster, so she is—and is not—responsible for giving substance to her dream.

Her 1831 version of the dream that inspired the novel makes clear what Shelley is so eager to disavow: the monster's creator, now referred to specifically as an artist, transgresses the bounds of propriety through his art. This transgression (now characterized as blasphemy) is followed by the artist's fear and revulsion, for he recognizes in his "odious handywork" the essential meaning of artistic creation: the "yellow, watery, but speculative eyes" that mirror the artist's own are the signs not only of transgression but of a fundamental deficiency common to creature and creator alike.

> I saw the pale student of unhallowed arts kneeling beside the thing he had put together. I saw the hideous phantasm of a man stretched out, and then, on the working of some powerful engine, show signs of life, and stir with an uneasy, half vital motion. Frightful must it be; for supremely frightful would be the effect of any human endeavour to mock the stupendous mechanism of the Creator of the world. His success would terrify the artist; he would rush away from his odious handywork, horror-stricken. He would hope that, left to itself, the slight spark of life which he had communicated would fade; that this thing, which had received such imperfect animation, would subside into dead matter; and he might sleep in the belief that the silence of the grave would quench for ever the transient existence of the hideous corpse which he had looked upon as the cradle of life. He sleeps; but he is awakened; he opens his eyes; behold the horrid thing stands at his bedside, opening his curtains, and looking on him with yellow, watery, but speculative eyes. [P. 228]

The boldness with which Shelley once pursued metaphysical speculations now seems, first of all, a defiance of one's proper place—here the male's in relation to God, but also, by extension, woman's in relation to the family. Clearly here, as in the thematic emphasis of the novel, Shelley expresses the tension she feels between the self-denial demanded by domestic activity and the self-assertiveness essential to artistic creation. Before 1816, she explains, she did not respond to Percy's encouragement that she write because "travelling, and the cares of a family, occupied [her] time" (pp. 223–24). Now that she has pursued his designs, she finds literary production to be a perverse substitute for a woman's natural function: a "hideous corpse" usurps what should be the "cradle of life."[25]

But the "speculative" monster is also an objectification of the artist's creative self, and as such it raises disturbing associations for the real Mary Shelley. Because this society tends to objectify women in cultural forms ranging from symbols of property to poetic muses, the temptation to think of oneself as an object constitutes a particular-ly seductive danger for women.[26] Certainly Mary Shelley's personal testimony proves that self-objectification was both an alluring and a terrifying temptation for her for some very specific reasons. In her culture, objects and nature and women and the literal, as versions of the Other in opposition to which the Subject seeks definition, are all on the same side of the conceptual axis.[27] And for Shelley, as we have seen, the common denominator of all of these is death. Objec-tification for Shelley therefore means not only conforming to the masculine stereotype of women but, more ominously, exiling herself into the object world of nature—ironically, "maternal nature"—which harbors both the murderous egotism Shelley feared in herself and the deadly blight of the literal. As Mary Shelley imagines her female self, she gives her own conflicted energy the form of a mon-ster, a vivified corpse that is capable of commanding pity but that, in all its actions and despite its intentions, destroys every living being it touches. And as she imagines the act of creativity, she imagines exiling her own imaginative energy into a landscape that is fatal to figuration and that freezes all attempts to transform or disguise the self. In such a world, the monster—and, by extension, the female artist—is doomed; in the object world of nature, even one who longs to speak and who acquires eloquence from the tablescraps of patriar-chal culture, finds that language loses its power to create more than curiosity or revulsion.

As this description suggests, however, the terror that Shelley associ-ates with artistic creation comes not just from the guilt of exceeding one's proper role or from the fatal claims of the literal; it comes also from the fear of failure that accompanies such presumption. The creation Shelley imagines is "odious," "horrid," "hideous," imper-fectly animated—a failure for all to see. Earlier in the 1831 introduc-tion she had also suggested that the anxiety generated by artistic creation emanates in large part from its profoundly public nature. There she distinguished between her youthful, private fantasies of pure imagination ("waking dreams . . . which had for their subject the formation of a succession of imaginary incidents" [p. 222]) and the stories she actually wrote down, the "close imitations" she shared with her childhood friend, Isabel Baxter. "My dreams were at once more fantastic and agreeable than my writings," she explains. "The airy flights of . . . imagination," in fact, she considers her only "true compositions," for what she wrote was in "a most common-place style." Whereas Mary Wollstonecraft, in *The Rights of Woman* at least, conceived of writing as confrontation with authorities, for Shelley, to write is necessarily to imitate, and her models, almost all masculine, are both intimidating and potentially judgmental of her audacious foray into their domain. Thus Shelley automatically anticipates their censure of what seems even to her to be the monstrous inadequacy of her objectified self. The fear of public scrutiny and judgment lies behind most of Shelley's disclaimers of the artistic enterprise: "What I wrote was intended at least for one other eye—my childhood's companion and friend; but my dreams were all my own; I accounted for them to nobody; they were my refuge when annoyed—my dearest pleasure when free" (p. 223). For Mary Shelley, when the imagination is placed in the service of a text, a discomforting transformation occurs: what had been a harmless pastime becomes tantamount to a transgression, and, fueling the attendant guilt, the fear surfaces that if she does compete she will be found inadequate. Only the unbound and therefore nonbinding imagination can escape censure and thus protect the dreamer against exposure and pain.

Shelley's distinction between imagination and imaginative creation would have surprised many of her male contemporaries. In his "Defence of Poetry," for example, Percy Shelley does not even consider the possibility of keeping imaginative insights private, for, in his theory, poets have a profoundly public responsibility; they are the "unacknowledged legislators of the world."[28] Percy's description centers on the self-expressive function of art; he derives his authority from a masculine tradition of poet-prophets and his self-confidence from the social approval generally accorded to masculine self-assertion. Lacking the support of both tradition and public opinion, however, and lacking her mother's determination, Mary Shelley separates the permissible, even liberating expression of the imagination from the more egotistical, less defensible act of public self-assertion.[29] For Mary Shelley, the imagination is properly a vehicle for escaping the self, not a medium of personal power or even self-expression. She therefore associates the imagination with images of flight, escape, and freedom; writing she associates with monstrosity, transgression, and failure. If her male peers would have found this distinction incomprehensible, her mother would have understood it all too well; for Shelley's ideal "art" is very like the "feminine" artistry that Wollstonecraft criticized in *Maria*: it not only lacks "substance," but it is completely ineffectual as well.

Mary Shelley did not, of course, wholly reject the artistic enterprise, no matter how genuine her anxieties and no matter how abject her apologies. As we will see, by 1831 Shelley was an established professional author; she was supporting herself and her son almost exclusively by writing; and her numerous reviews and stories, as well as her three novels, had earned her a considerable reputation. Nor does she totally disavow kinship with her younger self, the more defiant Mary Godwin. It is with felt intensity that Shelley vividly recalls her feeling of power when, having dared to imagine a "fright-ful . . . success," the younger Mary triumphantly silenced her male critics: "Swift as light and as cheering was the idea that broke in upon me. 'I have found it!' . . . On the morrow I announced that I had *thought of a story*" (p. 228). But in 1831, the mature Mary Shelley is able to countenance the creation of *Frankenstein*—and, in effect, the crea-tion of her entire artistic role—only because she can interpret these creations as primarily the work of other people and of external circumstances. Thus Shelley "remembers" (sometimes inaccurately) the origin of *Frankenstein* in such a way as to displace most of the responsibility for what might otherwise seem willful self-assertion; essentially she offers a story that depicts the young Mary Godwin as a creation of others, a pawn, like Frankenstein, of forces larger than herself. Twice she insists on Percy's role in her project, his repeated desire that she "prove [herself] worthy of [her] parentage, and enrol [herself] on the page of fame": "He was for ever inciting me to obtain literary reputation," she adds (p. 223). She also (incorrectly) recalls the pressure her companions at Diodati exerted on her to produce a ghost story for their contest. The degree of embarrassment she records and the vividness of this inaccurate recollection suggest both the extent to which she internalized the expectations she assumed her companions would have and how important it was that the impetus for her creativity should come from outside. "*Have you thought of a story? I was* asked each morning, and each morning I was forced to reply with a mortifying negative."[30] To protect herself, however, Shelley assures herself and the reader that she never entered directly into competition with her intimidating male companions. "The illus-trious poets," Byron and Percy Shelley, soon tired of the "platitude of prose," and "poor Polidori" is hardly worth considering (perhaps because both poets openly ridiculed the doctor). "The machinery of a story" is the humblest of all inventions, she continues, diminishing her accomplishment to what she now considers its appropriate stat-ure. All invention, in fact, she reduces to mere piecework: "invention, it must be humbly admitted . . . can give form to dark, shapeless substances, but it cannot bring into being the substance itself" (p. 226). Even the "substance" of her story, she is quick to add, comes from external sources: initially, her dream was inspired by a conver-sation between Byron and Percy, "to which [Mary] was a devout but nearly silent listener." Finally, Shelley dramatizes her own contribu-tion to these ideas ("moulding and fashioning") as if it were nearly involuntary:

> When I placed my head on my pillow, I did not sleep, nor could I be said to think. My imagination, unbidden, possessed and guided me, gifting the suc-cessive images that arose in my mind with a vividness far beyond the usual

5

"Ideal and Almost Unnatural Perfection"
Revising Mary Shelley

MARY SHELLEY'S RETREAT from unorthodoxy, which is evident even in the supposedly unorthodox 1818 *Frankenstein,* was neither immediate nor complete. Yet the differences between her first novels and her last three are so marked that the seven novels could almost have been written by two different persons. Shelley's contemporaries noted this. Whether they were shocked (and slightly titillated) by her imaginative audacity or were frankly irate at what seemed to be her betrayal of Percy's radical ideals, Shelley's acquaintances recorded their conviction that she was, in some sense, simply not what she seemed to be. "Your writing and your manner are not in accordance," Lord Dillon observed in 1829.

> I should have thought of you—if I had only read you—that you were a sort of my Sybil, outpouringly enthusiastic, rather indiscreet, and even extravagant; but you are cool, quiet, and feminine to the last degree—I mean in delicacy of manner and expression. Explain this to me.[1]

Leigh Hunt, who had known Shelley longer than most of her new London friends, thought her double character was amusing enough to be captured in rhyme:

> And Shelley, four-famed—for her parents, her lord,
> And the poor lone impossible monster abhorred.
> (So sleek and so smiling she came, people stared,
> To think such fair clay should so darkly have dared.)[2]

But Edward Trelawny, Percy Shelley's friend and fellow rebel, found nothing to joke about in Mary's "delicacy" and "sleekness." "Mary was the most conventional slave I have ever met," he complained bitterly to Claire after Shelley's death; "she was devoid of imagination and Poetry—she felt compunction when she had lost him [Percy]—she did not understand or appreciate him."[3]

Shelley's contemporaries were responding to the expertise with which she eventually came to exploit the discrepancies permitted by—in fact, inherent in—the paradigm of feminine propriety. For

Shelley, divided, as we have seen, by her conflicting desires for self-assertive originality and conventional self-effacement, gradually learned how to use this paradigm to transform the feelings that surfaced in her early works. Essentially, Shelley took advantage of both the artificiality and the paradoxes of the Proper Lady. Once she accepted the paradox—and, by extension, the fiction—inherent in the conventional definition of femininity, she was able to revise the unacceptable facets of herself and her past so that "Mary Shelley" would seem to be only what a lady should be. And, equally important, by using the forms of power implicit in this ideal, she found an acceptable way to express her aggression against the persons she felt had driven her to her adolescent excesses. Whether her exploitation of the artifice of propriety was conscious or not is unclear, and to a certain extent the question is unimportant; for in either case Shelley was simply responding to personal and cultural pressures to conform to a model of behavior that, by making paradox "natural," made dissembling all but inevitable.

The events and emotions that Mary Shelley experienced in her young adulthood were, to say the least, not the sort that middle-class moralists sanctioned or even openly discussed. In the turbulent years between the two editions of *Frankenstein,* Mary Shelley lived almost completely outside the conventional definitions of what a woman should be or do. Percy Shelley's idealistic notions of love and perfectibility encouraged her to be a self-made woman of a kind very different from the one her mother aspired to be. But even without the influence of Percy's radical idealism, the series of domestic catastrophes Shelley suffered between 1816 and 1822 was in itself sufficient to set her apart from her peers even in a period in which untimely deaths—and infant deaths—were not uncommon.[4] Almost as soon as Mary and Percy returned to England in 1816, for example, they were greeted with tragedy: on 9 October, Fanny Imlay, Mary's half-sister, was found dead of an overdose of laudanum. Two months later, on 15 December, they were informed of another suicide: the body of Percy's wife Harriet, possibly pregnant, had been pulled from the Serpentine on 10 December. Anxious to adopt his two children by Harriet and to regain Godwin's approval, Percy and Mary were married on 30 December. But while their marriage succeeded in reconciling Godwin to his "criminal" daughter, it did not convince the courts that the "highly immoral" Percy Shelley had reformed; the couple was denied custody of the children in March 1817. In September of that year Mary gave birth to another child, Clara, and on 11 March of the next year, anxious to place Claire's child (Clara Allegra Byron, born in January 1817) under Byron's protection and to still the persistent rumors that Percy was the father of this child, Percy,

Mary, Claire, and the three children set off for Italy. On that same day, *Frankenstein* was published.

In Italy the tragedies continued. In September 1818, the baby, Clara, died in Mary's arms, and in June 1819, William—the beloved little "Wilmouse"—fell ill with malaria and died. Now "Childless & for ever miserable," Mary Shelley felt despondent, devoid of will: "Let us hear . . . anything you may have done about the tomb," she wrote from Leghorn to a friend at Rome, "near which I shall lie one day & care not—for my own sake—how soon—I shall recover that blow—I feel it more now than at Rome—the thought never leaves me for a single moment—Everything on earth has lost its interest to me."[5] Another child, Percy Florence, was born to the Shelleys in November, and Mary had difficulty shaking off her chronic anxieties about his health. Three years later, in April 1822, Allegra Byron, whom Lord Byron had placed in a convent in Bagnacavello, died of typhus. Claire was briefly, intensely distraught, and Mary, who was pregnant for a fifth time and remembering her own maternal anguish, was again cast into a deep depression. "I was not well in body or mind," she later explained to Maria Gisborne. "My nerves were wound up to the utmost irritation, and the sense of misfortune hung over my spirits. . . . I repeated to myself all that another would have said to console me, & told myself the tale of love peace & competence which I enjoyed—but I answered myself by tears—did not my William die? & did I hold my Percy by a firmer tenure?" (*MSL,* 1:244, 246; 15 August 1822). Early in June, Mary Shelley suffered a near-fatal miscarriage, and only Percy's packing her in ice saved her life. Then, during the next weeks, everyone in the seaside house was troubled by Percy's recurring nightmares. Mary later described one of these as follows: Percy "went to . . . his window that looked on the terrace & the sea & thought he saw the sea rushing in. Suddenly his vision changed & he saw the figure of himself strangling me" (*MSL,* 1:245; 15 August 1822). In the midst of such agitation, the Shelleys and their companions, Edward and Jane Williams, began to look forward to the arrival of Marianne and Leigh Hunt as promising change and perhaps calm for the nervous household. On 1 July, Percy and Edward Williams set out in a boat for Leghorn, to meet the Hunts. A storm broke out on 8 July, as Percy and Edward were beginning their return voyage, and on 26 July, Percy's friend Edward Trelawny broke the news to Mary and Jane that the bodies of their husbands had been found.

The Last Man

Despite the personal catastrophes that punctuated these years, Mary Shelley tried doggedly to live up to Percy's ideals. Indeed, the two novels that she composed before his death—*Mathilda* and *Valperga*—suggest that Shelley was willing to explore subjects considerably more daring than the egotistical ambition she had dramatized in *Frankenstein*. The short *Mathilda*, for instance, is about a father's incestuous love for his daughter, and *Valperga*, which follows the career of Castruccio, the medieval prince of Lucca, introduces infidelity, a woman's sexual passion, and, in the speeches of Beatrice, the seventeen-year-old prophetess, outspoken blasphemy. In both of these novels, Shelley's ambivalence, not only about her father and Percy Shelley but about herself, is dramatized more explicitly than in the 1818 *Frankenstein*. Yet she seems to have felt no inhibitions about giving either work to the men most directly implicated. She read *Mathilda* to Percy, the Gisbornes, and the Williamses; she also sent it eagerly to her father,[6] and, when she sent *Valperga* to him, she was already anticipating a favorable response: "I long to hear some news of it," she wrote Godwin, "as with an authors vanity I want to see it in print & hear the praises of my friends" (*MSL*, 1:218; 9 February 1822). *Mathilda* was not published during Shelley's lifetime, at least partly because Godwin found the subject "disgusting and detestable,"[7] and *Valperga*, which finally appeared in 1823 in a version extensively altered by Godwin, was greeted mostly with censure. "It is impossible to read [the chapter containing Beatrice's creed]," complained *Blackwood's* reviewer "without sorrow that any English lady should be capable of clothing such thoughts in such words."[8]

Only in Shelley's third full-length novel, *The Last Man*, do we begin to see extensive use of the literary strategies that marked her final abandonment of Percy's aesthetic ideals. Even so, *The Last Man* is far from being a conventional woman's novel, for, even after Percy's death, Mary Shelley continued to associate self-exploration and writing with the memory of her husband and with the image of herself he had supported and encouraged. Her journal for the year between Percy's death and her own departure for England reveals that she was trying desperately to preserve her best self by being true to his image of her:

> Oh my beloved Shelley! how often during those happy days—happy, though chequered—I thought how superiorly gifted I had been in being united to one to whom I could unveil myself, and who could understand me! Well, then, now I am reduced to these white pages, which I am to blot with dark imagery. As I write, let me think what he would have said if, speaking thus to him, he could have answered me. Yes, my own heart [her pet name for Percy], I would fain

know what to think of my desolate state; what you think I ought to do, what to think. I guess you would answer thus:—"Seek to know your own heart, and, learning what it best loves, try to enjoy that."[9]

"Literary labours, the improvement of my mind, and the enlargement of my ideas" are the answers her "own heart" returns, even more than caring for her child. As a consequence, the journal for most of the next year records Shelley's attempt to carry out this intellectual program—that is, to make herself a worthy representative of Percy Shelley. "I would endeavour to consider myself a faint continuation of his being," she wrote a few days later, "and, as far as possible, the revelation to the earth of what he was. Yet, to become this, I must change much, and above all I must acquire that knowledge and drink at those fountains of wisdom and virtue, from which he quenched his thirst." "You will be with me in all my studies, dearest love!" she addresses Percy; "Your voice will no longer applaud me, but in spirit you will visit and encourage me: I know you will. What were I, if I did not believe that you still exist?" (*MSJ*, pp. 182–83).

The England to which Mary Shelley returned in July 1823, in search of a publisher for Percy's posthumous poems and her own work, was a country not likely to welcome the radical ideals that Mary associated with Percy's memory. Having survived Napoleon's challenge, England was still recovering from the economic depression that followed the end of the war in 1815. A protective grain tariff, the Corn Law of 1815, had helped landowners survive the falling prices and unstable currency, but the same measure raised the price of bread and made the life of urban laborers hard and insecure. In rural areas of England, living conditions also deteriorated, at least partly because, while real wages for farm laborers stagnated or even declined between the 1790s and 1830, the rents they paid nearly doubled.[10] In 1815 and 1822 there were uprisings in East Anglia, the Peterloo Massacre occurred in Manchester in 1819, and throughout the country agitation spread for repeal of the Corn Laws and for election reforms. Licentious behavior at the Regency court had undermined the prestige of the crown, but the Tory government took extremely repressive measures to quell the social unrest: in 1817, all large public meetings were temporarily banned, and in November 1819, in the wake of the Peterloo Massacre, Parliament passed the notorious Six Acts, which, among other things, curtailed public gatherings, weakened the radical press, and facilitated the prosecution of disturbers of the peace. After 1822, reforms were gradually introduced, but there was certainly no dramatic return to the radical optimism briefly inspired by the French Revolution (even though such sentiment was momentarily rekindled among some intellectuals by the Greek crusade against the Ottoman Empire, which erupted in war in 1821).

The social disturbances that consolidated the British government's conservatism also brought pressure on middle-class women to conform to increasingly rigid standards of propriety. The close association of women with domestic harmony (which, as we have noted, developed in response to the French Revolution) seemed to make the gentler sex the guardians of social security. Moreover, what looked like the disintegration of working-class families made middle-class women themselves more anxious to defend their proper sphere. As factories gradually increased in number in the first decades of the century, the greater numbers of working mothers and children seemed to foretell the end of that most cherished middle-class institution, the family. Lord Ashley, seventh earl of Shaftesbury, worried that "domestic life and domestic discipline must soon be at an end; society will consist of individuals no longer grouped into families; so early is the separation of husband and wife, of parents and children."[11] In the context of such social chaos, middle-class women worked hard to protect themselves and their families from behavior associated with the lower classes. At the same time, as England's propertied classes gradually recovered from the economic threat of the first two decades of the century, they hired more servants to take over the household chores that many middle-class women had traditionally assisted in. It quickly became a mark of distinction for a woman not to know how to cook or even to be familiar with the inside of her own kitchen.[12] The cultivation of conspicuous inactivity was increasingly considered to be one of women's most honorable occupations, second only to the perfection of her traditional maternal virtues. The woman without a home, without a husband, and without even a male relative willing to act on her behalf was in a difficult position indeed.

Mary Shelley's anomalous social position was further complicated by the cloud of scandal that trailed her parents, her husband, her friends, and herself and by her aspirations for her surviving child, Percy Florence. Percy Florence stood to inherit his grandfather's title. Mary would not allow Sir Timothy to raise her son, but she was ambitious for Percy Florence in the most conventional sense of the word. Sir Timothy, however, disapproved of Mary as thoroughly as did the rest of polite society. When she returned to England, he at first refused to grant her or her son any allowance ("I think that her conduct was the very reverse of what it ought to have been"),[13] and when she published Percy's *Posthumous Poems,* he demanded that she suppress the edition and give up the meager stipend he had reluctantly allotted her.

In spite of England's conservatism and her own traditional ambitions for her son, the first extended literary work Shelley produced after returning to London is thematically more akin to her early novels than to her last three. Shelley's first winter in her home country was lonely and dreary, and she was filled with increasing doubts about her own intellectual and imaginative abilities. "My imagination is dead," she repeatedly lamented; "my ideas stagnate and my understanding refuses to follow the words I read" (*MSJ*, p. 192). Taking up in earnest the creative activity Percy had so encouraged no doubt seemed to her a means of retaining for as long as possible her precarious hold on the past. When that hold was further jeopardized by Byron's death in Greece in May 1824, Shelley set out to memorialize her friends and reinforce her own image of herself as Percy's worthy successor in a form appropriate to the intensity of her own feelings. The result was *The Last Man,* a "tale romantic beyond romance," as Mary had once called her life with Percy (*MSJ*, p. 186), for it relates the story of the gradual destruction of humanity from the point of view of the last man on earth.

Shelley's express desire may have been to honor Percy's life, but the disappointment and grief that characterize *The Last Man* actually condemn his political and personal optimism. Moreover, in *The Last Man,* the ambivalence that had begun to cloud her feelings about Percy shortly before his death surfaces in a form that challenges the adoration she now professes to feel. In this novel we see, more clearly than before, the way that what looks like an exploration of the self can serve as a defense of the self; and we also see the way that objectifying and compartmentalizing emotional complexities can obscure the ambivalence of one's feelings rather than generate anxiety. Shelley used these strategies to disown the resentment that stirs up guilt and also to court sympathy for herself as a suffering survivor. As she remarked, "The accumulating sorrows of days and weeks [were] forced to find a voice" (*MSJ*, p. 193).

The Last Man completes Shelley's chronicle of maturation and therefore constitutes a logical sequel to the 1818 *Frankenstein.* But, like *Mathilda* and *Valperga, The Last Man* disavows *Frankenstein's* condemnation of the egotist as origin and agent of destruction, for here, again, Shelley directs responsibility away from the artist-protagonist to impersonal forces. In many ways, *The Last Man* bridges the 1818 and 1831 *Frankensteins*; but, as we will see, only its critical and popular receptions begin to account for the dramatic turn against imaginative self-assertion that marks the rest of Shelley's career.

Like all of her early novels, *The Last Man* dramatizes the way that egotistical ambition threatens domestic harmony. Among its characters, the most obvious transgressor is Lord Raymond, the fictional counterpart of Byron. Counterposed to him is Adrian, an idealized version of Percy Shelley.

Raymond, whose "passions were violent,"

> looked on the structure of society as but a part of the machinery which
> supported the web on which his life was traced. The earth was spread out as
> an highway for him; the heavens built up as a canopy for him.

Adrian, on the other hand,

> felt that he made a part of a great whole. He owned affinity not only with
> mankind, but all nature was akin to him; the mountains and sky were his
> friends; the winds of heaven and the offspring of earth his playmates; while
> he the focus only of this mighty mirror, felt his life mingle with the universe
> of existence. His soul was sympathy, and dedicated to the worship of beauty
> and excellence.[14]

Raymond marries Perdita, the sister of Lionel Verney, the narrator,
who is Mary Shelley's own persona; but Raymond's political enthusiasm soon causes him to neglect, then betray, his wife. Further unify-
ing their small domestic circle, Verney marries Adrian's sister, Idris.
Ironically, only Adrian, with his indiscriminately sympathetic soul,
fails to establish a domestic relationship; he is "destined," as Shelley
phrases it, "not to find the half of himself."

Despite the fact that Shelley raises here, as she did in 1818, the
specter of murderous ambition, Raymond's personal transgressions
are not really responsible for the destruction that blasts domestic
harmony. The immediate agent of death is instead, the "PLAGUE"—an
infection that boils up not out of overweening human desire but out
of nature, and, beyond that, out of inscrutable fate or "Necessity."
Nothing any individual can do in any way affects this relentless force.
"Nature, our mother, and our friend, had turned on us a brow of
menace. She shewed us plainly, that, though she permitted us to
assign her laws and subdue her apparent powers, yet, if she put forth
but a finger, we must quake. She could take our globe . . . and cast
it into space, where life would be drunk up, and man and all his
efforts for ever annihilated" (p. 168). "Mother of the world!" Verney
exclaims in the throes of his anguish; "Servant of the Omnipotent!
eternal, changeless Necessity!" (p. 290).

Significantly, all the destructive forces in this novel—the "PLAGUE,"
Necessity, and nature—are feminine. This personification is one form
in which Shelley externalizes the pain, anger, and conflicted energy
she feels as a powerless woman; like the monster and the deadly ice
floes of *Frankenstein*, this destructive natural force is the essence of
female nature.[15] The difference here is that, in being split off from the
human ambition dramatized in *The Last Man*, this force is much more
detached from both Shelley's fictional persona and her authorial
"self." Typically in *The Last Man*, she distances whatever aggressive
emotions she may feel, either by apportioning them among the other

characters or by submerging them within loneliness and grief, emotions that attest to the sufferer's attachment to others, not to her self-indulgence. Shelley's fictionalization of such readily identifiable real-life prototypes as Byron and Percy Shelley is one facet of this defensive strategy. Even if she senses in herself the ambition Raymond embodies or the idealistic longings of Adrian, her readers, recognizing these characters as Byron and Percy Shelley, would attribute such emotions to them, not to Mary Shelley. For all intents and purposes, Shelley is placing herself on the outside of such emotions; as the witness, the auditor, of heroic passions and unconventional deeds, Shelley/Verney seems less the agent than the victim of unladylike feelings.

As another part of this defensive gesture, Shelley divides her own turbulent emotions among the attitudes implied toward several different characters. By separating her ambivalence toward someone like Percy, for example, into simpler emotions for two different characters, she can express two conflicting attitudes without directly investigating their relationship to each other or to Shelley's own image of herself. Thus, for example, her admiration for Percy is represented in the characterization of Adrian, but her reservations about his otherworldliness are expressed also, in her characterization of the second Percy-figure, the astronomer Merrival.[16] Merrival is "far too long sighted in his view of humanity to heed the casualties of the day" (p. 209); he continues analyzing the earth's axis even as the plague destroys all of London's citizens, including his own children. The preoccupied scientist is finally punished for neglecting domestic responsibilities, however, for on the death of his self-sacrificing wife he goes mad. Like the rebuke to Percy's political idealism, which implicitly governs the plot of The Last Man,[17] this criticism of his tendency to sacrifice present realities for future (im)possibilities allows Shelley to vent her hostility without really acknowledging it or considering its effects on her own life.

The ambivalence Mary felt for Percy Shelley no doubt had as many sources as it had incarnations. On the one hand, Percy had given the young Mary Godwin profound love, sympathy, and understanding at the very time when Godwin seemed most distant and judgmental. On the other hand, Mary seems never to have felt comfortable with the practical manifestations of Percy's idealistic notions about love. Periodically, she was simply—but intensely—jealous, as, for example, during her first pregnancy, when Percy seemed to spend too many late evenings talking with Claire, or, again, during the winter of 1820, when he reveled in his brief infatuation for the nineteen-year-old Emilia Viviani, or, again, during the last weeks of his life, when he seemed inordinately interested in Jane Williams. In retrospect,

Mary probably felt guilty about her suspicions and about the attitude of indifference her pain caused her to project. A number of her friends—Leigh Hunt, Edward Trelawny, then Jane Williams—accused her of having a "cold heart," and she anguished that Percy might have felt the same.[18] Yet the pain she had felt was also real, and no amount of retroactive remorse could totally efface its memory. Then, too, Percy had given Mary an image of herself that was compelling in many ways but in others was almost crippling. The image of a bold, imaginative, famous artist was difficult to live up to in the best of times—even for a man; for a woman, in these worst of times, such an ideal seemed not only unrealizable but frankly undesirable. No doubt Mary Shelley felt guilty about abandoning Percy's ideals; but she may well have equally resented the pressure this ideal exerted upon her. All of Mary Shelley's novels contain some trace of her attempts to come to terms with these conflicting feelings; but in the novels she wrote after Percy's death, her particular struggle was to submerge whatever anger she still felt in emotions that she— and the ideal of propriety that was replacing Percy's ideal—could countenance. For Shelley needed to be able to retain her cherished memories of Percy's love, but she also needed to live in the society she had chosen to rejoin.

In keeping with this design, Shelley's persona in *The Last Man*, Lionel Verney, voices not anger but resignation and pain. To escape the plague, the last citizens of England had sought "some natural Paradise, some garden of the earth" (p. 226), as if they could halt the ravages of the plague by returning to the origin of the species, back beyond childhood, beyond the Fall, into the womb of humanity. But their flight away from death, metaphorically back through time, demonstrates only how irreversible their collective fate is. Gradually stripped of all of humanity's civilizing accomplishments—of nations and social order, of science and the arts—the few survivors still find themselves *outside* the secret of their original purity, still fallen and like "our first parents expelled from Paradise" (p. 234). Their ultimate destination proves to be not some miraculous garden of innocence but humanity's lowest common denominator, a hideous equality before death (an equality surely more imaginable for a woman than the political equality Percy dreamed of). They realize this common bond only when they reach "the bones of the world" (p. 308; the phrase comes from Wollstonecraft's *Letters Written . . . in Sweden*), the rocks at the foot of Mont Blanc. As in *Frankenstein*, Shelley's presentation of this scene is almost supernaturally charged, for the setting represents for her nature's icy, indifferent heart, an "eternal sepulchre" that swallows up the bodies of most of the survivors and even the plague itself. Having reached this bleakness, Verney and his three remaining companions seem to pass beyond the origin of humanity, beyond human time, and into a new world, depopulated, but beautiful in its eerie silence, rich with the relics of dead civilizations, and replete with all the meaningless—because inhuman—treasures of the world.

The effect of dramatizing the destruction of humanity is to collapse the narrative until Verney/Mary Shelley fills the entire lens. In the empty world the plague leaves behind, Shelley's nightmare of her own maturity is fully dramatized; its defining characteristics, as the preceding stories of infidelity, jealousy, and death foretold, are pain, loss, and grief. Here Shelley does not envision further development for the individual or even a relief from suffering. Her version of maturity is not a process toward, or the achievement of, self-knowledge or self-fulfillment but a state of incompletion prolonged into eternity. The family, which seemed to promise mature relationships in *Frankenstein,* has been destroyed by fate; nothing remains but the isolated individual, who, in grieving loudly for others, weeps silently for him/herself. Grief is the one emotion about which Shelley feels no ambivalence, for its intensity is proof of her immortal love for her lost friends. In passage after passage she details Verney's grief, embellishing it with classical allusions, until it "fills all things, and, like light, it gives its own colours to all" (p. 325)—until, that is, it achieves mythic proportions. Increasingly, Shelley is swept up in what she calls "the grand conclusion":

> Arise, black Melancholy! quit thy Cimmerian solitude! Bring with thee murky fogs from hell, which may drink up the day; bring blight and pestiferous exhalations, which, entering the hollow caverns and breathing places of earth, may fill her stony veins with corruption, so that not only herbage may no longer flourish, the trees may rot, and the rivers run with gall—but the everlasting mountains be decomposed, and the mighty deep putrify, and the genial atmosphere which clips the globe, lose all powers of generation and sustenance. Do this, sad visaged power, while I write. [P. 318]

As in Wollstonecraft's two *Vindications,* Shelley's artificial rhetoric aspires to link her personal emotion to a venerable tradition. But whereas Wollstonecraft employed rhetorical formulas to control emotion, Shelley is using them primarily to legitimize—and even to inflate—feelings that are already very powerful. Predictably, this emotional self-indulgence has a highly ambiguous effect. Extracts from Shelley's journal of this period suggest that what had begun as a means of retaining contact with her heroic past and Percy's memory rapidly degenerated into an intensified anxiety about her own abilities and the effectiveness of what she was doing. "I have no great faith in my success," she lamented in September. "Composition is delightful, but if you do not expect the sympathy of your fellow creatures in what you write, the pleasure of writing is of short duration" (*MSJ,* p. 195).

Shelley was beginning to realize that imaginative communion with the past could not provide a surrogate for relationships, and, along with that, she was beginning to realize that writing (especially the kind of uninhibited flaunting of emotion she was given to) did not, as she had once feared, pose a threat to relationships but in fact *depended on* a sympathetic audience. In the absence of Percy's active support, Shelley found herself reduced to begging for sympathy from her audience. She continued to write even after her imaginative contact with Percy failed only because she tried to construct her narrative so that pity would be the only possible response. Yet even as she indulged her craving for sympathy and indulged her self-obsession, she despised herself for her vanity. In her journal she wrote: "Writing this is useless; it does not even soothe me; on the contrary, it irritates me by showing the pitiful expedient to which I am reduced" (*MSJ,* p. 196). By objectifying her grief in this way, she could see clearly the extent to which her sorrow was pure egotism.

In many ways, the development of Verney in *The Last Man* mirrors the defensiveness with which Shelley tries to deal with her emotions. His initial determination to explore his present psychological condition as well as his past rapidly diminishes in the course of his narrative. The deeper he probes into his own heart, the more repulsed he is by what he sees there, the more anxious he is to retreat into reverie or fantasy—even if such dreams are delusive. In Verney's increasing reluctance to examine himself, to fall into what he calls "the abyss of the present—into self-knowledge—into tenfold sadness" (p. 337), we can glimpse one facet of Shelley's growing hesitation about the feelings she has toward Percy's aesthetic ideal. The pity she seeks for herself through Verney is part of her simplification of her own emotional complexity. For although her characterization of Verney incorporates traits of both Frankenstein and the monster, the emotional affect he inherits from each emanates not from Verney's guilt but only from his pathos. In "I am a tree rent by lightning," he echoes Frankenstein (p. 329), and, catching sight of his reflection in a mirror, he sees in himself an incarnation of the monster: "My long and tangled hair hung in elf locks on my brow—my dark eyes, now hollow and wild, gleamed from under them—my cheeks were discoloured by the jaundice, which (the effect of misery and neglect) suffused my skin, and were half hid by a beard of many days' growth" (p. 331). All traces of ambition and egotism are gone; even the monstrosity that had been its symbol is now merely a realistic symptom of disease, brought on by "misery and neglect." In *The Last Man,* Shelley also invokes a comparison with "that monarch of the waste—Robinson Crusoe"; but here Defoe's hero is diminished by Verney's unrivaled suffering: "Yet he was far happier than I: for he could hope" (p. 326).

One of the reasons why Shelley, in treating her own suffering, rejects psychological complexity for a simplified indulgence of self-pity is that this strategy enables her to atone for her past transgressions even as she solicits sympathy for her present anguish. Here her ambivalence about the past is pronounced. Her defiant adolescence and its series of calamities had undeniably brought her much pain, but those years had also made her a distinguished person, had made her life romantic, had given her what seemed like a legitimate basis for prolonging her claim to sympathy. Shelley's attitude toward professional writing is tangled up with these emotions. She still sees writing as a means of keeping open an avenue to the past and of preserving the self Percy had convinced her was worthy, but increasingly she is also using her craft to manipulate her audience through her own self-presentation. Once more Verney's attitude toward writing illuminates Shelley's strategy. When Verney decides to become a writer, he initially extolls the way the occupation enlarges relationships: as an author he becomes the "father of all mankind," "an eager aspirant to the praise and sympathy of [his] fellow men." By addressing an imaginary reader (pp. 199, 230, 291, 318) he keeps the illusion of community alive, but his further comments reveal that writing is also a form of denying the present by manipulating his self-presentation. Through his imaginative exertions, Verney keeps the past vital, and, despite incursions of present grief, he manages to project a self that defies maturity and is, as a consequence, still loving and beloved: "There was a glade . . . there am I now; Idris, in youth's dear prime, is by my side—remember, I am just twenty-two, and seventeen summers have scarcely passed over the beloved of my heart" (p. 57). Writing, Verney claims, is "an opiate," but it is also a means of controlling the past and of enhancing his own present relation to it:

> Time and experience have placed me on an height from which I can comprehend the past as a whole; and in this way I must describe it, bringing forward the leading incidents, and disposing light and shade so as to form a picture in whose very darkness there will be harmony. . . ; mellowing the lurid tints of past anguish with poetic hues, I am able to escape from the mosaic of circumstance, by perceiving and reflecting back the grouping and combined colouring of the past. [Pp. 192–93]

Reclaiming the past enables Verney to achieve personal significance and self-definition; the notion of fate imposes a plot on the past and gives him the leading role. Even though he purports to be the willing servant of his materials, Verney "mellows" past emotion, just as Wollstonecraft used imaginative excursions to mitigate the boredom of long dinners in Sweden. The difference is, of course, that whereas in such passages Wollstonecraft exposed the resources and limitations of her persona, Shelley returns to her past to revise it. Taking Verney's "mellowing" one step further, Shelley imaginatively makes herself over into the person she now wishes she had been. In her introduction to *The Last Man,* Shelley announces that composing this story serves for her the same dual function that writing serves Verney: it simultaneously preserves the past and gives her imaginative power over it. As she remarks: "My labours have cheered long hours of solitude, and taken me out of a world, which has averted its once benignant face from me, to one glowing with imagination and power" (p. 4).

The most explicit example of Shelley's self-revision in *The Last Man* occurs in her dramatization of Adrian's death. Spared from the plague, Adrian dies—as Percy Shelley did—in a storm-tossed sea. But now Mary Shelley projects herself into that fateful memory, and in the process she imagines superhuman but futile efforts to save her husband's life.

> I thought I saw Adrian at no great distance from me, clinging to an oar; I sprung from my hold, and with energy beyond my human strength, I dashed aside the waters as I strove to lay hold of him. As that hope failed, instinctive love of life animated me, and feelings of contention, as if a hostile will combated with mine. I breasted the surges, and flung them from me, as I would the opposing front and sharpened claws of a lion about to enfang my bosom. When I had been beaten down by one wave, I rose on another, while I felt bitter pride curl my lip. [P. 323]

Shelley not only retroactively dramatizes her desire to save Percy's life; she also depicts her own survival as having been won precisely at the cost of repressing contending emotions. The "feelings of contention" here may literally refer to the power of the waves Verney battles, but Shelley's formulation of this struggle also suggests a contest between the egotistical "love of life" and the "hope" the drowning Adrian elicits from Verney. Along with her feminization of destructive forces, this moment comes closest to exposing the complexities of Shelley's residual feelings about the past and about Percy Shelley in particular. Had she been there, she suggests, her exertion for Percy's safety would have been "beyond [her] human strength." But, in a sense vivid to her imagination, his was "a hostile will"; the expectations Percy held for Mary were like the "sharpened claws of a lion about to enfang [her] bosom." Her response to his expectations, while tinged with regret, is now triumphantly defiant: "I breasted the surges," she exults, "and flung them from me. . . . When I had been beaten down by one wave, I rose on another."

Despite this moment of self-assertion, Verney responds to the situation in which he finally finds himself by the typically feminine gesture of humble resignation, the proud embrace of fatality. His responses are, in fact, so consistently feminine that one reviewer was provoked to ask why Mary Shelley did not write about being "*the last Woman.*"[19] Verney cries unrestrainedly when Raymond dies, and he finds his greatest fulfillment in protecting his own domestic tranquillity. Mary Shelley's use of a male persona suggests, then, not the wishful assumption of a stronger self but, simply, another strategy of indirection, intended to sanction her self-assertion and her demands for sympathy. As a man, Verney can indisputably deserve attention, and he is more justified than a woman would be in telling his story and inscribing his final message prominently in all the cities of the earth. Interestingly enough, Mary Shelley displaces many of her less praiseworthy traits onto female characters in the story, as if further to idealize Verney's persona. Perdita, for example, is sullen and withdrawn as a child, and Idris initiates the elopement with Verney and, in consequence, is rejected by her parent.

Shelley places her most elaborate strategy of indirection in the "Author's Introduction" to the text, a ruse which, as we have seen, she later used in revising *Frankenstein.* Here she defers responsibility for the story by claiming that she has only "faithfully transcribed" it from "Sibylline leaves." But she also reminds us that, like Verney's role in "bringing forward" the past, her contribution of "links" and "a consistent form" is crucial: "Sometimes I have thought, that, obscure and chaotic as they are, they owe their present form to me, their decipherer." Almost immediately, however, she qualifies this claim: "My only excuse for thus transforming them, is that they were unintelligible in their pristine condition" (p. 4).

In their "pristine condition" the fragments of *The Last Man* were leaves and pieces of bark covered with writing in a variety of languages—"ancient Chaldee, and Egyptian hieroglyphics" as well as English and Italian. Mary claims that she and Percy discovered these leaves in 1818, deep in the "gloomy cavern of the Cumaean Sibyl," and that, in the months since Percy's death, she has devoted herself to the task of translating them. The result of this elaborate narrative and temporal mediation is an ostentatious disengagement of Mary Shelley from a story that is patently autobiographical. For the leaves that Shelley claims to have found eight years before were theoretically written in the distant past, even before Virgil told of the Sibyl's existence. Yet they contain the history of the future, a narrative that describes the end of all possibility of relationship and that speaks, through Shelley, to readers who predate the events of the story they read. This extensive distancing of the emotion and events of *The Last Man* is Shelley's most complex strategy for simultaneously sanctioning and disavowing the publication of her most private grief. Like another incarnation of the Sybil, whom Lord Dillon would later imagine her to be, Shelley is and is not the subject of her own story, just as she is and is not the author of this most romantic of all tales.

SHELLEY HAD STAKED her emotional and financial security on *The Last Man,* and it proved to be a critical and popular disaster. *Blackwood's Magazine,* for example, complained of its "stupid cruelties," and *The London Magazine and Review* dismissed it with a single sentence: "The Last Man is an elaborate piece of gloomy folly—bad enough to read—horrible to write." *The Monthly Review* charged that it was "the product of a diseased imagination and a polluted taste," more qualified to be a lecture in the anatomy of illness than amusement for polite readers.[20] This nearly universal rejection of the persona that represented Shelley's uneasy truce with the past followed immediately on Sir Timothy Shelley's decision to suppress her edition of Percy's *Posthumous Poems,* and that, in turn, was followed by his angry withdrawal of her meager allowance and, the next summer, by what Mary believed to be a betrayal by her best friend, Jane Williams.[21] One effect of these rebuffs was to weld Mary Shelley's sense of personal guilt and disappointment to her attitude toward imaginative self-expression; more specifically, she now completely rejected the image of the boldly original artist that Percy had embodied and encouraged. From this time until her death, claiming to be motivated only by financial necessity, Shelley composed novels and stories carefully calculated to win public respect and economic returns—designed, that is, to earn acceptance by the society she had once defied and whose rejection was now proving so painful and so crippling.

Shelley's retreat from personal exposure, unorthodox subjects, and, consequently, from emotional investment in her writing suggests that her embrace of propriety—which had begun, tentatively, as early as 1818, in the original version of *Frankenstein*—now quickly intensified. There were, clearly, very practical reasons for distancing herself from the personality and behavior her society found offensive; quite simply, the failure of *The Last Man* threatened her with financial disaster. Claire Clairmont, for example, had recently lost her post as a governess because her employer had discovered her scandalous past. ("You may imagine this man's horror when he heard who I was; that the charming Miss Clairmont, the model of good sense, accomplishments, and good taste, was brought, issued from the very den of freethinkers").[22] In order to support herself successfully, a woman had no choice but to conform to social norms.

Claire Clairmont begrudged paying her dues to orthodoxy, but the vehemence of Shelley's conventionality suggests that, after *The Last Man,* she did not acquiesce simply in order to make money but was, instead, passionately interested in disavowing what she now agreed were the crimes of her youth (she once remarked in her journal that she considered her own "heavy sorrows" to be "the atonement claimed by fate" for Harriet Shelley's suicide [*MSJ*, p. 207]). Unlike Claire Clairmont, Mary did not insist that she was hiding her "real" personality from society's gaze.[23] She wanted to forge a *new* personality— one that would not offend but that could still incorporate the emotional needs that would not die. Thus, between 1829 and 1831, Shelley's dislike of personal exposure grew to "horror" as she struggled to revise her offensive past. The horror shows in her response to Edward Trelawny, who had asked for documents for a proposed life of Percy Shelley.

> There is nothing I shrink from more fearfully than publicity. . . . Could you write my husband's life, without naming me it were something—but even then I should be terrified at the rousing the slumbering voice of the public—each critique, each mention of your work, might drag me forward— Nor indeed is it possible to write Shelley's life in that way. Many men have his opinions— none fearlessly and conscientiously act on them, as he did—it is his act that marks him—and that—You know me—or you do not, in which case I will tell you what I am—a silly goose—who far from wishing to stand forward to assert myself in any way, now that I am alone in the world, have but the desire to wrap night and the obscurity of insignificance around me. This is weakness— but I cannot help it—to be in print—the subject of *men's* observations—of the bitter hard world's commentaries, to be attacked or defended!—this ill becomes one who knows how little she possesses worthy to attract attention— and whose chief merit—if it be one—is a love of that privacy which no woman can emerge from without regret. . . . I only seek to be forgotten. [*MWSL*, 2:13–14; April 1829]

Shelley both wants and does not want to be severed from her husband's story; his most memorable "fearless" act, she suggests, involved his relationship with her, and she wants to preserve that sign of love as integral to both their histories. Yet the implications of that act appall her, and once more she considers herself unworthy—now not of her parents' reputation or Percy's respect, but of society's attention. Dreading the public scandal she had once provoked, Shelley retreats with relief to the conventional feminine protection of obscurity.

Falkner

Mary Shelley's last three novels reveal the way in which stereotypical feminine propriety could disguise—and even accommodate— the kind of unladylike aggression she had expressed in the productions of her youth. These late novels, and Shelley's public statements about them, suggest that by 1830 she had totally rejected both Wollstonecraft's goal of "rest[ing] on [her] own" and Percy's ideal of artistic originality. Writing them occupied much less of Shelley's time and attention than the earlier works had, they were all written expressly for money, and Shelley speaks approvingly of them on two grounds only: she approves of *Perkin Warbeck* because it provides "no scope for *opinion*"[24] and of *Lodore* and *Falkner* because they deal with emotions that even the most Proper Lady would gladly own. Moreover, in each of these novels she either specifically revises incidents or emotions of her youthful life that she now considers unacceptable, or she explicitly justifies them to a reproving world. But countercurrents, present in each novel (and obtrusive in *Falkner*), reveal that the emotional complexity Shelley had once so freely acknowledged did not completely disappear when she reentered polite society. That Mary Shelley could continue to express unconventional feelings without being in any way "original" illuminates not only the ingenuity of her strategies for dealing with her persistent needs but also the complexity of the Proper Lady she effectively became.

Of the three late novels, *Falkner* most clearly reveals the compatibility between propriety and "unladylike" emotions. Ostensibly it is about fidelity, which Shelley called "the first of human virtues" (*MWSL*, 2:108; November 1835). Although the title character, Rupert Falkner, bears many resemblances to Edward Trelawny,[25] the fidelity his foster daughter Elizabeth expresses toward Falkner is clearly one version of the intense filial love Mary Shelley felt for William Godwin. Of her father, Mary had written in 1822 that "until I met Shelley I [could?] justly say that he was my God—and I remember many childish instances of the [ex]cess of attachment I bore for him."[26] Godwin apparently never satisfactorily returned Mary's love. He was distant during her childhood and disapproving during her adolescence; even after she and Percy were officially married, his attentions to her were less frequently expressions of love than remonstrations, wheedling complaints, and pleas for money. During Mary's long depression after young William's death, for example, Percy had to request a letter of consolation from Godwin, and the reply—an admonition against "selfishness and ill humour" in which Godwin warned Mary that her continued grief would cause her friends to "finally cease to love you, and scarcely learn to endure you"[27] —was so appalling that Percy rebuked this "hard-hearted person" for his insensitivity. And in May 1822, Percy began to intercept Godwin's letters because they "convey[ed] a supposition that she could do more than she does, thus exasperating the sympathy which she already feels too intensely for her fathers [financial] distress, which she would sacrifice all she posesses to remedy,—but the remedy of which is beyond her power."[28] After Percy's death, Godwin clearly felt that a barrier between him and his daughter had been removed, but once more his sympathy was tinged with self-pity. "You are now fallen to my own level; you are surrounded with adversity & with difficulty," he wrote; "& I no longer hold it sacrilege to trouble you with my adversities. We shall now truly sympathise with each other; & whatever misfortune or ruin falls upon me, I shall not now scruple to lay it fully before you."[29]

Mary Shelley was never fully able to free herself from the perhaps excessive sense of obligation she felt toward Godwin even when she recognized that his demands for support were increasingly unreasonable. However radical his youthful opinions may have been, he was obviously one important source of Mary's life-long allegiance to the conventional ideology of proper feminine behavior. As such, Godwin was directly opposed—in Mary's intellectual and emotional affiliations as well as in a more general sense—to both her mother and her lover. For any woman, at an unconscious level at least, redirecting her primary affiliation from her mother to her father to a lover is potentially traumatic; for Mary Shelley, this was particularly true. For in her case both the submerged conflict between her mother and her father and the more obvious conflict between her father and her lover were tied up with the conflict between propriety and originality—and thus with her own self-image. It was at least in part to resolve these fundamental psychological and social conflicts that Mary Shelley began to write *Falkner* in 1835.

The relationship that is initially foregrounded in *Falkner* is between a daughter and her father. Although the title character of the novel is not Elizabeth Raby's biological parent, their bond is in some ways even stronger, for Elizabeth's first gesture toward Rupert Falkner returns to an adult male the gift no daughter could give her father: life itself. Elizabeth is a little orphan who first sees Falkner as a distraught stranger, about to shoot himself. Grabbing his arm just as he pulls the trigger, she saves his life. Falkner then adopts Elizabeth, not simply from gratitude but because he discovers that the woman whose death he has caused was to have been Elizabeth's foster mother.

Like Elizabeth Lavenza, Elizabeth Raby grows up to epitomize feminine virtue. She becomes the type of "ideal and almost unnatural perfection. . . . She was intelligent, warm-hearted, courageous, and sincere. Her lively sense of duty was perhaps her chief peculiarity."[30] But like even the most proper young lady, Elizabeth soon meets and falls in love with a young man, Gerald Neville. Neville is nearly a savage when Elizabeth first meets him, for his mother, Alithea, had abandoned him when he was a child and, in retaliation, his father has now charged the missing woman with adultery. Neville has never lost faith in his mother, however, and he is attracted to the mirror image of his own fidelity in Elizabeth's love for Falkner. Responding to the young man and to her own inclinations, Elizabeth soon longs for some "link" to unite her "more than father" with her newest friend. Halfway through the first volume, Shelley makes it clear that the "link" indeed exists and that it will soon bring Elizabeth's two loves into a fateful confrontation.

> Little did she think of the real link that existed, mysterious, yet adamantine; that to pray for the success of one, was to solicit destruction for the other. A dark veil was before her eyes, totally impervious; nor did she know that the withdrawing it, as was soon to be, would deliver her over to conflicting duties, and struggles of feeling, and stain her life with the dark hues that now, missing her, blotted the existence of the two upon earth for whom she was most interested. [1:159–60]

Shelley's foreshadowing the conflict, and the terms in which she describes it, reveal that the heart of this novel is not to be the uncovering of the secret link but an exploration of its consequences, which are Elizabeth's "conflicting duties, and struggles of feeling." Indeed, before the end of the first volume, Shelley provides the reader with the background to which she has repeatedly alluded: the three women—Alithea (Neville's mother), the woman to whom Elizabeth's dying mother bequeathed her child, and the woman Falkner inadvertently destroyed—are all one and the same. Alithea was originally Falkner's beloved, yet at her father's insistence, and in Falkner's absence, she had married the uncouth Sir Boyville Neville. When Falkner returned to England, he had tried to force Alithea to abandon her husband and son for him; unable to persuade her, he had been driven to abduct her, only to have her escape, then drown while trying to rejoin her son. Obsessed with guilt, Falkner then fled England once more; and Alithea's husband, unable to locate his wife and unaware of her honorable death, initiated divorce proceedings on the grounds of adultery.

The entire second volume of *Falkner* focuses on the issue of fidelity: Alithea's impugned fidelity to her son, Neville's dogged fidelity to his mother's honor, and Elizabeth's fidelity to Falkner, which is now imperiled not only by her love for Neville but also by her strong identification with the wronged Alithea (2:89–91). Through an intricate series of coincidences, Shelley has simultaneously established fidelity as the highest of all virtues and placed that fidelity in the service of one who is patently blameworthy, who has been motivated throughout his life by "impetuosity and ill-regulated passions" (1:53), and whose past crimes now threaten to block Elizabeth's future happiness. Thus the barrier between Elizabeth's surrogate father and would-be lover is stronger than any a father's explicit disapproval could erect; for what both joins and divides the two men is simply "fate," and against fate Elizabeth cannot feel any self-righteous resentment. Because of the emphasis placed on fidelity, the solution to the dilemma cannot be that Neville, as Elizabeth's husband, be considered a second surrogate father for her (although Falkner proposes that at one point); the only satisfactory resolution is for both men to emulate Elizabeth's sacrifice of "inclination" to the higher principles of "duty." To bring this about, Neville ultimately represses his blind hatred of Falkner and sets out on a quest for the true story of his mother's death; then, after Falkner's eventual trial and exoneration, the two men join in the friendship necessary for "the happiness of the dearest and most perfect being in the world" (2:312). Only in the presence of such friendship can Elizabeth's two roles coalesce: she will marry Neville, but the couple will live with Elizabeth's "more than father" and devote their energies to "making him forget the past and rendering his future years calm and happy" (2:315).

Thus for—and through the example of—Elizabeth's love, two men master their strong passions and narrowly avert the crisis that Shelley had made to seem inevitable. Clearly, behind this knitting and unraveling of the central complication lies Shelley's exploration of the indirect but undeniable power of women. Not only Elizabeth, but Alithea before her, was willing to sacrifice love for duty, and the effect of such feminine heroism helps the more impetuous men subdue their desires and expand their definitions of both heroism and, ultimately, love. But despite Shelley's focus on the conflict between the two men and her explicit celebration of Elizabeth's self-denying and essentially passive role in effecting their reconciliation, the plot of the novel also suggests that, indirectly, Elizabeth is carrying out an office that is far more aggressive and passionate but is, at the same time, permitted, even sanctioned, by feminine propriety. In this novel, the father figure, Falkner, is actually being humbled by a daughter for crimes committed against the mother. In fact, as we explore the sources of energy of this novel, it seems clear that Mary Shelley is concerned at least as much with punishing the father as with defusing the threat he now poses to the daughter's future.[31]

The subplots of *Falkner* contain a number of examples of cruel, tyrannical fathers taking the place of loving mothers. Not only does the undemonstrative Sir Boyville prove a woefully inadequate substitute for Neville's beloved mother, but, before that, Alithea's own mother's death had left her dependent on a father whom Falkner describes as a "rude tyrant" (2:36). Falkner's mother also died when he was young, leaving him with memories of maternal caresses but the reality of a "rough and ill-tempered" father; "I am not going to dwell," he tells Elizabeth, "on those painful days, when a weak, tiny boy, I felt as if I could contend with the paternal giant; and did contend, till his hand felled me to the ground" (2:8).

Given this context, the adult Falkner can be seen as another trans-gressor into what should be the domain of maternal love. In his initial appearance he violates the young Elizabeth's daily communions with her mother's spirit, and Elizabeth's life-saving tug at Falkner's arm is in fact a gesture intended only to defend her mother's grave: "Oh go away!" the child cries to the trespassing man; "go away from mama!" (1:31). In the story that is gradually revealed, Falkner was twice the violator of the maternal bond: though not responsible for the death of Elizabeth's real mother, he has destroyed the woman who was to have been her surrogate mother and who was Neville's real mother. In a sense reminiscent of *Frankenstein,* the self-serving passions of the male destroy the happiness of innocent children. Falkner's passion, in fact, is his most salient characteristic; according to Shelley's explicit moralizing, even his devotion to Elizabeth is a willful, wishful indul-gence:

> He meditated doing rather what he wished, than what was strictly just. . . . What ills might arise to the orphan from his interweaving her fate with his—he, a criminal, in act, if not in intention—who might be called upon hereafter to answer for his deeds, and who at least must fly and hide himself—of this he thought not. . . . —and it was half unconsciously that he was building from them a fabric for the future, as deceitful as it was alluring. [1:52]

To the selfish passions of Falkner and the other fathers, Shelley contrasts the self-denying love of mothers. Her depiction, especially of Alithea, is frankly idealized, and the hyperbole suggests Shelley's most intense imaginative engagement. "The divine stamp on woman is her maternal character," she asserts (2:142), and she makes Eliza-beth respond to the history of Alithea by projecting herself imagina-tively into the older woman's feelings:

> To the last she [Alithea] was all mother; her heart filled with that deep yearning, which a young mother feels to be the very essence of her life, for the presence of her child. There is something so beautiful in a young mother's feelings. Usually a creature to be fostered and protected—taught to look to another for aid and safety; yet a woman is the undaunted guardian of her little child. She will expose herself to a thousand dangers to shield his fragile being from harm. . . . Readily, joyfully, she would give her own blood to sustain him. The world is a hideous desert when she is threatened to be deprived of him; and when he is near, and she takes him to the shelter of her bosom, and wraps him in her soft, warm embrace, she cares for nothing beyond that circle; and his smiles and infantine caresses are the life of her life. [2:91–92]

There is a curious—and compelling—division of imaginative sympa-thy here. In the pages just preceding this passage, Elizabeth, reliving

Alithea's last thoughts, clearly identifies with the dead mother; but as the passage itself progresses, the narrative consciousness moves closer to the sensibility of the child and projects itself into a "soft, warm embrace," where it is enclosed in a protecting circle of love. Thus, even as such passages celebrate womanly power, they also suggest the extent to which the narrative consciousness (whether we call it Elizabeth's or Mary Shelley's) longs for entry into just such a domain of maternal love. And it is this realm that the tyrannical fathers—Falkner among them—have violated.

In retaliation, Shelley imaginatively punishes the passionate father for his transgression. Elizabeth's love for her departed mother saves Falkner's life, but one effect of this intervention is to prolong Falkner's agony. In fact, the love that develops between Elizabeth and her surrogate father eventually serves to bring before him the crime he had tried to escape. It is obviously not part of Elizabeth's conscious design to make Falkner suffer, but the undeniable corollaries of Elizabeth's simultaneous love for Falkner and Neville are Falkner's admission of, and eventual trial for, his part in Alithea's death. Through Elizabeth, then, Falkner is doubly punished: he is called to personal and public account for his passionate behavior, and he is forced to seek forgiveness from the very person whose vengeance occasions his public humiliation. At the conclusion of the novel, Falkner's impetuous nature has been altogether subdued; still haunted by his sense of guilt, he is effectively reabsorbed into the domestic tranquillity he had once destroyed.

Thus Mary Shelley erects an apparently unassailable barrier between father and lover only to level it by female love, exemplary and compelling in its selflessness. Yet, despite its obvious structural importance, the confrontation between father and lover does not seem to occupy the emotional center of the novel. In the first place, Elizabeth never responds to her lover in a passionate way; in fact, her attractiveness comes precisely from the fact that her love replicates the one desire that propriety allows women to express freely—maternal love. In the second place, the threatened contest between the daughter's duty to her father and her love for another man primarily serves to remind us of another conflict that has already occurred. Behind the explicit cleaving to the father lies the dimly remembered and intensely idealized attachment to the mother. Thus Neville, the lover, cannot jeopardize what appears to be Elizabeth's primary emotional bond, for her real primary affection—for her mother—has already been violated by her tyrannical father.

Given Mary Shelley's complex relationships with William Godwin and with the legend of Mary Wollstonecraft, there seems to be ample justification for this kind of smoldering resentment against the father.

But the fact that she could not only harbor such aggressive feelings but also give voice to them—all the while endorsing, in every superficial respect, the values of the Proper Lady—exposes a more general point about the ideology of feminine propriety. For just as the hierarchy intrinsic to patriarchal society reinforces—psychologically as well as legally—women's inferiority, so the paradigm of propriety offers women compensatory power and, not incidentally, a legitimate avenue through which to act out what might seem to be impermissible, aggressive feelings.

In the models of maturation she introduced in *Frankenstein* and *The Last Man,* Mary Shelley revealed something of what growing up feels like to a young girl raised in patriarchal society. Twentieth-century feminists have recently begun to suggest why a young woman's psychological development might take such a course in such a society. Their explanation centers in a revision of Freud's theory of the oedipal conflict and an elaboration of the preoedipal development of the child. In this society, according to theorists like Nancy Chodorow, children of both sexes, partly for biological and partly for sociological reasons, form their initial, and in many ways their most influential, relationships with their mother. From the child's primary, preoedipal bond with the mother s/he ideally receives both the immediate satisfaction of physical and emotional needs and the foundation of the structured ego that will eventually be consolidated as "identity." For the male child, the critical moment of maturation occurs when this original heterosexual bond is threatened by the intervention of the rival father. In order to avoid confrontation with the stronger father, the boy represses his attachment to his mother and, in the "resolution" that is the basis of patriarchal society,[32] transfers his identification from his mother to his father. Identifying with his father assures the boy that he can eventually form another primary relationship with someone *like* his mother and thus protects him from traumatic loss. For the male child, then, the development of a strong social persona is at least theoretically possible; maturation is a relatively continuous process, marked primarily by the intervention of the father, which, paradoxically, first deprives the boy of power but then gives it back to him through the male's (superior) position in patriarchal society. Of course, the male's social and psychological maturation rarely culminates in complete autonomy; because his mature heterosexual love is derived from—and depends on the repression of—his original love for his mother, even the grown man remains particularly susceptible to the influence of a maternal figure. At least sensitive to, though no doubt not fully aware of, this male susceptibility, Mary Shelley and the paradigm of propriety to which she conformed exploited this vulnerability in the particular form of female power they imagined.

In patriarchal society, however, the process of maturation does not promise even qualified social autonomy for a girl. Like the boy, the girl originally identifies with the mother, but for her this preoedipal identification is more formative and long-lived than the boy's identification. Within this primary relationship the girl confronts such basic psychic issues as identity, love, dependence, and separation without the threat of an aggressive competitor. The father never poses a serious threat to her relationship with her mother; therefore the girl never needs to identify with him. Instead, her identification with her (socially) weak mother remains dominant, and the girl never develops the strong superego that would enable her to free herself from her original dependence.[33] The moment at which a girl transfers her love from her father to a (male) lover is a particularly critical juncture in this process, for choosing the man who will take the father's place necessitates a second identification with her mother and thus reinforces, rather than qualifies, the girl's sense of her own inferiority.

Despite the fact that during Shelley's historical period young people of both sexes had begun to have more control over the marriage choice, women's increased social power was not automatically accompanied by complete psychological freedom. Indeed, given this psychological configuration, which is much slower to change than its social counterpart, the very moment that should epitomize a girl's social power does not necessarily do so at all. Far from allowing her to express autonomous desire, in fact, this moment brings to the surface the complex facets of the girl's psychological immaturity. Within the institutions of patriarchal society, the apparent achievement of social self-determination is in fact false: as a wife the young woman will be as dependent as she was as a daughter. Nevertheless, the emotional demands of the situation are real: the moment of choice dictates that the woman take the initiative—or at least the responsibility—for rejecting her father and installing another man in his place. The consequence of these demands—in the face of the girl's inability to meet them—is the exposure of two critical aspects of the female situation: the girl sees that her relationship with her father has been largely idealized, and she intuits, however dimly, that the man she has idealized is, in fact, the tyrant of patriarchal society. For Mary Shelley, articulating the prerogatives of feminine propriety, these truths both delimit the opportunities for female self-expression and constitute the foundation for woman's power.

The reasons for a girl's idealization of the father, Nancy Chodorow suggests, involve both his general inaccessibility and the strength of her libidinal attachment to her mother. In patriarchal society, men are typically not responsible for child care; hence, the physical remoteness of the father allows the girl to project onto him the illusion that he is capable of satisfying perfectly all the needs that the real mother imperfectly fulfills. This illusion is necessary to the girl's ability to disengage herself even partially from her dependence on and identification with the mother. The young girl, Chodorow explains,

> (and the woman she becomes) is willing to deny her father's limitations (and those of her lover or husband) as long as she feels loved. She is more able to do this because his distance means that she does not really know him. The relationship, then, because of the father's distance and importance to her, occurs largely as fantasy and idealization, and lacks the grounded reality which a boy's relation to his mother has.[34]

In Mary Shelley's case, this idealized relationship was doubly determined because the father's psychological remoteness was intensified by Godwin's emotional distance and because the real mother had been replaced by a despised stepmother. Given this situation, it is not surprising that in Mary Shelley's own youth and in *Falkner* (and, in a slightly different sense, in *Frankenstein*) the motherless daughter's relationship with the father carries the burden of needs originally and ideally satisfied by the mother; in a sense, the relationship with each father is only an imaginative substitute for the absent relationship with the mother. But the young girl cannot recognize that this substitution has occurred until she has sufficient psychological security to risk the loss of her idealized version of her father—until, that is, another idealized male stands ready to replace him. Thus Mary Shelley characterizes the awakening of the daughter's romantic affection as the action that precipitates confrontation with the father. For Shelley, then, even though she may only intuit this, the central confrontation is not between the father and the lover but between the father and the daughter—or, more precisely, between the daughter's idealized version of the father and the other version of him she now sees.

The "other version" of the father is virtually the opposite of the idealized protector the young girl had imagined. The "real" father, Shelley's novel implies, is passionate and willful, and, as such, he is the destroyer of the mother, whose self-denying love was powerless before him. As guardian of patriarchal society, the father is the tyrant who blocks a woman's social and psychological maturity, destroys domestic tranquillity, and reduces both mother and daughter to "cyphers" within the home that should shelter them. For the daughter, the ambivalence this revelation awakens toward the father may then surface as anger, resentment, or—as a cover for these aggressions—as excessive and compensatory fidelity.

But within the woman's position of inferiority and dependence Mary Shelley identifies sources and resources of power—effective and acceptable means of expressing her female characters' (and her own) aggressive resentment and desires. When her heroine discovers the true nature of her father, she also discovers her own legitimate social office: as "representative" of her mother, Elizabeth Raby—like Elizabeth Lavenza before her—is to carry out the maternal role; she is to civilize, to socialize, passionate men. The expression of her anger, like the expression of her desire, must be indirect, but assuming the role of a mother affords Elizabeth both the satisfaction of retaliating against the father and the comfort of doing her social duty. The expression of these unconscionable wishes, of course, requires the illusion—though not the reality—of self-effacement. Thus in *Falkner* the punishment of the father is exacted on behalf of the wronged mother, not on behalf of the self. Moreover, the father openly ac-knowledges his guilt; Elizabeth does not have to accuse him, for Rupert Falkner interprets the daughter's mere presence as the sign of the punishment he deserves. The anger behind the daughter's revenge is therefore displaced, as is the desire to punish. Elizabeth does not consciously want or try to punish her stepfather; yet, be-cause she is presented as taking the place of the wronged mother, her very presence pricks the male's conscience and thus initiates the punishment she unconsciously desires. To further defuse her resent-ment, Shelley mediates this confrontation even more by displacing not only the parental relations involved but the biographical object of her resentment. In *Falkner,* both the wronged mother and the passionate father are surrogates for Elizabeth's biological parents; moreover, the guilty figure of William Godwin is conflated with the less emotionally charged figure of Edward Trelawny. Thus no explicit confrontation with the real father need occur (for Elizabeth or for Mary Shelley). The indirect expression of power permissible to a woman can effectively articulate her desire, no matter how unconven-tional her feelings might be.

As the legitimate agents for socializing men (a role in which nearly every late eighteenth- and early nineteenth-century moralist approv-ingly cast them), women could actually retaliate against their legal superiors. Within the paradigm of propriety, not only could passivity easily assume an aggressive form, as psychologists have long noted, but exercising influence could also focus and articulate personal (if unconscious) resentment in the name of social well-being. As we have seen, in their campaign to control aggressive female sexuality, late eighteenth-century and Victorian moralists reversed the late seven-teenth-century depiction of women; ironically, this reversal effectively provided women with a new vehicle for expressing their aggression—

a vehicle which, because it reinforced society's institutions rather than threatened them, may have permitted the expression of a greater range of emotions than its predecessor. As Proper Ladies, and acting in the name of duty, the very women who had initially been instructed to regulate their own passions eventually became the wardens of men's desires, authorized to punish the men society set over them.

It is at least partly because the paradigm of feminine propriety accommodates such aggression that it consolidated its power so quickly and has retained that power for so long. For Mary Shelley, as, no doubt, for many other women who led more conventional lives, this model of behavior answered nearly every need: it enabled her to win social approval, to channel her impermissible aggressions into acceptable expression, to retreat from public view, and yet to display her sense of her own self-importance in an indirect but effective form. Shelley's retreat from political prominence must be seen, then, not as simple cowardice but as part of a self-revision that permitted her to take refuge in—while taking full advantage of—the resources of her culture's ideology. That that ideology was restrictive, even crippling, is undeniable. But it is important for us to recognize that it did not altogether stifle desires or silence women who were willing to master its language of indirection.

THROUGHOUT THE REST OF HER LIFE, Mary Shelley continued to receive periodic entreaties from the friends of her youth to be what they once thought she was. "If you would but know your own value," Claire Clairmont cajoled her, and

> exert your powers you could give the men a most immense drubbing! You could write upon metaphysics, politics, jurisprudence, astronomy, mathematics—all those highest subjects which they taunt us with being incapable of treating, and surpass them; and what a consolation it would be, when they begin some of their prosy, lying, but plausible attacks upon female inferiority, to stop their mouths in a moment with your name.[35]

But Mary Shelley continued to refuse all such pleas that she become the spokesperson for any radical cause. Even though she maintained friendships with some of her less proper peers,[36] she was more comfortable "shut up," as she told Maria Gisborne. "I never walk out beyond my garden," she explained in 1834, "because I *cannot* walk alone—you will say I ought to force myself, so I thought once, and tried—but it would not do—the sense of desolation was too oppressive. . . . My heart beat with a sense of injury and wrong—I was better shut up" (*MWSL,* 2:87; 30 October 1834).

In this last passage it is difficult to know whether Shelley's "sense of injury and wrong" is directed against herself or the polite society that had judged her so harshly. Significantly, however, both may be true at the same time. In either case, Shelley's decision to be "shut up" is an appropriate response. For if the "injury" is her fault, then she needs to be "shut up" so as to commit no more transgressions; and if the "injury" is society's, then she must be "shut up" so as to stifle her anger as well as her pain. In both cases, Shelley seeks to be "shut up" by propriety as well as by the walls of her house. If she acts the way a Proper Lady is supposed to act, perhaps it will matter less what she feels. More to the point, if she acts the way a Proper Lady is supposed to act, even her unladylike feelings will be able to find their legitimate as well as their desired outlet.

After *The Last Man,* Mary Shelley never again trespassed on the masculine domain of metaphysical speculation. In fact, after *Falkner,* she wrote no more novels.[37] From all accounts, her creative self became her hidden self, separate from the Proper Lady she had outwardly become. "It is too often the case that authors talk too much of their writings," her friend and apologist Eliza Rennie declared, attempting to account for Shelley's "circumscribed fame . . . as a writer."

> Mrs. Shelley was the extremest reverse of this. In fact, she was almost morbidly averse to the least allusion to herself as an authoress. To call on her and find her table covered with all the accessories and unmistakable traces of *book-making,* such as copy, proofs for correction, etc., made her nearly as nervous and unself-possessed as if she had been detected in the commission of some offence against the conventionalities of society, or the code of morality. . . .
>
> I really think she deemed it unwomanly to print and publish; and had it not been for the hard cash which, like so many of her craft, she so often stood in need of, I do not think she would ever have come before the world as an authoress.[38]

Shelley's conviction that it was "unwomanly to print," that it was an "offence against the conventionalities of society," was a learned response, the result of the head-on collision between the aggressive desire epitomized by her mother and reinforced by Percy Shelley's Romantic ideals and, on the other hand, the conservative, conventional wisdom that delimited the woman's proper sphere. Mary Shelley's divided self was at least in part the product of this collision, and her uneasy career as a novelist maps out the practical and psychological battlefields where aggression squares off against inhibition. For a woman writer in the early nineteenth century, some version of this confrontation was almost inevitable. While few writers allowed their monstrosity as resonant a voice as Mary Shelley did, many other women followed her into the side streets where propriety permitted women to express desire, resentment, and even rage.

6

Ideological Contradictions and the
Consolations of Form
The Case of Jane Austen

READING JANE AUSTEN'S NOVELS in the context of the works of
Mary Wollstonecraft and Mary Shelley reminds us that Austen also
lived through and wrote about the crisis of values that dominated late
eighteenth- and early nineteenth-century English society. Austen's
perspective on this crisis was, of course, markedly different from
those of the other two women, for whereas both the lower middle-
class Wollstonecraft and the emigrée Shelley witnessed the radicals'
challenge to propriety from outside its eminent domain, Austen spent
her entire life in the very heart of propriety. Austen never traveled
as widely as either Wollstonecraft or Shelley, she never flamboyantly
defied propriety, and she never wrote to support herself or anyone
else. Perhaps partly as a consequence of her limited experience,
Austen did not choose to write about politics, nature, or metaphysics,
and she assiduously avoided the highly imaginative, melodramatic
incidents that so fascinated her contemporaries.

Yet for all the obvious differences between her life and aesthetic
interests and theirs, Jane Austen did concern herself with many of the
same issues as Wollstonecraft and Shelley—with the process of a
young girl's maturation, for example, and, more important, with the
complex relationship between a woman's desires and the imperatives
of propriety. Considering Austen's novels from the perspective of
these issues and in terms of the debate already set out in the works
of Wollstonecraft and Shelley enables us to recognize what the challenge to traditional values looked like from the inside and how an
artistic style could constitute part of a defense against this challenge.
As we will see, Austen's class position placed her firmly in the middle
of the crisis of values we have been examining. As with Wollstonecraft and Shelley, Austen's gender and her decision to write profes-
sionally focused the contradictions inherent in this crisis. What is new
is that Austen's aesthetic choices—her style and her subject matter—
can be seen as "solutions" to some of the problems that neither
Wollstonecraft nor Shelley could solve. My analysis of Austen's work

therefore comes last not because this order is faithful to chronology but because her novels culminate a sequence of stages of female insight and artistic achievement. We can never fully "explain" genius, but in considering the ways in which Austen both completes Wollstonecraft's analysis of female inhibition and perfects Shelley's attempt to make propriety accommodate female desire, we can better understand her accomplishment and some of the functions her artistic strategies served.[1]

Our access to Jane Austen's personal attitudes to historical events and to propriety will always be blocked by her sister Cassandra, who destroyed many of Austen's letters and censored numerous others; moreover, the letters that did survive at times convey contradictory opinions and, what is perhaps even more confusing, almost always employ a decidedly ambiguous tone.[2] When an individual work by Wollstonecraft or Shelley seems morally or stylistically ambiguous, surviving letters or journals help provide a background for interpretation; and the psychological or aesthetic complexities that appear in their fiction and nonfiction alike can be clarified in the same way. But the incompleteness and opacity of Austen's personal record often compound the notorious instability of her novelistic irony, thus leading us further into confusing (if delightful) ambiguity. When Austen tells the obsequious James Stanier Clarke, for example, that "I think I may boast myself to be, with all possible vanity, the most unlearned and uninformed female who ever dared to be an authoress" (*JAL,* 2:443; 11 December 1815), we feel certain that she pretends to diminish herself at her silly correspondent's expense. But when she tells her nephew that she cannot manage his "strong, manly, spirited Sketches" upon the canvas of her art—"the little bit (two Inches wide) of Ivory on which I work with so fine a Brush, as produces little effect after much labour" (*JAL,* 2:468–69; 16 December 1816)—it is difficult to determine exactly how much of her self-depreciation is genuine, how much is simply encouragement for the young writer, and how much is the mock vanity of a self-confident miniaturist. The Austen legacy has been further complicated, of course, by the officious concern of her relatives. In addition to Cassandra's excessive concern for propriety, the efforts of her brother and nephews to beatify "Aunt Jane" for Victorian readers has also blurred our hindsight and has no doubt generated, in some cases, as much overcompensation as accurate evaluation.

Lady Susan

In the absence of extensive biographical documentation, then, Austen's juvenilia provide a logical point of departure. Indeed, her most extended early work, *Lady Susan* (composed c. 1793–94),[3] places her precisely "between" Wollstonecraft and Shelley and broadly establishes the aesthetic and ethical issues that were to occupy her for the remainder of her career. *Lady Susan* is an epistolary satire that takes to task both the ideal of "natural" propriety, which Mary Wollstonecraft also challenged, and the suggestion, similarly rejected by Mary Shelley, that individual desire is, automatically, socially constructive. In the course of *Lady Susan,* Austen seems to agree with *both* Wollstonecraft and Shelley; for, like Shelley, she insists on the destructive potential of individual desire, and, like Wollstonecraft, she points to the way in which the contradictions of social manners may distort the constructive energies women do possess. Because of the hypocrisy implicit in propriety, Austen suggests, there can be no victors: society cannot afford to unleash the energy inherent in female desire, yet the morality by which society controls desire destroys the individual and threatens society itself. In many ways the "heroine" of *Lady Susan* is Austen's version of the energy that Shelley was to call a "monster"; but because Lady Susan's society is almost as repressive and barren as the one depicted in Wollstonecraft's *Maria,* Austen's presentation of this creature is even more ambiguous than Shelley's dramatization of the monster in 1818.

The first two letters that appear in *Lady Susan* establish the unmistakable tone and range of the heroine's voice. Recently widowed, immediately ejected from her "particular" friend's house for her outrageous flirtations, Lady Susan Vernon writes first to her brother, Charles Vernon, to whom she displays only her "winningly mild" countenance. "My kind friends here are most affectionately urgent with me to prolong my stay," she assures him, "but their hospitable & chearful dispositions lead them too much into society for my present situation & state of mind."[4] She is looking forward, she says, to meeting her new "Sister" in the "delightful retirement" of the country. But the reader, more privileged than Mr. Vernon, immediately receives another version of these "facts." In the next letter, addressed to her confidential friend, Alicia Johnson, Lady Susan explains that "the Females of the Family are united against me"; "the whole family are at war" (pp. 244, 245). "Charles Vernon is my aversion, & I am afraid of his wife," she acknowledges; nevertheless, out of necessity, she is off to visit them in "that insupportable spot, a Country Village" (pp. 246, 245–46). Already we see that Lady Susan uses her letters to manipulate reality—to create it, in fact; for we can assume that she plays on Mrs. Johnson's prejudices against propriety almost as consistently as she plays on her brother's simpleminded belief that "truth" has only one face and a single voice.

In Lady Susan's adroit manipulation of "truth" Austen is dramatizing the way that the gap between appearance and reality, which is intrinsic to the paradoxical configuration of propriety, generates a crisis of moral authority. And the remarkable success Susan enjoys with most of her audience for most of the novel suggests the gravity of this crisis. Because her retreat to the country enhances the impression she cultivates of being both virtuous and unavailable, Susan sustains the interest of both of her town admirers and adds to them Reginald De Courcy, Mrs. Vernon's brother and the heir to his family's estate. Susan is able to manipulate others chiefly because she knows that the use of language is an art capable of generating plausible, internally consistent, but wholly malleable fictions—just as the manners of propriety can. Thus she reverses Reginald's initial prejudices against her simply by revising the "facts" on which her notoriety is based, and she prejudices the Vernons against her own daughter Frederica so as better to control the child and then almost manages to make this timid daughter marry the man she herself has chosen for her—her own cast-off suitor, Sir James Martin. Lady Susan freely admits to the pleasure her quick wit and creative pen afford: "If I am vain of anything," she preens, "it is of my eloquence. Consideration & Esteem as surely follow command of Language, as Admiration waits on Beauty" (p. 268). In the end she fails to control reality completely only because the people she has successfully duped—Mrs. Manwaring and Reginald, Frederica and Mrs. Vernon—escape the closed system of her rhetoric by talking to each other. "Horrid" facts obtrude, and her victims conspire to drive Susan out of both family circles. Ultimately, Susan, without a pen or audience, has no influence because she has no vehicle or context by which to create her "self."

Throughout the novel, Lady Susan also aspires to maintain a related but equally precarious balance: she wants to retain the power to exercise her aggressive energies and, at the same time, the reputation for propriety that gives her that power. "Those women are inexcusable," she scoffs, "who forget what is due to themselves & the opinion of the World" (p. 269). The principle that Lady Susan overlooks but that Jane Austen underscores is that, given the nature of female desire, these two "dues" are incompatible. Susan's fidelity to herself would entail indulging her apparently insatiable appetite for attention; yet the "World" will not grant that appetite free expression or substantial gratification. Lady Susan, in other words, is trapped in the very paradox of propriety that she thought she could exploit; because it demands indirection, propriety effectively distorts the desires it seemed to accommodate.

Despite her apparently indomitable wit, Lady Susan also finds herself thwarted by another irony of the female situation. She seems to be a woman of the mind and to pride herself on her ability to dominate not only other people and their perceptions of reality but emotion itself. Susan's sharpest comments are reserved for women who, like her own daughter and Mrs. Manwaring, experience and express strong feeling without inhibition or art. Of her daughter Susan despairs: "I never saw a girl of her age, bid fairer to be the sport of Mankind. Her feelings are tolerably lively & she is so charmingly artless in their display, as to afford the most reasonable hope of her being ridiculed & despised by every Man who sees her." "Artlessness will never do in Love matters," she continues, "& that girl is born a simpleton who has it either by nature or affectation" (p. 274). Yet despite her professed preference for art over spontaneity, Austen hints that Susan yearns for a genuine contest—perhaps even for defeat by an emotion that prudence cannot master. She will not marry the "contemptibly weak" Sir James, she vows, for all his wealth: "I must own myself rather romantic in that respect, & that Riches only, will not satisfy me" (p. 245). Initially she is aroused by Reginald precisely because he seems a worthy antagonist. "There is something about him that rather interests me," she admits; "a sort of sauciness, of familiarity which I shall teach him to correct. . . . There is exquisite pleasure in subduing an insolent spirit, in making a person pre-determined to dislike, acknowledge one's superiority" (p. 254). The problem here is that even though Susan insists that power resides in the mind, she fears that it may actually originate in emotion. Noting the perceptible increase in Frederica's affection for Reginald, Susan admits to "not feeling perfectly secure that a knowledge of *that* affection might not in the end awaken a return. Contemptible as a regard founded only on compassion, must make them both, in my eyes, I [feel] by no means assured that such might not be the consequence" (p. 280).

Beneath Lady Susan's artful self-presentation, then, lurk fears and desires she can neither conceal nor acknowledge. Her boasts of the power of art belie a fascination not only with the "romantic" love that drives her daughter to defy her but even with the fear that compels Frederica to run away from Sir James. Similarly, Susan's need to be flattered hides her persistent anxiety that neither she nor the "World" is as admirable as she wants to believe, and her impatience with spontaneity cloaks her fear that its real liability is just what she says it is: if one is not loved in return, the lover may ridicule, despise, and make sport of a woman's heart.

Despite her aggressive hostility to feminine stereotypes, Lady Susan conforms precisely to the typical female the mid-eighteenth-century moralists described: she is vain, obsessed by men, dominated by her appetites, and, finally, incapable of creating any identity independent of the one she tries to denounce.[5] Ironically, her aggressiveness only affirms the vulnerability she prides herself on having overcome, and she is finally caught in the most fatal paradox of female feeling: to express love is to risk rejection, yet never to acknowledge feeling is to court isolation and the hollow victory of having successfully repressed desire.

Part of the problem, Austen implies, is that society fails to provide any power adequate to Lady Susan. Even in this patriarchal society there are simply no men strong enough either to engage or resist her irrepressible energy. The novel is consistently dominated by women, despite Susan's preoccupation with men. Mr. Vernon seems oblivious to what is happening beneath his roof; Reginald's father, even when told of Susan's plot, refuses to believe that such women exist; Sir James, Mr. Manwaring, and Reginald are simply dupes of Susan's wiles. Only the women are capable of grasping the implications of her exuberance or of doing anything about it. Even timid Frederica three times defies her mother; Mrs. Manwaring finally overthrows Susan by pursuing her husband to London; and Mrs. Vernon consistently proves herself capable not only of understanding Susan's art but of matching it with machinations of her own. As Lloyd W. Brown has noted, the only real contest in *Lady Susan* is between the heroine and Mrs. Vernon; Reginald and Frederica constitute the pawns and the spoils. Like Lady Susan, Mrs. Vernon seeks to control the emotions and the futures of these two young people; both women are egotists, who use their epistolary art to manipulate "reality," and only they can fully comprehend any desire other than avarice.[6]

By the end of the story, the failure of every moral authority in Susan's society threatens to subvert any didactic effect this novel might have seemed to promise. On the one hand, *Lady Susan* constitutes an attack on propriety, which, paradoxically, Austen presents as both restrictive and permissive. Such morality, Austen suggests, is inadequate not because it has misrepresented female nature but because its attempt to control desire has served only to distort this powerful force, to drive it into artful wiles and stratagems that are often both socially destructive and personally debilitating. On the other hand, because the world Austen depicts contains neither adequate outlets for this energy nor a paternal authority capable of mastering it, we cannot imagine what constructive form Susan's exuberance could take—or, for that matter, what social or moral institution could control it. Because Susan's energy exceeds the capacity of the world she inhabits, it is necessarily destructive—not only of the foolish men but of innocent young persons like Frederica and, ultimately, of Lady Susan herself.[7]

Despite its destructive tendencies and effects, however, Lady Susan's energy—like that of Shelley's monster—remains the most attractive force in this novel. And, as in *Frankenstein,* the power of this attraction is reinforced by the epistolary form, which allows us not only to engage ourselves with Lady Susan's intellect but to sympathize with her conflicting feelings as well. Even though the letters Mrs. Vernon writes supply another perspective on Susan's schemes, her judgments are no more "objective" or authoritative than Susan's whims—especially given her personal grudge against Susan. Similarly, the final agent of "justice"—Mrs. Manwaring—comes from the household that was, initially, so easily duped, and she too, like Mrs. Vernon, retaliates from personal motives, not to save some absolute system of disinterested values. In a novel that lacks a spokesperson for such values, the epistolary form generates moral anarchy; Austen does not establish a genuinely critical position within the fiction but depends instead on an implicit contrast between the values presented and those the satire presumes but does not formulate. Within the moral consensus of a family such allusiveness might well suffice, and we can imagine Austen reading *Lady Susan* to her amused family circle. But without this consensus there is no moral authority because there is no narrative authority. In the laissez-faire competition the epistolary *Lady Susan* permits, the reader will identify with whatever character dominates the narration or most completely gratifies the appetite for entertainment. In *Lady Susan* this character is, of course, the dangerous heroine.

So compelling and so complete is this heroine's artful power that the only way Austen can effectively censure her is to impose punishment by narrative fiat. Predictably, this entails disrupting the epistolary narrative and ridiculing not just the correspondents but the morally anarchic epistolary form itself. "This Correspondence," Austen playfully announces in the "Conclusion," ". . . could not, to the great detriment of the Post office Revenue, be continued longer. Very little assistance to the State could be derived from the Epistolary Intercourse of Mrs. Vernon & her niece" (p. 311). She then abruptly summarizes the fate of the characters: Mrs. Vernon and Mrs. Manwaring triumph, and Frederica and her mother reverse positions in almost every important respect: the daughter marries Reginald, and Lady Susan is reduced to marrying the suitor whom Frederica has now cast off, Sir James Martin. But Austen will not allow even this summary to have final authority, for in her final reference to Lady Susan she leaves her in exactly the same moral vacuum in which we found her: "Whether Lady Susan was, or was not happy in her second Choice—I do not see how it can ever be ascertained—for who would take her assurance of it, on either side of the question?" (p. 313).

Austen's final ambivalence here suggests an attempt to accomplish the same feat to which Lady Susan aspired: to obtain both "what is due to [herself] & the opinion of the World." What is due to herself as an artist is uninhibited self-expression; the "opinion of the World" requires conclusive moral order. Austen seems reluctant to deny the power or attraction of female energy, perhaps because it is too close to the creative impulse of her own wit; nor does she fully condone the indulgence of that energy, for its destructive potential is undeniable. By allowing herself and her reader imaginative engagement with her heroine, Austen seems to satisfy the prerogatives of desire; by abruptly severing that engagement, she aspires to reassert the system of social principles whose authority Lady Susan has so effectively challenged.

THE NARRATIVE IMPASSE at the conclusion of *Lady Susan* is in many ways reminiscent of the problems that beset Wollstonecraft's *Maria*: the appeal of female feeling competes with Austen's reservations about it almost as dramatically as Wollstonecraft's attraction to "romantic expectations" jeopardizes her critique of sentimentalism. In both cases, one consequence of this aesthetic ambiguity is uncertainty for the reader as to the moral ground of the novels. Just as *Maria* seems to hover between irony and wholehearted sentimentalism, so *Lady Susan* occupies the gray area between satire and direct social criticism. But the intervention of the unmistakable narrative voice at the end of *Lady Susan,* while necessitated by a version of *Maria's* tonal uncertainty, points to one essential difference between these two writers— a difference that becomes more marked during Austen's subsequent career. The "solution" Wollstonecraft offers in *Maria* involves two extreme gestures: on the one hand, she rejects social institutions that inhibit individual feeling; on the other hand, she redefines human emotions so that they transcend social institutions altogether. By contrast, Austen brings individual desire into confrontation with social institutions in order first to discipline anarchic passion and then to expand the capacity of such institutions to accommodate educated needs and desires. One reason *Maria's* conclusion remains blocked is that everything in the sections Wollstonecraft finished suggests her desire to segregate the realistic depictions of corrupt society from her romantic effusions of passion. The conclusion of *Lady Susan,* on the other hand, for all its contrivance, suggests an impulse to contain even momentary fantasies of unmitigated power within the twin controls of aesthetic closure and social propriety. In this sense, Jane Austen resembles Mary Shelley more than Mary Wollstonecraft. But the balance of her sympathies, along with the aesthetic solutions she developed to convey them, take her beyond the artistic achievement of either of the other two.

The division of sympathies we see in *Lady Susan* bears a particularly interesting relationship to Jane Austen's complex social and economic position during this period of change. As we have already seen, the period between 1775 and 1817, the years of Austen's life, was punctuated by challenges to the traditional hierarchy of English class society and, as a consequence, to conventional social roles and responsibilities. William Wordsworth's 1817 survey of the preceding thirty years summarizes the chaotic impact of these changes:

> I see clearly that the principal ties which kept the different classes of society in a vital and harmonious dependence upon each other have, within these 30 years, either been greatly impaired or wholly dissolved. Everything has been put up to market and sold for the highest price it would buy. . . . All . . . moral cement is dissolved, habits and prejudices are broken and rooted up, nothing being substituted in their place but a quickened self-interest.[8]

In England, the decisive agent of this change was not just the French Revolution but the more subtle, more gradual, dissemination of the values and behavior associated with capitalism—first, agrarian capitalism in the mid- and late eighteenth century, then, in the early nineteenth century, industrial capitalism, as money made itself felt in investment and capital return. As we have seen, by the first decades of the nineteenth century, birth into a particular class no longer exclusively determined one's future social or economic status, the vertical relationships of patronage no longer guaranteed either privileges or obedience, and the traditional authority of the gentry, and of the values associated with their life-style, was a subject under general debate. In the midst of such changes, the assumptions that had theoretically been shared by eighteenth-century moralists and their audiences seemed increasingly problematic, requiring refinement and defense if not radical change. As the literature and political debates of this period unmistakably reveal, the crisis in imaginative and moral authority was pervasive and severe; even conservative writers generally abandoned arguments about absolute truths in favor of discussions in which one set of principles was defended against a contrary but equally coherent system of values.[9]

As the daughter of a country clergyman with numerous and strong ties to the landed upper gentry, Jane Austen was involved in this crisis of authority in an immediate and particularly complex way. As Donald J. Greene has conclusively demonstrated, Jane Austen was acutely aware of her kinship to several prominent families, among them the Brydges, who were earls and lords of Chandos, and the lords Leigh of Stoneleigh.[10] More immediately, as a clergyman Austen's father belonged to the lesser realms of the gentry, and Jane and her siblings all benefited more or less directly from the patronage that traditionally reinforced the gentry's hegemony. One of Austen's brothers, Edward, was adopted by the wealthy Knight family, of Kent, and, as heir to the valuable estate of Godmersham, he was eventually able to provide a home at Chawton Cottage for Jane, her mother, her sister, and their friend Martha Lloyd. Two of Austen's other brothers, James and Henry, became clergymen, and her two youngest brothers, Francis and Charles, entered the British navy and eventually became admirals; Francis in fact became a knight. Thus Jane Austen was raised in the heart of middle-class society; she shared its values, and she owed her own position to the bonds of patronage that cemented traditional society, even though her immediate resources never permitted her fully to emulate the gentry's life-style.

In keeping with this class affiliation, Jane Austen's fundamental ideological position was conservative; her political sympathies were generally Tory, and her religion was officially Anglican; overall, she was a "conservative Christian moralist," supportive of Evangelical ethical rigor even before she explicitly admitted admiring the Evangelicals themselves.[11]

But neither the external evidence of Austen's social position nor the internal evidence of her novels supports so strict a delineation of her sympathies. In the first place, even the traditional practices of paternalism were influenced during this period by the rhetoric and practices of individualism. (To give but one relevant example: promotion in such prestigious professions as the navy could result from individual effort and merit [as *Persuasion* indicates]; at other times it depended on the interest of a patron [as William Price learns in *Mansfield Park*]). In the second place, the role played by Austen's class in the rise of capitalism was particularly complicated; for the agricultural improvements that preceded and paved the way for early industrial capitalism were financed and initiated in many cases by the landowning gentry, yet the legal provisions of strict settlement and entail were expressly designed to prohibit land from becoming a commodity susceptible to promiscuous transfer or easy liquidation. Despite the fact that the landowning gentry participated in the expansion of agrarian capitalism, their role was passive, not active; as a consequence, their values and life-style were not extensively altered until the more radical and rapid expansion of industrial capitalism began in the first decades of the nineteenth century. When that occurred, the gentry were suddenly awakened to the implications of the changes to which their patterns of expenditure had contributed.[12] From the more vulnerable position of the lower levels of the gentry, Jane Austen was able to see with particular clarity the marked differences between the two components of the middle class: the landed gentry and the new urban capitalist class.[13] The division of sympathies that occurs in her novels when middle-class daughters get rewarded with the sons of landed families emanates at least partly from Austen's being both involved in and detached from these two middle-class groups at a moment when they were implicitly competing with each other.

IN AUSTEN'S VERY EARLY WORKS, like *Lady Susan,* this division of sympathies characteristically leads either to broad farce or to the tonal uncertainties of parody.[14] As her career progresses, however, we see Austen gradually develop aesthetic strategies capable of balancing her attraction to exuberant but potentially anarchic feeling with her investment in traditional social institutions. This balance is embodied in the thematic material she chooses and the rhetorical stance she adopts. At their most sophisticated, Austen's rhetorical strategies harness the imaginative energy of her readers to a moral design; she thus manages to satisfy both the individual reader's desire for emotional gratification and the program of education prescribed by traditional moral aestheticians.

To understand why Austen assumed that a novel could simultaneously gratify the cravings of the imagination and provide moral instruction, it is useful to turn to Samuel Johnson, Austen's favorite eighteenth-century essayist. According to Johnson, novel-reading is an active, not passive, enterprise, for it aggressively engages the imagination of its young reader. Novels, Johnson explains,

> are the entertainment of minds unfurnished with ideas, and therefore easily susceptible of impressions; not fixed by principles, and therefore easily following the current of fancy; not informed by experience, and consequently open to every false suggestion and partial account. . . . If the power of example is so great, as to take possession of the memory by a kind of violence, and produce effects almost without the intervention of the will, care ought to be taken that, when the choice is unrestrained, the best examples only should be exhibited; and that which is likely to operate so strongly, should not be mischievous or uncertain in its effects.[15]

Johnson's wariness about the power of the imagination should remind us of Mary Shelley; for, as different as these two writers were, they shared a profound anxiety about the insatiable hunger of the imagination. Johnson's answer to this anxiety was to compose not novels but moral essays that were characterized by a tremendous respect for reason's antagonist. Mary Shelley's solution, as we have seen, was simultaneously less evasive and less effective. In fact, her novels represent the two dangers to which imaginative engagement might lead. At one extreme, as the 1818 *Frankenstein* proves, a "romantic" novel might so thoroughly activate the imagination as to undermine all moral authority; at the other extreme, as in *Falkner,* the moral novel might so dogmatically focus the imagination that all subversive exuberance would be driven into the background of the fiction, only to return to the forefront in troubling reminders of what cannot be contained.

To a certain extent, Jane Austen shared this ambivalence with regard to the imagination. When Anne Elliot advises Captain Benwick in *Persuasion* to admit "a larger allowance of prose in his daily study" so as to "rouse and fortify" a mind made "tremulous" by immersion in Romantic poetry, she is warning against the "susceptibility" of the indulged imagination.[16] But while Austen might well agree with John-son that novels should "serve as lectures of conduct, and introduc-tions into life," her major works are not as defensive as either his *Rasselas* or Shelley's *Falkner*; they do not, that is, "initiate youth by mock encounters in the art of necessary defence."[17] Instead, Austen attempts to convert the pleasure generated by imaginative engage-ment into a didactic tool. As the "productions" that provide "more extensive and unaffected pleasure than those of any other literary corporation in the world," novels are best suited for such education. For in the best novels, Austen continues in *Northanger Abbey*, "the greatest powers of the mind are displayed, . . . the most thorough knowledge of human nature, the happiest delineation of its varieties, the liveliest effusions of wit and humour are conveyed to the world in the best chosen language."[18]

Sense and Sensibility

The narrative impasse reached in Wollstonecraft's *Maria* and the Scylla and Charybdis of Shelley's aesthetic choices remind us that achieving such a balance was not easy. Jane Austen's first published novel, *Sense and Sensibility* (1811), suggests how persistent this problem proved to be for her early in her career.[19] *Sense and Sensibility* is a much darker novel than any of the juvenilia or the parodic *Northanger Abbey* (1818), and we might speculate that one origin of its somber tone and the eruptions of anarchic feeling that punctuate it lies in the anxiety with which Austen viewed individualism's challenge to paternalism. For in *Sense and Sensibility*, as, in a slightly different way, in *Lady Susan* and *Northanger Abbey*, the most fundamental conflict is between Aus-ten's own imaginative engagement with her self-assertive characters and the moral code necessary to control their anarchic desires.

In the greater part of *Sense and Sensibility*, Austen's aesthetic strate-gies endorse the traditional values associated with her "sensible" heroine, Elinor Dashwood. One of these strategies consists in measur-ing all of the characters (including Elinor) against an implicit, but presumably authoritative, moral norm. As early as the second chap-ter, in that free, indirect discourse that is the hallmark of her mature style, Austen shadows the opinion of a single fallible character with this implicit moral standard.[20] Irony in *Sense and Sensibility* arises for the most part from the novel's action; the dialogue between Mr. and Mrs. John Dashwood points up as surely as any overt narrative commentary the parsimony behind their dwindling good will. But our response to this dialogue is initially shaped by such sentences as the following: "To take three thousand pounds from the fortune of their dear little boy, would be impoverishing him to the most dreadful degree"; "How could he answer it to himself to rob his child, and his only child too, of so large a sum?"[21] The hyperbole expressed in the words "impoverishing," "dreadful," and "rob" conveys both the strategy of Mrs. Dashwood's rhetoric and its absurdity, and the repeated use of the word "child" suggests how effective she is in manipulating John Dashwood's generosity. Because these sentences belong to the narrative and not to direct dialogue, they mimetically convey the tone of the conversation and simultaneously judge it by reference to an implicit system of more humane values—the undeniably Christian values that one should love one's neighbor as one's self and that the man who hoards treasures in this world (or the woman who encourages him to do so) will never get into the kingdom of heaven.

But despite this ground of Christian principles, nearly everything in the plot of *Sense and Sensibility* undermines the complacent assumption that they are principles generally held or practically effective. Almost every action in the novel suggests that, more often than not, individual will triumphs over principle and individual desire proves more compelling than moral law. Even the narrator, the apparent voice of these absolute values, reveals that moral principles are qualified in practice. The narrator's prefatory evaluation of John Dashwood, for example—"he was not an ill-disposed young man, unless to be rather cold hearted, and rather selfish, is to be ill-disposed" (p. 5)—directs our attention most specifically to the way in which what should, in theory, be moral absolutes can, and in practice do, shade off into infinite gradations and convenient exceptions. Is it always morally wrong to be "rather" selfish, especially in a society in which such selfishness is the necessary basis for material prosperity? What efficacy will moral absolutes have in such a society? How could Elinor's patient, principled fidelity win the passive, principled Edward if it were not, finally, for Lucy Steele's avarice?

A second strategy that is apparently designed to forestall such questions by aligning the reader's sympathies with Elinor's "sense" involves the juxtaposition of Elinor and her sister Marianne at nearly every critical juncture in the novel. Consistently, Elinor makes the prudent choice, even when doing so is painful; almost as consistently, Marianne's decisions are self-indulgent and harmful, either to herself or to someone else. But this neat design is less stable than an absolute and authoritative moral system would seem to require. Many readers have found Marianne's "spirit" more appealing than Elinor's cautious, prim, and even repressive reserve, and they have found Marianne's passionate romance with Willoughby more attractive than the prolonged frustration to which Elinor submits. That such preferences may be in keeping with at least one countercurrent of the novel is suggested by the fact that whenever Austen herself explicitly compares the two putative heroes—Colonel Brandon and Edward Ferrars—with the less moral, more passionate Willoughby, it is Willoughby who is appealing. On two occasions when Willoughby is expected but one of the more subdued lovers appears instead, the disappointment is unmistakable; and when the reverse situation occurs, in the climactic final encounter between Elinor and Willoughby, Elinor is aroused to a pitch of complex emotion we never see Edward inspire in anyone. Moreover, Willoughby repeatedly bursts into the narrative with "manly beauty and more than common gracefulness," but Edward and Brandon seem inert fixtures of the plot, incapable of energetic galantry and attractive only to the most generous observer. The initial description of each of them is dominated by negative constructions and qualifying phrases, and even Elinor cannot unreservedly praise the man she wants to marry. "At first sight," she admits, "his address is certainly not striking; and his person can hardly be called handsome, till the expression of his eyes, which are uncommonly good, and the general sweetness of his countenance, is perceived. At present, I know him so well, that I think him really handsome; or, at least, almost so" (p. 20). Colonel Brandon, "neither very young nor very gay," is "silent and grave" much of the time (p. 34), and his "oppression of spirits," like Edward's chronic depression, can scarcely compete with Willoughby's charm.

The most telling dramatization of the contest between the potentially anarchic power of feeling and the restraint that moral principles require takes the form of a conflict within Elinor herself. This scene, in the final volume, owes much to conventional eighteenth-century didactic novels, but Austen's placing it at a moment when the generally self-disciplined Elinor is unusually susceptible to emotion gives it a particularly complicated effect. Colonel Brandon has presented a living to Edward Ferrars, and Elinor is finally, but sadly, reconciled to the fact that her lover will marry someone else. In the midst of this personal disappointment, she is also particularly sensitive to her sister's condition, for Marianne, whose own romantic disappointment had sent her into a dangerous decline, has just been declared out of danger. Elinor's "fervent gratitude" for this news is especially great because of the joy and relief it will bring to her mother, whose arrival is expected at any moment. It is this hectic peace—as Marianne sleeps quietly upstairs and a violent storm assaults the house—that Willoughby invades when he melodramatically steps into the drawing-room.

Elinor's first response is "horror" at his audacious intrusion; but before she can leave the room, Willoughby appeals to something even more powerful than Elinor's "honour": her curiosity. Elinor is momentarily captivated by Willoughby's "serious energy" and "warmth," and she listens "in spite of herself" to the story he unfolds—the chronicle of his passions, both honorable and base. At the end of his dramatic recital, Willoughby asks Elinor for pity, and, even though she feels it is her "duty" to check his outburst, she cannot repress her "compassionate emotion." It is this emotion that governs her judgment of Willoughby—a judgment that verges disconcertingly on rationalization:

> Elinor made no answer. Her thoughts were silently fixed on the irreparable injury which too early an independence and its consequent habits of idleness, dissipation, and luxury, had made in the mind, the character, the happiness, of a man who, to every advantage of person and talents, united a disposition naturally open and honest, and a feeling, affectionate temper. The world had made him extravagant and vain—Extravagance and vanity had made him cold-hearted and selfish. [P. 331]

When Willoughby departs, he leaves Elinor in an even greater "agitation" of spirits, "too much oppressed by a croud of ideas . . . to think even of her sister."

> Willoughby, in spite of all his faults, excited a degree of commiseration for the sufferings produced by them, which made her think of him as now separated for ever from her family with a tenderness, a regret, rather in proportion, as she soon acknowledged within herself—to his wishes than to his merits. She felt that his influence over her mind was heightened by circumstances which ought not in reason to have weight; by that person of uncommon attraction, that open, affectionate, and lively manner which it was no merit to possess; and by that still ardent love for Marianne, which it was not even innocent to indulge. But she felt that it was so, long, long before she could feel his influence less. [P. 333]

One purpose of this episode is clearly to dramatize the odds against which Elinor's "sense," or reason, ultimately triumphs and therefore to increase, not undermine, our admiration for that faculty. But a second effect of the passage is to subject the reader to the same temptation that assails Elinor. Because the presentation is dramatic and because, for a moment at least, the character whose judgment has thus far directed our own hesitates in her moral evaluation, the reader is invited to judge Willoughby not by reference to an objective

standard but by his immediate appeal to our imaginative, sympathetic engagement. As Elinor temporizes, the moral principle for which
she otherwise speaks seems dangerously susceptible to circumstances, to the appeal of "lively manners," and to the special pleading
of aroused female emotion.

Jane Austen seems anxious to control the moral anarchy that
strong appeals to feeling can unleash; yet, significantly, she does not
exclude passion from the novel, nor does she so completely qualify
it as to undermine its power. Instead, Austen attempts to bend the
imaginative engagement it elicits in the reader to the service of moral
education. To do so, she restricts the reader's access to the romantic
plot by conveying its details and its emotional affect only through
indirect narration. At the beginning of the novel, for example, the
incident in which Willoughby rescues Marianne is summarized by the
dispassionate narrative persona, who supplies sentimental clichés but
not Marianne's response to her rescue: "The gentleman offered his
services, and perceiving that her modesty declined what her situation
rendered necessary, took her up in his arms without farther delay"
(p. 42). Similarly, the episode in which Willoughby cuts and kisses a
lock of Marianne's hair is given to Margaret to relate (p. 60), and the
emotional specifics of Willoughby's farewell at Barton Cottage can be
deduced only from their aftermath (p. 82). Most of Marianne's outbursts of passion to Willoughby are confined to letters, which are
concealed from the reader until after Willoughby has snubbed Marianne. In fact, the only emotionally charged encounter between the
lovers that Austen presents dramatically is their final meeting at the
London ball, and there Marianne's passion is transmuted by Willoughby's silence into the terrible muffled scream that both voices
and symbolizes her thwarted love. So careful is Austen to keep the
reader on the outside of such "dangerous" material that she embeds
the most passionate episodes within other, less emotionally volatile
stories. Thus the story of the two Elizas—related, as we will see, by
a character whose relationship to the tale immediately activates our
judgment—is contained within the story of Marianne's passion for
Willoughby—a relationship whose emotional content is conveyed to
the reader more by innuendo, summary, and indirection than by
dramatic presentation. And this second story, in turn, is contained
within the story of the relationship that opens and closes the novel—
Elinor's considerably less demonstrative affection for Edward. By
embedding these stories in this way, Austen seeks to defuse their
imaginative affect and increase their power to educate the reader:
from the fates of the two Elizas we learn to be wary of Marianne's
quick feelings, and from the consequences of Marianne's self-indulgent passion we learn to value Elinor's reserve.

Instead of being allowed to identify with Marianne, then, for most of the novel we are restricted to Elinor's emotional struggles. This enables Austen to dramatize the complexities of what might otherwise seem an unattractive and unyielding obsession with propriety; it also permits her to filter the two stories of illicit passion through a character whose judgment generally masters emotion. That the passion bleeds from the narrators of these two tales into Elinor's "sense" attests to the power of this force and to the dangerous susceptibility that, without proper control, might undermine the judgment of even the most rational reader.

Austen also attempts to control the allure of Marianne's romantic desires by refusing to consider seriously either their social origin or their philosophical implications. As Tony Tanner has pointed out, Austen really avoids the systematic examination of "sensibility" that the novel seems to promise.[22] The novel begins like a novel of social realism. In the first paragraphs the narrator sounds like a lawyer or a banker; family alliances, the estate that is the heart of paternalistic society, even the deaths of loved ones, are all ruthlessly subordinated to the economic facts. Given this introduction, the reader has every reason to believe that the most important fact—that Mrs. Dashwood will have only five hundred pounds a year with which to raise and dower her daughters—will govern the futures of Elinor, Marianne, and Margaret. And given this probable development, the reader can understand why romantic fantasies are appealing. It is no wonder that Marianne—facing a life of poverty, the spiritual banality of relatives like the John Dashwoods, and the superficial urbanities of a neighborhood composed only of the Middletons and Mrs. Jennings—turns to Cowper for imaginative compensation; nor is it surprising that she fancies (in accordance with the promises of romantic novels) that her beauty will win the heart and hand of an errant knight. Beneath Marianne's effusions on nature and her passionate yearning for a hero lies the same "hunger of imagination" that Mary Wollstonecraft tried and failed to analyze in *Maria*. But to take Marianne's passions and longings seriously on their own terms would be to call into question the basis of Christian moral authority, the social order that ideally institutionalizes that authority, and, finally, the capacity of orthodox religion or society to gratify imaginative desires.[23] Elinor's sense, despite its admirable capacity to discipline and protect the self, cannot begin to satisfy this appetite, and no other social institution in the novel does any better. Instead of taking this implicit criticism to its logical conclusion, as Wollstonecraft tried to do, Jane Austen defuses its threat by directing our judgment away from bourgeois society and toward the self-indulgent individual. Austen caricatures just enough of Marianne's responses to nature and

love to make her seem intermittently ridiculous, and, when her desires finally explode all social conventions, Austen stifles her with an
illness that is not only a result but also a purgation of her passion.
At the end of the novel, Austen ushers Marianne into Brandon's
world of diminished desires in such a way as to make Marianne
herself negate everything she has previously wanted to have and to
be.

> Marianne Dashwood was born to an extraordinary fate. She was born to
> discover the falsehood of her own opinions, and to counteract, by her conduct,
> her most favourite maxims. She was born to overcome an affection formed so
> late in life as at seventeen, and with no sentiment superior to strong esteem
> and lively friendship, voluntarily to give her hand to another! . . . Marianne
> could never love by halves; and her whole heart became, in time, as much
> devoted to her husband, as it had once been to Willoughby. [Pp. 378-79]

To further defuse the questions raised by Marianne's assertive
subjectivity, Austen seconds the opinion of eighteenth-century moralists that women's appetites are particularly dangerous and more akin
to inexplicable natural forces than to socialized—hence socializable—
responses. Except for Elinor, nearly all of the women in *Sense and
Sensibility* are given to one kind of excess or another. Mrs. John
Dashwood and her mother, Mrs. Ferrars, attempt to dominate the
opinions, the professions, and even the emotions of the men who are
closest to them; Willoughby's aunt, who is empowered by money
and age, is even more tyrannical; and Sophia Grey, Willoughby's
fiancée, enacts her passion and her will when she commands Willoughby to copy her cruel letter for Marianne. Austen implies that
these women are exceptional only in the extent of their power, not
in the force of their desires. The narrator describes a "fond mother,"
for example, as "the most rapacious of human beings" (p. 120)—a
description borne out by the monomanical Lady Middleton—and she
refers lightly to the "suffering" endured by every lady who has the
"insatiable appetite of fifteen" (p. 33). Until her compassion is necessary to the plot, even Mrs. Jennings seems dominated by a single
uncontrollable desire, the hunger to live vicariously through the romantic attachments of her young friends.

Austen's female characters certainly do not monopolize passion,
nor are their little contrivances finally more destructive than Willoughby's deceit. But the implications of her characterizations of such
women can be identified by contrasting them with her presentation
of male characters. Austen consistently provides men's behavior with
a realistic explanation by describing the social or psychological contexts that shaped it. Mr. Palmer's general contempt, Elinor concludes
(without any narrative qualification), "was the desire of appearing

superior to other people" (p. 112)—a desire that is an understandable compensation for Palmer's initial error: "his temper might perhaps be a little soured by finding, like many others of his sex, that through some unaccountable bias in favour of beauty, he was the husband of a very silly woman" (p. 112). Austen's comparable references to Mrs. Palmer's history are both cursory and curt: her mantelpiece, the narrator informs us, is adorned with "a landscape in coloured silks of her performance, in proof of her having spent seven years at a great school in town to some effect" (p. 160). Austen also more extensively explains the differences between the Ferrars brothers than between the oldest Dashwood sisters; she makes no attempt to account for the temperamental contrast between Elinor and Marianne but carefully attributes the differences between Robert and Edward to their education. The only female character Austen appears to explain is Lucy Steele. Initially, Lucy's "deficiency of all mental improvement" seems to be the effect of her neglected education: "Lucy was naturally clever; her remarks were often just and amusing . . . but her powers had received no aid from education, she was ignorant and illiterate, and her deficiency of mental improvement . . . could not be concealed from Miss Dashwood" (p. 127). Soon we discover, however, that this "explanation" is really only Elinor's generous and erroneous first impression. Austen explicitly ridicules the notion that Lucy's "want of liberality" could be "due to her want of education" by having Edward cling to this rationalization to the end. But in jilting Edward for his brother Robert, Lucy conclusively proves herself inherently flawed. Like Shelley's 1831 characterization of Frankenstein, and like both portrayals of the monster, female nature appears to be fated, fixed. Austen's final comments on Lucy are decisive: her behavior exposes "a wanton ill-nature" (p. 366), characterized by "an earnest, an unceasing attention to self-interest" (p. 376).

The harshness with which Austen disposes of Lucy Steele exceeds the necessities of the plot, but it is perfectly in keeping with her moral design. For, like Shelley, Austen wants to convince the reader that female nature is simply inexplicable and that propriety must restrain this natural, amoral force. At least one other set of female characters also supports this argument, but, paradoxically, the episode in which they appear alludes not to an innate female nature but to the constraints imposed on women by patriarchal society. Because of this, the episode threatens to subvert the argument for propriety it theoretically should support. The characters are the two Elizas, and their story belongs to Colonel Brandon.

Colonel Brandon relates the story of the two Elizas to Elinor ostensibly to persuade her to warn Marianne about Willoughby. But both the hesitations with which he interrupts his narrative and the fact that he focuses not on the second Eliza (Willoughby's victim) but on her mother ("his" Eliza) suggest that Brandon does not fully recognize his own motives for telling the story. As the tale unfolds, it becomes clear that Brandon's deepest intention is to warn Marianne about the dangerous nature of her own passion; paradoxically, however, the overall effect of the episode is to reveal to the reader the depth—and consequences—of *Brandon's* sexual anxiety.[24] This anxiety, initially aroused by the first Eliza, is now being reactivated by Marianne. But there is one critical difference between the two situations: unlike the first Eliza, Marianne's passion is not for Brandon but for Willoughby. Thus Brandon's anxiety is doubly displaced: it is a past fear of too much emotion *and* a present fear of too little love. The first Eliza *did* love him, Brandon asserts, as if to enhance his own appeal, but she could not withstand her guardian's pressure to marry Brandon's older brother, heir to the family's encumbered estate. As he tells the story, Brandon stumbles over the details that wounded him most:

> "My brother did not deserve her; he did not even love her. I had hoped that her regard for me would support her under any difficulty, and for some time it did; but at last the misery of her situation, for she experienced great unkind-ness, overcame all her resolution, and though she had promised me that nothing——but how blindly I relate! I have never told you how this was brought on. We were within a few hours of eloping together for Scotland. The treachery, or the folly, of my cousin's maid betrayed us. I was banished . . . and she was allowed no liberty, no society, no amusement, till my father's point was gained. I had depended on her fortitude too far, . . . —but had her marriage been happy, . . . a few months must have reconciled me to it. . . . This however was not the case. My brother had no regard for her. . . . The conse-quence of this, upon a mind so young, so lively, so inexperienced as Mrs. Brandon's, was but too natural. . . . Can we wonder that with such a husband to provoke inconstancy, and without a friend to advise or restrain her . . . she should fall? Had I remained in England, perhaps—but I meant to promote the happiness of both by removing from her for years. . . . The shock which her marriage had given me," he continued, in a voice of great agitation, "was of trifling weight—was nothing—to what I felt when I heard, about two years afterwards, of her divorce. It was *that* which threw this gloom,-even now the recollection of what I suffered—". . . . [Pp. 205–06; ellipses added]

The story begins and ends in Eliza's infidelity to Brandon; only as an extension of this does her infidelity to her husband matter, only as the origin of his pain does Eliza's unhappiness figure. The weakness of this woman—and her sexual abandon—are "natural," according to Brandon; only the presence of a male guardian could have pro-tected her from herself. Once Eliza has fallen, her fate is so predictable (and disturbing) that it warrants only summary description—except in regard to Brandon's own misery:

So altered—so faded—worn down by acute suffering of every kind! hardly could I believe the melancholy and sickly figure before me, to be the remains of the lovely, blooming, healthful girl, on whom I had once doated. What I endured in so beholding her—but I have no right to wound your feelings by attempting to describe it—I have pained you too much already. [P. 207]

Given the fate of the mother, Brandon is not surprised at the fall of the second Eliza, the daughter, who has been bequeathed to his protection. At seventeen, her mother's fatal year and Marianne's current age, she too evaded her male guardian and ran away with Willoughby. Now pregnant, abandoned, poor, and miserable, this Eliza is a second monument to the passionate excesses of women.

The intense anxiety that Brandon betrays here is produced by his fear of female sexual appetite. If female sexuality had caused the first Eliza to betray him, how vulnerable might the excitable Marianne be to Willoughby, who had seduced the second Eliza? Yet Brandon expressly admires Marianne for the very passion that occasioned the downfall of the two Elizas. Brandon wants Marianne to be emotionally responsive, but he wants her sexuality to answer only to his command. When Elinor wishes that Marianne would renounce sentimental prejudices, Brandon's response is swift: "No, no, do not desire it,—for when the romantic refinements of a young mind are obliged to give way, how frequently are they succeeded by such opinions as are but too common, and too dangerous! I speak from experience" (pp. 56–57). The allusion is clearly to the first Eliza; Brandon fears that beneath the "romantic refinements" of the girl lurks a woman's sexual appetite, which is both "common" and "dangerous." Better far to keep women innocent, to protect them from themselves—and to protect men from their "natural" volatility.

The anxieties Brandon unwittingly reveals suggest that Austen at least intuits the twin imperatives that anchor patriarchal society: men want women to be passionate, but, because they fear the consequences of this appetite, they want to retain control over its expression. This anxiety explains why women in this society must experience so problematic a relation to their own desire. In order to win the husband necessary to their social position, women must gratify both of men's desires by concealing whatever genuine emotions they feel so as to allow men to believe that *they* have all the power. Women must use indirection, in other words, the allure of "romantic refinements," and the subterfuges of manners and modesty in order to arouse male desires and assuage male anxieties.

The implications of this passage are very close to those Mary Wollstonecraft specifically addresses in both *The Rights of Woman* and *Maria*. But in *Sense and Sensibility* Jane Austen will no more pursue the criticism of patriarchy that is inherent in this insight than she will pursue the grim reality that is implicit in the narrator's account of the Dashwood's economic situation. Despite its gestures toward realism, *Sense and Sensibility* repeatedly dismisses the analysis of society that realism might imply and instead embraces the idealism of romance. But Austen's idealism never completely banishes her realistic impulse either. Instead, Austen retains both "principles" and romance. Thus Marianne debunks her own youthful romance, and the novel as a whole endorses the "heroism" (the word itself appears on pp. 242 and 265) of Elinor's self-denial. Nevertheless, Austen rewards both characters at the conclusion of the novel precisely in terms of romantic love and of lives lived happily ever after.

Some of the tensions that we finally feel in *Sense and Sensibility* emerge, then, from the conflict between the realism in which the action is anchored and the romantic elements that Austen harnesses to this realism. Throughout, she attempts to use realism to control the imaginative excesses that romances both encourage and depict: not only does the point of view repress the romantic plot, but Austen also suggests that Elinor's self-denial—her refusal to reveal Lucy Steele's secret and her willingness to help Edward even to her own disadvantage—ultimately contributes to her own happiness as well as to the happiness of others. The prerogatives of society, Austen suggests, sometimes make secrecy and repression necessary; but if one submits to society, every dream will come true. The last part of this formulation reminds us, of course, that, just as Austen uses realism to control the irresponsible and morally anarchic imagination, she also enlists the power of the reader's wishes to buttress her moral design. Theoretically, if her readers will submit to a version of the frustration Elinor suffers or even the compromise to which Marianne grows accustomed, their wish for a happy ending will be legitimized and gratified. This fusion of realism and romance in the service of aesthetic closure decisively distinguishes between Wollstonecraft's *Maria* and Austen's early novels. For notwithstanding her imaginative engagement in "romantic expectations," Wollstonecraft's persistent goal is to criticize the social institutions that seem to her to thwart female feeling. Jane Austen, on the other hand, despite her recognition of the limitations of social institutions, is more concerned with correcting the dangerous excesses of female feeling than with liberating this anarchic energy. Her turn to aesthetic closure enables her to dismiss many of the problems her own divided sympathies have introduced. That the need for such closure grows out of society's inability to grant happiness to everyone in the terms it promises is a problem that can remain unexamined because it is, ideally, irrelevant to this fiction. The most troubling aspect of *Sense and Sensibility* is Austen's inability to establish narrative authority because she is

ambivalent toward both realism and romance. Her inability to establish moral authority is clearly related to this ambivalence. But its
complexities and implications are more clearly apparent in her next
novel, *Pride and Prejudice*.

Pride and Prejudice

In *Pride and Prejudice* (1813) the challenge that feeling and imaginative energy offer to moral authority is particularly persistent and
problematic, for it is posed by the heroine herself. As the outspoken
champion of the prerogatives of individual desire, Elizabeth Bennet
should jeopardize both the social order, which demands self-denial,
and the moral order, which is based on absolute Christian principles.
Yet, despite the dangers she seems to embody, Elizabeth Bennet was
Jane Austen's special favorite. "I think her as delightful a creature as
ever appeared in print," she wrote to Cassandra (*JAL*, 2:297; 29
January 1813). And, as a favorite, Elizabeth is handsomely rewarded:
she marries the richest man in all of Jane Austen's novels and is
established as mistress of Pemberley, one of those great country
estates that superintend and stabilize patriarchal society. In fact, Elizabeth's triumph signals the achievement of the balance that characterizes Austen's mature novels, for it is the result, on the one hand, of
the gradual transformation of social and psychological realism into
romance and, on the other, of a redefinition of romance. Essentially,
Austen legitimizes romance by making it seem the corrective—not
the origin or the product—of individualism. By such narrative magic,
Austen is able to defuse the thematic conflict between sense and
sensibility—or reason and feeling, or realism and romance—that
troubled her earlier works. What is more, by forcing her reader to
participate in creating the moral order that governs the novel's conclusion, Austen is able to make this aesthetic "solution" seem, at least
momentarily, both natural and right.

Pride and Prejudice depicts a world riven by ethical relativity, a fact
that both mocks any pretense to absolute moral standards and enhances the quality of everyday life in a small country village. "The
country," Darcy remarks, "can in general supply but few subjects for
such a study. In a country neighbourhood you move in a very confined
and unvarying society." "But people themselves alter so much," pert
Elizabeth responds, "that there is something new to be observed in
them for ever."[25] This principle of infinite variety within apparent
unity extends from the object of study to the observer, of course; the
fact that Elizabeth can praise Bingley for his compliance when he
offers to remain at Netherfield and call that same trait weakness when
he stays away (pp. 50, 135) tells us more about Elizabeth's desires than

the principle of tractability. And the fact that Elizabeth can excuse Wickham for preferring a practical marriage when she will forever blame Charlotte for making the same choice reveals more about Elizabeth's personal investment in these two situations than Jane Austen's views on matrimony or money. Judgment is always inflected—modulated—by personal desire, Austen suggests, just as vision is always governed by perspective. "Principles" are often merely prejudices, and prejudices simply project one's own interests onto the shifting scene outside so as to defend and reinforce the self.

Ideally, in such a world, conventions of propriety and morality make living together possible by compensating for the competing desires of individuals and by stabilizing standards of judgment and value. But in *Pride and Prejudice,* as in Austen's other novels and, presumably, in her society as well, social conventions no longer necessarily serve this end; instead, as Wollstonecraft complained, social institutions have ossified until they threaten to crush the desire from which they theoretically grew and which they ought to accommodate. Beside the arrogant Miss Bingley, parading around the drawing room in hopes of catching Darcy's eye, or Mr. Collins, pompous embodiment of unyielding propriety itself, Elizabeth's impulsiveness, outspokenness, and generosity seem admirable and necessary correctives. When she bursts into Netherfield to see her sick sister, for example, the mud on her skirts becomes completely irrelevant beside the healthiness of her unself-conscious concern for Jane. That Miss Bingley despises Elizabeth for what she calls "conceited independence" simply enhances our sympathy for conceit and independence, if these are the traits Elizabeth embodies. And when Elizabeth refuses to be subdued by Lady Catherine, whether on the subject of her music or her marriage, we feel nothing but admiration for her "impertinence"—if this is what her energy really is.

Yet the juxtaposition of Elizabeth's lively wit with this pretentious and repressive society cuts both ways; for if the vacuity of her surroundings highlights her energy, it also encourages her to cultivate her natural vivacity beyond its legitimate bounds. As the novel unfolds, we begin to recognize that Elizabeth's charming wit is another incarnation of willful desire, which, by rendering judgment unstable, contributes to moral relativity. As Elizabeth embellishes her surroundings with imaginative flourishes, we begin to see that indulging the imagination can harm others and that it in fact serves as a defense against emotional involvement. Through this juxtaposition, then, Austen is able to enlist the reader's initial imaginative engagement with Elizabeth in the service of moral education—an education for the reader, which shadows (but does not correspond precisely to) Elizabeth's own education, and which schools the imagination by means of its own irrepressible energy.

One of the first indications that Elizabeth's quick wit and powerful feelings may be unreliable moral guides emerges in her initial conversation with George Wickham. Until this moment, Elizabeth's companions and the settings in which she has appeared have enhanced her charm and appeal. But as soon as Elizabeth enters into her intimate conversation with Wickham, Austen encourages us to recognize that something is wrong. The problem here is not that a responsive young woman is attracted to a handsome young militia man; instead, the problem is that Elizabeth is unconsciously using Wickham to reinforce her prejudice against Darcy and is, as a consequence, allowing herself to be used by Wickham to reinforce his own false position. There are no disinterested or straightforward emotions in this scene; what appears to be Elizabeth's simple response to Wickham's physical and emotional charm is actually being fed by the subterranean force of her anger at Darcy. Elizabeth is flattered by Wickham's particular attention to her, but she is equally aroused by the fact that his story justifies her anger at Darcy. As a consequence of this double flattery, Elizabeth is blinded to the impropriety of this stranger's intimacy, she is seduced into judging on the grounds of Wickham's "countenance" rather than some less arbitrary principle, and she is encouraged to credit her feelings instead of testing her perceptions against reality.

The action of *Pride and Prejudice* generally reveals that, despite what looks like a generous overflow of irrepressible energy, Elizabeth's "liveliness" is primarily defensive.[26] More specifically, her "impertinence" is a psychological defense against the vulnerability to which her situation as a dependent woman exposes her. Elizabeth's prejudice against Darcy is so quickly formed and so persistent because, at the first assembly, he unthinkingly confronts her with the very facts that it is most in her interest to deny. "She is tolerable," Darcy concedes, rejecting Bingley's overtures on Elizabeth's behalf, "but not handsome enough to tempt *me*; and I am in no humour at present to give consequence to young ladies who are slighted by other men" (p. 12).

Despite the fact that Elizabeth's "playful disposition" enables her to turn this "ridiculous" remark against Darcy, his cool observation continues to vex and haunt her for much of the novel and to govern not only her anger toward Darcy but also her "mortification" at the antics of her family. It has this effect for two closely related reasons. First of all, in spite of her professed unconcern, Elizabeth, like everyone else, is immediately attracted to this handsome, eminently eligible bachelor, and, if only for a short time, he engages her natural romantic fantasies. We discover this later, when Darcy offers to make her dream come true and Elizabeth retorts by acknowledging that, though she once considered him as a possible husband, she no longer does so: "I had not known you a month," she exults, inadvertently acknowledging the longevity of her fantasy, "before I felt that you were the last man in the world whom I could ever be prevailed on to marry" (p. 193). But, given Elizabeth's social position and economic situation, even to dream of marrying Darcy is an act of imaginative presumption. The second reason for her lingering pain, then, is that Darcy's rejection deflates not only her romantic fantasies of marriage to a handsome aristocrat but, more important, the image of herself upon which such fantasies are based.

Darcy's casual remark suggests that the fact that Elizabeth is momentarily without a partner indicates that she will always be so "slighted," that her "tolerable" beauty will never attract the permanent partner she desires. And this remark strikes very close to home. For the inevitable result of an entail in a household more blessed with daughters than frugality is, at best, a limited choice of suitors; at worst, the Bennet's shortage of money for dowries and their equivocal social position foretell spinsterhood, dependence on a generous relative, or, most ominous of all, work as a governess or lady's companion. Austen never lets the reader or Elizabeth forget how very likely such a future is. Darcy lays the groundwork for this scenario when, alluding to their uncles in trade and law, he remarks that such connections "must very materially lessen [the sisters'] chance of marrying men of any consideration in the world" (p. 37). Even closer to home, when Charlotte Lucas rejects romance, she does so for its opposite, the matter-of-fact assessment that a "comfortable home" is more substantial than romantic fantasies. Elizabeth's mother is even more brutally frank. "If you take it into your head," she warns Elizabeth, "to go on refusing every offer of marriage in this way, you will never get a husband at all—and I am sure I do not know who is to maintain you when your father is dead" (p. 113). In the context of such dark realism, even Mr. Collins's compensatory retaliation sounds ominously like a self-evident truth. "Your portion is unhappily so small," he smugly informs Elizabeth, "that it will in all likelihood undo the effects of your loveliness and amiable qualifications" (p. 108).

Elizabeth chooses to ignore all of these warnings, of course, because, with the arrogance born of youth, natural high spirits, and intellectual superiority, she believes herself too good for such a fate. But Darcy challenges her self-confidence, and, in the disappointment he indirectly inflicts on Jane, he proves himself capable of bringing the Bennet family face to face with undeniable reality. In the face of real dependence and practical powerlessness, Elizabeth grasps at any possible source of power or distinction. As she confides to Jane in a moment of telling self-awareness, wit and prejudice have been her two sources of power, two means of distinguishing herself:

I meant to be uncommonly clever in taking so decided a dislike to him, without
any reason. It is such a spur to one's genius, such an opening for wit to have
a dislike of that kind. One may be continually abusive without saying any thing
just; but one cannot be always laughing at a man without now and then
stumbling on something witty. [Pp. 225–26]

From this statement, Elizabeth's psychological economy is clear: she
directs her intelligence toward defending herself against emotional
vulnerability; she bases her moral judgments at least partially on her
defensiveness; and she rationalizes both the romantic fantasies with
which she consoles herself and the forays of wit with which she
protects herself as spontaneous effusions of a lively and superior
mind.

Such criticism of Elizabeth's "liveliness" is elaborated by Austen's
characterizations of both Mr. Bennet and Lydia. Elizabeth is her
father's favorite daughter, and Mr. Bennet's witty intelligence clearly
reinforces and feeds off Elizabeth's superiority. But Mr. Bennet is
finally a failure, for he is lax when it comes to the social duties that
are most important to the Bennet family as a whole and to Elizabeth
in particular. Like Elizabeth's society in general, Mr. Bennet's character is a moral vacuum; his "indolence and the little attention he has
[given] to what was going forward in his family" (p. 283) finally
permit, if they do not encourage, Lydia's rebellion. Mr. Bennet tries
to make light of his moral irresponsibility by describing social relations as an amusing game. "For what do we live," he asks rhetorically,
"but to make sport for our neighbours, and laugh at them in our
turn?" (p. 364). But the pain that unthinking Lydia visits on the rest
of the family proves conclusively how serious—and how selfish—his
evasion really is.

Just as her father's defensive intelligence refracts and exaggerates
Elizabeth's intellectual "liveliness," so Lydia's wild, noisy laughter
helps clarify Elizabeth's "impertinence." But perhaps the most important function of Lydia's story derives from its placement. For Austen
positions the announcement of Lydia's elopement so as to precipitate
the second, and most important, stage of Elizabeth's education. Through
Darcy's letter, Elizabeth has already learned that she was wrong
about both Wickham and Darcy, but Darcy's proposal and her angry
rejection have, if anything, increased, not lessened, her pride and
sense of superiority. "Vanity, not love, has been my folly," Elizabeth
exclaims at the moment of this first "humiliation" (p. 208); but, on
second thought, she is deeply flattered by the great man's attentions,
and, since she does not regret her decision, she is free to bask in the
triumph his proposal gives her over his "pride," over his "prejudices," and over Lady Catherine and Miss Bingley as well. Thus, even
though she feels that her own "past behaviour" constitutes "a con-

stant source of vexation and regret" (p. 212), Elizabeth visits Pemberley with her vanity very much intact: "at that moment she felt, that
to be mistress of Pemberley might be something!" (p. 245). This
dream of what she might have been is jolted into the present and then
into the future when Darcy suddenly appears, proves courteous to the
very relatives he had previously slighted, and then invites Elizabeth
back to Pemberley to meet his sister. At this moment, Elizabeth
realizes that her "power" is even greater than she had dared imagine
it to be.

> She respected, she esteemed, she was grateful to him, she felt a real interest
> in his welfare; and she only wanted to know how far she wished that welfare
> to depend upon herself, and how far it would be for the happiness of both that
> she should employ the power, which her fancy told her she still possessed, of
> bringing on the renewal of his addresses. [P. 266]

While this reflection is neither cool nor calculating, it does suggest
that Elizabeth feels herself more superior than ever—not so much to
Darcy as to love.

Jane's letter arrives when Elizabeth is basking in this self-
confidence; its effect is to strip her of self-control, self-assurance, and
her confident superiority over feeling. In Darcy's presence she bursts
into tears and then, suddenly recognizing what she now believes she
has lost, she realizes that true power belongs not to the imagination
but to love: "Her power was sinking; every thing *must* sink under such
a proof of family weakness. . . . The belief of his self-conquest . . .
afforded no palliation of her distress. It was, on the contrary, exactly
calculated to make her understand her own wishes; and never had
she so honestly felt that she could have loved him, as now, when all
love must be vain" (p. 278).

Elizabeth's fantasies no longer seem as wild or romantic as they
once did, but, before her wish can be fulfilled, she must be "humbled" by her own sister—not only so that she (and the reader) will
recognize the pernicious effects of Lydia's passionate self-indulgence,
but so that Elizabeth herself will understand how intimately her own
fate is bound up in the actions and characters of others. Individualism
is not simply morally suspect, Austen suggests; it is also based on a
naïve overestimation of personal autonomy and power. To pretend
that one can transcend social categories or refuse a social role (as Mr.
Bennet does) is not only irresponsible; it also reveals a radical misunderstanding of the fact that, for an individual living in society, every
action is automatically linked to the actions of others. And to believe
that one can exercise free will, even when parents do not intercede,
is to mistake the complex nature of desire and the way in which social
situation affects psychology and self-knowledge.

Yet, despite its sobering implications, the "mortification" of Elizabeth's vanity does not constitute a rebuke to the premises or promises
of romance, as Marianne's illness does in *Sense and Sensibility*. Instead,
in order to convert the power of romance into a legitimate corrective
for harsh realism, Austen redeems romance by purging it of all traces
of egotism. As we have already seen, to believe that one's beauty and
wit will captivate a powerful lord is really a form of vanity. But
Elizabeth's actual romantic fantasies about Darcy are short-lived; the
only dashing young man she fantasizes extensively about is Wickham.
Elizabeth's response to her aunt's query about Wickham may be only
half serious, but her confusion does reveal the extent of her susceptibility.

> At present I am not in love with Mr. Wickham; no, I certainly am not. But he
> is, beyond all comparison, the most agreeable man I ever saw—and if he
> becomes really attached to me—I believe it will be better that he should not.
> I see the imprudence of it.—Oh! *that* abominable Mr. Darcy!—My father's
> opinion of me does me the greatest honor, and I should be miserable to forfeit
> it. My father, however, is partial to Mr. Wickham. In short, my dear aunt, I
> should be very sorry to be the means of making any of you unhappy; but since
> we see every day that where there is affection, young people are seldom
> withheld by immediate want of fortune from entering into engagements with
> each other, how can I promise to be wiser than so many of my fellow creatures
> if I am tempted, or how am I even to know that it would be wisdom to resist?
> All that I can promise you, therefore, is not to be in a hurry. I will not be in
> a hurry to believe myself his first object. When I am in company with him, I
> will not be wishing. In short, I will do my best. [Pp. 144–45]

Just as Elizabeth's prejudice against Darcy originally fed her admiration for Wickham, now her attraction to the young soldier focuses her
resentment against Darcy: if Wickham's story is true, after all, Darcy
has been directly (although inadvertently) responsible for preventing
a marriage between Elizabeth and Wickham. But Austen does not
allow this or any other romance to develop or capture Elizabeth's
imagination; indeed, when she dismisses this particular suitor, she
does not ridicule either the claims or the attractions of romance.
Instead, when Wickham declares for the wealthy Miss King, Elizabeth
remains undisturbed, and the entire issue of romantic love is simply
pushed to the periphery of the narrative. Wickham's decision to
marry for money does, after all, leave Elizabeth's vanity intact. "His
apparent partiality had subsided, his attentions were over, he was the
admirer of some one else. Elizabeth was watchful enough to see it all,
but she could see it and write of it without material pain. Her heart
had been but slightly touched, and her vanity was satisfied with
believing that *she* would have been his only choice, had fortune
permitted it" (p. 149).

Elizabeth's eventual love for Darcy is legitimate because it springs not from the vanity we ordinarily associate with romantic expectations but precisely from the mortification of pride. Yet because Elizabeth only belatedly realizes that she loves Darcy, her humbling does not entail a rejection of romantic love. Indeed, unaccountable, uncontrollable romantic love continues to play a role in *Pride and Prejudice* —in *Darcy's* desire for Elizabeth. This passion, which Austen notes but does not dwell on, is the subtextual force behind much of the action. In response to love, Darcy overcomes his prejudices against Elizabeth's connections, proposes to her, returns to her even after hope seems gone, and eventually brings about the marriages of three of the Bennet daughters. The narrative does not focus on the development or pressures of this passion; even when Elizabeth playfully asks Darcy for an account of his love, her mocking celebration of "impertinence" deflects any explanation he might have given. Romantic love remains the unexamined and unaccountable source of power in a novel preoccupied with various forms of social and psychological power and powerlessness. It not only overcomes all obstacles; it brings about a perfect society at the end of the novel.

The romantic conclusion of *Pride and Prejudice* effectively dismisses the social and psychological realism with which the novel began. Elizabeth's "impertinence" may have originated in her need to dispel the vulnerability of her dependent situation, but when marriage with Darcy cancels all the gloomy forecasts about Elizabeth's future, Austen no longer suggests a possible relationship between social causes and psychological effects. Elizabeth's "liveliness" persists, of course, but it is purified of its defensiveness and its egotism. In essence, in awarding Elizabeth this handsome husband with ten thousand pounds a year, Austen is gratifying the reader's fantasy that such outspoken liveliness *will* be successful in material terms, but she earns the right to do so precisely because Elizabeth's first fantasy of personal power is *not* rewarded. *Pride and Prejudice,* in other words, legitimizes the reader's romantic wishes by humbling the heroine's vanity. At the level of the plot, power is taken from egotism and given to love; at the level of the reading experience, power seems miraculously both to emanate from and to reward individualistic desire.

Darcy and Elizabeth, then, learn complementary lessons: he recognizes that individual feelings outweigh conventional social distinctions; she realizes the nature of society's power. Their marriage purports to unite individual gratification with social responsibility, to overcome the class distinctions that elevated Lady Catherine over the worthy Gardiners, and to make of society one big happy family. The last pages of *Pride and Prejudice* describe family connections radiating throughout society, closing the gap between geographical locations,

social classes, and temperamental differences. The union that concludes this novel reestablishes the ideal, paternalistic society that Mr.
Bennet's irresponsibility and Wickham's insubordination once seemed
to threaten. With Darcy at its head and Elizabeth at its heart, society
will apparently be able to contain the anarchic impulses of individualism and humanize the rigidities of prejudice, and everyone—even
Miss Bingley—will live more or less happily in the environs of Pemberley, the vast estate whose permanence, prominence, and unique
and uniquely satisfying fusion of individual taste and utility, of nature
and art, symbolize Jane Austen's ideal.[27]

AUSTEN IS ABLE TO EFFECT an aesthetic resolution of what is essentially
a moral dilemma partly because the realistic elements in her portrayal of the situation are so carefully contained. As in *Sense and Sensibility,*
Austen simply does not explore to the full the social or psychological
implications of her realism. Darcy, Charlotte Lucas, Mr. Collins, and
Mrs. Bennet all warn Elizabeth that her impertinence will probably
result in spinsterhood, but Austen does not imperil the integrity of
the romantic ending by dramatizing the perils of such a future in a
character like Jane Fairfax, Miss Bates, or Mrs. Smith. But even
beyond curtailing the extent of her realism, Austen controls the
response of her readers by drawing them into a system of values that
seems, by the end of the novel, both "natural" and right. She can
generate this system of common values because one of the fundamental principles of her art is to assume that the relationship between an
author and an audience is ideally (if not automatically) a version of
the relationship she knew best: the family.

The model of the family governs Jane Austen's art in at least three
important ways. To begin with, her own personal family served as
her first and most appreciative audience. Like the Brontës after her,
Jane Austen wrote her first stories for the amusement of her family;
most of her surviving juvenilia are dedicated to her siblings or cousins, and it is easy to imagine these stories and plays being read in the
family circle, with various members contributing jokes from time to
time. Austen's first longer works—*First Impressions* (later *Pride and
Prejudice*) and *Elinor and Marianne* (later *Sense and Sensibility*)—were also
apparently family entertainments, and, even after she became a published author, she continued to solicit and value the responses of her
family as she composed and revised her novels.[28] For Austen, the
entire enterprise of writing was associated with hospitality and familial bonds. Her letters reveal that she sometimes half-jokingly talked
of her novels as her "children" and of her characters as if they were
family friends. She assured her sister, for instance, that she could "no
more forget" *Sense and Sensibility* "than a mother can forget her

sucking child" (*JAL*, 2:272; 25 April 1811); she referred to *Pride and Prejudice* as her "own child" (*JAL*, 2:297; 29 January 1813); and she pretended to find a portrait of Jane Bingley exhibited in Spring Gardens: "There never was a greater likeness," Austen playfully announced; "She is dressed in a white gown, with green ornaments, which convinces me of what I had always supposed, that green was a favourite colour with her" (*JAL*, 2:310; 24 May 1813).[29]

The fact that Austen's completed novels and the activity of writing itself were part of the fabric of her family relationships helps to explain why she was able to avoid both the aggressive polemicism that Mary Wollstonecraft employed and the enfeebling defensiveness to which Mary Shelley resorted. Austen actively wondered what her readers thought of her novels, and she regretted that her works did not receive adequate critical attention, but she never seems to have imagined an audience openly hostile to either her novels or herself, as both Wollstonecraft and Shelley did, for different reasons. But in addition to providing a hospitable transitional area between her private imagination and the public bookstall, Jane Austen's experience of a close and supportive family also provided models both for the way an individual's desires could be accommodated by social institutions and for the context of shared values that an author could ideally rely on to provide a moral basis for art.

The notion of the family that served Jane Austen as a model for the proper coexistence of the individual and society was essentially patriarchal, supportive of, and supported by, the allegiances and hierarchy that feminine propriety implied. Its smallest unit—the marriage—embodied for Austen the ideal union of individual desire and social responsibility; if a woman could legitimately express herself *only* by choosing to marry and then by sustaining her marriage, Austen suggests, she *could*, through her marriage, not only satisfy her own needs but also influence society. For the most part, the culminating marriages in Austen's novels lack the undercurrents of ambivalence that characterize Shelley's depictions of even happy marriages. This is true in part because the energies of Austen's heroines are not so rigorously channeled by propriety into self-denial either before or after marriage. As *Sense and Sensibility* suggests, however, Austen does discipline female energies, but, increasingly, she also suggests that the psychological toll exacted by patriarchal society from women is too high. The fact that almost all of the peripheral marriages in her novels are dissatisfying in one way or another seems to indicate that Austen recognized both the social liabilities that Wollstonecraft identified and the psychological complexities that Shelley intuited. Nevertheless, and especially in *Pride and Prejudice*, the most idealistic of all of her novels, marriage remains for Austen the ideal paradigm of the most perfect fusion between the individual and society.

As the actual basis and ideal model of the contract between an author and an audience, the family also promised a context of shared experiences, assumptions, and values against which the writer could play and to which he or she could eventually return. And it is in this sense—and for this reason—that the moral relativism theoretically unleashed by individualism does not necessarily undermine Austen's conservative moral pattern or her didactic purpose. For if an author can assume a set of basic assumptions and values, such as family members share, then he or she can depend on the reader's returning with the narrator to that common ground, in spite of liberties to stray that have been permitted in the course of the fiction. In fact, given the common ground, these liberties often contribute to the didactic design of the novel, for they foster the illusion that challenges to ethical and aesthetic authority are actually being engaged and defeated in their own terms.

In *Pride and Prejudice* Austen tries to ensure that her readers will share a common ground by making them participate in constructing the value system that governs the novel. This participation is a necessary part of reading *Pride and Prejudice* because Austen combines a predominantly dramatic presentation of the action with an irony so persistent that it almost destroys narrative authority.[30] Even what looks like omniscient commentary often turns out, on closer inspection, to carry the accents of a single character. The famous first sentence of the novel, for example—"It is a truth universally acknowledged, that a single man in possession of a good fortune, must be in want of a wife"—points to the radical limitations of both "truth" and "universally." Masquerading as a statement of fact—if not about all unmarried men, then certainly about a community that collectively assumes it to be true—this sentence actually tells us more about Mrs. Bennet than anyone else. In such local instances, irony allows us a certain freedom of interpretation even when it teases us to test our "first impressions" against our developing understanding of individual characters and the priorities of the novel as a whole.

As Wayne Booth has noted, irony forces the reader not only to participate in interpretation and evaluation but to choose one *system* of values over another.[31] And it is through the value system developed in the overall action of the novel that Austen hopes to counter the relativism that the localized ironies might permit.[32] We can see this principle at work in Charlotte Lucas's argument about marriage. The narrator, conveying Charlotte's thoughts indirectly, takes no explicit stand on her position: "Without thinking highly either of men or of matrimony, marriage had always been her object; it was the only honourable provision for well-educated young women of small fortune, and however uncertain of giving happiness, must be their pleasantest preservative from want" (pp. 122–23). Certainly this statement illuminates the limitations of Charlotte's romantic expectations, but is it meant to be an authoritative assessment of reality? Or is Elizabeth's indignant rejoinder more authoritative? "You must feel, as well as I do," she exclaims to Jane, "that the woman who marries him, cannot have a proper way of thinking" (p. 135). Elsewhere Elizabeth's "proper way of thinking" has proved self-interested. Is this case any different? And how are we, finally, to decide?

In such passages, Austen is both permitting momentary freedom of choice and demonstrating the vertigo that accompanies it. But through the unfolding action of the novel she seems to qualify this freedom by endorsing one option over the other: Mr. Bingley and Mr. Darcy *do* both want and need wives; the love matches Elizabeth believed in *do* come about, despite all the odds against them. And, most important, the paternal order established at the end of the novel both embodies an authoritative system of values and abolishes the apparent discrepancy between individual desire and social responsibility. Jane Austen's irony, then, enables her to reproduce—without exposing in any systematic way—some of the contradictions inherent in bourgeois ideology; for by simultaneously dramatizing and rewarding individual desire *and* establishing a critical distance from individualism, she endorses both the individualistic perspective inherent in the bourgeois value system *and* the authoritarian hierarchy retained from traditional, paternalistic society. Moreover, by allowing her reader to exercise freedom of judgment in individual instances while controlling the final value system through the action as a whole, Austen replicates, at the level of the reading experience, the marriage of romantic desire and realistic necessity that she believed was capable of containing individualism's challenge to traditional authority.

In *Pride and Prejudice* this strategy effectively focuses what had remained two distinct narrative parts in *Lady Susan* and two competing centers of authority in *Northanger Abbey* and *Sense and Sensibility*. The closure of *Pride and Prejudice* is thus aesthetically successful, but whether it insures a comparable ideological resolution is doubtful. For at the level of the plot Austen can grant moral authority to feeling by stripping desire of egotism, but she cannot guarantee that every reader will be as educable as Elizabeth or that all expressions of feeling will be as socially constructive as Elizabeth's desire for Darcy. This problem is raised specifically in *Pride and Prejudice* by Lydia, and Austen never really dismisses this character or the unruly energy she embodies:

> Lydia was Lydia still; untamed, unabashed, wild, noisy, and fearless. She turned from sister to sister, demanding their congratulations, and when at length they all sat down, looked eagerly round the room, took notice of some

little alteration in it, and observed, with a laugh, that it was a great while since
she had been there. [P. 315]

Even Austen's concluding comment on Lydia acknowledges that she
finally finds a place within the same society that Elizabeth superintends. "In spite of her youth and her manners," the narrator informs
us, Lydia "retained all the claims to reputation which her marriage
had given her" (p. 387).

Austen's tacit assumption that her readers will renounce the moral
anarchy epitomized in Lydia and generated by the pattern of localized
ironies would be accurate only if her audience already shared her
own experiences and values. For the purposes of her art, Austen
makes this assumption because it allows her to contain not only
individual interpretations but also the social criticisms implicitly raised
in the course of *Pride and Prejudice*. In fact, this assumption enables
her to bring the real experiences of her readers to bear on her
narrative in such a way as to underscore the necessity of the aesthetic
solution, which pushes aside social realism and criticism. Austen's
contemporary readers would no doubt have been all too familiar with
the facts and pressures that made Charlotte Lucas's cool assessment
of marriage reasonable, and, merely by alluding to this shared experience, Austen enhances the gratification that Elizabeth's improbable
success provides. Thus she introduces the specters of spinsterhood,
dependence, and compromise less to explore the social strictures of
Elizabeth's situation than to invoke the reality that makes her own
consoling art necessary. The inadequacy of the aesthetic solution to
the social problems it supposedly answers remains implicit but un-
problematic; for it is precisely the gap between imaginative desire and
social reality—a gap that still exists—that makes the escape into
romance attractive to all readers and probably made Austen's contemporaries, in particular, anxious to believe that Elizabeth's happiness was available to every daughter of the middle class.

The special resonance and impact that her contemporaries sensed
in the statements and situations of Austen's novels are dim or absent
altogether for twentieth-century readers. But even the experiences
Austen's contemporaries shared with her, merely by virtue of their
historical, geographical, and class proximity, would not have guaranteed a common set of values. For, as we have seen, in this period of
social turmoil even the dominant system of values was characterized
by internal tensions and contradictions—stresses that reflected the
competition between bourgeois individualism and old patterns of
patronage and also the inevitable gap between the promises of individualism and the general inequalities and personal repressions that
bourgeois society requires. Given the structure of bourgeois society,
the system of absolute Christian principles that is the foundation of

Austen's novels necessarily had to have its everyday, functional version, which allowed one to be "rather" selfish in pursuit of material prosperity as long as one practiced charity and thought good thoughts. It is precisely the latitude of interpretations permitted by this compromise of ethical and moral absolutes that finally imperils the didactic design of *Pride and Prejudice*. For the family of readers that Austen posited did not necessarily exist; even in her own day, the consensus of values she needed to assume was as wishful a fiction as Elizabeth Bennet's marriage to Darcy.

Because of the sophistication of her narrative skills, the romance Austen dramatizes at the end of *Pride and Prejudice* seems not only right but plausible. But it is plausible only because, in this novel, Austen separates the power to gratify and discipline desire from the conditions that generate and frustrate that desire. The power moves from society to the realm of art; in *Pride and Prejudice* Austen substitutes aesthetic gratification—the pleasures of the "light and bright and sparkling" plays of wit—for the practical solutions that neither her society nor her art could provide. That we do not more often feel shortchanged by this sleight-of-hand attests to the power of her artistry and to the magnitude of our own desire to deny the disturbing ideological contradictions that have made such imaginative compensation necessary.

7

"The True English Style"

IN MANY WAYS Jane Austen's last three completed novels and the unfinished *Sanditon* continue the didactic program adumbrated as early as *Lady Susan* and artistically worked out in *Pride and Prejudice:* to demonstrate how feeling can be schooled into a constructive and reliable moral authority. Nevertheless, in *Mansfield Park* (1814), *Emma* (1815), *Persuasion* (1818), and *Sanditon* Austen devotes increasingly critical attention to the social situations and conventions that shape—and, as often as not, thwart or deform—female desire. In *Lady Susan, Northanger Abbey,* and *Sense and Sensibility,* female desire is a natural force that is, at best, morally ambiguous; at worst, it is a force capable of distorting reality, of disrupting social relations, and of turning back on itself to fester or erupt in destructive sicknesses of body and mind. But in *Pride and Prejudice* and, more consistently, in her last novels, as Austen begins to consider some of the reasons why female desire takes these disastrous directions, she begins to be less ambivalent toward this source of personal energy and distress. In doing so, Austen moves beyond both Mary Wollstonecraft's aggressive criticism of social institutions and Mary Shelley's defensive castigation of female energy. For in exploring the relationship between social situations and psychology, Austen suggests the way in which ideology is internalized and even psychologized. But because she does not wholly reject either social institutions or the power of individual desire, she is able to imagine the possibility of both personal moral education and institutional reform. As a result, she is able to explore the institutional repressions that so enraged Mary Wollstonecraft and the psychological complexities that so intimidated Mary Shelley. In her last novels Austen is as insistent as ever on the epistemological and ethical anarchy that unchecked individualism can produce, but she is now more intent on showing how individual feeling can become moral and how it can—and must—make room for itself within the very social institutions that threaten to destroy it. Austen never again constructs as idealistic a romance as the one that concludes *Pride and*

Prejudice, but in these last novels she does continue to try to salvage romance—both romantic love and the form of wish-fulfillment itself. For only by making romance speak to and answer propriety can she hope to fuse individual desire with social responsibility.

Austen's increasing concern with the connection between the social and the psychological was no doubt fueled by the series of personal disappointments she experienced between 1798 and 1809. Probably because of the personal turbulence of this period, Cassandra has left few letters to detail Jane Austen's precise responses, but the facts of this period and the novels and letters that we do have suggest that Austen was increasingly aware of the implications of her position as a single, dependent woman in a society threatened by sweeping social and economic changes. It was also at this time that she began to develop a sense of herself as a professional writer, a woman telling stories not only for the amusement of her immediate family but for the edification of an audience desperately in need of reform. Paradoxically, the vulnerability of one position reinforced the strength of the other; for as Jane Austen became more aware of what it meant to be a woman in her society, she became more anxious to explore in realistic terms the treacherous facts that made the position of women so complicated.

The great trauma of these years began when Austen's father decided to retire to Bath, the resort city that Jane had always disliked. According to family tradition, this decision, announced dramatically to Jane in late 1800, caused her to faint, and the move, which took place in May 1801, completely disrupted the stability of her domestic life; among other things, it necessitated the disposal of all of her most valued possessions—the family furniture, her piano, and her books. Her letters that survive from this period reflect a resolute determination to be cheerful, but her depiction of Bath in *Persuasion* alerts us to the feelings embedded in the letters' comic forecasts of what life at Bath will be like. The family, Austen jokes, will ensure their comfort with "a steady Cook, & a young giddy Housemaid, with a sedate, middle aged Man, who is to undertake the double office of Husband to the former & sweetheart to the latter."[1] Sometime during the Austens' residence at Bath, Jane probably suffered another severe personal disappointment as well. According to the story Cassandra passed on to their niece Caroline, Jane, during one of these summers, probably while the family was vacationing in Devon, fell deeply in love for the first time in her life. The gentleman's feelings were reportedly as strong as hers, but, before he could visit her again, he fell ill and died.[2] In the winter of 1802, Austen had a second brush with romance, this time apparently with Harris Bigg-Wither, the twenty-one-year-old neighbor of her brother James at Steventon. As

Caroline tells the story, Jane actually accepted Bigg-Wither's proposal but, after a sleepless night, she reversed her decision the next morning. At twenty-seven, Jane Austen seems voluntarily to have embraced the fact that she would be a spinster for the rest of her life.

The personal disturbances continued. On 16 December 1804, Jane Austen's birthday, her close friend Mrs. Lefroy was killed in a riding accident. One month later, on 21 January 1805, Austen's father died suddenly after an illness of only forty-eight hours. The blow this last death dealt to the family was severe—especially for the three women. Not only did they suffer emotional loss, but the Reverend Austen's death also destroyed their personal security, for it left Mrs. Austen, Cassandra, and Jane an annual income of only £460 and no permanent residence of their own.[3] As a temporary measure, the three women moved to furnished lodgings in Bath, where they were joined by Jane's friend Martha Lloyd. But Bath did not offer an affordable or a desirable home, and during the next several years the women were visitors in the houses of such friends or relatives as Jane's brother Frank at Southampton and Edward's family at Godmersham in Kent. Not until after Edward's wife died in 1808 and Edward offered his mother the cottage at Chawton in Hampshire did the women find a permanent home.

During these years Austen also suffered what turned out to be a second setback in her attempt to become a published writer. *First Impressions,* the first version of *Pride and Prejudice,* had been submitted to the London publisher Cadell and rejected by return post in 1797. In 1803, in what seemed at last to be the launching of a career, Jane's father sold *Susan* (later *Northanger Abbey*) to Crosby & Cox for £10. The publisher advertised the novel but failed to print it, and Henry Austen eventually had to buy it back in 1816. Austen probably composed the fragment known as *The Watsons* during this period, but the reception her two manuscripts had received and her own unsettled emotional and domestic situation were not conducive to sustained composition. "You mu[st be] aware that in another person's house one cannot command one's own time or actions," she noted in 1814 (*JAL,* 2:423; November or December 1814). When she did finally get Thomas Egerton of the Military Library interested in *Sense and Sensibility,* Henry had to guarantee, if not advance, the printing costs (between £100 and £200). Jane was so uncertain of the novel's success that she saved a contingency fund from her small resources so that she could reimburse Henry if it failed.

Among her contemporaries Jane Austen never achieved the popularity that novelists like Maria Edgeworth, Fanny Burney, Walter Scott, or Mary Shelley enjoyed, nor were her earnings from her novels large. During her lifetime, her four published novels earned her less than £700; this was at a time when Maria Edgeworth could command between £1,500 and £2,000 per novel.[4] Only *Pride and Prejudice* went into three editions, and, even though her first two novels were widely enough read and reviewed to achieve the (dubious) honor of attracting the prince regent's attention, Austen could never count on her novels to support her or permit her to change her personal situation. Yet her letters suggest that she increasingly had a sense of herself as a public figure and respectable writer. Her first responses to having her identity as an author known were humorously self-deprecating: "I should like to see Miss Burdett very well," she wrote in 1813, "but that I am rather frightened by hearing that she wishes to be introduced to *me*.—If I *am* a wild Beast, I cannot help it" (*JAL*, 2:311; 24 May 1813). By the fall of that year, however, Austen was thinking about exploiting publicity rather than shrinking from it.

> I was previously aware of what I sh^d be laying myself open to—but the truth is that the Secret has spread so far as to be scarcely the Shadow of a secret now—& that I beleive [*sic*] whenever the 3^d appears, I shall not even attempt to tell Lies about it.—I shall rather try to make all the Money than all the Mystery I can of it.—People shall pay for their knowledge if I can make them. [*JAL* 2:340; 25 September 1813]

By November, Austen was joking, with considerably more self-confidence, that "I do not despair of having my picture in the Exhibition at last—all white & red, with my Head on one Side;—or perhaps I may marry young Mr. D'arblay" (*JAL*, 2:368; 3 November 1813). Austen cared about the sales and reviews of her novels as well as the opinions of her friends and family.[5] Yet, in writing to Cassandra that

> I do not write for such dull elves
> As have not a great deal of ingenuity themselves,
>   [*JAL*, 2:298; 29 January 1813]

Austen reveals that she preferred a small, discriminating audience to having to gratify her readers' expectations.

That Jane Austen did have a sense of her role as a professional author, writing primarily for an intelligent audience, becomes an important factor in our understanding of her last novels. Though she was obviously enamored of the wit, the charm, and the relative popularity of *Pride and Prejudice,* she now desired to turn to "a complete change of subject" (*JAL*, 2:298; 29 January 1813), and that fact, and the particular subject she chose, suggest that she was now beginning to sense that irony, and the moral ambiguity it often entailed, would blur her more serious didactic design.[6] Perhaps because her own personal experience was showing her both the perils of the female situation and the inadequacy of escaping into the purely aesthetic consolation of romance, she wanted to use her art to confront some of the problems that made romantic escape attractive. In order to do so, Austen withheld from her readers both the "playfulness and epigrammatism" of *Pride and Prejudice* (*JAL,* 2:300; 4 February 1813) and the immediate gratification provided by a heroine with whom it was flattering—and rewarding—to identify. Austen was aware that doing so might cost her what popularity she had acquired. She acknowledged, for example, that *Mansfield Park* was "not half so entertaining" as her last novel (*JAL,* 2:317; 3 July 1813), and she predicted that those who appreciated *Pride and Prejudice* would find *Emma* "inferior in wit" (*JAL,* 2:443; 11 December 1815). But Austen was beginning to see that challenging her readers' expectations and desires was a necessary first step toward reforming the social practices that currently helped to frustrate female self-expression and fulfillment. By educating her readers to the dangers of uninhibited desire, Austen might be able to convince them that the controls exercised by the institutions of patriarchal society were necessary. By then suggesting that principled feeling could, in turn, reform these social institutions, she could argue that discipline was not only necessary but desirable. Particularly through dramatizing such "principled" yet passionate heroines as Fanny Price and Anne Elliot, Austen would be able to show how bourgeois ideology could be purged of its contradictions and how, when it was so reformed, it could accommodate female feeling without driving a woman's energy into self-destructive or anarchic forms.

Mansfield Park

Beside the charming, outspoken Elizabeth Bennet, Fanny Price holds little appeal for many readers, but as a response to the complex dangers threatening the values of traditional society, she promises a more convincing solution than Elizabeth Bennet could offer. For though Elizabeth's impertinence could be schooled into love, the individualistic energy she represented was ominously akin to one of the primary antagonists of social order. By contrast, Fanny Price is outwardly everything a textbook Proper Lady should be; she is dependent, self-effacing, and apparently free of impermissible desires. If so ideal an exemplar of femininity could be made both sympathetic and powerful, Austen would be able to demonstrate how traditional society could be regenerated from within its own values and institutions.

The necessity of moral regeneration is established by Austen's depicting the dangers threatening class society as more numerous and more potent than they had seemed in her earlier novels. In

Mansfield Park the danger is not confined to a single avaricious male or to a female who indulges anarchic desire; instead, internal decay undermines the health of the landed gentry even as dangerous outsiders invade Mansfield's expansive grounds. In many ways, Mansfield Park seems a citadel in a turbulent world; compared to London or Portsmouth, Mansfield enjoys quiet and order, everyone has his or her own place and possessions, everyone is cared for, and the labor necessary to sustain this life goes on unseen, miraculously efficient and apparently part of the natural order of things. But in other ways the shadow of the outside world falls across Mansfield Park more darkly than in Austen's earlier novels. Sir Thomas departs for Antigua and returns, a changed man, to a home strangely disrupted in his absence; Portsmouth, Fanny Price's birthplace, home of the twin specters of poverty and selfishness, is an ever-present reminder of the past that was and the future that so easily might be; and London, with its casual morality and its confusion of rank, is always close by, always ready to disgorge more people like the Crawfords, hungry for whatever diversion the quaint country estate can yield.

The Crawfords epitomize the external challenge to Mansfield Park and the values it ideally superintends; for though Henry Crawford owns an estate in Norfolk, he does not fulfill his patriarchal responsibilities until love for Fanny inspires him to reform. He and his sister have been raised to practice London habits: they maintain that anything can be got with money and that morality is simply a matter of convenience or inclination, not of principle. "Nothing ever fatigues me," Mary Crawford cavalierly remarks, "but doing what I do not like."[7] But the Crawfords are so openly welcomed to Mansfield that it is difficult to believe that this external threat is in any way decisive. Indeed, the secure, stable life at Mansfield has already begun to deteriorate before the Crawfords arrive. When the novel opens, the extravagance of Tom Bertram, heir to the estate, has already squandered his brother's patrimony (the Norwood living), and Tom's continuing thoughtlessness so undermines the family's wealth that his father must go to Antigua to shore up the family holdings there. Tom's general fecklessness also causes him to associate with decadent gentlemen like Yates, and it eventually leads to the overindulgence and fever that almost deprive Mansfield Park of its heir. The decay has not originated with Tom, however, for Sir Thomas has raised his children with an unhealthy combination of restraint and indulgence that has given them—especially his daughters—an idiosyncratic education instead of the principles of "duty" they should have learned. "They had never been properly taught to govern their inclinations and tempers, by that sense of duty which can alone suffice" (p. 463).

The threat to the traditional habits and values that had originally

sprung from humanity's dependence on the land is posed most generally in *Mansfield Park* by an ethics based on convenience, ready cash,
and individual pleasure. *Lovers' Vows,* the play rehearsed at Mansfield
in Sir Thomas's absence, brings together all the elements and agents
of this threat and unleashes within the great house itself the anarchic
energies that social conventions ideally restrain. The play itself, as
numerous critics have pointed out, is an example of "Continental
political radicalism expressed in the conventions of sentimental comedy";[8] it denounces the entire upper class and substitutes for the
values traditionally associated with the landed classes the morality
based on individual desire that Hannah More so roundly berated.
The rehearsals of this play at Mansfield liberate each character's
repressed desires, preoccupations, or anxieties, and the fact that the
anticipated performance necessitates physical alterations in the house,
and the lesson that emotion, once indulged, will inevitably find an
outlet, also point to the dangers this new ethic poses.

Austen's graphic depiction of the moral deterioration within the
landed gentry suggests her growing awareness that she might need
to create a family of readers with a common set of values instead of
merely assuming that such readers already existed. To do so, she
makes her heroine embody and enforce ideal principles and then
humanizes these principles so that they perfectly accommodate desire. Austen's goal is to make propriety and romantic desire absolutely congruent. By showing how self-effacement can yield self-
fulfillment, she will imaginatively purge ideology of the inequities and
self-interest that currently make the expression of individual desire
dangerous to society as a whole.

One function of the novel's plot is to redeem propriety by distinguishing between conduct based on absolute, selfless principles and
the superficial accomplishments that serve merely to display the self.
In the contrasts she establishes between Fanny Price and Mrs. Norris,
Maria Bertram, or Mary Crawford, Austen is essentially exposing the
fundamental paradox of propriety, separating its ideal substance
from the surface that belies this substance. Fanny's grave self-effacement, for example—"I can never be important to any one" (p. 26)—is
followed immediately by the passive aggression that is its other face.
"What could I do with Fanny?" Mrs. Norris whimpers. "Me! A poor
helpless, forlorn widow, unfit for any thing" (p. 28). Maria Bertram
repeatedly proves that the "duty" that Fanny so rigorously interprets
is susceptible to a more "liberated" reading. "Being now in her
twenty-first year," the narrator tells us, "Maria Bertram was beginning to think matrimony a duty; and as a marriage with Mr. Rushworth would give her the enjoyment of a larger income than her
father's . . . it became, by the same rule of moral obligation, her

evident duty to marry Mr. Rushworth if she could" (pp. 38–39). As skillfull as Mrs. Norris and Maria Bertram are at exploiting the paradoxes of propriety, their accomplishments are overshadowed by Mary Crawford's ability not only to use manners for flirting but to convince Edward, the novel's sternest moralist, that her "liveliness" and beauty merit their own ethical yardstick. Edmund reveals Mary's influence when he lectures Fanny that "The right of a lively mind, . . . seizing whatever may contribute to its own amusement or that of others, [is] perfectly allowable, when untinctured by ill humour or roughness" (p. 64).

When we see the hypocrisy that propriety allows so graphically demonstrated in these characters, and when we see its subversive potential explode in Maria's final revolt, we cannot help but contrast and prefer quiet Fanny's fidelity to a more rigid code of behavior. But Austen does not propose so straightforward a reversal of "accomplishments" into "conduct," for neither the social implications of propriety nor its psychological function is so simple. Indeed, one of the most significant of Austen's achievements in *Mansfield Park* is the way that she uses psychological realism, briefly introduced in *Pride and Prejudice,* to explore the complex appeal and limitations of propriety.

Like *Sense and Sensibility, Mansfield Park* opens with a summary history that anchors the subsequent action. Here, however, the economic factors that affect the characters have much more extensively developed psychological implications, for the story of the ambitions and achievements of the three Ward sisters actively helps to explain the formation of Fanny Price's personality. In the background story, each of the sisters acts out one of the possible fates that romantic expectations can lead to in bourgeois society. One sister has "the good luck" to succeed in the competitive business of getting a husband: she "captivate[s] Sir Thomas Bertram, of Mansfield Park" (p. 3). A second sister, her expectations no doubt reinforced by her sister's success, "had used to look forward to" a similar future of consequence and luxury, but her romantic expectations are frustrated by the cruel disproportion between promises and possibilities: "there certainly are not so many men of large fortune in the world, as there are pretty women to deserve them," the narrator explains, and this Miss Ward is "obliged to be attached to the Rev. Mr. Norris," a man "with scarcely any private fortune," but conveniently placed so as to benefit from Sir Thomas's patronage. The third sister—Fanny's mother—for reasons never extensively explored, completely rejects the romantic fantasies that have shaped her sisters' ambitions. "To disoblige her family," she marries a man "without education, fortune, or connections," a lieutenant of marines whose profession places him beyond the pale of Sir Thomas's generosity.

This brief history of the fate of romantic expectations provides the context in which we will eventually interpret Fanny's more modest desires. More immediately, it helps explain the origin of the defenses that Fanny consolidates upon her arrival at Mansfield Park. Significantly, of the three sisters, neither Fanny's mother nor her patron aunt, Lady Bertram, proves as influential as Mrs. Norris, the sister whose hopes have been thwarted by society's inability to satisfy the expectations romance has generated. "Having married on a narrower income than she had been used to look forward to," the narrator explains,

> she had, from the first, fancied a very strict line of economy necessary; and what was begun as a matter of prudence, soon grew into a matter of choice, as an object of that needful solicitude, which there were no children to supply. Had there been a family to provide for, Mrs. Norris might never have saved her money; but having no care of that kind, there was nothing to impede her frugality, or lessen the comfort of making a yearly addition to an income which they had never lived up to. Under this infatuating principle, counteracted by no real affection for her sister, it was impossible for her to aim at more than the credit of projecting and arranging so expensive a charity; though perhaps she might so little know herself, as to walk home to the Parsonage after this conversation, in the happy belief of being the most liberal-minded sister and aunt in the world. [Pp. 8–9]

Needing to be needed, needing to express her "spirit of activity," yet lacking any vehicle for expression more meaningful than accumulating capital or "projecting" charity, Mrs. Norris is a typical victim of the discrepancy between romantic expectations and social possibilities. Her irritating officiousness focuses this discrepancy, for it is really a woman's imaginative energy misdirected by her dependence and social uselessness. To the extent that Mrs. Norris becomes an artist manquée, she does so because she has been deprived of an appropriate profession by the strictures society has placed on the very imagination it has aroused.

Mrs. Norris arranges for Sir Thomas to adopt Fanny Price as a means of reinforcing what meager power she has. For just as the office of patron flatters Sir Thomas (and thus indirectly enhances Mrs. Norris's value), so the activity of moral instructor reinforces Mrs. Norris's tenuous sense of her own superiority—especially when the lessons she prescribes all project onto her little niece the worthlessness, inferiority, and indebtedness she is so anxious to deny in herself. Fanny's "education" begins as soon as she enters her aunt's charge: "Mrs. Norris had been talking to her the whole way from Northampton of her wonderful good fortune, and the extraordinary degree of gratitude and good behaviour which it ought to produce" (p. 13).

The fact that Austen so fully details the origins of Fanny's timidity demonstrates how the behavior associated with propriety can answer very pressing psychological needs. Young Fanny is effectively pushed and pulled into becoming a textbook Proper Lady. On the one hand, she is driven to self-effacement and passivity by Mrs. Norris's admonitions about the "evil" of ingratitude, by Sir Thomas's stern and wary disapproval, and by her female cousins' "easy indifference." On the other hand, she is drawn toward propriety by the only attention she receives—the indolent tolerance of Lady Bertram and the more discriminating approval Edmund seems to offer. What we later see of Fanny's first home in Portsmouth suggests that she has thus far received little attention or guidance. Thus, when Edmund begins to notice her and to initiate her education, Fanny is anxious to please—because pleasing Edmund accords her her only sense of personal value or success. Twice Austen informs us that, in every important respect, Edmund has "formed [Fanny's] mind" (pp. 64, 470). While Austen only alludes to the actual process of this moral and intellectual education—we must understand it from the results it produces in Fanny's behavior and from Edmund's discussion of the clergy at Southerton—we can infer that its principles were strict and that Fanny has been carefully taught how to distinguish the *"conduct"* that is the "result of good principles" from mere "refinement and courtesy . . . the ceremonies of life" (p. 93).

Fanny's embrace of propriety is, therefore, intimately bound up with her defense against rejection, and it is likewise linked to her ideas about love. Even though she has never had the kind of romantic expectations that are her cousins' birthright, her greatest ambition still involes romance and love. For her, the ultimate reward of propriety would be simply to be loved by the man who has made her what she is. Yet, because she has taken her model of propriety not from other women or from books but from a man whose vocation incarnates absolute virtue, Fanny Price knows only one dimension of propriety. From her education by Edmund she acquires neither the superficial accomplishments her cousins perfect nor the knowledge of how to make propriety express the desire she feels. More specifically, in direct contrast to both Mary Crawford and her cousins, Fanny does not know how to make propriety express her sexuality and thus earn her the romance that is theoretically its reward. When Fanny's modesty and susceptibility finally do arouse a man's attention—and every moralist assured young women that these traits would produce this result—the poor girl does not know how to defend herself from Henry Crawford or how to make her real desires known.

In presenting the psychological and social origins of propriety and the costs that it can exact, Austen alerts her readers to complexities of the ethical code that the conservative moralists overlooked. But

Austen does so in order to endorse this code; dramatizing the emotional turmoil hidden behind Fanny's impassive face generates sympathy for the principles Fanny consistently struggles to defend. For,
even more than Maria or Mary, Fanny is a character besieged by
intense feelings; and, even more than Catherine Morland or Marianne Dashwood, she is a heroine of feeling. Numerous critics have
commented on Fanny's sensitivity to nature and to art; throughout
the novel her responses are a veritable barometer of the emotional
undercurrents of the action, and her periodic outbursts of "agitation"—whether induced by pain or by intense joy—mark the moral
turning points of the plot. That for most of the novel only the reader
recognizes the extent and direction of Fanny's passion enhances our
sense of her isolation and the complexity of what might look to her
fellow characters like unyielding self-righteousness. Because we—and
no one else—see Fanny's struggles to bring her strong feelings into
line with propriety, we are asked to appreciate the difficulties of her
task and thus to share in the triumph of her eventual accomplishment.

In order to give Fanny's feelings moral authority and power, Austen subjects her to two tests, each of which pits her hard-earned
principles against what should be a bulwark of patriarchal values. In
the first of these trials, Fanny must choose between the principles
Edmund has inculcated in her and the love he has aroused. This test
is particularly difficult for Fanny because, despite Edmund's initial
severity, *his* principles have given way to love for Mary Crawford. The
dilemma is brought to a crisis for Fanny by Edmund's decision to act
in *Lovers' Vows*. Fanny knows that she loves Edmund, and she knows
that acting in this play, in Sir Thomas's absence, is wrong. Yet, so
entangled are her "disinterested" principles in all kinds of self-interested feelings and fears that, for a moment, we are allowed to glimpse
the complexities involved in even the best of intentions. Realizing that
at least *she* will be spared the embarrassment of acting—but only
because Mary Crawford has spoken in her defense—Fanny abandons
herself to tumultuous emotions that border on self-pity:

> She was safe; but peace and safety were unconnected here. Her mind had been
> never farther from peace. She could not feel that she had done wrong herself,
> but she was disquieted in every other way. Her heart and her judgment were
> equally against Edmund's decision; she could not acquit his unsteadiness; and
> his happiness under it made her wretched. She was full of jealousy and agita-
> tion. . . . Every body around her was gay and busy, prosperous and impor-
> tant. . . . She alone was sad and insignificant; she had no share in any thing;
> she might go or stay. [Pp. 159–60]

By this point in the novel, Fanny has become Edmund's conscience,
a silent reminder of the principles he is now violating. But in scenes

like this one Austen reminds us that, though conscience may be authoritative and even reliable, it does not take its stand without effort and pain.

In this case, and at the moment when her resolution is most hard-pressed, Fanny is spared, by Sir Thomas's return, from having to choose between love and principle. But in her second trial she *is* required to assert herself, and now against an even more intimidating authority figure. Just as Edmund allowed his passion to undermine his judgment, so Sir Thomas now lets his pride overwhelm his grow- ing affection for Fanny. Henry Crawford's proposal is in itself easy for Fanny to reject, but disappointing Sir Thomas is extremely pain- ful. For her fidelity to her feelings, Fanny is called "self-willed, obsti- nate, selfish, and ungrateful" (p. 319)—all the qualities she has struggled to avoid—and she is exiled to Portsmouth, which has long since ceased to be her home. It is in Portsmouth, however, that Fanny finally begins to gain the same confidence in her feelings that Ed- mund taught her to have in principles. Empowered by her compara- tive wealth and stimulated by the "potent" appeal of books, Fanny takes the initiative for the first time when she purchases a silver knife to resolve her sisters' quarrel. Feeling her love answered by Susan's gratitude, she is emboldened to undertake her sister's education: "she [gives] advice" to Susan, as Edmund had once done for her, and she joins a circulating library to increase Susan's knowledge even more. "Amazed at being any thing *in propria persona,* amazed at her own doings in every way" (p. 398), Fanny finally realizes that she *is* impor- tant and that her deepest feelings really will point out her proper duty.

For Jane Austen, the "heroism of principle" is the most important lesson of *Mansfield Park.* In the course of the novel Fanny must learn two things: to understand her feelings enough to be able to distin- guish between selfishness and self-denying love, and to trust her feelings enough to be willing to act on them, even when they contra- dict more traditional, but less authentic, authority. Strengthened by the confederacy of principle and feeling, Fanny is ultimately able to superintend the moral regeneration of Mansfield Park; simply by the "comfort" her quiet example provides, she is able to arrest the moral cancer that has spread from Sir Thomas's combined neglect and indulgence. Significantly, Fanny's prominence at the end of the novel is perfectly in keeping with what moralists described as woman's proper role: her actions are always indirect, and she finally engages Edmund's love, not by aggressively exposing Mary's treachery, but through the irresistible appeal of her constant love. Edmund is always allowed to sense his own superiority; his love for Fanny is founded on her "most endearing claims of innocence and helplessness," and she soon grows necessary to him "by all his own importance with her" (p. 470). Fanny also becomes a dutiful daughter to Sir Thomas— "the daughter that he wanted"—a salve to his damaged ego and a "rich repayment" for his initial generosity.

Through these two tests of Fanny's character, Austen effectively strips propriety of its potential for selfishness and its tempting offer of invisibility and crowns it with romantic love. As Fanny finally exemplifies it, "the heroism of principle" is tough-minded and tender-hearted; its struggles and its victories are, in many ways, more difficult and more rewarding than those any contemporary moralist described. But it is important to recognize that Austen can engineer Fanny's triumph only by skillfully managing any trial that would actually pit Fanny's principles against feeling. To avoid such confron-tations completely would be to undermine the authority that Fanny's arduous defense of principle has earned, but to dramatize them would be to risk losing the consensus about values that the action aspires to establish. Austen solves the dilemma by alluding to possibilities she never allows to enter her fictional world. For example, she informs the reader that, had Fanny's "affection" not been engaged by Ed-mund, she would eventually have been "persuaded into love" by Henry Crawford (p. 231); but Austen never lets the reader forget that Fanny's heart *is* prepossessed by Edmund, and Henry succumbs to Maria's wiles before Fanny's feelings square off against her principles. Similarly, Austen acknowledges Mary Crawford's powerful appeal; indeed, even Fanny feels "a kind of fascination" for Mary's charms (p. 208). But Austen tries not to let our emotional response to Mary undermine the values that Fanny represents. Many of the narrator's overt comments underscore the contrast between Mary and Fanny precisely in order to reinforce these values: Mary "had none of Fanny's delicacy of taste, of mind, of feeling; she saw nature, inani-mate nature, with little observation" (p. 81). In order to ensure that the reader will censure this character who constantly threatens to escape narrative control, Austen awards the final, harsh assessment of Mary to the character who has most thoroughly succumbed to her charms: "Hers is not a cruel nature," Edmund explains, fumbling for a formula that will negate his love; "The evil lies yet deeper; in her total ignorance, unsuspiciousness of there being such feelings, in a perversion of mind. . . . Hers are faults of principle, Fanny, of blunted delicacy and a corrupted, vitiated mind" (p. 456).

A genuine contest between feelings and principles would finally challenge the power—and, implicitly, the moral authority—of Fanny's triumph. Austen therefore cannot admit into her fictional world any graphic dramatization of the forces that made this triumph so con-trived. Antigua and everything it represents—poverty, slavery, the challenge to authority that the slave uprising posed—all of these things remain distant, vague; Sir Thomas returns from Antigua chastened and changed, but we never know why or how the change occurred. Similarly, the "guilt and misery" to which the narrator alludes in the final chapter are conveniently left offstage; Maria may suffer constant anguish, but her suffering is relegated to "another country, remote and private," for Austen cannot acknowledge that the society she is so anxious to defend can either accommodate Maria's passion or punish it, remorselessly, forever. Finally, Austen alludes to but does not dramatize the complete disintegration of the family, the institution upon which her ideal society is based. The following narrative aside interrupts the description of the reunion between Fanny and William, for only their surprisingly resilient love can contradict the possibility that Austen's lament introduces. "Even the conjugal tie is beneath the fraternal," the narrator tells us.

> Children of the same family, the same blood, with the same first associations and habits, have some means of enjoyment in their power, which no subsequent connections can supply; and it must be by a long and unnatural estrangement, by a divorce which no subsequent connection can justify, if such precious remains of the earliest attachments are ever entirely outlived. Too often, alas! it is so.—Fraternal love, sometimes almost every thing, is at others worse than nothing. [P. 235]

If there were, finally, no family bonds, impervious to the effects of distance or time, there would be no basis for the society Austen wants to defend or for the consensus she counts on to anchor her moral and narrative authority. The notion that such bonds might disappear must be admitted in order to be emphatically dismissed by both the narrator and the novel's action; even the exiled Maria remains under Sir Thomas's protection, and, at the novel's conclusion, every character can be appropriately "placed" for all time by the narrator. Indeed, in one sense or another, the whole world seems "within the view and patronage of Mansfield Park."

Ideally, the values epitomized by Fanny and centered in Mansfield Park will, by the end of the fiction, be shared by all of Austen's readers. To effect this consensus, Austen employs another version of the narrative strategy she used in *Pride and Prejudice*. Here, as there, most of the action is dramatic, and here, by manipulating sequences of perspectives on certain important events, Austen duplicates the interpretive freedom that she achieved there through irony. Thus, for example, when Edmund initially begins to love Mary, we are given the opinions of Edmund, Mary, and Fanny without authoritative narrative commentary. Similarly, the account of the ball that Sir Thomas organizes after his return is narrated in turn by Mary, Fanny,

Sir Thomas, and Edmund; and Henry Crawford's proposal is presented from the points of view of Henry, Fanny, and Sir Thomas.

In *Pride and Prejudice* ironic ambiguity is in the end dispelled by the
narrative closure, and in *Mansfield Park* the relativity of multiple points
of view is ultimately abolished by the prominence and authority
Austen gives to Fanny's perspective. The episodes in which our correct judgment is most critical are all narrated from Fanny's point of
view because, even before she has learned to trust her moral intuitions, hers are the standards by which we are asked to judge. For this
reason, Fanny's perspective dominates the scene in Southerton Park,
the debate about the theater, and the rehearsal between Amelia and
Anhalt. Because Fanny participates in these episodes only reluctantly,
if at all, the reader is protected from the dangerous emotional cur-
rents they introduce. Instead, because Fanny's emotional struggles
are foregrounded, we are encouraged to exercise our imaginative
sympathy in the cause of self-denying principles, not self-serving
passions.

Austen also seeks to control the reader's judgment through her use
of symbolism. Unlike Shelley's symbolism in *Frankenstein,* Austen's
symbols do not multiply the diverse and sometimes contradictory
interpretations an event or object may inspire. Instead, they multiply
the contexts in which individual incidents or objects can repeat their
single meaning. For example, the fact that William's cross will fit only
the chain that Edmund gives her has the same implication for Fanny's
life as it has for her choice of jewelry. Similarly, the key to the gate
at Southerton, the gambits in the game of Speculation, and the most
elaborate symbol of all, the play-within-the-novel, extend their influence
simply by virtue of the symbolic status Austen accords them.[9]

In spite of the strategies by which Austen tries to shore up her
narrative authority and make Fanny's principles both imaginatively
and morally appealing, many readers have found *Mansfield Park* Austen's most problematic novel. Part of the problem finally seems to
stem from the inherent difficulty of distinguishing between Fanny's
emotions, which are moral, and the emotions of the other characters,
which often are not. Austen demonstrates that feeling is an extremely
powerful force, but she cannot unequivocally grant or deny its inherent morality. We know that Maria's passion is uncontrollable and
destructive, and we see Edmund's desire subvert his judgment; but
when Mary Crawford is drawn to Edmund despite her coldest calcula-
tions, or when Henry begins to love Fanny in spite of himself, what
value are we supposed to grant their affections?

The difficulty of determining the morality of feeling emanates, of
course, from the fundamental ambivalence toward the individual that
constitutes the heart of *Mansfield Park*. On the one hand, the moral

regeneration Austen dramatizes within the world of the novel is initiated by an individual. Indeed, Sir Thomas's climactic insight seems to ratify an ethic based on individual effort within an essentially competitive world: he realizes "the advantages of early hardship and discipline, and the consciousness of being born to struggle and endure" (p. 473). On the other hand, the materialism and ethical relativity that are the theoretical corollaries of individualism have consistently been shown by Austen to be dangerous—potentially subversive to the patriarchal authority and practical patronage that Mansfield Park ideally represents. The inherent contradiction of Austen's proposed "solution"—individual reform, leading to individuals protecting society against individualism—is ultimately as disruptive to the ethical closure of the novel as it is inadequate to real behavior in a real society.

A second factor that jeopardizes the novel's didactic scheme is related to the nature of the authority that Fanny finally represents. In order to persuade the reader of the severity of the challenge to paternalism and its values, Austen must dramatize both the internal moral decay of the landed gentry and the powerful individualism of the Crawfords. But even though Fanny triumphs at the end of the novel, the qualities of passivity, reserve, and self-depreciation she embodies make it difficult to understand how she has overcome either the Bertram's moral inertia or the Crawfords' anarchic power. Fanny emerges victorious simply because the others falter: Tom drinks himself into illness, Mary exposes her callousness, Maria seduces Henry, and Sir Thomas, in loneliness and despair, recalls Fanny to Mansfield Park. And Edmund finally falls in love with Fanny simply because she is faithfully, silently *there* when his feelings are in "that favourable state which a recent disappointment gives" (p. 470).

These same qualities threaten to undermine our engagement with Fanny Price and therefore our acceptance of the moral authority she ideally represents. Only if we find Fanny's internal struggle more absorbing than Mary Crawford's energetic wit will we finally value self-denial over self-indulgence. The novel's point of view encourages us to identify with Fanny, but, because she is so passive, we are accorded no vicarious experience of the power her principles have to conquer anything but her own desires. In fact, our sense of triumph comes not from Fanny but from the tone and machinations of the narrator, whose vitality is far closer to Mary Crawford's energy than to Fanny's passivity. In other words, the imaginative energy that first encourages us and then enables us to enter into a fiction is defused by the passivity of the character with whom we are asked to identify. If our identification with Fanny *could* be rendered complete, we would—like Mansfield Park itself—be reformed by an internal agent (the principled imagination), not by an external and authoritarian teacher. But as long as her example contradicts the energy we seek and express in imaginative activity, it is difficult to imagine how Fanny might engage readers who do not already share her principles and priorities.

Persuasion

The tension between the stable communal values ideally at the heart of patriarchal society and the moral relativity implied by the individualistic defense of that society is implicit in all of Jane Austen's mature novels, but nowhere do its polarities emerge into such stark relief as in *Persuasion,* Austen's last completed work. In *Persuasion,* the fact that the social and ethical hierarchy superintended by the landed gentry is in a state of total collapse is clear not only from the fiscal and moral bankruptcy of Sir Walter Elliot but also from the epistemological relativity that is emphasized both thematically and formally. On the one hand, the individualism that is implicit in relativity is granted narrative and even moral authority by the quality of the narration: the centralizing narrative authority taken for granted in the earlier novels has almost completely disappeared from *Persuasion,*[10] and in its place, we find a style inflected at nearly every level by the subjectivity of the heroine. But on the other hand, at the level of the novel's action we repeatedly see the personal and social consequences of this epistemological relativism. Unlike *Emma,* its immediate predecessor, *Persuasion* is punctuated by dramatic changes of locale, and each time that Anne Elliot is forced to move she experiences the vertiginous realization that "a removal from one set of people to another, though at a distance of only three miles, will often include a total change of conversation, opinion, and idea."[11] Like Fanny Price, Anne Elliot has known her share of loss. In her twenty-seven years, she has learned that the first lesson of relativity involves "knowing our own nothingness beyond our own circle." But the second lesson takes her beyond Fanny's experience, for the action of *Persuasion* proves that no judgment is absolute and that even such "objective" principles as "duty" may be susceptible to personal interpretation and abuse. Finally, the complexities of this tension are dramatized more explicitly here than in any previous Austen novel, for the self-confidence, "ardour," and even "imprudence" that make Frederick Wentworth "a dangerous character" in Lady Russell's terms are the very qualities that facilitate his personal success; what is more, in this most historically specific of all Austen's novels, they help save England from Napoleon's threat.[12]

In *Persuasion* Austen introduces the consequences of this tension by exploring the relationship between "manners" and "duty"—in other words, by raising once more the basic issue of propriety. The first facet of this relationship is obvious—and obviously problematic. Given the subjectivity of perception on which the novel insists, it is clear that each individual's experience is personal and unique. It follows from this that ethical judgment will be based at least initially on appearances and that all moral evaluation will be at least implicitly subjective. The reader is exposed to the moral vertigo that results from this when Austen presents one character—William Walter Elliot—to two others—Anne Elliot and Lady Russell. Anne's early evaluation of Mr. Elliot is based on the appeal of his "manners": "his manners were so exactly what they ought to be," she muses, "so polished, so easy, so particularly agreeable" (p. 143). But it is difficult for the reader to know whether Anne's assessment is morally authoritative or whether it is colored by her response to his flattery. We are further perplexed when, in the next chapter, Lady Russell's judgment of Elliot endorses Anne's:

> Every thing united in him; good understanding, correct opinions, knowledge of the world, and a warm heart. He had strong feelings of family-attachment and family-honour, without pride or weakness; he lived with the liberality of a man of fortune, without display; he judged for himself in every thing essential, without defying public opinion in any point of worldly decorum. He was steady, observant, moderate, candid; never run away with by spirits or by selfishness, which fancied itself strong feeling; and yet, with a sensibility to what was amiable and lovely, and a value for all the felicities of domestic life, which characters of fancied enthusiasm and violent agitation seldom really possess. [Pp. 146–47]

The problem for Anne, Lady Russell, and the reader is that Mr. Elliot has exploited the paradox of propriety by completely detaching manners from their ethical underpinnings.[13] In the absence of an objective, authoritative standard by which to judge such behavior, and deprived of access to Mr. Elliot's hidden motivation, how are we to know what to make of such a character?

It is at least partly to avoid dealing with this problem that Austen never allows Anne to become seriously interested in Mr. Elliot; indeed, she almost immediately informs the reader why Anne does not succumb to him: "Mr. Elliot was rational, discreet, polished,—but he was not open. There was never any burst of feeling, any warmth of indignation or delight, at the evil or good of others. This, to Anne, was a decided imperfection" (p. 161). The problem with this narrative ruse, of course, is that it foregrounds the subjectivity whose moral relativity we have just been led to suspect. Eventually Mr. Elliot will be betrayed by Mrs. Smith, who *can* expose his secret motive. But it is important to keep in mind that our first and lasting evaluation of him is influenced not by reference to authoritative knowledge or an objective assessment of "manners" but simply by Anne's subjective preference for "feeling" and "warmth."

To resolve the problems introduced by this implicit contradiction, Austen relies on the fact that, by the time Mr. Elliot becomes an issue, the reader will recognize that Anne's intuitions are meant to be morally responsible and hence authoritative. Certainly, as the novel opens, Anne Elliot comes closer than any other Austen heroine to being educated in both principles and feeling. Like Elinor Dashwood and Fanny Price, Anne has from her youth internalized sound moral principles; but, more surely than either of them, she has also experienced and fully acknowledged the demands of her heart. Austen's opening description of Anne's maturity summarizes her unusual career: "She had been forced into prudence in her youth, she learned romance as she grew older—the natural sequal of an unnatural beginning" (p. 30). This statement effectively suspends our estimation of Lady Russell's original admonition to "prudence," but it does not really explain how Anne's belated "romance" has acquired moral authority. Especially given the vanity with which the desires of Sir Walter, Elizabeth, and William Elliot are inflected and the instability of the romantic inclinations of Benwick and Louisa Musgrove, the reader must wonder why Anne's desires are more reliable.

This question of the authority of Anne's intuitions and inclinations introduces a second aspect of the paradox of propriety. As in *Mansfield Park,* Austen suggests in *Persuasion* that "proper" behavior may have a psychological dimension that neither eighteenth-century moralists nor more conventional authors like Mary Shelley described. This, she implies, may be the most significant paradox of propriety—not that conforming to superficial manners can enable one to express desire indirectly, but that even sincere fidelity to "objective" principles may actually provide a way of answering personal needs, that doing one's "duty" may be a means of protecting oneself against both pain and unreasonable desire, and that virtuous behavior may afford substitute gratifications for the pleasure it seems to deny. Because the reader does not directly witness Anne's first and in many ways most important conflict—the struggle between her first love for Wentworth and Lady Russell's "prudence"—we are encouraged to accept her decision as one of the premises of the action and to evaluate it more by its consequences than by the principle that inspired it. In other words, instead of focusing on the correctness of Anne's first decision, or on the issue of personal autonomy it involved, we are asked to understand *how,* given that decision, Anne was able to discipline her personal feelings. The explanation is that she *did* gratify her personal desire— her desire, that is, to help Wentworth before gratifying herself. Austen tells us that Lady Russell's argument—that marriage to Wentworth was "a wrong thing . . . hardly capable of success, and not deserving it"—finally influenced Anne less than her confidence that, in denying Wentworth, she was actually "consulting his good, even more than her own." "The belief of being prudent, and self-denying principally for *his* advantage, was her chief consolation, under the misery of a parting—a final parting" (p. 28). Anne has been able to displace her own desire not simply by reference to an objective principle but by convincing herself that her love for Wentworth would be more adequately expressed by denying what they both so badly want.

One practical difficulty with traditional Christian self-denial is that in the world of *Persuasion* no one but Anne adheres to the morality of which it is a part. But a second and closely related difficulty is that if, in the absence of an objective standard of moral absolutes and a consensus about ethical norms, an individual can identify "duty" only by the personal satisfaction it yields, then "principle" may easily shade over into unrecognized self-interest or self-defense. "How quick come the reasons for approving what we like," the narrator announces early in the novel (p. 15). Austen raises the specter of this ethical chaos again when she discusses the psychological function of Anne's other performances of "duty." When Mary asks Anne to Uppercross Cottage, for example, Anne leaps at the chance to act in compliance with the wishes of anyone else, to act according to any rule that, because it exists outside herself, seems to be authoritative and reliable. She is simply "glad to be thought of some use, glad to have any thing marked out as a duty" (p. 33).

As Austen describes Anne's situation, however, it becomes clear that one reason Anne is so anxious to be dutiful is that the approbation that ideally attends selflessness is the only recognition Anne is likely to receive. In this regard, Anne's situation is much like that of Fanny Price. Repeatedly Austen points out that, except for the compassion she receives from Lady Russell, Anne enjoys almost no domestic encouragement or support. "Excepting one short period of her life," the narrator tells us, "she had never, since the age of fourteen, never since the loss of her dear mother, known the happiness of being listened to, or encouraged by any just appreciation or real taste" (p. 47). When she is left behind by the Musgroves, to nurse their child, Anne experiences "as many sensations of comfort, as were, perhaps, ever likely to be hers. She knew herself to be of the first utility to the child" (p. 58). The problem with this fusion of "duty" and "happiness" is twofold. On the one hand, because the "satisfaction of knowing herself extremely useful" (p. 121) is virtually the only happiness Anne has, she is driven to Christian virtue at least partly out of personal need; on the other hand, because this "satisfaction" is virtually her only assurance that what she does is right, Anne will be prone to identify "duty" primarily by the pleasure it brings. Like Mary Wollstonecraft in her two *Vindications*, Austen never calls into question the authority of Anne's "satisfaction" or her implicit religious ethic. But Austen's exploration of such consolation is more troubling than Wollstonecraft's, for, by showing us Mary, who happily tempers "duty" with personal convenience, and Mr. Elliot, for whom " 'to do the best for himself ' passe[s] as a duty" (p. 202), Austen implicitly raises the question of how the selfless definition of duty can be distinguished from its self-serving twin.

Austen raises these questions, but she leaves them unanswered. With consummate narrative skill, she completely displaces the problem of the basis and nature of Anne's moral discrimination by foregrounding the difficulty with which Anne exercises her moral intuition. Because Anne's situation and her feelings are both given as premises of the plot, Austen can focus on the inevitable confrontation between repressive social conventions and an individual's desires—and this confrontation, unlike the ideologically charged question of duty, *can* be resolved realistically and in the terms of traditional values. Austen never actually examines the process by which Anne's feelings become moral, but because she does focus briefly on the emotional and psychological complexities of self-denial, she conveys the impression that Anne's first acquiescence to "duty" must have entailed soul-searching and a difficult weighing of alternatives. As in *Mansfield Park,* Austen asks us to sympathize with (although *not* to experience vicariously) the principle of self-denial. But unlike the earlier novel, *Persuasion* takes us beyond the subduing of desire to its struggle against social restraint. In doing so, it dramatizes the *power* of principled feeling and thus gives us an idea, not only of what this power ideally should be, but of how its triumph might actually come about.

Austen focuses on the conflict between social conventions and moral desire by dramatizing it not only at the level of content but at the level of the narrative development itself. At this formal level, Austen provides two narrative lines. The "private" plot of the novel corresponds to—and contains the story of—Anne's love for Wentworth. The "public" plot corresponds to repressive social conventions and contains the accounts of the interactions between the Elliots and Lady Russell, the Musgroves and their friends, Mr. Elliot and his relatives, and so on. Typically, the private plot is repressed, although increasingly it competes with the public plot for the reader's attention; the overall narrative action of *Persuasion* involves the gradual emergence of the private plot into the public sphere and its eventual triumph, just as the overall content involves the ultimate victory of personal needs and desires over social conventions. Thus the first three chapters of the novel confine the reader to the public plot, the domain of social intercourse, which originally stifled Anne's emotions and into which her feelings will soon surface again. Even these chapters contain allusions to the hidden, private plot, but that plot does not emerge into visibility until the end of chapter 3, when we are suddenly exposed to Anne's turbulent consciousness: "A few months more, and *he,* perhaps, may be walking here" (p. 25). Only at this point do we begin to understand why Anne so intensely dislikes Bath and why she knows not only who Admiral Croft is but where he has seen action. And only at this point do we recognize that Anne is not a secondary character but the heroine and that it is *her* plot—along with her desire—that is being repressed by the bustling vanity of her loquacious relatives.

What we are seeing here is Jane Austen's most sophisticated version of the narrative technique she had employed at least as early as the conclusion of *Lady Susan.* Essentially, it consists of shifting between different levels or planes of the fiction so that the problems or contradictions raised at one level can be symbolically "resolved" by foregrounding another, nonproblematic level. In *Lady Susan* this "resolution"—which is actually only a displacement—consists in the complete dismissal of the principal character, the thematic tensions, and the epistolary form itself. In *Pride and Prejudice,* to give another example, it consists in foregrounding romance conventions in order to displace complexities raised by the introduction of realistic social and psychological details. And, in *Persuasion,* it consists in the double movement whereby the thematic contradictions raised by the problems of individualism and morality are displaced by foregrounding other, apparently equivalent, thematic complexities and by shifting the reader's imaginative engagement to the conflict between the public and the private plots.

Austen makes the conflict between repressive society and Anne's desire seem as important as the epistemological conundrum it displaces by emphasizing the odds against Anne's happiness. Nearly all the events of the first part of the public plot reinforce the anxiety we share with Anne that her love for Wentworth will be frustrated a second time. Louisa Musgrove actively pursues Wentworth, circumstances rarely bring the two estranged lovers together, Wentworth seems determined to misunderstand Anne, and Anne repeatedly retreats from exposure by defining her "duty" as self-effacement. She wants, she says repeatedly, only "to be unobserved" (p. 71), "not to be in the way of any body" (p. 84). Austen further underscores the likelihood that Anne's romantic hopes will be denied by giving us one revealing glimpse into Wentworth's consciousness. This passage constitutes one of the very few departures from the narrative's participation in Anne's point of view; and, even though we eventually recognize its defensive tenor, it immediately serves to convince the reader that any struggle between Anne's sense of propriety and her feelings would inevitably lead to frustration and pain. "He had not forgiven Anne Elliot," the narrator tells us. "She had given him up to oblige others. It had been the effect of over-persuasion. It had been weakness and timidity. . . . Her power with him was gone for ever" (p. 61).

The turning point in *Persuasion*—both in Captain Wentworth's feelings and, as a consequence, in the dilemma that is foregrounded for the reader—occurs in the episode at Lyme. Before this episode, Wentworth has insisted that he does not love Anne, and thus the reader—confined, largely, to Anne's subjective point of view—has remained engaged in the heroine's attempts to master her still active desire, not so much in the name of some authoritative principle but because circumstances—reality—make such self-discipline necessary. In order for the critical shift in the narrative to take place, two things must happen: Wentworth must realize that he still loves Anne, and this recognition must be conveyed to the reader. Only then will the primary conflict be located between the private and the public plots instead of between selfish and moral desire or between feeling and necessity; for only then will both lovers struggle to make social conventions express and accommodate their feelings. The delicate handling of this series of revelations generates the tension and the power of *Persuasion*.

Two illuminations are necessary for Wentworth to realize that his well-mannered politeness toward Anne is actually the stirring of his old love: he must be reminded of Anne's powerful physical attractions, and he must learn to distinguish between simple selfishness in the name of principle and the genuine self-command that Anne can place in the service of others. Wentworth learns each of these lessons at Lyme. His desire for Anne is reawakened by Mr. Elliot's open admiration of her, for Wentworth suddenly sees Mr. Elliot as a rival. Then his appreciation for Anne is given new meaning when Louisa, taking Wentworth's own ideal of "firmness" to its destructive extreme, jumps precipitously from the stile.

Eventually we discover that Anne's selfless and competent attendance on the stricken Louisa has been instrumental in reanimating Wentworth's love, but we cannot immediately be sure of his feeling for Anne because Austen removes the heroine—and, with her, the reader—to Bath. But even though we are still basically confined to Anne's perspective, the two episodes immediately preceding Louisa's accident provide the reader with vantage points for seeing Anne that materially enhance our appreciation of her. In doing so, these episodes settle once and for all any lingering questions about the moral authority of Anne's feelings, and thus they reinforce our hopes (if not our expectations) that her altogether admirable desire will ultimately be rewarded. The meaning each of these episodes has for Anne is slightly different from the meaning it has for the reader. In the first—Wentworth's dialogue with Louisa about the nut—Anne understands only that the man she loves is rejecting her more "persuadable" character for Louisa's greater "firmness." The attentive reader, however, will hear that Wentworth's endorsement of "firmness" actually has a very personal stress. "It is the worst evil of too yielding and indecisive a character," he explains, "that no influence over it can be depended upon" (p. 88). From this statement it is clear that Wentworth does not really want "firmness"; he merely wants to be the one whose "influence" is longest felt. The second episode involves Anne's conversation with Captain Benwick. In his tenacious grief Anne sees only a mirror image of her own lingering sorrow, and, in the "allowance of prose" she recommends, she sees only the medicine she has ineffectively administered to herself. But contrasting Anne's public self-command with Benwick's demonstrative and even occasionally eloquent suffering, we recognize how far Anne Elliot really is from indulging the pain she cannot help but feel. These two events reduce Anne to her lowest emotional state, for just as the first convinces her that Wentworth will never love her, the second shows her unequivocally that her love for him is not yet dead. For the reader, however, these episodes establish the context in which Anne's self-command at Louisa's side can be properly appreciated.

In contrast to the emotional turmoil liberated in Lyme, Bath seems stultifying, claustrophobic. Its occupants and its formalities are artificial and repressive: Mr. Elliot's careful manners are of a piece with the "white glare of Bath," and, significantly, the only truth eventually emanates from Mrs. Smith's "dark bedroom," where Anne finally discovers Mr. Elliot's secret history. Anne's immediate problem in Bath is simply to stifle her feelings once again and to correct her first impression of William Walter Elliot. But Austen makes the month-long "imprisonment" in Bath occupy but three short chapters so that Anne will soon know what the reader has already begun to suspect: that Wentworth will not marry Louisa, that he is "unshackled and free." Suddenly, emissaries from the country begin to pour into Bath, and, when Wentworth himself arrives, Austen sets in motion the intricate, almost musical movement through which, point counterpoint, Anne gradually discovers and elicits Wentworth's love.

In order to effect the resolution that will finally bring the private plot into public view, Austen forces Anne to take the initiative, to act on her own feelings and her intuition of Wentworth's answering desires. Just as Anne's ministrations in Lyme were completely in keeping with the behavior proper to a lady, so her self-assertion now is gentle, almost shy; in other words, she acts only indirectly and only as opportunity allows. "Making yet a little advance," she greets Wentworth warmly at the Rooms (p. 181), and she uses their polite conversation to voice heartfelt emotions whose significance only he will fully understand: "one does not love a place the less for having suffered in it," she says, referring to their shared past (p. 184). From Wentworth's response, Anne realizes that "he must love her" (p. 186), and she sets out to dispel the only remaining impediment to their happiness: Wentworth's misinterpretation of her relationship with Mr. Elliot. Fortified by the information Mrs. Smith has given her, Anne resolves to be "more direct" with Mr. Elliot and more assertive with Captain Wentworth. She seizes an "opportunity" to "decidedly" voice her disinclination to accompany Mr. Elliot (p. 229), she openly alludes to her former relationship with Wentworth ("I am not yet so much changed" [p. 225]), and, in her conversation with Captain Harville, after she becomes aware that Wentworth is listening, she "eagerly" claims the "privilege" for her sex of "loving longest, when existence or when hope is gone" (p. 235).

Thus Anne struggles to make social conventions accommodate and communicate her feelings, and Captain Wentworth does the same. Significantly, Austen makes the final reconciliation between Anne and Wentworth depend on the self-reliant commander's accepting the "penance" and anguish of the typical female situation: discovering that others assume he is courting Louisa, Wentworth is hemmed in by social conventions, forced to wait passively while circumstances dictate his fate. Even after Louisa's turn to Benwick permits him once more to "exert" himself and follow Anne to Bath, he is still restricted to the feminine position of helpless onlooker and overhearer; and, when he finally takes decisive action, he does so indirectly, by writing to Anne under the cover of another letter, just as she had communicated with him under the cover of her conversation with Harville.

More than any previous Austen novel, *Persuasion* dwells on the reciprocity of love between man and woman. Wentworth's "agitation" is at least as frequently noted as Darcy's, but here the man's agitation is the counterpart of the woman's, not its illustrative opposite. Perhaps even more important, however, is the fact that in *Persuasion* Austen is more attentive than ever before to the "situation" of women, and, by placing Wentworth in that situation, she both makes him do "penance" for his unthinking flirtation and alerts the reader to the frustration such restrictions can generate for anyone. Through the character of Mrs. Croft and Anne's conversation with Captain Harville, Austen also addresses the implications of woman's social situation—again more explicitly than in any of her novels. Recogniz-

ing that women are "rational creatures," Austen acknowledges that
they are not always treated as such, either because of the patriarchal
prerogatives that relegate "all the Marys and Elizabeths" to the single
category of "wife" (p. 4) or because of the superficial dictates of
propriety, which insists that "fine ladies" have "no *right*" to comfortably endure hardships (p. 69), that all women with ruddy faces are
"frights," and that the "model of female excellence" should take no
initiative and have no desires of her own (p. 159). As Austen depicts
them in this novel, women are imprisoned (p. 137), confined (p. 141),
"surrounded and shut in" (p. 188), and legally crippled, sometimes
physically crippled, by the actions of men. The artifices of society
make such restriction inevitable for every sensitive individual, but
Austen does not let us forget that women's position is especially cruel.
Acknowledging that women love with special force, Anne will *not*
grant Captain Harville's point that fidelity is in woman's "nature."
"It is, perhaps, our fate rather than our merit," she explains. "We
cannot help ourselves. We live at home, quiet, confined, and our
feelings prey upon us. You are forced on exertion. You have always
a profession, pursuits, business of some sort or other, to take you
back into the world immediately, and continual occupation and change
soon weaken impressions" (p. 232). Jane Austen does not sound so
very different from Mary Wollstonecraft here;[14] if she does not aggressively agitate for reform, she nevertheless rejects both the deter-
minist argument from nature and the definition of a Proper Lady,
which makes a woman psychologically and emotionally dependent.

In *Persuasion,* Mrs. Smith exists to remind us both how restrictive
a woman's situation can be and, no matter how severe that restriction, how resilient a woman's emotions are. "Here was that elasticity
of mind," Anne remarks to herself, "that disposition to be comforted,
that power of turning readily from evil to good, and of finding
employment which carried her out of herself, which was from Nature
alone" (p. 154). Significantly, Mrs. Smith's "power" epitomizes female
indirection; through Nurse Rooke she learns the secrets of the most
private rooms of Bath, and she takes advantage of the momentary
incapacities of others to lighten the burden of her own physical
affliction. As unsavory as some critics have found her,[15] Mrs. Smith
serves as the necessary secret agent of *Persuasion,* analogous to Mrs.
Norris in *Mansfield Park* and Miss Bates in *Emma.* Because of her, the
novel's private plot surfaces and finally shatters the complacent round
of evening parties and formal concerts. Mrs. Clay and Mr. Elliot are
flushed, temporarily, from Sir Walter's home, and, more satisfying,
the romantic first love of Anne and Wentworth, now proved worthy
through endurance and trial, moves the lovers into the prominence
they have long held for the reader.

The conclusion of *Persuasion,* as many critics have noted,[16] does not promise general social reform, an authoritative system of values, or even "happiness ever after" for one loving couple. Kellynch will still eventually descend to Mr. Elliot, Mrs. Clay may even preside over the great hall, and the "dread of a future war" is as much Anne's legacy as domestic affection is. For Austen, despite the gratification of romance, Anne's happiness is less complete than Elizabeth's, Fanny's, or Emma's: "Anne had no Uppercross-hall before her, no landed estate, no headship of a family" (p. 250). And because she will not attain to these, her society can look forward to no internal reformation. Captain Wentworth can restore Mrs. Smith's West Indian property, but he cannot put Anne in her mother's place. For Austen, individual education no longer seems powerful enough to initiate social improvement; when she celebrates the culminating happiness of Anne Elliot and Frederick Wentworth, it is in the context of the present disarray—and, implicitly, the future disarray—of family and class.

Yet in some respects, because *Persuasion* promises less, it achieves more. As Nina Auerbach has pointed out, *Persuasion* endorses possibilities never before entertained in Austen's novels. Instead of attempting to reform the landed gentry, Austen shows that money—and, along with it, power—is passing from this class to those who actively labor (and who, not incidentally, by laboring defend England). Significantly, the naval officers in *Persuasion* are "associated with nature, openness, hospitality, romance,"[17] and, by granting them social prominence, Austen endows individual feeling with a new power. And because the question of the *moral* authority of individual feeling is not so pressing here as in *Mansfield Park* or even *Emma,* empowering it seems to presage general social reform, if only through the gradual erosion of the mannered repression epitomized by William and Elizabeth Elliot. In *Persuasion,* Austen also devotes more attention to social groups whose absence is so conspicuous—and essential—in her earlier novels. Mrs. Smith and Nurse Rooke make more than token appearances, and at least twice Austen mentions anonymous groups of workers going about their ordinary business or only briefly interrupted by their social superiors. When Louisa falls, for example, there suddenly appear "workmen and boatmen" who have gathered "to be useful if wanted, at any rate, to enjoy the sight of a dead young lady, nay, two dead young ladies, for it proved twice as fine as the first report" (p. 111). What is remarkable about this passage is not its proof that Austen was aware of the lower classes but the fact that it contains—at least momentarily—the workmen's point of view ("nay, two dead young ladies"). Near the beginning of the novel, Austen's allusion to the lower classes is more stylized, but here again—as so seldom before—we glimpse a group of people who are not defined by their relation to the upper classes, who are neither agents of the central characters nor even particularly interested in them. Walking from Uppercross to Winthrop, Anne and her friends make the "gradual ascent through large enclosures, where the ploughs at work, and the fresh-made path spoke the farmer, counteracting the sweets of poetical despondence, and meaning to have spring again" (p. 85).

Such brief asides do not, of course, significantly widen the focus of Jane Austen's art, although they do generate the impression of realistic depth that was first introduced in *Emma* through allusions to such characters as William Larkin. But in *Persuasion* these receding depths do not simply expand the sphere of influence of the upper classes as they do in *Emma*. Instead, they are subtle reminders of the limitations of that influence; in some fundamental sense, the vanity of Sir Walter Elliot is not only foolish but irrelevant, for his preening arrogance no more affects the behavior of his social inferiors than poetic pretensions alter the inexorable rhythms of nature. In *Persuasion* Austen suggests that the landed classes have forfeited their moral authority partly through extravagance and a failure of social responsibility. But their gradual displacement is also partly the consequence of the more general challenge to the stable system of values they ideally represented. This challenge is both political and epistemological; that the lower classes not only exist in their own right but have a distinct point of view provides a social context and content for the epistemological relativity implicit in the very title of *Persuasion*.

It is important to appreciate the direction of Austen's last completed novel, but it is also necessary to look once more at the inherent contradictions of the resolution she proposes. Even if the peace and happiness promised at the conclusion of *Persuasion* are but temporary and limited, the novel's fundamental predication of a private sphere that can accommodate personal desire and yield personal fulfillment perpetuates many of the problems raised by Austen's earlier works. And here we need to remember that these problems are not the stigmata of aesthetic failure but indices of contradictions within ideology itself. Essentially, *Persuasion* advances the argument, proposed as early as *Pride and Prejudice*, that personal feeling can be a moral force within society. In the earlier novel the way of life eventually ratified by desire was that of the landed gentry; in *Persuasion*, feeling is put in the service of—and is gratified by—the much less certain life-style of those who earn their social position by personal effort. In *Pride and Prejudice* Elizabeth Bennet's aggressive energy had to be chastened into love by circumstances and by Fitzwilliam Darcy; in *Persuasion*, Anne Elliot's persistent love prevails, finally triumphing over both her lover's pride and the institutional inhibitors that would disguise or deny it altogether. Still, by using individual feeling to inaugurate moral reform and by rewarding desire with the conventional prizes of bourgeois society—marriage and (implicitly) a family—Austen is finally reproducing an unresolved (and, in these terms, unresolvable) contradiction inherent in her culture's values. This contradiction centers in a promise that is invariably fused to the demands of propriety; it centers, that is, in the concept of romantic love.

As we have repeatedly seen, romantic love purports to be completely "outside" ideology. It claims to be an inexplicable, irresistible, and possibly biological attraction that, in choosing its object, flouts the hierarchy, the priorities, and the inequalities of class society. Romantic love seems to defy self-interest and calculation as completely as it ignores income and rank; as a consequence, if it articulates (or can be educated to articulate) an essentially unselfish, generous urge toward another person, it may serve as an agent of moral reform: Louisa Musgrove might become a more serious person through loving Benwick, just as Henry Crawford seems launched on a significant course of moral improvement by his love for Fanny Price. But it is crucial to recognize that the moral regeneration ideally promised by romantic love is as individual and as private as its agent. In fact, the fundamental assumption of romantic love—and the reason it is so compatible with bourgeois society—is that the personal can be kept separate from the social, that one's "self" can be fulfilled in spite of—and in isolation from—the demands of the marketplace.

Once one accepts this division of society into separate spheres, it is possible to argue that the gratification of personal desire will inaugurate social reform only if one assumes a social organization that structurally accommodates influence. At the lowest level, this organization is represented by the nuclear family; at a higher level, it is the patriarchal society modeled on the family. If this concentric arrangement of "spheres" (which is, of course, actually a hierarchy of power) is disrupted or even seriously challenged—as it was during Jane Austen's lifetime—then the movement from individual fulfillment to social improvement becomes problematic. Ironically, even as the importance of imagining some program for social reform increases, the gap between the private and the public seems to widen and—completing the circle—the more necessary it becomes to believe that at least in the privacy of one's own home, the comfort of one's own family, and the personal gratification of one's own love, there can be deeply felt, hence "substantial," satisfactions.

In connection with Wollstonecraft's *Maria* I have already noted that "romantic expectations" offer one socially acceptable form of imaginative (or spiritual) transcendence—a form of symbolic gratification that proves particularly elusive for women because of the restrictions bourgeois society places on their sexuality. And, in connection with Mary Shelley's late novels, I noted that even the promise of such symbolic gratification can prevent women from aggressively challenging society's failure to provide opportunities for fulfillment in the material terms that the society so clearly endorses. Austen's novels now alert us to yet another liability of romantic love: its illusion of personal autonomy. Given the fact that living together in society necessarily requires dependence and compromise, the belief that one can withdraw or simply gratify oneself is morally irresponsible, psychologically naïve, and, finally, practically untrue. Even Mrs. Smith has Nurse Rooke to connect her to the public world of Bath; even outspoken heroines like Elizabeth Bennet and Emma Woodhouse do not always know their own hearts; and, as Anne Elliot's prolonged and problematic courtship of Wentworth proves, even the strongest, most self-aware desire must be defined within other social relationships, which are also configurations of power.

In retaining the premises and promises of romantic love even as she makes this point, Jane Austen perpetuates one of the fundamental myths of bourgeois society. For the model of private gratification that romantic love proposes can disguise the inescapable system of economic and political domination only by foregrounding the few relationships that flatter our desire for personal autonomy and power. But the notion that romantic relationships actually have the kind of social power this emotional prominence suggests is only a fiction: in the absence of institutions that actually link the private and the public spheres, romantic relationships, by their very nature, cannot materially affect society. What is even more distressing, they cannot provide women with more than the kind of temporary and imaginative consolation that serves to defuse criticism of the very institutions that make such consolation necessary. For by focusing on courtship, the myth of romantic love tends to freeze the relationship between a man and a woman at its moment of greatest intensity, when both partners are seen (and see themselves) in the most flattering light, and—what is perhaps most important—when women seem to exercise their greatest power. Romantic love, in other words, seems to promise to women in particular an emotional intensity that ideally, compensates for all the practical opportunities they are denied. All that it can actually yield, however, is the immediate gratification of believing that this single moment of apparent autonomy will endure, that the fact that a woman seems most desirable when she is most powerful will continue on in marriage and in society. In Jane Austen's society, of course, romantic love did not alter the institutions of marriage or property or female dependence. Even the private gratification available in the domestic sphere could not live up to the intensity and power promised by romantic love; for, as a wife and mother, a woman could at best act indirectly: through her children, through sacrifice, through duty. Romantic love, finally, had its most vital, most satisfying existence, not in society, but in art.

The problems these ideological contradictions generate in Jane Austen's novels should be clear by now. In order to give individual feeling moral authority—in order, that is, to place romance in the service of propriety, social reform, and realism—Austen must posit the existence of separate spheres within her fiction. These separate spheres exist at the level of content and form, and, at each level, the "private" sphere is theoretically linked to the "public" sphere by the influence bred of contiguity. But these private spheres are in fact qualitatively different from the public spheres. The public spheres activate expectations generated by her readers' actual experiences in class society; they are governed by psychological and social realism and the iron law of cause and effect. The private spheres are different indeed. They open out onto romance; they activate and feed off expectations generated by reading other romantic novels; they arouse and satisfy desire. Each of Jane Austen's novels contains these special pockets of romance, not just in their most obtrusive form—those fairy-tale marriages that stop realism dead in its tracks—but in unexpected, out-of-the-way places as well. In *Persuasion,* for example, Mrs. Smith remains miraculously, inexplicably cheerful, against all the odds of her social situation, even though, in the same novel, Elizabeth Elliot withers on much less barren soil; and in *Mansfield Park* Fanny and William Price keep domestic affection alive, even though we see it atrophy and die in both squalid Portsmouth and immaculate Mansfield Park. At the level of form, Austen's dividing her fiction into public and private spheres means that all the potentially subversive content is relegated to the margins of the action or to a carefully confined arena. Paradoxically, the "private," romantic spheres of her novels—Marianne's passion for Willoughby, Darcy's love for Elizabeth, Fanny's yearning for Edmund, Emma's recognition of love, and Anne's fidelity to Wentworth—must all be rigorously contained, whether by narrative distancing, as in *Sense and Sensibility,* by circumstantial frustration, as in *Mansfield Park* and *Persuasion,* or by obscuring the heroine's virtues by other, less admirable, traits, as in *Pride and Prejudice* and *Emma.* This separation is essential. It protects romance from the necessarily deflating power of reality, but in the end it ensures that the demands of reality will be taken seriously, not merely repressed or imaginatively escaped. For the private sphere, though it is the location and source of the greatest fulfillment Austen can imagine, nourishes the subjectivity that is potentially fatal to the claims of other people, to morality, and, implicitly, to society itself.

Significantly, Jane Austen's solution to this problem is almost exactly the same as the one proposed by Mary Wollstonecraft for precisely the opposite problem. Indeed, for a social critic like Wollstonecraft, who believed that the innate moral goodness of feeling was perverted by social inequalities and restrictions, the central question was this: How can any individual raised in a corrupt society escape society's influence sufficiently to inaugurate reform? Her solution was to posit a separate symbolical sphere where "substantial" values miraculously distinguish themselves from their debased twins. For a conservative like Jane Austen, the central problem is reversed. Believing that individual feeling is at least potentially anarchic, she asks how any individual can be trusted to initiate reform, or even, in a society devoid of objective moral standards, how any individual can identify the values it is crucial to endorse. Her solution, of course, is identical to Wollstonecraft's: she posits a separate sphere—sometimes populated by herself and her family of readers, sometimes by only a single fictional couple—in which absolute values survive intact and are intuitively recognized as authoritative and just.

In the absence of institutional opportunities for power, Jane Austen can effect the aesthetic resolution she desires only by *asserting* that the private sphere of domestic relationships can remain autonomous and yet retain a unique and powerful moral dimension. The resolution is only symbolic, of course, and, as we have seen, it can be achieved only by repressing or displacing any question that might jeopardize it. The fact that Austen's novels contain almost no examples of marriages that the reader would want to emulate, despite their inevitable culmination in a happy marriage, summarizes both the price of such symbolic resolution and its attractions. For, on the one hand, for Austen to move chronologically, realistically, from the suspended promise of romantic love to a dramatization of the power relations inherent in marriage (dynamics she portrays elsewhere with ruthless wit) would be to risk depriving romantic love of its capacity to engage our imaginations by offering us flattering images of socially acceptable (if unavailable) power. Even more damaging, it would call into question the consoling assumption that the emotional gratifications of love make up for the absence of other forms of self-expression; it would also cast doubt on the enabling belief that the self-denial that society demands can yield the fulfillment that every person desires. But, on the other hand, freezing the narratives precisely at the height of emotional intensity endorses the promises of romantic love and, in doing so, enjoins the reader to imitate the moral love the hero and heroine promise to bring to fruition in society. What is equally important, the model of female power inherent in the premises of romantic love provides Jane Austen the artist with a legitimate paradigm for the self-assertion with which she not only expresses her own desires but works in the service of moral reform.

The division of society and morality into separate public and private spheres was a solution particularly attractive to women. Because bourgeois society defined women in terms of their relationships (specifically, their conjugal or familial relationships), because they were granted power within the "proper sphere" of the home, and because the theory of "influence" postulated a model for the dissemination of domestic virtues throughout society, women had a particular investment in conceptualizing their space as special and as containing special moral authority. More generally, however, we should remember that the cultural ideology that encompassed both propriety and romantic love had at its heart the same separation of spheres that we see in women's novels. For bourgeois ideology held out the promise that every individual would have an equal opportunity to work for equal material rewards—a promise that the limitations of natural resources and the inherent inequalities of class society rendered patently false. The existence of a private sphere, replete with the resources of boundless love and uncritical sympathy, promised a compensatory substitute for other kinds of unavailable gratification—for men as well as women. Not incidentally, of course, the home further reinforced bourgeois ideology through this compensatory gratification, for it provided competitive labor with both an end and a means—both a goal to defend, and, within the patriarchal family, a nursery for the habits of propriety and the promises of romantic love.

Conclusion

IN THE COURSE of this book, many of the contradictions inherent in bourgeois society have surfaced. These contradictions have become visible in the themes of the works I have examined, in disruptions within the novel's form, and in the conflict between expectations generated at one level of a narrative and resolutions offered at another. The same contradictions have also appeared within the general "content" of the writers' lives and in the "form" of their professional careers. Perhaps the most fundamental contradiction to emerge in all of these areas is the discrepancy between the promises of bourgeois ideology and the satisfactions that life in bourgeois society actually yields. This contradiction is not, of course, uniquely felt by women writers, by women, or even by people living in late eighteenth- or early nineteenth-century English society. Indeed, it constitutes one version of the gap that always opens between desire and possibility—most specifically, the gap that opens wide between the possibilities promised by the ideology of bourgeois individualism and the rewards possible in a world where resources are limited and power is unequally held.

But in the ways I have tried to indicate in this book, in the early nineteenth century this most general of all contradictions was experienced in an intense form by women and, particularly, by women writers; for the cultural pressure to conform to the image of proper (or innate) femininity directly contradicted the demands of professional authorship. The three women whose works I have examined in detail responded to this collision of expectations in a variety of ways. Mary Wollstonecraft tried to confront directly and aggressively the political inequalities perpetuated in the name of propriety. Mary Shelley struggled to adapt to propriety so perfectly that she could disappear into the Proper Lady and use the complexities of that stereotype to channel her own impermissible resentment and rage. Jane Austen turned her creative energies to the reformation of propriety in the hope of finding within its codes an acceptable form for a

241

woman's desires and a reinforcement for the social order she cherished. In the variety of these women's imaginative and life choices I have tried to explore the range of individual responses to ideology available to them in their historical moment. Their social position, personal situation, education, experience, and such unaccountable qualities as "genius" all combined to make their individual responses to society and ideology unique and sometimes startling in their ingenuity and creativity.

Despite this variety, the recurrence of certain basic features in these writers' works and lives suggests that their responses were all shaped by the dynamics of the ideological situation that, as women, they all shared. For the paradoxical commands of propriety—that desire express itself through modesty, that power be deflected into influence, that fulfillment be won through meekness—and its paradoxical promise—that romantic love will crown a youth of self-control, self-effacement, and self-denial—combined to make indirection and accommodation the most effective strategies for self-expression, whether these strategies were adopted consciously or unconsciously, and whether they appeared in life or in art. Before we leave these three women, it is worth looking once more at the persistence and the price of such indirection—the opportunities it opened and the possibilities it denied.

The forms that indirection and accommodation take as strategies for living are different from the forms they take in art, if for no other reason than the fact that social relationships and public activity permit less freedom than the symbolic realm of art permits. But life choices and aesthetic choices are, both of them, attempts to "resolve" felt social contradictions. Thus Mary Shelley's retreat from her adolescent audacity into a life of conscientious self-effacement reveals her desire to discover a socially acceptable form for her antisocial aggression, and Jane Austen's perfection of a witty, deliciously sharptongued narrative alter ego suggests that she was attempting to enlarge the boundaries of the life she led as a properly devoted and self-denying daughter and aunt. In the imaginative creations of both these women, indirection also frequently appears as substitution, as resolutions blocked at one level of a narrative and then displaced by other subjects that are more amenable to symbolic transformation. We saw this, for example, in Wollstonecraft's importation of a religious resolution into the political analysis of *The Rights of Men,* in Shelley's substitution of the issue of fidelity for the more ambiguous issue of female autonomy in *Falkner,* and in Austen's imposition of a romantic resolution on the realistic premise of *Pride and Prejudice.* But the continuities between life and art are perhaps even more clearly delineated by the "themes" that cross over from one domain

*idea of romantic
love, proper
lady

sentimentalism
controlled
women's
behavior

to the other. Thus sentimentalism, as Mary Wollstonecraft pointed
out in *The Rights of Woman,* governed actual women's behavior, values,
and conceptions of themselves; and, as she demonstrated—less happily—in *Maria,* these sentimental values and goals necessitated evasions damaging both to aesthetic closure and to happiness in the real
world. By the same token, ideal romantic love was no doubt dreamed
of by actual girls, as Wollstonecraft's early letters suggest and the
young Mary Godwin's romantic escapade proved; yet introducing the
ideal of romantic love in a socially realistic fiction requires either
freezing the narrative at the climactic moment of marriage—as Austen always does—or abandoning realism altogether—as *Maria, Frankenstein,* and *Pride and Prejudice* do in such different ways.

Both the aesthetic closure of narrative and the imaginative
gratification of sentimentalism or romantic love are, in one respect
at least, compensations for the more material, more practical rewards
that bourgeois ideology endorses, seems to promise, and then denies.
The practical problem with these compensatory, substitute gratifications is that, no matter how imaginatively satisfying they are, they
finally prove debilitating to their real adherents; to put it most simply,
they deflect criticism from the social institutions they ultimately serve.
As Mary Wollstonecraft recognized, sentimentalism purports to gratify the senses it inflames by offering first vicarious titillation and then
the ennobling reward of spiritual transcendence. Yet because of the
position and definition of women in bourgeois society, the actual
rewards of sentimentalism prove meager and false, consisting, as they
do, of extreme susceptibility to every passing emotion, cultivated
helplessness, and even sexual frustration. Romantic love similarly
promises women emotional fulfillment and the legitimation of their
autonomy, their intensity of feeling, and even their power; but, given
the actual power relations institutionalized in society, such rewards
are short-lived. Romantic love makes women dream of being swept
off their feet; it ends by reinforcing the helplessness that makes
learning to stand on their own two feet unlikely.

The consequences of habitual indirection were undoubtedly serious in personal terms, in political terms, and in terms of the "unfolding of genius." Even so, we should not overlook the fact that these
three women (and many more) *were* able to accommodate their creative energies to the imperatives of propriety sufficiently to exploit
the opportunities for self-expression that existed in their time. In one
sense, the idea that facilitated their self-expression—the illusion that
art constitutes a discrete, apolitical domain—simply reinforces bourgeois ideology; for in guaranteeing the kind of private sphere that
found expression in Austen's novels, art provided women (and men)
an arena for action apparently protected from the demands of the

material world, hospitable to the most personal desires and fantasies, and capable of being even further confined, if necessary, to a separate "self" or under covering sheets of blotting paper. But in another sense, even if art seems safely protected from material and practical concerns, even if its resolutions are at best symbolic, the imaginative gratification yielded by creating and reading literature is genuine in being deeply felt. Even if it cannot by itself resolve social contradictions, art can pursue the utopian dream of restoring at least a symbolic experience of fulfillment to a world sadly lacking in opportunities for other kinds of satisfaction.[1] Indirection itself is a symbolic action, and, as such, it creates imaginative freedom where there would otherwise be only inhibition, restraint, and frustration. Mary Wollstonecraft's ability, in *The Rights of Woman,* to identify many of the ideological complexities of her society reveals an extraordinary degree of critical insight, and her capacity to record faithfully the process of self-creation in her *Letters Written . . . in Sweden* suggests one of the ways in which even a fledgling subjectivity can produce effective art. For all her defensiveness, Mary Shelley also reveals a remarkable degree of creativity, not just in the 1818 *Frankenstein,* where the ambiguity of symbolism opens a space for both self-expression and self-doubt, but in such conventional novels as *Falkner,* where her ability to pack the marginal areas of her fictions—the minor characters, the subplots, the latent psychological complexities—with important material permits her to expose her complex, often contradictory, desires. In this context, Jane Austen's aesthetic accomplishment also takes on a new dimension; for not only are the strategies we have long associated with her creative "genius" now seen to be extraordinarily complicated responses to an ideological dilemma, but her fictions themselves can be seen as imaginative spaces into which she invites her readers in the hope of collectively, symbolically, reforming the world they share.

To argue that works of literature participate in ideology is not to argue that they are ruthlessly determined, that the concerns they dramatize are practiced deceits, or that the comforts they offer do not console and gratify their readers. But to argue that literature participates in ideology *is* to argue that all works are acts of communication and that, as such, they involve not only a speaker and an audience but an "occasion" as well. The first "occasion" of any work is its historical situation, a situation defined not just by its position in time, in literary history, or in the history of ideas but by the dynamic interplay of collective and personal needs, priorities, ideals, and preoccupations within the society in which it was produced. As a social act—and, inevitably, as a political act—the literary work spoke to and now speaks of its moment in social history; it does not simply articulate its producer's unique and inimitable style.

And this, of course, leads to the relationship that exists between interpretations of the kind offered in this book and our own ideological situation. For if all works of literature participate in ideology, then all works of criticism do too. One of the things we discover when we begin to look at literature from this perspective is the extent to which criticism tends to select and rewrite the texts it examines in terms of its own implicit ideology.[2] Indeed, the continuing popularity of works like *Frankenstein* and Jane Austen's novels can be seen to be related to the fact that these works contain a degree of indeterminacy that makes them hospitable to a wider range of ideological positions than does the explicit didacticism of Wollstonecraft's *Vindications* or even the culturally specific wish-fulfillments of Shelley's late novels. As the history of critical reception reveals, succeeding generations have been able to interpret the "nonideological" or "mythic" qualities of *Frankenstein* in a variety of ways, consistent with their own preoccupations and needs, just as critics have been able to depict Jane Austen either as "Aunt Jane" or as a practitioner of "regulated hatred," depending on their own ideological positions.

In choosing to analyze these three writers in detail rather than more popular women writers like Anne Radcliffe or Maria Edgeworth, I have reproduced the ideological bias of my own contemporaries instead of trying to reenter or reflect that of my subjects (a task which seems to me daunting, if not impossible). But it is this very gap between me and my subjects that has yielded what seem to me to be two of the most important results of my analysis. In the first place, the changes that have occurred in the past century and a half have brought into visibility issues that Wollstonecraft, Shelley, and Austen never explicitly formulated and might not even have considered important to their social situation, much less to their artistic styles. Such hindsight as I have employed may result in lapses of sensitivity, but I think that it has allowed me to interpret three writers of the past in terms that (while not necessarily superior and certainly not absolute) are sufficiently different from the terms they used in interpreting themselves that they yield exciting insights and explanations. In the second place, just as the present casts new light on the past, so light from the past returns to illuminate our own situation. Even if we have moved beyond the age of industrial capitalism, and even if such conceptual revolutions as the civil rights movement and the women's movement have altered the ways some of us think about old questions, many of the same configurations of power I have examined in this book still characterize American society. Perhaps more important, many of the same values and inhibitions persist, sedimented deep in the layers of our culture and our unconsciousness. The psychological experience of many women still replicates the patterns I

Notes

Preface

1. Joseph Glanvill, "Against Confidence in Philosophy and Matters of Specula-tion," in *Essays on Several Important Subjects in Philosophy and Religion* (1676), quoted by Donald Greene, "Latitudinarianism and Sensibility: The Genealogy of the 'Man of Feeling' Reconsidered," *Modern Philology* 75, no. 2 (November 1977): 169–70.

2. Edwin Hood, *The Age and Its Architechts,* quoted by Walter E. Houghton, *The Victorian Frame of Mind, 1830–1870* (New Haven: Yale University Press, 1957), p. 352.

3. Margaret George, "From 'Goodwife' to 'Mistress': The Transformation of the Female in Bourgeois Culture," *Science & Society* 37, no. 2 (Summer 1973): 155–56.

4. Quoted by Ralph M. Wardle, *Mary Wollstonecraft: A Critical Biography* (Lawrence: University of Kansas Press, 1951), p. 136.

5. For a discussion of the persistent political ramifications of equating "female" with "feminine," see Catherine A. MacKinnon, "Feminism, Marxism, Method, and the State: An Agenda for Theory," *Signs: Journal of Women in Culture and Society* 7, no. 3 (Spring 1982): 515–44.

6. Condorcet, quoted by Madelyn Gutwirth, *Madame de Staël, Novelist: The Emer-gence of the Artist as Woman* (Urbana: University of Illinois Press, 1978), p. 22.

7. Hester Lynch Thrale Piozzi, *Thraliana: The Diary of Mrs. Hester Lynch Thrale, 1776–1809,* 2 vols., ed. Katherine C. Balderston (Oxford: Clarendon Press, 1942), 1:421–22.

8. William Law, *A Serious Call to a Devout and Holy Life. Adapted to the State and Conditions of all Orders of Christians* (London: William Innys, 1729), p. 365.

9. "Clarissa is not a performance to be read with eagerness and laid aside for ever, but will be occasionally consulted by the busy, the aged, and the studious," Johnson argued in urging Richardson to append an index (*The Letters of Samuel Johnson,* ed. R. W. Chapman, 3 vols. [Oxford: Clarendon Press, 1952], 1:35–36).

10. Sandra M. Gilbert and Susan Gubar, *The Madwoman in the Attic: The Woman Writer and the Nineteenth-Century Literary Imagination* (New Haven: Yale University Press, 1979), pp. 27–36.

11. *The Ladies Library, Written by a Lady,* 3d ed., 3 vols. (London: Jacob Tonson, 1722), 1:4.

12. In *Freud on Schreber: Psychoanalytic Theory and the Critical Act* (Amherst: University of Massachusetts Press, 1982), C. Barry Chabot argues persuasively that the assump-tion that an individual's life is a more or less cohesive whole is a necessary first postulate of *any* psychological or social analysis. Moreover, he continues, far from perpetuating the "illusion" of the autonomous individual, this assumption necessari-ly links the psychological and the social. "The theory of the cohesive life is not a denial of the social formation of the individual, not a covert piece of bourgeois

ideology. . . . The individual lives at the intersection of social vectors, is both constituted by them and constitutes them; the psychological is always (already) social, and
the social can only be constituted psychologically. Any attempt to grasp this interpen-
etration solely from one side or the other must reify the relationship, and thereby
hopelessly mystify understanding" (p. 92).

13. For pertinent discussions of the concept of "ideology," see Terry Eagleton,
Criticism and Ideology: A Study in Marxist Literary Theory (London: New Left Books, 1976),
pp. 11–63; Terry Eagleton, *Marxism and Literary Criticism* (Berkeley: University of
California Press, 1976), pp. 3–27; Fredric Jameson, *The Political Unconscious: Narrative
as a Socially Symbolic Act* (Ithaca: Cornell University Press, 1981), pp. 17–23, 58–102;
and Raymond Williams, *Marxism and Literature* (Oxford: Oxford University Press,
1977), pp. 55–74. For discussions of the relationship between social relations and
psychology, see Juliet Mitchell, *Psychoanalysis and Feminism: Freud, Reich, Laing, and
Women* (New York: Random House, 1975), pp. 401–6, and Nancy Chodorow, *The
Reproduction of Mothering: Psychoanalysis and the Sociology of Gender* (Berkeley: University
of California Press, 1978).

14. See Jameson, *The Political Unconscious,* p. 77.

15. Cora Kaplan also underscores the "contradiction posed by women's writing
as simultaneously a historical record of their oppression and a definite mark of their
defiance" ("The Indefinite Disclosed: Christina Rossetti and Emily Dickinson," in
Women Writing and Writing about Women, ed. Mary Jacobus [New York: Barnes &
Noble, 1979], p. 64).

16. Virginia Woolf, "Women and Fiction," in *Collected Essays,* ed. Leonard Woolf,
4 vols. (London: Chatto & Windus, 1966), 2:141.

Chapter One

1. Thomas Gisborne, *An Enquiry into the Duties of the Female Sex,* 4th ed. (London:
T. Cadell, Jr. & W. Davies, 1799), pp. 122–23.

2. Quoted in Robert Palfrey Utter and Gwendolyn Bridges Needham, *Pamela's
Daughters* (New York: Macmillan, 1936), p. 25.

3. Mary Astell, *A Serious Proposal to the Ladies for the Advancement of Their True and
Great Interest,* 4th ed. (1701; rpt., New York: Source Books Press, 1970), p. 35.

4. Joseph Swetnam, quoted by David J. Latt, "Praising Virtuous Ladies: The
Literary Image and Historical Reality of Women in Seventeenth-Century England,"
in Marlene Springer, ed., *What Manner of Women: Essays on English and American Life
and Literature* (New York: New York University Press, 1977), p. 43.

5. Harold Perkin, *The Origins of Modern English Society, 1780–1880* (London: Routledge & Kegan Paul, 1969), p. 85.

6. According to Perkin (ibid., p. 85), the "ultimate motivation" for aspiring
members of the middle classes "was a dynastic one: to found a family, to endow
them splendidly enough to last for ever, and to enjoy a vicarious eternal life in the
seed of one's loins." In an essay on the social causes of the Industrial Revolution,
Perkin quotes this statement from T. R. Malthus's *Principles of Political Economy:* "the
desire to realize a fortune as a permanent provision for a family is perhaps the most
general motive for the continued exertions of those whose incomes depend upon
their own personal skill and efforts" (Harold Perkin, "The Social Causes of the British
Industrial Revolution," *Transactions of the Royal Historical Society* 5th ser. 18 [1968]: 139).

7. See James Boswell, *Journal of a Tour to the Hebrides,* ed. Allan Wendt (1785: rpt.,
Boston: Houghton Mifflin/Riverside, 1965), p. 250.

8. Jean-Jacques Rousseau, *Emile,* trans. Barbara Foxley (New York: Dutton/
Everyman, 1974), pp. 324–25.

9. Sir William Blackstone, *Commentaries of the Laws of England, Book the First* (Oxford, 1765), p. 442, quoted in Sandra M. Gilbert and Susan Gubar, *The Madwoman in the Attic: The Woman Writer and the Nineteenth-Century Literary Imagination* (New Haven: Yale University Press, 1979), p. 155. Essentially, a married woman in the eighteenth century was legally nonexistent. She could not take even the smallest legal step on her own: she could own no property unless it had been settled on her by her father, her husband, or a male relative; she could not sue for a divorce; and, in the event that her husband left her, she could not even visit her children. The first laws to affect materially the legal position of married women were these: the Infant's Custody Act (1839), which allowed women to petition the court for custody over children under seven years old and for visiting rights over older children; the Matrimonial Causes Act (1857), which, in the case of a separation, granted women possession of property they had contributed to their marriages; and the Married Woman's Property Act (1870), which finally granted reforms in educational opportunities and political rights (though not, of course, the right to vote).

10. See Alice Clark, *Working Life of Women in the Seventeenth Century* (London: George Routledge & Sons, 1919), and Margaret George, "From 'Goodwife' to 'Mistress': The Transformation of the Female in Bourgeois Culture," *Science & Society* 37, no. 2 (Summer 1973): 157–61.

11. Women like Margaret Fell Fox were quick to prove this. The debate over women's right to speak in church or preach the Scripture was taken up on one side by the Quakers and, in particular, by Fox's *Womens Speaking Justified by the Scriptures*. On the other, more typical side, were the Abington Baptists, who answered the question "How far women may speak in the church?" thus: "They may not so speak as that their speaking shall show a not acknowledging of the inferiority of their sex and so be an usurping authority over the man" (quoted by Christopher Hill, *Milton and the English Revolution* [New York: Viking Press, 1977], p. 118).

12. Daniel Rogers, *Workes* (Cambridge, Eng., 1609–13), p. 303, cited by Keith Thomas, "The Double Standard," *Journal of the History of Ideas* 20 (April 1959): 213. Gilbert Burnet, *The Earl of Rochester* (1680), cited by Hill, *Milton*, p. 120.

13. Astell, *A Serious Proposal*, p. 1.

14. *The Ladies Library, Written by a Lady,* 5th ed., 3 vols. (London: J. & R. Tonson, 1739), 2:73.

15. Clara Reeve, quoted by J. M. S. Tompkins, *The Popular Novel in England, 1770–1800* (Lincoln: University of Nebraska Press, 1961), p. 154.

16. Robert Southey, quoted by E. P. Thompson, *The Making of the English Working Class* (1963; New York: Random House/Vintage, 1966), p. 369.

17. Hannah More, quoted by Muriel Jaeger, *Before Victoria* (London: Chatto & Windus, 1956), p. 29. For further discussions of Evangelicalism, see ibid., pp. 36–52; Thompson, *Making of the English Working Class,* chap. 2; and Maurice J. Quinlan, *Victorian Prelude: A History of English Manners, 1700–1830* (1941; rpt., New York: Columbia University Press, 1965), pp. 53–56 and passim.

18. For a discussion of the social role of Evangelical sects, see E. P. Thompson, *The Making of the English Working Class,* esp. chap. 2.

19. See Perkin, *Origins,* pp. 185–214.

20. *Blackwood's Edinburgh Magazine* 27 (1830): 876, quoted by Perkin, *Origins,* p. 285.

21. "Female Character," *The Ladies' Magazine* 1, no. 5 (May 1828): 197.

22. See Nancy F. Cott, *The Bonds of Womanhood: Woman's "Proper Sphere" in New England, 1770–1830* (New Haven: Yale University Press, 1977), p. 69.

23. Louis A. Landa, "Pope's Belinda, The General Emporie of the World, and the Wondrous Worm," *South Atlantic Quarterly* 70, no. 2 (Spring 1971): 234–35.

24. For discussions of women as consumers, see Neil McKendrick, "Home Demand and Economic Growth: A New View of the Role of Women and Children in

the Industrial Revolution," in *Historical Perspectives: Studies in English Thought and Society in Honor of J. H. Plumb,* ed. Neil McKendrick (London: Europa, 1974), pp. 152–210, and Perkin, "The Social Causes," pp. 123–43.

25. The standard discussion of this subject is H. J. Habakkuk's "Marriage Settlements in the Eighteenth Century," *Transactions of the Royal Historical Society* 4th ser. 32 (London: Royal Historical Society, 1950): 15, 21, 27, 29.

26. Ibid., p. 18.

27. Ibid., p. 21.

28. Mary Ann Radcliffe, *The Memoirs of Mrs. Mary Ann Radcliffe. In Familiar Letters to Her Female Friend* (Edinburgh: Printed for the Author, 1810), p. 432. In *Sir Roger de Clarendon,* Clara Reeve cites the "suitable" formula for dowries: "A bride should bring her husband a dowry large enough to enable him to pay his younger brothers and sisters their portions under his father's will, without altering his own style of living" and, presumably, without encumbering his estate (see Tompkins, *Popular Novel,* pp. 165–66).

29. The decline in the number of eligible bachelors was partly the result of late seventeenth-century wars and partly a consequence of strict settlement, which forced many younger sons to conserve money by remaining single or to augment their portion by entering, or marrying into, the professional classes. See Habakkuk, "Marriage," pp. 23, 24.

30. Samuel Richardson, *Clarissa, Or, the History of a Young Lady,* 4 vols. (London: Dutton/Everyman, 1932), 1:54.

31. See Hester Lynch Thrale Piozzi, *Thraliana: The Diary of Mrs. Hester Lynch Thrale, 1776–1809,* ed. Katherine C. Balderston, 2 vols. (Oxford: Clarendon Press, 1942), 1:54.

32. Sir William Temple, *An Essay on Popular Discontents: Miscellanea, The Third Part* (1750), p. 268, quoted by Habakkuk, "Marriage," p. 25.

33. Lawrence Stone, in *The Family, Sex, and Marriage in England, 1500–1800* (New York: Harper & Row, 1977), argues that the proportion of "companionate marriages" increased during the eighteenth century. See especially chap. 8.

34. Mrs. Griffith, *The History of Lady Barton* (1771), quoted by Tompkins, *Popular Novel,* p. 147.

35. See, for example, Mary Wollstonecraft, *Maria; or the Wrongs of Woman* (1798), and Hannah More, *Coelebs in Search of a Wife* (1809).

36. Richard Allestree, Preface to *The Ladies Calling,* 12th ed. (Oxford: n.p., 1727), n.p.

37. Piozzi, *Thraliana,* 1:547. She was reading *Spectator* 217.

38. Miss Hatfield, *Letters on the Importance of the Female Sex: With Observations on Their Manners, and on Education* (London: J. Adlard, 1803), pp. 20–21.

39. The first English periodical for women was probably the *Ladies' Mercury,* published briefly by John Dunton in 1693; it was followed by the *Ladies' Diary; or, Women's Almanack* in 1704, and then by such diverse periodicals as the *Visiter* in 1723, the *Ladies' Journal* in 1727, the *Parrot* in 1728, the *Lady's Magazine; or, Universal Repository* in 1733, the *Female Spectator* in 1744, the *Lady's Weekly Magazine* in 1747, the *Ladies' Magazine; or, Universal Entertainer* in 1749, the *Old Maid* in 1755, and the *Lady's Museum* in 1760. For further discussion of such magazines, see Cynthia L. White, *Women's Magazines, 1693–1968* (London: Michael Joseph, 1972), esp. pp. 30–32, and Bertha Monica Stearns, "Early English Periodicals for Ladies (1700–1760)," *PMLA* 48 (1933): 38–60. General periodicals that occasionally appealed specifically to women include *The Tatler, The Spectator,* Johnson's *Rambler* and *Idler,* and *The Gentleman's Magazine.*

40. I owe the research for this comparison to Tad Anderson. His unpublished essay, "Sexual Roles in Late Eighteenth-Century England: A Comparison of the

January 1793 issues of *Lady's Magazine* and *Gentleman's Magazine*" (Yale College, 1978), has been instrumental in helping me formulate these observations.

41. *Gentleman's Magazine* 43 (January 1793).

42. *Lady's Magazine* 24 (January 1793).

43. "Female Character," p. 196 (See n. 21, above).

44. Adam Smith, *The Theory of Moral Sentiments,* 10th ed., 2 vols. (London: T. Cadell & W. Davies, 1804), 1:400.

45. Daniel Defoe, "Essay upon Several Projects: Or, Effectual Ways for Advancing the Interests of the Nation" (1702), in *The Complete Works of Daniel Defoe,* 3 vols. (London: John Clements, 1843), 3:42. See also Bernard Mandeville, *The Virgin Unmask'd: Or, Female Dialogues betwixt an Elderly Maiden Lady and Her Niece, on Several Diverting Discourses on Love, Marriage, Memoirs, and Morals, &c. of the Times,* 2d ed. (London: G. Strathan, 1724), p. 117. and Jonathan Swift, "The Lady's Dressing Room" (1730), rpt. in *The Writings of Jonathan Swift,* ed. Robert A. Greenberg and William Bowman Piper (New York: Norton, 1973), pp. 535–38.

46. See James Boswell, *The Life of Johnson,* ed. George B. Hill, 6 vols. (1887 ed.), 5:226 n.

47. *The Polite Lady: Or a Course of Female Education. In a Series of Letters, from a Mother to Her Daughter,* 2d ed. (London: Newberry & Carnan, 1769), p. 267.

48. Allestree, *Ladies Calling,* p. 14.

49. Gisborne, *Enquiry,* pp. 228–29.

50. Hannah More, *Strictures on the Modern System of Female Education,* 2d ed., 2 vols. (London: T. Cadell, Jr. & W. Davies, 1799), 2:166.

51. More, ibid., p. 71.

52. Gisborne, *Enquiry,* pp. 33–34.

53. *The Polite Lady,* pp. 191–92.

54. *The Ladies Library,* 1:162.

55. *The Polite Lady,* p. 205; Hannah More, *Strictures,* 2:12; *Spectator* 81, in *The Spectator with Notes and a General Index,* 2 vols. (New York: Samuel Marks, 1826), 1:109.

56. See Ellen Pollak, "Re-Reading *The Rape of the Lock*: Pope and the Paradox of Female Power," *Studies in Eighteenth-Century Culture,* vol. 10, ed. Harry C. Payne (Madison: University of Wisconsin Press, 1981), pp. 429–44), and Peggy Kamuf, "Rousseau's Politics of Visibility," *Diacritics* 5, no. 4 (Winter 1975): 51–56.

57. *The Ladies Library,* 1:128.

58. Allestree, *Ladies Calling,* p. 6.

59. Ibid., p. 15.

60. *The Polite Lady,* pp. 184, 186–87.

61. Dr. Gregory, *A Father's Legacy to His Daughters,* 4th ed. (1762; London: W. Strahan, T. Cadell, and Edinburgh: J. Balfour & W. Creech, 1774), p. 28.

62. More, *Strictures,* 2: 66–67.

63. James Fordyce, *Sermons to Young Women,* 4th ed., 2 vols. (London: A. Millar & T. Cadell, 1767), 1:99.

64. In Fanny Burney's novel, Reverend Villars assumes that Evelina can be "read." When Evelina, lost in thought about Lord Orville, asks her guardian if he has been reading, Villars replies, "Yes, my child;—a book that both afflicts and perplexes me" (*Evelina* [1778; New York: Norton, 1965], p. 248).

65. Unlike Anna Howe, Clarissa knows that reputation is not essential to her "self." Despite the fact that her reputation has long been ruined, it is only after the rape that she laments to Anna: "*I,* my *best self,* have *not* escaped!" (*Clarissa,* 3:321).

66. Tony Tanner, *Adultery in the Novel: Contract and Transgression* (Baltimore: Johns Hopkins University Press, 1980), pp. 163–64.

67. Gregory, *Legacy,* pp. 58–60.

68. Allestree, *Ladies Calling*, p. 156.

69. When Clarissa declares that, although she will not marry Mr. Solmes, her "heart is free," her parents are frankly incredulous. Either her heart must be "prepossessed," they assert, or it must be theirs to dispose of. They cannot conceive of the possibility that a young girl might know and "own" her own heart.

70. See Isaac Kramnick, "Children's Literature and Bourgeois Ideology: Observations on Culture and Industrial Capitalism in the Later Eighteenth Century," in *Culture and Politics from Puritanism to the Enlightenment*, ed. Perez Zagorin (Berkeley: University of California Press, 1980), pp. 203–40.

71. Gorges Edmond Howard, *Aphorisms and Maxims on Various Subjects for the Good Conduct of Life, &c.* (n.p., n.d.), p. 332.

72. *The Polite Lady*, p. 58.

73. Sarah Pennington, *An Unfortunate Mother's Advice to Her Absent Daughters. In a Letter to Miss Pennington* (London: S. Chandler, 1761), pp. 71–72.

74. Miss Hatfield, *Letters on the Importance of the Female Sex: With Observations on Their Manners, and on Education* (London: J. Adland, 1803), p. 4.

75. Reynald Morryson, "On Female Association," *Gentleman's Magazine* 80 (June 1810): 531.

76. More, *Strictures*, 1:59–61.

77. Abigail Mott, *Observations on the Importance of Female Education, and Maternal Instruction, with Their Beneficial Influence on Society. By a Mother.* (New York: Mahlon Day, 1825), p. 16.

78. Piozzi, *Thraliana*, 2:909. Mrs. Thrale's concern about social stability increased during the turbulent last decade of the century. In 1795, for example, she worried over "the Distress upon the poorer Sort in ev'ry Town & Country—I hear the Brewhouses are stopt in London; a violent, & so far as I know a *new* Event, manifesting heavy pressure upon the publick. Handbills too of an inflammatory Nature posted on our Church Doors at Streatham in Surry—*demanding*, not *requesting* Relief for the lower Orders—terrifie one whilst they shew and indeed openly confess, that France in her Conduct—shall serve as Example to Britain—so here are Famine & Insurrection threatening us *within*, whilst Invasion is avowedly the Design of our Neighbour the French—*without*" (ibid.).

79. Laetitia Matilda Hawkins, *Letters on the Female Mind, Its Powers and Pursuits. Addressed to Miss H.M. Williams, with Particular Reference to Her Letters from France*, 2 vols. (London: Hookham & Carpenter, 1793), 2:141–42.

80. Hawkins even fears at one point that talk of equal rights is a plot of Frenchwomen to seduce Englishmen away from their wives. See ibid., 2:200.

81. More, *Strictures*, 1:6.

82. Arthur Young, *An Enquiry into the State of the Public Mind* (1798), quoted by Quinlan, *Victorian Prelude*, p. 98.

83. More, *Strictures*, 2:39.

84. John Ruskin, "Of Queens' Gardens," in *Sesame and Lilies* (New York: John Wiley & Son, 1865), p. 92.

85. Samuel Johnson, *The Rambler*, vol. 4 of *The Yale Edition of the Works of Samuel Johnson*, ed. W. J. Bate and Albrecht B. Strauss (New Haven: Yale University Press, 1969), pp. 133–34.

86. More, *Strictures*, 2:1, 12.

87. Gilbert and Gubar, *Madwoman*, pp. 3–7.

88. Ian Watt, in *The Rise of the Novel* (1957; rpt. Berkeley: University of California Press, 1964), claims (p. 298) that the majority of eighteenth-century novels were written by women.

89. Tompkins, *Popular Novel*, p. 120, including note 3.

90. Robert Halsband, "Ladies of Letters in the Eighteenth Century," in *The Lady of Letters in the Eighteenth Century,* ed. Irvin Ehrenpreis and Robert Halsband (Los Angeles: University of California Press, 1969), pp. 32–33.

91. Lady Mary Wortley Montagu, quoted by Halsband, "Ladies," p. 38.

92. Among Montagu's published works are an essay on smallpox inoculation (1722), a defense of Walpole's ministry (*The Nonsense of Common-Sense,* 1737), an attack on Pope (*Verses to the Imitator of Horace,* 1733), an attack on Swift (*The Dean's Provocation for Writing the Lady's Dressing Room,* 1733), and an *Answer* to James Hammond's amorous poem to Catherine Dashwood (1733).

93. See Halsband, "Ladies," p. 47.

94. Piozzi, *Thraliana,* 2:730.

95. More, *Strictures,* 2:26.

96. See Tompkins, *Popular Novel,* pp. 116–71, esp. p. 129.

97. Piozzi, *Thraliana,* 1:146.

98. Ibid., p. 158.

99. "I believe there are really very infamous Things done by the Managers with regard to the female Wits: the poor Girls are so easily brow beaten, & dare not tell how Mr Such a one treated their Piece with Contempt for fear of incurring more Contempt; so then Mr Such a one lays it by as worthless, & in a Year or two, (especially if the Wench dies,) brings out a Play of his own upon her Plot, or with a Character from her performance as suits him best" (ibid., p. 421).

100. See Tompkins, *Popular Novel,* pp. 126–27.

101. More, *Strictures,* 2:13–14.

102. Ibid., p. 21.

103. Jane West, *Letters to a Young Lady* (1802), quoted by Claire Tomalin, *The Life and Death of Mary Wollstonecraft* (London: Weidenfeld & Nicolson, 1974), p. 247.

104. Catherine Maria Sedgwick, quoted by Cott, *The Bonds of Womanhood,* p. 166 (see n. 22, above).

105. Mary Shelley, *Frankenstein, or The Modern Prometheus,* ed. James Rieger (1818; Indianapolis: Bobbs-Merrill, 1974), p. 222.

106. Halsband, "Ladies," p. 35.

107. See Ida Beatrice O'Malley, *Women in Subjection: A Study of the Lives of Englishwomen before 1832* (London: Duckworth, 1933), pp. 179–99, for a discussion of similar accomplishments on the part of other women.

108. A number of important feminist critics have begun to recognize and discuss this female indirection. In addition to Spacks and Gilbert and Gubar, whom I cite below, see also Carolyn Heilbrun and Catharine Stimpson, "Theories of Feminist Criticism: A Dialogue," in *Feminist Literary Criticism: Explorations in Theory,* ed. Josephine Donovan (Lexington: University Press of Kentucky, 1975), pp. 61–73, and Elaine Showalter, *A Literature of Their Own: British Women Novelists from Brontë to Lessing* (Princeton: Princeton University Press, 1977).

109. Gilbert and Gubar have also pointed out that the "hidden story" of much women's writing is the quest for self-definition. See *Madwoman,* p. 76.

110. Patricia Meyer Spacks, "Reflecting Women," *Yale Review* 63 (Autumn 1973): 27–30.

111. Radcliffe, *Memoirs,* pp. 478–79 (see n. 28, above).

112. These two kinds of plots dominate eighteenth-century novels by men as well. Contrast, for example, Richardson's *Clarissa* with Fielding's *Tom Jones.*

113. For a discussion of Fanny Burney as a novelist, see Patricia Meyer Spacks, *Imagining a Self: Autobiography and Novel in Eighteenth-Century England* (Cambridge, Mass.: Harvard University Press, 1976), pp. 158–92, and Lillian Bloom and Edward A. Bloom, "Fanny Burney's Novels: The Retreat from Wonder," *Novel* 12, no. 3 (Spring 1979): 215–35.

114. Gilbert and Gubar call this feminine alter ego the "madwoman in the attic" after Charlotte Brontë's Bertha. See *Madwoman,* esp. pp. 73–79.

115. See Judith Wilt, "He Could Go No Farther: A Modest Proposal about Lovelace and Clarissa," *PMLA* 92, no. 1 (January 1977): 19–32.

116. See Terry J. Castle, *"Amy,* Who Knew my Disease: A PsychoSexual Pattern in Defoe's *Roxana,*" *ELH* 46 (1979): 81–96.

117. See *Madwoman,* p. 73.

118. According to Nancy Chodorow, the psychic maturation of a young girl neither repeats nor simply reverses the oedipal configuration that Freud identified in young boys. Like the boy, the girl originally identifies with the mother; but, for her, this *pre*oedipal identification is more formative and more long-lasting than the boy's identification. When the girl's father does become important, it is "in the context of a bisexual relational triangle. . . . A girl usually turns to her father as an object of primary interest from the exclusivity of the relationship to her mother, but this libidinal turning to her father does not substitute for her attachment to her mother. Instead, a girl retains her preoedipal tie to her mother . . . and builds oedipal attachments to both her mother and father upon it" (*The Reproduction of Mothering: Psychoanalysis and the Sociology of Gender* [Berkeley: University of California Press, 1978], pp. 192–93. If Chodorow is correct, it may well be the case that a woman's psychological relation to authority may involve accommodation rather than confrontation; in other words, it may be more in keeping with her psychological development to identify with and accept a number of role models instead of trying to usurp the place of her authoritative forebears. See also Juliet Mitchell, *Psychoanalysis and Feminism: Freud, Reich, Laing, and Women* (1974; New York: Random House/Vintage, 1975), pp. 377–81.

119. For a provocative discussion of parody, see George Levine, "Translating the Monstrous: *Northanger Abbey,*" *Nineteenth-Century Fiction* 30, no. 3 (December 1975): 335–50.

120. See Mary Poovey, "Ideology and *The Mysteries of Udolpho,*" *Criticism* 21, no. 4 (Fall 1979): 329–30.

121. Gilbert and Gubar, *Madwoman,* p. 85.

122. Patricia Meyer Spacks, "Self as Subject: A Female Language," in *In/Sights: Self-Portraits by Women,* compiled by Joyce Tenneson Cohen (Boston: D. R. Godine, 1978), p. 110.

Chapter Two

1. *Collected Letters of Mary Wollstonecraft,* ed. Ralph M. Wardle (Ithaca and London: Cornell University Press, 1979), p. 60; 4 June 1773–16 November 1774. All references in text and notes will be to this edition (cited as *MWL,* with page number and date).

2. See Emily W. Sunstein, *A Different Face: The Life of Mary Wollstonecraft* (Boston: Little, Brown, 1975), pp. 3–20. Wollstonecraft once said to William Godwin that her father had *not* been trained in any profession; the implication is that she wanted to overlook his initial inferior social position (see William Godwin, *Memoirs of Mary Wollstonecraft,* ed. W. Clark Durant [London and New York: Constable, 1927], pp. 8–9).

3. See Wollstonecraft's letters of January 1784 to her sister Everina, *MWL,* pp. 86–89.

4. Wollstonecraft's jealousy makes its appearance in the thinly disguised account of her relationship with Fanny in *Mary, A Fiction* (1788) and in her letter of January 1784 to Everina (*MWL,* pp. 88–89).

5. Ralph M. Wardle, Margaret George, and Margaret Walters give particular attention to Wollstonecraft's tendency to adopt roles. See Wardle, *Mary Wollstonecraft:*

A Critical Biography (Lawrence, Kans.: University of Kansas Press, 1951), pp. 15, 66, 69, 75, 86; George, *One Woman's "Situation": A Study of Mary Wollstonecraft* (Urbana and Chicago: University of Illinois Press, 1970), pp. 41, 63–76; and Walters, "The Rights and Wrongs of Women: Mary Wollstonecraft, Harriet Martineau, Simone de Beauvoir," in *The Rights and Wrongs of Women,* ed. Juliet Mitchell and Ann Oakley (Harmondsworth, Eng.: Penguin Books, 1976), pp. 312–13.

6. For a discussion of Johnson's circle, see Claire Tomalin, *The Life and Death of Mary Wollstonecraft* (London: Weidenfeld & Nicolson, 1974), pp. 66–82.

7. Wollstonecraft's only formal education consisted of a brief attendance at the Beverley day school. She did read some classics with the Reverend Clare during 1774 and no doubt continued informal study with Dr. Richard Price while she taught in and superintended her school at Newington Green (1784–85).

8. Mary Jacobus also notes Wollstonecraft's defiance of her female nature: "A plain-speaking utilitarian speaks not so much *for* women, or *as* a woman, but *against* them—over their dead bodies, and over (having attempted to cast it out) the body of the text too" ("The Difference of View," in *Women Writing and Writing about Women,* ed. Mary Jacobus [New York: Barnes & Noble, 1979], pp. 14–15).

9. Edmund Burke, *Reflections on the Revolution in France* (1790; Garden City: Anchor Press/Doubleday, 1973), p. 89.

10. *Monthly Review,* January 1791; quoted in James T. Boulton, *The Language of Politics in the Age of Wilkes and Burke* (London: Routledge & Kegan Paul, 1963), p. 168.

11. *A Vindication of the Rights of Men, in a Letter to the Right Honourable Edmund Burke; Occasioned by His "Reflections on the Revolution in France"* (London: J. Johnson, 1790; facsimile edition, Gainesville, Fla.: Scholar's Facsimiles & Reprints, 1960), pp. iii–iv. (All subsequent references are to this edition.) The implication that someone else urged the publication of her work is, in fact, misleading. When Wollstonecraft stopped writing, midway through the project, Johnson was willing to relieve her of the task. His diffidence, predictably, challenged her to prove that she could finish the book, and she hurried to complete it.

12. Gary Kelly points out that Wollstonecraft's style and organization are illuminated by Kenneth Burke's notion of "repetitive form." See Kelly, "Mary Wollstonecraft as *Vir Bonus,*" *English Studies in Canada* 5, no. 3 (Autumn 1979): 286.

13. Wollstonecraft's attack on Burke's rhetoric has been discussed by James Boulton, *The Language of Politics,* pp. 169–70, and by Gary Kelly, "Mary Wollstonecraft as *Vir Bonus,*" pp. 281–83.

14. Kelly briefly alludes to the "masculine" and "feminine" terms of Wollstonecraft's argument. See his "Mary Wollstonecraft as *Vir Bonus,*" pp. 282, 289.

15. In a letter of January 1784, Wollstonecraft does suggest a theological explanation: "The mind of man is formed to admire perfection and perhaps our longing after it and the pleasure we take in observing a shadow of it is a *faint line* of that image that was first stamped on the soul" (*MWL,* p. 87). William Wordsworth proposes the model of the child's relationship with its mother in *The Prelude.*

16. *A Vindication of the Rights of Woman* (1792; New York: Norton, 1975), p. 136. This text, which is published in the Norton Critical Editions Series, is based on the second edition of 1792. All of my citations of this work are to this text.

17. The first quotation is from *The Rights of Men,* p. 29; the second is from *The Rights of Woman,* p. 14.

18. Edmund Burke also associates energy with the bourgeoisie and a sort of decorous indolence with the aristocracy. Explicitly, he allies himself with the latter, but the nature of his images and the contradictions in his argument have led Isaac Kramnick, very understandably, to suspect some ambivalence. See Kramnick, *The Rage of Edmund Burke: Portrait of an Ambivalent Conservative* (New York: Basic Books, 1977), esp. pp. 143–68.

19. Burke, *Reflections on the Revolution in France*, p. 89.

20. See, for example, Boulton, *The Language of Politics*, pp. 174–75.

21. *The Rights of Woman*, p. 58. Subsequent references will appear in the text.

22. For a discussion of this aspect of *The Rights of Woman*, see Janet M. Todd, "The Language of Sex in *A Vindication of the Rights of Woman*," *Mary Wollstonecraft Newsletter* 1, no. 2 (April 1973): 10–17.

23. Rousseau, *Emile*, trans. Barbara Foxley (New York: Dutton/Everyman, 1974), p. 324.

24. For a discussion of the role Milton plays in the writings of other nineteenth- and twentieth-century women, see Sandra M. Gilbert and Susan Gubar, *The Madwoman in the Attic: The Woman Writer and the Nineteenth-Century Literary Imagination* (New Haven: Yale University Press, 1979), pp. 187–212.

25. Nina Auerbach also discusses Wollstonecraft's anxiety about the "subtle sexual contagion" of women's schools. See her *Communities of Women: An Idea in Fiction* (Cambridge, Mass.: Harvard University Press, 1978), pp. 14–15.

26. See Patricia Meyer Spacks, "Ev'ry Woman is at Heart a Rake," *Eighteenth-Century Studies* 8, no. 1 (Fall 1974): 38.

Chapter Three

1. See Claire Tomalin, *The Life and Death of Mary Wollstonecraft* (London: Weidenfeld & Nicolson, 1974), p. 131. While in France, Wollstonecraft also began to speak less critically about sexuality. To a Frenchwoman who claimed to lack sexual appetite, Wollstonecraft replied, "Tant pis pour vous, madame, c'est un défaut de la nature" (quoted by Tomalin, p. 132).

2. William Godwin, *Memoirs of Mary Wollstonecraft*, ed. William Clark Durant (London and New York: Constable, 1927), p. 84.

3. Amelia Alderson, quoted by Ralph M. Wardle, *Mary Wollstonecraft: A Critical Biography* (Lawrence, Kans.: University of Kansas Press, 1951), p. 274.

4. *Letters Written during a Short Residence in Sweden, Norway, and Denmark* (1796), edited by Carol H. Poston (Lincoln, Neb., and London: University of Nebraska Press, 1976), p. 5. All subsequent references will be to this edition.

5. See *A Vindication of the Rights of Men* (London: J. Johnson, 1790; facsimile edition, Gainesville, Fla.: Scholar's Facsimiles & Reprints, 1960), p. iv.

6. See Mitzi Myers, "Mary Wollstonecraft's *Letters Written . . . in Sweden*: Toward Romantic Autobiography," in *Studies in Eighteenth-Century Culture*, ed. Roseann Runte (Madison: University of Wisconsin Press, 1979), pp. 169–70.

7. See ibid., pp. 178–79; Carol H. Poston, "Introduction" to *Letters Written . . . in Sweden*, pp. xvi–xvii; and Florence Boos, "Review of Wollstonecraft's *Letters Written . . . in Sweden*, ed. Carol H. Poston," *Eighteenth-Century Studies* 10 (Winter 1976–77): 280–81.

8. Even though many liked the *Letters*, Wollstonecraft's contemporaries reacted strongly—and generally negatively—to the less orthodox theology this work contained. A reviewer for *The Monthly Magazine and American Review*, for instance, argued that we "may date her lapse from that dignity of character which before distinguished her" to this period, when she "discarded all faith in christianity. . . . From this period she adored [God] . . . not as one whose interposing power is ever silently at work on the grand theatre of human affairs, causing eventual good to spring from present evil, and permitting nothing but for wise and benevolent purposes; but merely as the first great cause and vital spring of existence" (*The Monthly Magazine* 1, no. 1 [1799]: 331).

9. Myers, "Mary Wollstonecraft's *Letters*," p. 170.

10. Ibid., p. 173.

11. Ibid., p. 170.

12. The letters to Imlay are reprinted in *Collected Letters of Mary Wollstonecraft* (*MWL*), pp. 289–314. When the publication of these private letters made Wollstone-craft's illicit relationship with Imlay public, the positive reception some reviewers had given to the *Letters Written . . . in Sweden* gave way to general condemnation.

13. See *MWL*, p. 309; 9 August 1795.

14. See ibid., pp. 310–12; 26 August–25 September 1795.

15. See ibid., pp. 313–14; 27 September 1795.

16. Perhaps the most notable opinion Wollstonecraft preserved in defiance of Godwin's skepticism was her religious faith in "God, or something, consolatory [*sic*] in the air" (*MWL*, p. 394; 21 May 1797).

17. Godwin, *Memoirs*, p. 111.

18. Godwin states that Wollstonecraft believed the "purpose and structure of the . . . work . . . capable of producing an important effect" (Godwin's Preface to *Maria, or the Wrongs of Woman* [1798; New York: Norton, 1975], p. 5). Mitzi Myers also explores the difficulty Wollstonecraft had in reconciling purpose and structure; see her "Unfinished Business: Wollstonecraft's *Maria*," *Wordsworth Circle* 11, no. 2 (Spring 1980): 107–14.

19. *Maria, or the Wrongs of Woman* (1798; New York: Norton, 1975), p. 8. All subsequent references will be to this edition.

20. In her essay, "The Difference of View" (in *Women Writing and Writing about Women*, ed. Mary Jacobus [New York: Barnes & Noble, 1979], pp. 10–21) Mary Jacobus points out many of these same hesitations and contradictions; but even though she recognizes *Maria's* stylistic collapse ("Marginalised, the language of feeling can only ally itself with insanity—an insanity which, displaced into writing, produces a moment of imaginative and linguistic excess over-brimming the container of fiction, and swamping the distinction between author and character" [p. 15]), she interprets this collapse as a radical critique of masculine literary conventions. Indeed, Jacobus sees in Wollstonecraft's elision of narrator and character a Utopian gesture, a genuinely revolutionary moment pointing toward (if not fully achieving) a new kind of feminist writing. "A mental convulsion breaches the impasse between undifferen-tiated disappearance into a 'male' text and the prison of sensibility. Rejecting the essentialism that keeps women subjected as well as subjective, it also rejects mastery and dominance. Madness imagined as revolution, or the articulation of Utopian desire ('a demand for something—they scarcely knew what'), represent gestures past the impasse played out in Mary Wollstonecraft's prose. In writing, such gestures may release possibilities repressed by a dominant ideology or its discourse. The transgres-sion of literary boundaries—moments when structures are shaken, when language refuses to lie down meekly, or the marginal is brought into sudden focus, or intelligi-bility itself refused—reveal not only the conditions of possibility within which women's writing exists, but what it would be like to revolutionise them. In the same way, the moment of desire (the moment when the writer most clearly installs herself in her writing) becomes a refusal of mastery, an opting for openness and possibility, which can in itself make women's writing a challenge to the literary structures it must necessarily inhabit" (p. 16). Jacobus is not claiming that Wollstonecraft was fully aware of such possibilities, but her analysis still seems to me to superimpose twenti-eth-century feminist aesthetics onto Wollstonecraft's work. Judged by the aesthetic standards Wollstonecraft would have recognized, the narrative collapse of *Maria* signals failure, not the birth of a new form. I think we can see this, in part, in Wollstonecraft's repeated attempts to revise the manuscript and in her tendency to fall back on catchphrases and stock incidents from sentimental novels every time she sought an alternative to the emotional claustrophobia she identified in patriarchal

institutions. I find it more convincing to interpret her depiction of Jemima as an intimation of a revolutionary alternative. The fact that Wollstonecraft invokes senti-mentalism to dismiss this character reinforces my argument that she saw sentimen-talism as part of the solution, not part of the problem.

This disagreement notwithstanding, Jacobus' argument bears some interesting similarities to the one I present here.

21. Eighteenth-century moralists frequently connected sentimentalism, imagina-tive "animation," and sexual agitation. In her *Rights of Woman,* for example, Mary Wollstonecraft herself connected indulged sensibility and "vice": "women subjected by ignorance to their sensations," she declared, "and only taught to look for happi-ness in love, refine on sensual feelings, and adopt metaphysical notions respecting that passion, which lead them shamefully to neglect the duties of life, and frequently in the midst of these sublime refinements they plump into actual vice" (*A Vindication of the Rights of Woman,* p. 183). Hannah More was even more vehement about the danger of sensibility. "Perhaps," she warned her readers in 1799, "if we were to inquire into the remote cause of some of the blackest crimes which stain the annals of mankind, profligacy, murder, and especially suicide, we might trace them back to their original principle, an ungoverned Sensibility" (Hannah More, *Strictures on the Modern System of Female Education,* 2d ed., 2 vols. [London: T. Cadell, Jun. & W. Davies, 1799], 2:102–3).

22. Tony Tanner, *Adultery in the Novel: Contract and Transgression* (Baltimore: Johns Hopkins University Press, 1979), p. 15.

23. Rousseau discusses this paradox in his *Lettre à d'Alembert,* vol. 4 of *Correspon-dance générale de J.-J. Rousseau,* ed. Théophile Dufour, 21 vols. (Paris: Armand Colin, 1924).

24. In his *Keywords: A Vocabulary of Culture and Society* (New York: Oxford University Press, 1976), Raymond Williams explains that the word *sensibility* was, throughout the eighteenth century, informed by its root affiliation with *sensible* and that it was closely associated with both *sentimental* and *sentiments.* "The significant development in 'sense' was the extension from a process to a particular kind of product: 'sense' as good sense, good judgment, from which the predominant modern meaning of *sensible* was to be derived. . . . *Sensibility* in its C18 uses ranged from a use much like that of modern 'awareness' (not only 'consciousness' but 'conscience') to a strong form of what the word appears literally to mean, the ability to feel. . . . The associa-tion of *sentimental* with *sensibility* was then close: a conscious openness to feelings, and also a conscious consumption of feelings" (*Keywords,* pp. 235–38). For a discussion of the physiological basis for sentimentalism see George S. Rousseau, "Nerves, Spirits, and Fibres: Towards Defining the Origins of Sensibility," in *Studies in the Eighteenth Century,* vol. 3, ed. R. F. Brissenden and J. C. Eade (Canberra: Australian National University Press, 1976), pp. 137–57.

25. To see Wollstonecraft's ambivalence about the imagination, compare these two statements of hers: (1) "One great cause of misery in the present imperfect state of society is, that the imagination, continually tantalized, becomes the inflated wen of the mind, draining off nourishment from the vital parts" (from *An Historical and Moral View of the Origin and Progress of the French Revolution and the Effect It has Produced in Europe,* quoted in *A Wollstonecraft Anthology,* ed. Janet M. Todd [Bloomington: Indiana University Press, 1977], p. 126); (2) the imagination "is the mother of senti-ment, the great distinction of our nature, the only purifier of the passions. . . . The imagination is the true fire, stolen from heaven, to animate this cold creature of clay, producing all those fine sympathies that lead to rapture, rendering men social by extending their hearts" (*MWL,* p. 263; 22 September 1794).

26. "The mighty business of female life is to please, and restrained from entering into more important concerns by political and civil oppression, sentiments become events" (*A Vindication of the Rights of Woman,* p. 183).

27. The appeal of sentimental novels is graphically conveyed by Hannah More: "Such is the frightful facility of this species of composition, that every raw girl, while she reads, is tempted to fancy that she can also write. . . . And as Corregio [*sic*], on first beholding a picture which exhibited the perfection of the Graphic art, prophetically felt all his own future greatness, and cried out in rapture, 'And I too am a painter!' so a thorough paced novel-reading Miss, at the close of every tissue of hackney'd adventures, feels within herself the stirring impulse of corresponding genius, and triumphantly exclaims, 'And I too am an author!' The glutted imagination soon overflows with the redundance of cheap sentiment and plentiful incident, and by a sort of arithemetical proportion, is enabled by the perusal of any three novels, to produce a fourth; till every fresh production, like the progeny of Banquo, is followed by Another, and another, and another!" (*Strictures on the Modern System of Female Education,* 1:184–85).

More is equally eloquent on the danger of sentimental novels. Such works, she argues, "teach, that chastity is only individual attachment; that no duty exists which is not prompted by feeling; that impulse is the main spring of virtuous actions, while laws and religion are only unjust restraints" (ibid., p. 35).

28. Mary Ann Evans [George Eliot], "Margaret Fuller and Mary Wollstonecraft," in *Essays of George Eliot,* ed. Thomas Pinney (New York: Columbia University Press, 1963), pp. 199–200.

Chapter Four

1. *Mary Shelley's Journal,* ed. Frederick L. Jones (Norman: University of Oklahoma Press, 1947), pp. 204–6. Subsequent references will be to this volume.

2. Claire Clairmont, quoted by Mrs. Julian Marshall in *The Life and Letters of Mary Wollstonecraft Shelley,* 2 vols. (London: Richard Bentley & Son, 1889), 2:248.

3. We have already seen this at work in *Maria.* One passage from her novel *Mary* will suffice to demonstrate Wollstonecraft's persistent desire to analyze the place her own distress occupies in the prevalent ideological configuration. This novel is sometimes hyperbolically sentimental, and Wollstonecraft ends by endorsing Mary's sentiment (partly, no doubt, because it specifically recapitulates her own love and grief for Fanny Blood). Yet passages like the following urge us to exercise the kind of judgment that she cannot yet consistently apply to herself. The narrator describes novels as "those most delightful substitutes for bodily dissipation" and then continues: "If my readers would excuse the sportiveness of fancy, and give me credit for genius, I would go on and tell them such tales as would force the sweet tears of sensibility to flow in copious showers down beautiful cheeks, to the discomposure of rouge, &c. &c. Nay, I would make it so interesting, that the fair peruser should beg the hair-dresser to settle the curls himself, and not interrupt her" (*Mary, a Fiction,* ed. Gary Kelly [1798; London: Oxford University Press, 1976], pp. 2, 3).

4. Discussing a woman whose husband is more well known than she is presents a problem when it comes to names. In Mary Shelley's case, this difficulty is compounded by the fact that she referred to her husband as "Shelley" and by the fact that she was still Mary Godwin during the early part of their relationship. I refer to Mary Shelley as "Shelley"—even when discussing events before her marriage—except when clarity demands that I designate her simply as "Mary." The five children in the household she grew up in included, in addition to herself, Charles and Mary Jane (who is also called Jane and Claire) Clairmont, children of Mary's stepmother either out of wedlock or by a former marriage; Fanny Imlay, daughter of Mary Wollstonecraft and Gilbert Imlay; and William Godwin, son of Mary's stepmother and William Godwin.

5. Shelley, letter of 30 October 1834, cited in the Introduction to *The Letters of Mary Wollstonecraft Shelley,* ed. Betty T. Bennett, 2 vols, (Baltimore: Johns Hopkins University Press, 1980), 1:xiii (hereafter cited as *MSL*). In Frederick Jones's edition of the letters, this phrase appears in a letter of 17 November 1834 (*The Letters of Mary Wollstonecraft Shelley,* ed. Frederick L. Jones, 2 vols. [Norman: University of Oklahoma Press, 1944], 2:88) (hereafter cited as *MWSL*).

6. Godwin, letter to William Baxter; 8 June 1812, quoted by Muriel Spark in *Child of Light: A Reassessment of Mary Wollstonecraft Shelley* (Hadleigh, Essex: Tower Bridge, 1951), p. 19.

7. See "Mary Shelley's Introduction to the Third Edition (1831)" in *Frankenstein, or The Modern Prometheus,* ed. James Rieger (1818 and 1831; Indianapolis and New York: Bobbs-Merrill, 1974; Phoenix Paperback ed., Chicago: University of Chicago Press, 1982), p. 223. All future references to *Frankenstein* will be to this edition (abbreviated as *F*), which follows the 1818 text and provides the 1831 revisions in a convenient appendix.

8. *The Elopement of Percy Shelley and Mary Wollstonecraft Godwin as Narrated by William Godwin,* published with a commentary by H. Buxton Forman (London: Privately printed, 1911), pp. 10, 16.

9. "I return your cheque," Godwin wrote to Percy in 1816, "because no consideration can induce me to utter a cheque drawn by you and containing my name. . . . I hope you will send me a duplicate of it by the post which will reach me on Saturday morning. You may make it payable to Joseph Hume or James Martin, or any other name in the whole directory" (quoted by R. Glynn Grylls in *Mary Shelley: A Biography* [New York: Oxford University Press, 1938], p. 55).

10. *The Letters of Percy Bysshe Shelley,* ed. Frederick L. Jones, 2 vols. (Oxford: Clarendon Press, 1964), 1:402.

11. See, especially, Sandra M. Gilbert and Susan Gubar, *The Madwoman in the Attic: The Woman Writer and the Nineteenth-Century Literary Imagination* (New Haven: Yale University Press, 1979), pp. 222–24; Betty T. Bennett, Introduction to *MSL,* 1:xii–xiii; and U. C. Knoepflmacher, "Thoughts on the Aggression of Daughters," in *The Endurance of "Frankenstein": Essays on Mary Shelley's Novel,* ed. George Levine and U. C. Knoepflmacher (Berkeley: University of California Press, 1979), pp. 88–119.

12. "A philosophical wanton," *The European Magazine* had called Wollstonecraft, who advocated principles that, according to the *Anti-Jacobin Review,* were "as old as prostitution" (*The European Magazine, and London Review, Containing the Literature, History, Politics, Arts, Manners & Amusements of the Age* 33 [January–June 1798]: 246; the *Anti-Jacobin Review and Magazine; or, Monthly Political and Literary Censor* 1 [July–December 1798]: 97). One of the most amusing responses to Wollstonecraft's works appears in *The Lady's Monthly Museum, or Polite Repository of Amusement and Instruction.* A reader, one "J. M.," a mother of four daughters, complains that *The Rights of Woman* has destroyed her family. "For some days after they [her daughters] had read that fatal book I thought they had lost their senses. . . . Their father, unhappily, was infected with the same madness, and encouraged them in it. The equality of the sexes is rung in my ears from morning till night." One of the daughters, Harriet, takes up horseracing; she loses "all that softness so amiable in a woman, and not unfrequently is seen rubbing down her horse like a stable-boy." Maria, "naturally of a more sedate turn than her sister, applies herself to books . . . and declares herself a disciple of Zoroaster." Clara begins a course of anatomical study "and, one evening disguised in a suit of boy's cloaths, went to a Lecture on that horrid subject. Since which she thinks she herself is able to dissect," her mother laments; "and I now cannot keep dog or cat alive in the house." And Lucy, the youngest, whom the mother hoped, "from her sweet infantile sprightliness, would have been the delight of my life, is now an animal with the boisterous roughness of the other sex, and the feminine weakness

of her own." She swears she will obtain military training "and is positive that she has in her arm strength sufficient to knock an ox down." Recently, Lucy challenged a man who offended her to a duel, and, when he declined, she "cursed him for a cowardly puppy, not worth her vengeance." J. M. obviously intends this letter to serve as a warning to mothers and daughters attracted to Wollstonecraft's philosophy or character: "In my family they may see it in practice; and see, also, how odious and ridiculous it makes my children to all who know them, excepting those who are so silly as themselves" (*Lady's Monthly Museum* 3 [December 1799]: 433-34, 435). Numerous novels, poems, and satires, among them Maria Edgeworth's *Belinda* (1801), George Walker's *The Vagabond* (1798), Richard Polwhele's "The Unsex'd Females" (1798), and Thomas Taylor's *A Vindication of the Rights of Brutes* (1792), pilloried Mary Wollstonecraft in a more permanent and readily accessible form than these reviews. Even though Ralph M. Wardle points out that by 1812 the name of Wollstonecraft was no longer automatically synonymous with female villainy, the young Mary Godwin was undoubtedly very familiar with the reception Wollstonecraft's writing and life had received (see Wardle, *Mary Wollstonecraft: A Critical Biography* [Lawrence, Kans.: University of Kansas Press, 1951], p. 331).

13. For a discussion of Percy Shelley's participation in the revision of *Frankenstein,* see Rieger's Introduction. Rieger goes so far as to assert that Percy's "assistance at every point in the book's manufacture was so extensive that one hardly knows whether to regard him as editor or minor collaborator" (*F,* p. xviii). The microfilms of the *Frankenstein* manuscript, which I have examined in Duke University's Perkin Library (Abinger Collection, reel 11), suggest that, while Percy made many marginal suggestions and probably helped recopy the manuscript, his contributions were largely stylistic and grammatical.

14. *Quarterly Review,* January 1818, quoted by Grylls, *Mary Shelley,* p. 316.

15. Grylls, *Mary Shelley,* p. 315.

16. Shelley's reading of her contemporaries' egotism, while certainly colored by the inhibitions that she, as a woman, had internalized, is an understandable interpretation. For example, Coleridge's depiction of the artistic act as a repetition of "the eternal act of creation in the infinite I AM" appropriates godlike power for the poet, whatever Coleridge's self-doubts might have been in practice. The Byron of *Childe Harold,* parading his bleeding heart before all of Europe, also conveys the impression of his own importance, and Percy Shelley's image of the artist as priest-lawgiver-prophet assumes that the poet is all-powerful, or ought to be. In *The Madwoman in the Attic* Gilbert and Gubar discuss this masculine image of the poet and the "anxiety of authorship" it causes in women. Although I think that the dilemma was intensified by the contradictions between the Romantic image of the artist as creator and the conventional ideal of the self-effacing woman, I essentially agree with Gilbert and Gubar's perceptive analysis of the self-doubts this image caused women, who read into male poets' claims more confidence than their poems sometimes reveal (see *Madwoman,* esp. pp. 45-64, and the discussion of *Frankenstein,* pp. 213-47). For another, quite different, interpretation of the treatment of domesticity in *Frankenstein,* see Kate Ellis, "Monsters in the Garden: Mary Shelley and the Bourgeois Family," in *The Endurance of "Frankenstein,"* pp. 123-42 (see n. 11, above). In this same collection of essays, Lee Sterrenburg points out the extent to which *Frankenstein* is a criticism of Godwin's optimistic political theories ("Mary Shelley's Monster: Politics and Psyche in *Frankenstein,*" *The Endurance,* pp. 143-71), and Peter Dale Scott discusses *Frankenstein* as an ambivalent response to Percy Shelley ("Vital Artifice: Mary, Percy, and the Psychopolitical Integrity of *Frankenstein,*" *The Endurance,* pp. 172-202).

17. Shelley seems to be answering, among others, William Godwin and David Hartley.

18. Contrast, for example, the final scene of *Frankenstein* with Percy Shelley's depiction of the same scene in "Mont Blanc." For Percy, nature is also a citadel of death.

> there, many a precipice,
> Frost and the Sun in scorn of mortal power
> Have piled: dome, pyramid, and pinnacle,
> A city of death, distinct with many a tower
> And wall impregnable of beaming ice.
> Yet not a city, but a flood of ruin
> Is there, that from the boundaries of the sky
> Rolls its perpetual stream; vast pines are strewing
> Its destined path, or in the mangled soil
> Branchless and shattered stand.
>   [103–11]

Yet, unlike Percy, Mary Shelley does not envision this landscape humanized by imaginatve power. Here is Percy Shelley again:

> And what were thou, and earth, and stars, and sea,
> If to the human mind's imaginings
> Silence and solitude were vacancy?
>   [142–44]

19. Although there are significant complexities in *The Prelude,* Wordsworth's model of maturation reminds us of Freud's paradigm of oedipal confrontation. Mary Shelley, on the other hand, implies the kind of psychological accommodation Nancy Chodorow describes as the female equivalent of male confrontation. See Chodorow, *The Reproduction of Mothering: Psychoanalysis and the Sociology of Gender* (Berkeley: University of California Press, 1978), pp. 192–93; see also above, p. 254, n. 118. For a discussion of Wordsworth's oedipal struggle against traditional social forms, see Michael H. Friedman, *The Making of a Tory Humanist: William Wordsworth and the Idea of Community* (New York: Columbia University Press, 1979), pp. 4–5 and passim. Mary Shelley would have had an even more obvious and immediate example of male oedipal relations in Percy Shelley's open rebellion against his father, his father's religion, his father's class, and the university that institutionalized this authority.

20. For a discussion of the chains of signification that make up *Frankenstein,* see Peter Brooks, "Godlike Science / Unhallowed Arts: Language and Monstrosity in *Frankenstein,*" *New Literary History* 9 (1978): 591–605.

21. Mary Shelley, Preface to the *Second Collected Edition of Percy Shelley's Poetry* (1839), in *Shelley: Poetical Works,* ed. Thomas Hutchinson, new edition corrected by G. M. Matthews (London: Oxford University Press, 1970), p. xxi.

22. "A Defence of Poetry, or Remarks Suggested by an Essay Entitled 'The Four Ages of Poetry,' " in *Shelley's Poetry and Prose,* ed. Donald H. Reiman and Sharon B. Powers, Norton Critical Edition (New York: W. W. Norton, 1977), p. 486.

23. "Defence of Poetry," pp. 487–88.

24. See Reiger's Introduction to the Bobbs-Merrill edition, pp. xxii–xxiii.

25. Ellen Moers, in *Literary Women: The Great Writers* (Garden City: Doubleday/Anchor, 1977), proposes that *Frankenstein* is specifically "a birth myth," that the novel is "most feminine . . . in the motif of revulsion against newborn life, and the drama

of guilt, dread, and flight surrounding birth and its consequences" (p. 142). While Moers's insights seem to me suggestive, I think her equation of the monster and the newborn too limiting. Child-bearing is only one kind of extension or projection of the self, and Shelley conflates several meanings in this central incident.

26. Margaret Homans, "Dreaming of Children: Literalization in *Jane Eyre* and *Wuthering Heights*" (unpublished essay, Yale University, 1979), pp. 1-2. According to Homans, women "cannot participate in [the dualism of self and other, or of self and object] as subjects as easily as men can. The feminine self is on the same side of that dualism with what is traditionally other. Women who do conceive of themselves as subjects—that is, present, thinking women rather than 'woman'—must continually guard against fulfilling those imposed definitions by being transformed back into objects."

27. See Margaret Homans, *Women Writers and Poetic Identity: Dorothy Wordsworth, Emily Brontë, and Emily Dickinson* (Princeton: Princeton University Press, 1980), pp. 12-29.

28. "Defence of Poetry," p. 508.

29. Shelley's endorsement of the liberated imagination is clear both from her portrait of Clerval, "a boy of singular talent and fancy" who gives up his childish composition of stories to become simply a connoisseur of natural beauty (p. 159), and from this journal entry of 1834: "My imagination, my Kubla Khan, my 'pleasure dome,' occasionally pushed aside by misery but at the first opportunity her beaming face peeped in and the weight of deadly woe was lightened" (*MSJ*, p. 203).

30. In his Introduction (p. xvii), Rieger explains that Shelley is incorrect in remembering this mortification: "Polidori's *Diary* . . . records on 17 June, 'The ghost-stories are begun by all but me.'"

Chapter Five

1. Lord Dillon, quoted by R. Glynn Grylls, *Mary Shelley: A Biography* (London: Oxford University Press, 1938), pp. 211-12.

2. Leigh Hunt, "Blue-Stocking Revels" (1837), quoted ibid., p. 211, n. 2.

3. Edward Trelawny, quoted by Elizabeth Nitchie, *Mary Shelley: Author of "Frankenstein"* (New Brunswick: Rutgers University Press, 1953), p. xii.

4. For other discussions of the effect these domestic tragedies might have had on Shelley's works, see Ellen Moers, *Literary Women: The Great Writers* (Garden City, N.Y.: Doubleday/Anchor, 1977), pp. 140-51, and U. C. Knoepflmacher, "Thoughts on the Aggression of Daughters," in *The Endurance of "Frankenstein,"* ed. George Levine and U. C. Knoepflmacher (Berkeley: University of California Press, 1979), pp. 88-119.

5. *The Letters of Mary Wollstonecraft Shelley*, ed. Betty T. Bennett, 2 vols. (Baltimore: Johns Hopkins University Press, 1980), 1:100; 27 June 1819. Hereafter cited as *MSL*.

6. See Elizabeth Nitchie, Introduction to *Mathilda*, in *Studies in Philology*, Extra Series 3 (Chapel Hill: University of North Carolina Press, 1959), pp. x-xi.

7. Quoted, ibid., p. xi.

8. Quoted by Grylls, *Mary Shelley*, p. 318.

9. *Mary Shelley's Journal*, ed. Frederick L. Jones (Norman: University of Oklahoma Press, 1947), p. 181. Hereafter cited as *MSJ*.

10. See Harold Perkin, *The Origins of Modern English Society, 1780-1880* (London: Routledge & Kegan Paul, 1969), p. 126.

11. Quoted ibid., p. 150, from E. Hodder, *The Life and Work of the 7th Earl of Shaftesbury*.

12. In Jane Austen's *Pride and Prejudice,* Mrs. Bennet informs Mr. Collins with a good deal of self-righteous pride that "they were very well able to keep a good cook, and that her daughters had nothing to do in the kitchen."

13. Sir Timothy Shelley, quoted by Mrs. Julian Marshall, *The Life & Letters of Mary Wollstonecraft Shelley,* 2 vols. (London: Richard Bentley & Son, 1889), 1:66.

14. Mary Shelley, *The Last Man* (1826), ed. Hugh J. Luke, Jr. (Lincoln: University of Nebraska Press, 1965), p. 31. Subsequent references are to this edition.

15. See Sandra M. Gilbert and Susan Gubar, *The Madwoman in the Attic: The Woman Writer and the Nineteenth-Century Literary Imagination* (New Haven: Yale University Press, 1979), pp. 246–47.

16. See Luke, Introduction to *The Last Man,* p. xiv.

17. Lee Sterrenburg points out that in *The Last Man* Mary Shelley "takes up a set of nature metaphors—diseases and plagues—which previous writers had used as hopeful symbols of the revolutionary process. She reinterprets these symbols in a pessimistic and apocalyptic way, and, in so doing, rejects the meliorative political views of her parents' generation. . . . The monsterlike holocaust that descends upon the Greek revolution in *The Last Man* is a graphic fictional rebuttal of Percy's political views" ("*The Last Man:* Anatomy of Failed Revolutions," *Nineteenth-Century Fiction* 33, no. 3 [June 1978]: 328, 345). See also Robert Lance Snyder, "Apocalypse and Indeterminacy in Mary Shelley's *The Last Man,*" *Studies in Romanticism* 17, no. 4 (Fall 1978): 435–52.

18. See *MSJ,* p. 185. See also *The Letters of Mary W. Shelley,* ed. Frederick L. Jones, 2 vols. (Norman: University of Oklahoma Press, 1944), 2:351, hereafter cited as *MWSL.*

19. The review, which appeared in *The London Gazette and Journal of Belles Lettres, Arts, Sciences, &c.* (February 1826), is quoted by Sterrenburg, "*The Last Man,*" p. 328.

20. See Luke, Introduction to *The Last Man,* p. viii.

21. Mary considered the widow of Edward Williams to be her closest friend and partner in sorrow. Jane was apparently less loyal; during this summer Mary discovered that Jane had been spreading rumors that Mary had failed Percy and that, during the last weeks of his life, he had turned to Jane for comfort.

22. Claire Clairmont, quoted by Marshall, *The Life & Letters of Mary Wollstonecraft Shelley,* 1:158.

23. "Nothing can equal Mrs. Mason's kindness to me," Claire wrote. "Hers is the only house, except my Mother's, in which all my life I have always felt at home. . . . I have no need to disguise my sentiments; to barricade myself up in silence, as I do almost with everybody, for fear they should see what passes in my mind, and hate me for it, because it does not resemble what passes in theirs" (quoted ibid., 1:250).

24. Trying to interest the publisher John Murray in *Perkin Warbeck,* Shelley argued that the novel dealt with "an historical subject of former times [which] must be treated in a way that affords no scope for *opinion,* and I think you will have no reason to object to it on that score" (*MWSL,* 1:371; 19 February 1828).

25. On the resemblance between Falkner and Trelawny, see Muriel Spark, *Child of Light: A Reassessment of Mary Wollstonecraft Shelley* (Hadleigh, Essex: Tower Bridge, 1951), p. 126; Elizabeth Nitchie, *Mary Shelley,* p. 123.

26. Quoted by Nitchie, Introduction to *Mathilda,* p. 83, n. 23.

27. Quoted by Spark, *Child of Light,* p. 62.

28. *The Letters of Percy Bysshe Shelley,* ed. Frederick L. Jones, 2 vols. (Oxford: Clarendon Press, 1964), 2:428; 29 May 1822.

29. Ibid., 2:460; 6 August 1822. (This letter of Godwin's is published in Appendix V.)

30. *Falkner, A Novel. By the Author of "Frankenstein," "The Last Man," &c.* (New York: Harper & Bros., 1837), p. 59. All subsequent references are to this edition.

31. See Knoepflmacher, "Thoughts," p. 59.

32. Juliet Mitchell, *Psychoanalysis and Feminism: Freud, Reich, Laing, and Women* (1974; New York: Random House/Vintage, 1975), pp. 377–81.

33. See ibid., pp. 112, 117.

34. Nancy Chodorow, *The Reproduction of Mothering: Psychoanalysis and the Sociology of Gender* (Berkeley: University of California Press, 1978), p. 195.

35. Claire Clairmont, quoted by Marshall, *Life & Letters of Mary Wollstonecraft Shelley*, 1:266–67.

36. Mary Shelley maintained relationships, for example, with Isabel Robinson Douglas and Mary Diana Dods. See Bennett, Introduction, *MSL*, 1:xix and 533–34, n. 2.

37. Although Mary Shelley wrote no more novels, she did continue to write such nonfiction as biographical sketches for the Reverend Dionysius Lardner's *Cabinet Cyclopedia* and her travelogue, *Rambles in Germany and Italy* (1844). But these productions did not require the same kind of emotional investment that writing novels did; Shelley refers to it as "quieter work" (*MWSL*, 2:200; 20 September 1843) and as "a source of interest and pleasure" (ibid., 2:83; 17 July 1834).

38. Eliza Rennie, *Traits of Character*, 2 vols, (London, 1860), 1:113, quoted by Marshall, *Life & Letters of Mary Wollstonecraft Shelley*, 1:315–16.

Chapter Six

1. The most extensive discussion of Austen's treatment of propriety is Jane Nardin's *Those Elegant Decorums: The Concept of Propriety in Jane Austen's Novels* (Albany: State University of New York Press, 1973). Nardin's analysis is extremely perceptive and discriminating, but, finally, I cannot accept the degree of conscious intention she attributes to Austen (see pp. 10–11). The most telling recent analysis of the contradictions in Austen's novels, and thus a reading more in keeping with my own, is Igor Webb's *From Custom to Capital: The English Novel and the Industrial Revolution* (Ithaca and London: Cornell University Press, 1981), pp. 49–70, 101–21, 158–61.

2. One example of Austen's apparent self-contradiction is evident in her opinions about Evangelicalism. On 24 January 1809 she told Cassandra: "You have by no means raised my curiosity after *Caleb* [Hannah More's *Coelebs in Search of a Wife*];—My disinclination for it before was affected, but now it is real; I do not like the Evangelicals." On 18 November 1814, however, she informed Fanny Knight that "I am by no means convinced that we ought not all to be Evangelicals, & am at least persuaded that they who are so from Reason and Feeling, must be happiest & safest" (*Jane Austen's Letters to Her Sister Cassandra and Others*, ed. R. W. Chapman, 2 vols. [Oxford: Clarendon Press, 1932], 1:256; 2:410; hereafter cited as *JAL*). Austen might simply have changed her opinion; on the other hand, she might have been making distinctions we can no longer confidently reconstruct.

3. The one extant copy of *Lady Susan* is a fair copy that bears the watermark 1805. Chapman acknowledges, however, that the transcription of the novel could easily have postdated its composition by a number of years. B. C. Southam, in *Jane Austen's Literary Manuscripts: A Study of the Novelist's Development through the Surviving Papers* (London: Oxford University Press, 1964), pp. 45–62, presents a strong case for the earlier date.

4. *Lady Susan*, vol. 6 of *The Works of Jane Austen*, ed. R. W. Chapman (London: Oxford University Press, 1954), p. 243. (Volumes 1–5 appeared in the second edition of the *Works*, published in 1926.)

5. See Lloyd W. Brown, "Jane Austen and the Feminist Tradition," *Nineteenth-Century Fiction* 28 (1973): 334, and Sandra M. Gilbert and Susan Gubar, *The Madwoman in the Attic: The Woman Writer and the Nineteenth-Century Literary Imagination* (New Haven: Yale University Press, 1979), p. 118.

6. See Lloyd W. Brown, *Bits of Ivory: Narrative Techniques in Jane Austen's Fiction* (Baton Rouge: Louisiana State University Press, 1973), pp. 147–48, 153.

7. Gilbert and Gubar point out that one way in which Austen attempts to control our sympathy for Lady Susan is by making her cruelty to Frederica exceed the demands of the plot. See *Madwoman,* pp. 155–56.

8. William Wordsworth, letter to Daniel Stuart, 1817, quoted by Alistair M. Duckworth, *The Improvement of the Estate: A Study of Jane Austen's Novels* (Baltimore: Johns Hopkins University Press, 1971), p. 81.

9. For a discussion of the spirit of "party" and the "contrary systems of thought" typical of the literature of this period, see L. J. Swingle, "The Poets, the Novelists, and the English Romantic Situation," *Wordsworth Circle* 3 (1979): 218–28, and David Simpson, *Irony and Authority in Romantic Poetry* (Totowa, N.J.: Rowman & Littlefield, 1979).

10. Donald J. Greene, "Jane Austen and the Peerage," *PMLA* 68 (1953): 1017–31; reprinted in *Jane Austen: A Collection of Critical Essays,* ed. Ian Watt (Englewood Cliffs, N.J.: Prentice-Hall, 1963), pp. 156–57.

11. See Marilyn Butler, *Jane Austen and the War of Ideas* (Oxford: Clarendon Press, 1975), pp. 161–67, 284–85, and Duckworth, *The Improvement,* pp. 2–80. For another discussion of Jane Austen's religion, see Warren Roberts, *Jane Austen and the French Revolution* (New York: St. Martin's Press, 1979), pp. 109–54.

12. See Terry Lovell, "Jane Austen and the Gentry: A Study in Literature and Ideology," *The Sociology of Literature: Applied Studies,* ed. Diana Laurenson (Hanley, Eng.: Wood Mitchell & Co., 1978), pp. 20–21.

13. See ibid., p. 21.

14. For an excellent discussion of the complexities of parody, see George Levine, "Translating the Monstrous: *Northanger Abbey,*" *Nineteenth-Century Fiction* 30 (1975): 337.

15. Samuel Johnson, *Rambler* 4, in *The Yale Edition of the Works of Samuel Johnson,* ed. W. J. Bate and Albrecht B. Strauss, 14 vols. (New Haven: Yale University Press, 1969), 3:21, 22.

16. *Persuasion,* in *The Works of Jane Austen,* 5:101.

17. Johnson, *Rambler* 4, pp. 23, 21.

18. *Northanger Abbey,* in *The Works of Jane Austen,* 5:37, 38. Patricia Meyer Spacks also points out that education in an Austen novel requires imaginative engagement; see her "Muted Discord: Generational Conflict in Jane Austen," in *Jane Austen in a Social Context,* ed. David Monaghan (Totowa, N.J.: Barnes & Noble, 1981), pp. 170, 174, 177–78.

19. The precise order in which Austen composed her major works is unknown, but B. C. Southam, having consulted Cassandra's original memorandum and the surviving manuscripts, argues persuasively for the following chronology: *Elinor and Marianne*—completed before 1796; *First Impressions*—October 1796–August 1797; *Sense and Sensibility,* the revision of *Elinor and Marianne*—begun November 1797, revised again at Chawton 1809–10; *Northanger Abbey,* originally entitled *Susan*—c. 1798–99, never substantially revised; *Pride and Prejudice,* the revision of *First Impressions*—conducted in 1809–10 and 1812; *Mansfield Park*—February 1811–June 1813; *Emma*—21 January 1814–29 March 1815; *Persuasion*—8 August 1815–6 August 1816 (Southam, *Jane Austen's Literary Manuscripts,* pp. 52–58). The dates given in parentheses in my text are the publication dates.

20. For a discussion of Austen's "free, indirect speech," see Norman Page, *The Language of Jane Austen* (New York: Barnes & Noble, 1972), pp. 123 ff.

21. *Sense and Sensibility,* in *The Works of Jane Austen,* 1:8.

22. Tony Tanner, Introduction to the Penguin edition of *Sense and Sensibility* (Harmondsworth, Eng., 1969), p. 32.

23. See Tanner, ibid., p. 30.

24. I am indebted to Patricia Meyer Spacks and to her Yale College seminar on Jane Austen for many of the observations about this episode.

25. *Pride and Prejudice*, in *The Works of Jane Austen*, 2:42–43.

26. Bernard J. Paris makes this point in *Character and Conflict in Jane Austen's Novels: A Psychological Approach* (Detroit: Wayne State University Press, 1978), pp. 118–39. While many of my observations are consistent with Paris's reading, I disagree with his central thesis that Elizabeth can be treated as a "real" person throughout the novel. It is precisely Austen's aborting of psychological realism that interests me.

27. See Duckworth, *The Improvement of the Estate*, pp. 123–26 (see n. 8, above).

28. In 1799, for instance, Austen remarked to her sister Cassandra, "I do not wonder at your wanting to read 'First Impressions' again" (*JAL*, 1:52; 8 January 1799); her letters also show her sharing *Mansfield Park* with her brother Henry before its publication, and she kept a list of the responses her family and friends made to that novel and to *Emma*. See "Opinions of *Mansfield Park* and *Emma*" in *The Works of Jane Austen*, 6:431–39. For another discussion of the relationship between Austen's composition and her family, see Mary Lascelles, *Jane Austen and Her Art* (Oxford: Clarendon Press, 1939), pp. 4, 146.

29. Austen's niece Catherine Hubback commented that her aunt "always said her books were her children" (quoted by R. W. Chapman, *Jane Austen: Facts and Problems* [Oxford: Clarendon Press, 1948], p. 67), and from her nephews we learn that Austen supplied her family with information about her characters' "after-life": "In this tradition any way we learned that Miss Steele never succeeded in catching the Doctor; that Kitty Bennet was satisfactorily married to a clergyman near Pemberley, while Mary obtained nothing higher than one of her uncle Phillips' clerks, and was content to be considered a star in the society of Meriton; that the 'considerable sum' given by Mrs. Norris to William Price was one pound; that Mr. Woodhouse survived his daughter's marriage, and kept her and Mr. Knightley from settling at Donwell, about two years; and that the letters placed by Frank Churchill before Jane Fairfax, which she swept away unread, contained the word 'pardon' " (J. E. Austen-Leigh, *A Memoir of Jane Austen* [London: Macmillan, 1906], pp. 148–49). Julia Prewitt Brown also discusses the importance of the family for Austen; see her *Jane Austen's Novels: Social Change and Literary Form* (Cambridge, Mass.: Harvard University Press, 1979), p. 9.

30. One of the best discussions of this function of irony is in Nardin, *Those Elegant Decorums*, pp. 4–11.

31. See Wayne C. Booth, *A Rhetoric of Irony* (Chicago: University of Chicago Press, 1974), p. 44 and passim.

32. See A. Walton Litz, *Jane Austen: A Study of Her Artistic Development* (New York: Oxford University Press, 1965), p. 108.

Chapter Seven

1. *Jane Austen's Letters to Her Sister Cassandra and Others*, ed. R. W. Chapman, 2 vols. (Oxford: Clarendon Press, 1932) 1:99; 3 January 1801. Subsequent references in the text are to this work.

2. See R. W. Chapman, *Jane Austen: Facts and Problems* (Oxford: Clarendon Press, 1948), pp. 64–69, and Jane Aiken Hodge, *Only a Novel: The Double Life of Jane Austen* (New York: Coward, McCann & Geoghegan, 1972), pp. 80–81.

3. The income bequeathed by Mr. Austen was only £210 per annum. Edward promised his mother an additional £100 per year, and Frank, James, and Henry each pledged £50 per year. Their payment, of course, depended on the vicissitudes of their own fortunes, which, especially in the wake of Henry's bankruptcy, were far from stable.

4. For a discussion of the publishing and sales of Austen's novels, see Hodge, *Only a Novel,* pp. 120–25, 207.

5. She even collated the responses of her friends and family to *Mansfield Park* and *Emma.* See *The Works of Jane Austen,* ed. R. W. Chapman (London: Oxford University Press, 1953), 6:431–39.

6. A. Walton Litz, citing "A Fragment, written to inculcate the practice of Virtue" from *Volume the First* of Austen's juvenilia, comments: "[Her] reaction against this passage shows a developing awareness of the danger inherent in ironic methods, the possibility that mockery of pretensions will become a mockery of the solid virtues those pretensions distort. In *Pride and Prejudice* irony can be turned into an agency for self-knowledge, but in *Mansfield Park* we see that it can also be a buttress for cynicism" (*Jane Austen: A Study of Her Artistic Development* [New York: Oxford University Press, 1965], p. 116).

7. *Mansfield Park,* in *The Works of Jane Austen,* ed. R. W. Chapman, 6 vols. (London: Oxford University Press, 1923), 3:68. Hereafter cited in the text by page numbers.

8. See Avrom Fleishman, *A Reading of "Mansfield Park": An Essay in Critical Synthesis* (Minneapolis: University of Minnesota Press, 1967), p. 27.

9. See Lloyd W. Brown, *Bits of Ivory: Narrative Techniques in Jane Austen's Fiction* (Baton Rouge: Louisiana State University Press, 1973), pp. 81–96, and Alistair M. Duckworth, *The Improvement of the Estate: A Study of Jane Austen's Novels* (Baltimore: Johns Hopkins University Press, 1971), pp. 59–60.

10. Norman Page describes the style of *Persuasion* as a "style in which narrative, comment, dialogue (presented in various ways) and interior monologue very frequently and unobtrusively merge into one another" (*The Language of Jane Austen* [New York: Barnes & Noble, 1972], p. 49).

11. *Persuasion,* in *The Works of Jane Austen,* 5:42. Subsequent references in the text are to this edition.

12. In *Jane Austen and the War of Ideas* (Oxford: Clarendon Press, 1975), Marilyn Butler argues that Austen presents Wentworth critically, that he is a "well-intentioned but ideologically mistaken hero" whose "personal philosophy approaches revolutionary optimism and individualism" (p. 275). But this interpretation needs to be qualified both by Austen's approving treatment of the naval meritocracy in *Persuasion* and by the personal pride she took in her own brothers' advances in the navy.

13. Duckworth also discusses Austen's loss of "faith in manners." See *The Improvement of the Estate,* pp. 181–82.

14. See Lloyd W. Brown, "Jane Austen and the Feminist Tradition," *Nineteenth-Century Fiction* 28 (1973): 321–38, and Nina Auerbach, "O Brave New World: Evolution and Revolution in *Persuasion,*" *ELH* 39 (1972): 112–28.

15. See, for example, Duckworth, *The Improvement of the Estate,* p. 192.

16. E.g., Duckworth; see ibid., p. 183.

17. Auerbach, "O Brave New World," p. 117.

Conclusion

1. Fredric Jameson, *The Political Unconscious: Narrative as a Socially Symbolic Act* (Ithaca: Cornell University Press, 1981), p. 81.

2. See ibid., p. 58.

Selected Bibliography

Chapter 1. The Proper Lady

Primary Sources

[Allestree, Richard.] *The Ladies Calling.* 12th impression. Oxford: n.p., 1727.

Appleton, Elizabeth. *Private Education; or A Practical Plan for the Studies of Young Ladies. With an Address to Parents, Private Governesses, and Young Ladies.* 3d rev. ed. London: Colburn, 1816.

Arblay, Fanny Burney d'. *The Journals and Letters of Fanny Burney.* Edited by Joyce Hemlow. 2 vols. Oxford: Oxford University Press, 1972. (This is a continuing project. So far, ten volumes have been published, but I have used only the first two.)

Astell, Mary. *A Serious Proposal to the Ladies for the Advancement of Their True and Great Interest.* Reprint ed. New York: Source Books Press, 1970. (Originally published in 1701.)

Bentham, Jeremy. *An Introduction to the Principles of Morals and Legislation.* Oxford: Clarendon Press, 1876.

Boswell, James. *Journal of a Tour to the Hebrides.* Edited by Allan Wendt. Boston: Houghton Mifflin/Riverside, 1965.

———.*Life of Johnson.* Edited by R. W. Chapman. New edition, corrected by J. D. Fleeman. New York: Oxford University Press, 1970.

Burke, Edmund. *A Philosophical Enquiry into the Origin of Our Ideas of the Sublime and Beautiful.* Edited by James T. Boulton. Notre Dame: University of Notre Dame Press, 1968.

———.*Reflections on the Revolution in France.* Garden City, N.Y.: Doubleday/Anchor, 1973.

Darrell, William. *A Gentleman Instructed in the Conduct of a Virtuous and Happy Life. Written for the Instruction of a Young Nobleman.* London: E. Evets, 1704.

Defoe, Daniel. "Essays upon Several Projects: Or, Effectual Ways for Advancing the interests of the Nation." Pp. 42–44 in *The Complete Works of Daniel Defoe,* vol. 3. London: John Clements, 1843.

———.*The Family Instructor.* 15th ed. London: C. Hitch & L. Hawes, G. Keith, W. Johnston & T. Longman, 1715.

———.*A Treatise Concerning the Use and Abuse of the Marriage Bed.* London: T. Warner, 1727.

Fordyce, James. *Sermons to Young Women.* 2 vols. 4th ed. London: A. Millar & T. Cadell, 1767.

The Gentleman's Magazine. Selected issues. London, 1731–1907.

Gisborne, Thomas. *An Enquiry into the Duties of the Female Sex.* 4th ed. London: T. Cadell, Jr. & W. Davies, 1799.

Gregory, Dr. John. *A Father's Legacy to His Daughters*. 4th ed. London: W. Strahan, T. Cadell, 1774.

Hatfield, Miss. *Letters on the Importance of the Female Sex: With Observations on Their Manners, and on Education*. London: J. Adlard, 1803.

Hawkins, Laetitia Matilda. *Letters on the Female Mind, Its Powers and Pursuits. Addressed to Miss H. M. Williams, with Particular Reference to Her Letters from France*. 2 vols. London: Hookham & Carpenter, 1793.

Howard, Gorges Edmond. *Aphorisms and Maxims on Various Subjects for the Good Conduct of Life, &c*. N.p., n.d.

Hume, David. *Theory of Politics*. Edited by Frederick Watkins. New York: Nelson, 1951.

⸺⸺.*A Treatise of Human Nature*. Edited by Ernest C. Mossner. Harmondsworth, Eng.: Penguin Books, 1969.

Instructions for a Young Lady, in Every Sphere and Period of Life. Edinburgh: A. Donaldson, 1773.

Johnson, Samuel. *The Letters of Samuel Johnson*. Edited by R. W. Chapman. 3 vols. Oxford: Clarendon Press, 1952.

⸺⸺.*The Rambler*. In *The Yale Edition of the Works of Samuel Johnson*, vol. 4. Edited by W. J. Bate and Albrecht B. Strauss. New Haven: Yale University Press, 1969.

Kames, Henry Home, Lord. *Loose Hints upon Education, Chiefly concerning the Culture of the Heart*. 2d ed. Edinburgh: John Bell, 1782.

The Ladies Library, Written by a Lady. 3 vols. 3d ed. and 5th ed. London: J. & R. Tonson, 1722, 1739.

Ladies' Magazine. Selected issues. Boston: 1828–36.

Lady's Magazine. Selected issues. London: 1770–1830.

Law, William. *A Serious Call to a Devout and Holy Life. Adapted to the State and Condition of All Orders of Christians*. London: William Innys, 1729.

Locke, John. *Two Treatises of Government*. Edited by Peter Laslett. Cambridge, Eng.: At the University Press, 1960.

Mandeville, Bernard. *The Virgin Unmask'd: Or, Female Dialogues betwixt an Elderly Maiden Lady and Her Niece, on Several Diverting Discourses on Love, Marriage, Memoirs, and Morals, &c. of the Times*. 2d ed. London: G. Strathan, 1724.

More, Hannah. *Coelebs in Search of a Wife. Comprehending Observations on Domestic Habits and Manners, Religion and Morals*. 2 vols. London: T. Cadell & W. Davies, 1809.

⸺⸺.*Strictures on the Modern System of Female Education*. 2 vols. 2d ed. London: T. Cadell, Jr. & W. Davies, 1799.

⸺⸺.*The Works of Hannah More*. 7 vols. London: H. Fisher, R. Fisher & P. Jackson, 1834.

Mott, Abigail. *Observations on the Importance of Female Education, and Maternal Instruction, with Their Beneficial Influence on Society. By a Mother*. New York: Mahlon Day, 1825.

Pennington, Sarah. *An Unfortunate Mother's Advice to Her Absent Daughters. In a Letter to Miss Pennington*. London: S. Chandler, 1761.

Piozzi, Mrs. Hester Lynch Thrale. *Thraliana: The Diary of Mrs. Hester Lynch Thrale, 1776–1809*. Edited by Katherine C. Balderston. 2 vols. Oxford: Clarendon Press, 1942.

The Polite Lady: Or a Course of Female Education. In a Series of Letters, from a Mother to Her Daughter. 2d ed. London: Newberry & Carnan, 1769.

Radcliffe, Mrs. Mary Ann. *The Memoirs of Mrs. Mary Ann Radcliffe. In Familiar Letters to Her Female Friend*. Edinburgh: Printed for the Author, 1810.

Reeve, Clara. *Plans of Education: With Remarks on the Systems of Other Writers. In a Series of Letters between Mrs. Darnford and Her Friends*. London: T. Hookham & J. Carpenter, 1792.

Richardson, Samuel. *Clarissa, or the History of a Young Lady.* 4 vols. London: Dutton/ Everyman, 1932.

Rousseau, Jean-Jacques. *Emile.* Translated by Barbara Foxley. New York: Dutton/ Everyman, 1974.

Ruskin, John. "Of Queens' Gardens." Pp. 74–119 in John Ruskin, *Sesame and Lilies.* New York: John Wiley & Son, 1865.

Shelley, Mary Wollstonecraft Godwin. *Frankenstein, or the Modern Prometheus.* The 1818 and 1831 texts, edited by James Rieger. Indianapolis; Bobbs-Merrill, 1974. Phoenix Paperback ed., Chicago: University of Chicago Press, 1982.

Smith, Adam. *The Theory of Moral Sentiments.* 2 vols. 10th ed. London: T. Cadell & W. Davies, 1804.

The Spectator, with Notes and a General Index. 2 vols. New York: Samuel Marks, 1826.

Wakefield, Priscilla. *Reflections on the Present Condition of the Female Sex, with Some Suggestions for Its Improvement.* 1798. Reprint, edited by Gina Luria. New York: Garland Press, 1974.

Wollstonecraft, Mary. *A Vindication of the Rights of Woman.* 1792. Reprint, edited by Carol H. Poston. New York: Norton, 1975.

Secondary Sources

Berger, D. G., and Wenger, M. G. "The Ideology of Virginity." *Journal of Marriage and the Family* 35 (1973): 666–76.

Bloom, Lillian D., and Bloom, Edward A. "Fanny Burney's Novels: The Retreat from Wonder." *Novel* 12 (1979): 215–35.

Bodek, Evelyn Gordon. "Salonières and Bluestockings: Educated Obsolescence and Germinating Feminism." *Feminist Studies* 3 (1976): 185–99.

Bogel, Fredric V. "The Rhetoric of Substantiality: Johnson and the Later Eighteenth Century." *Eighteenth-Century Studies* 12 (1979): 457–80.

Bond, Donovan H., and McLeod, W. Reynolds, eds. *Newsletters to Newspapers: Eighteenth-Century Journalism.* Morgantown: School of Journalism, West Virginia University, 1977.

Brissenden, R. F. *Virtue in Distress.* New York: Harper & Row, 1974.

Castle, Terry J. "*Amy,* Who Knew My Disease: A PsychoSexual Pattern in Defoe's *Roxana.*" *ELH* 46 (1979): 81–96.

Chabot. C. Barry. *Freud on Schreber: Psychoanalytic Theory and the Critical Act.* Amherst: University of Massachusetts Press, 1982.

Chodorow, Nancy. *The Reproduction of Mothering: Psychoanalysis and the Sociology of Gender.* Berkeley: University of California Press, 1978.

Clark, Alice. *Working Life of Women in the Seventeenth Century.* London: George Routledge & Sons, 1919.

Clinton, Katherine B. "Femme and Philosophe: Enlightenment Origins of Feminism." *Eighteenth-Century Studies* 8 (1974–75): 283–99.

Copeland, Edward. "What's a Competence? Jane Austen, Her Sister Novelists, and the 5%'s." *Modern Language Studies* 9 (1979): 161–68.

Cott, Nancy. *The Bonds of Womanhood: Woman's "Proper Sphere" in New England, 1770–1830.* New Haven: Yale University Press, 1977.

Davis, Natalie Zemon. " 'Women's History' in Transition: The European Case." *Feminist Studies* 3 (1976): 83–103.

George, Margaret. "From 'Goodwife' to 'Mistress': The Transformation of the Female in Bourgeois Culture." *Science & Society* 37 (1973): 152–77.

Gilbert, Sandra M., and Gubar, Susan. *The Madwoman in the Attic: The Woman Writer and the Nineteenth-Century Literary Imagination.* New Haven: Yale University Press, 1979.

Greene, Donald. "Latitudinarianism and Sensibility: The Genealogy of the 'Man of Feeling' Reconsidered." *Modern Philology* 75 (1977): 159–83.

Gubar, Susan. "The Female Monster in Augustan Satire." *Signs* 3 (1977): 380–94.

Gutwirth, Madelyn. *Madame de Staël, Novelist: The Emergence of the Artist as Woman.* Urbana: University of Illinois Press, 1978.

Habakkuk, H. J. "Marriage Settlements in the Eighteenth Century." *Transactions of the Royal Historical Society* 4th ser. 32 (1950): 15–30.

Halsband, Robert. "Ladies of Letters in the Eighteenth Century." In *The Lady of Letters in the Eighteenth Century,* edited by Irvin Ehrenpreis and Robert Halsband. Los Angeles: University of California Press, 1969.

Hays, H. R. *The Dangerous Sex: The Myth of Feminine Evil.* New York: G. P. Putnam's Sons, 1964.

Heilbrun, Carolyn, and Stimpson, Catharine. "Theories of Feminist Criticism: A Dialogue. Pp. 61–73 in *Feminist Literary Criticism: Explorations in Theory,* edited by Josephine Donovan. Lexington: University Press of Kentucky, 1975.

Hill, Christopher. *Milton and the English Revolution.* New York: Viking Press, 1977.

———.*Puritanism and Revolution: Studies in Interpretation of the English Revolution of the Seventeenth Century.* London: Mercury Books, 1962.

Houghton, Walter E. *The Victorian Frame of Mind, 1830–1870.* New Haven: Yale University Press, 1957.

Jaeger, Muriel. *Before Victoria.* London: Chatto & Windus, 1956.

Kamuf, Peggy. "Inside *Julie's* Closet." *Romantic Review* 69 (1978): 296–306.

———."Rousseau's Politics of Visibility." *Diacritics* 5 (1975): 51–56.

Kaplan, Cora. "The Indefinite Disclosed: Christina Rossetti and Emily Dickinson." Pp. 61–79 in *Women Writing and Writing about Women.* edited by Mary Jacobus. New York: Barnes & Noble, 1979.

Kramnick, Isaac. "Children's Literature and Bourgeois Ideology: Observations on Culture and Industrial Capitalism in the Later Eighteenth Century." Pp. 203–40 in *Culture and Politics from Puritanism to the Enlightenment,* edited by Perez Zagorin. Berkeley: University of California Press, 1980.

———.*The Rage of Edmund Burke: Portrait of an Ambivalent Conservative.* New York: Basic Books, 1977.

Landa, Louis A. "Pope's Belinda, the General Emporie of the World, and the Wondrous Worm." *South Atlantic Quarterly* 70 (1971): 215–35.

Laslett, Peter. *The World We Have Lost.* 2d ed. New York: Scribner's, 1971.

Latt, David J. "Praising Virtuous Ladies: The Literary Image and Historical Reality of Women in Seventeenth-Century England." Pp. 39–64 in *What Manner of Women: Essays on English and American Life and Literature,* edited by Marlene Springer. New York: New York University Press, 1977.

MacKinnon, Catherine A. "Feminism, Marxism, Method, and the State: An Agenda for Theory." *Signs: Journal of Women in Culture and Society* 7, no. 3 (Spring 1982): 515–44.

Mason, Shirlene. *Daniel Defoe and the Status of Women.* St. Alban's, Vt.: Eden Press, 1978.

McKendrick, Neil. "Home Demand and Economic Growth: A New View of the Role of Women and Children in the Industrial Revolution." Pp. 152–210 in *Historical Perspectives: Studies in English Thought and Society in Honor of J. H. Plumb,* edited by Neil McKendrick. London: Europa Publishers, 1974.

McKenzie, Alan T. "The Articulated Evil of Augustan Humanism." *Modern Language Studies* 9 (1979): 150–59.

McNamara, J. Ann. "Sexual Equality and the Cult of Virginity in Early Christian Thought." *Feminist Studies* 3 (1976): 145–58.

Miller, Nancy K. "Emphasis Added: Plots and Plausibilities in Women's Fiction."
   PMLA 96 (1981): 36–47.
———."The Exquisite Cadavers: Women in Eighteenth-Century Fiction." *Diacritics*
   5 (1975): 37–43.
———.*The Heroine's Text: Readings in the French and English Novel, 1722–1782.* New
   York: Columbia University Press, 1980.
Mitchell, Juliet. *Psychoanalysis and Feminism: Freud, Reich, Laing, and Women.* New York:
   Random House, 1975.
Okin, Susan Moller. *Women in Western Political Thought.* Princeton: Princeton Universi-
   ty Press, 1979.
O'Malley, Ida Beatrice. *Women in Subjection: A Study of the Lives of Englishwomen before
   1832.* London: Duckworth, 1933.
Perkin, Harold. *The Origins of Modern English Society, 1780–1880.* London: Routledge
   & Kegan Paul, 1969.
———."The Social Causes of the British Industrial Revolution." *Transactions of the
   Royal Historical Society* 5th ser. 18 (1968): 123–43.
Pollak, Ellen. "Comment on Susan Gubar's 'The Female Monster in Augustan Sat-
   ire.' " *Signs* 3 (1978): 728–33.
———."Re-reading *The Rape of the Lock*: Pope and the Paradox of Female Power."
   Pp. 429–44 in *Studies in Eighteenth-Century Culture,* vol. 10, edited by Harry C. Payne.
   Madison: University of Wisconsin Press, 1981.
Poovey, Mary. "Ideology and *The Mysteries of Udolpho.*" *Criticism* 21 (1979): 307–30.
Quinlan, Maurice J. *Victorian Prelude: A History of English Manners, 1700–1830.* New
   York: Columbia University Press, 1965.
Rougemont, Denis de. *Love in the Western World.* Translated by Montgomery Belgion.
   Rev. ed. New York: Harper & Row, 1956.
Rousseau, George S. "Nerves, Spirits, and Fibres: Towards Defining the Origins of
   Sensibility." Pp. 137–57 in *Studies in the Eighteenth Century,* vol. 3, edited by R. F.
   Brissenden and J. C. Eade. Canberra: Australian National University Press, 1976.
Shorter, Edward. "Capitalism, Culture, and Sexuality: Some Competing Models."
   Social Science Quarterly 53 (1972): 338–56.
Showalter, Elaine. *A Literature of Their Own: British Women Novelists from Brontë to Lessing.*
   Princeton: Princeton University Press, 1977.
Spacks, Patricia Meyer. " 'The Dangerous Age': Adolescence in Fielding, Richardson,
   Goldsmith, Burney & Smollett." *Eighteenth-Century Studies* 11 (1978): 417–38.
———."Ev'ry Woman Is at Heart a Rake." *Eighteenth-Century Studies* 8 (1974): 27–46.
———.*Imagining a Self: Autobiography and Novel in Eighteenth-Century England.* Cam-
   bridge, Mass.: Harvard University Press, 1976.
———."Reflecting Women." *Yale Review* 63 (1973): 26–42.
———."Self as Subject: A Female Language." Pp. 110–14 in *In/Sights: Self-Portraits
   by Women,* compiled by Joyce Tenneson Cohen. Boston: D. R. Godine, 1978.
Springer, Marlene, ed. *What Manner of Women: Essays on English and American Life and
   Literature.* New York: New York University Press, 1977.
Stearns, Bertha Monica. "Early English Periodicals for Ladies (1700–1760)." *PMLA* 48
   (1933): 38–60.
Stone, Lawrence. *The Family, Sex, and Marriage in England, 1500–1800.* New York:
   Harper & Row, 1977.
Tanner, Tony. *Adultery in the Novel: Contract and Transgression.* Baltimore: Johns Hop-
   kins University Press, 1980.
Taylor, Gordon Rattray. *The Angel-Makers: A Study in the Psychological Origins of Historical
   Change, 1750–1850.* London: Heinemann, 1958.
Thomas, Keith. "The Double Standard." *Journal of the History of Ideas* 20 (1959):
   195–216.

Thompson, E. P. *The Making of the English Working Class.* New York: Random House/
  Vintage, 1966.
Tompkins, J. M. S. *The Popular Novel in England: 1770–1800.* Lincoln: University of
  Nebraska Press, 1961.
Utter, Robert Palfrey, and Needham, Gwendolyn Bridges. *Pamela's Daughters.* New
  York: Macmillan, 1936.
Watt, Ian. *The Rise of the Novel.* Berkeley: University of California Press, 1957.
White, Cynthia L. *Women's Magazines, 1693–1968.* London: Michael Joseph, 1972.
Wilt, Judith. "He Could Go No Farther: A Modest Proposal about Lovelace and
  Clarissa." *PMLA* 92 (1977): 19–32.
Wood, Neal. "The Aesthetic Dimension of Burke's Political Thought." *Journal of
  British Studies* 4 (1964): 41–64.
Woolf, Virginia. "Women and Fiction." Pp. 141–48 in Virginia Woolf, *Collected Essays,*
  vol. 2, edited by Leonard Woolf. London: Chatto & Windus, 1966.

Chapters 2 and 3. Mary Wollstonecraft

Primary Sources
Wollstonecraft, Mary. *Collected Letters of Mary Wollstonecraft.* Edited by Ralph M. War-
  dle. Ithaca: Cornell University Press, 1979.
————.*Letters Written during a Short Residence in Sweden, Norway and Denmark.* Edited
  by Carol H. Poston. Lincoln: University of Nebraska Press, 1976.
————.*Maria, or The Wrongs of Woman.* Edited by Moira Ferguson. New York: Norton,
  1975.
————.*Mary, A Fiction.* Edited by Gary Kelly. London: Oxford University Press, 1976.
————.*A Vindication of the Rights of Men, in a Letter to the Right Honourable Edmund Burke;
  Occasioned by His "Reflections on the Revolution in France."* Facsimile ed. Gainesville,
  Fla: Scholar's Facsimiles & Reprints, 1963.
————.*A Vindication of the Rights of Woman.* Edited by Carol H. Poston. New York:
  Norton, 1975.
————.*A Wollstonecraft Anthology.* Edited by Janet M. Todd. Bloomington: Indiana
  University Press, 1977.

Secondary Sources
Auerbach, Nina. *Communities of Women: An Idea in Fiction.* Cambridge, Mass.: Harvard
  University Press, 1978.
Boos, Florence. "Review of Wollstonecraft's *Letters Written . . . in Sweden,* ed. Carol
  H. Poston." *Eighteenth-Century Studies* 10 (1976–77): 280–81.
Boulton, James T. *The Language of Politics in the Age of Wilkes and Burke.* London:
  Routledge & Kegan Paul, 1963.
Evans, Mary Anne [George Eliot]. "Margaret Fuller and Mary Wollstonecraft." Pp.
  199–206 in *Essays of George Eliot,* edited by Thomas Pinney. New York: Columbia
  University Press, 1963.
Fairchild, Hoxie Neale. *The Noble Savage: A Study in Romantic Naturalism.* New York:
  Russell & Russell, 1961.
George, Margaret. *One Woman's "Situation": A Study of Mary Wollstonecraft.* Urbana and
  Chicago: University of Illinois Press, 1970.
Godwin, William. *Memoirs of Mary Wollstonecraft.* Edited by W. Clark Durant. London:
  Constable, 1927.
Jacobus, Mary. "The Difference of View." Pp. 10–21 in *Women Writing and Writing
  about Women,* edited by Mary Jacobus. New York: Barnes & Noble, 1979.
Jones, Howard Mumford. *Revolution and Romanticism.* Cambridge: Harvard University
  Press, 1974.

Kelly, Gary. "Mary Wollstonecraft as *Vir Bonus.*" *English Studies in Canada* 5 (1979): 275–91.

Myers, Mitzi. "Mary Wollstonecraft's *Letters Written . . . in Sweden*: Toward Romantic Autobiography." Pp. 165–85 in *Studies in Eighteenth-Century Culture,* edited by Roseann Runte. Madison: University of Wisconsin Press, 1979.

————."Unfinished Business: Wollstonecraft's *Maria.*" *Wordsworth Circle* 11 (1980): 107–14.

Poston, Carol H. Introduction to Mary Wollstonecraft, *Letters Written . . . in Sweden,* edited by Carol H. Poston. Lincoln: University of Nebraska Press, 1976.

"Reflections on the Character of Mary Wollstonecraft Godwin." *The Monthly Magazine and American Review* 1 (1799): 330–35.

Sapiro, Virginia. "Feminist Studies and the Discipline: A Study of Mary Wollstonecraft." *University of Michigan Papers in Women's Studies* 1 (1974): 178–200.

Sunstein, Emily W. *A Different Face: The Life of Mary Wollstonecraft.* Boston: Little, Brown, 1975.

Todd, Janet M. "The Language of Sex in *A Vindication of the Rights of Woman.*" *Mary Wollstonecraft Newsletter* 1 (1973): 10–17.

Tomalin, Claire. *The Life and Death of Mary Wollstonecraft.* London: Weidenfeld & Nicolson, 1974.

Walters, Margaret. "The Rights and Wrongs of Women: Mary Wollstonecraft, Harriet Martineau, Simone de Beauvoir." Pp. 304–78 in *The Rights and Wrongs of Women,* edited by Juliet Mitchell and Ann Oakley. Harmondsworth, Eng.: Penguin Books, 1976.

Wardle, Ralph M. *Mary Wollstonecraft: A Critical Biography.* Lawrence: University of Kansas Press, 1951.

Williams, Raymond. *Keywords: A Vocabulary of Culture and Society.* New York: Oxford University Press, 1976.

Chapters 4 and 5. Mary Shelley

Primary Sources

Godwin, William. *The Elopement of Percy Shelley and Mary Wollstonecraft Godwin as Narrated by William Godwin.* With commentary by H. Buxton Forman. Privately printed, 1911.

Shelley, Mary Wollstonecraft Godwin. *Falkner, A Novel.* New York: Harper & Bros., 1837.

————.*The Fortunes of Perkin Warbeck, A Romance.* 3 vols. London: Henry Colburn, 1830.

————.*Frankenstein, or the Modern Prometheus.* Edited by James Rieger. Indianapolis: Bobbs-Merrill, 1974.

————.*The Last Man.* Edited by Hugh J. Luke, Jr. Lincoln: University of Nebraska Press, 1965.

————.*The Letters of Mary Wollstonecraft Shelley.* 2 vols. Edited by Betty T. Bennett. Baltimore: Johns Hopkins University Press, 1980.

————.*The Letters of Mary W. Shelley.* 2 vols. Edited by Frederick L. Jones. Norman: University of Oklahoma Press, 1944.

————.*Lodore.* New York: Wallis & Newell, 1835.

————.*Mary Shelley's Journal.* Edited by Frederick L. Jones. Norman: University of Oklahoma Press, 1947.

————.*Mathilda.* Edited by Elizabeth Nitchie. In *Studies in Philology,* Extra Series 3. Chapel Hill: University of North Carolina Press, 1959.

————.*My Best Mary: The Selected Letters of Mary Wollstonecraft Shelley.* Edited by Muriel Spark and Derek Stanford. London: Allan Wingate, 1953.

————.*Valperga: Or, the Life and Adventures of Castruccio, Prince of Lucca.* 3 vols. London: G. & W. B. Whittaker, 1823.

Shelley, Percy Bysshe. "A Defence of Poetry, or Remarks Suggested by an Essay Entitled 'The Four Ages of Poetry.' " Pp. 478–508 in *Shelley's Poetry and Prose,* edited by Donald H. Reiman and Sharon B. Powers. New York: Norton, 1977.

————.*The Letters of Percy Bysshe Shelley.* 2 vols. Edited by Frederick L. Jones. Oxford: Clarendon Press, 1964.

————.*Shelley: Poetical Works.* Edited by Thomas Hutchinson. New edition, corrected by G. M. Matthews. London: Oxford University Press, 1970.

Secondary Sources

Anti-Jacobin Review and Magazine; or Monthly Political and Literary Censor 1 (1798): 91–102.

Brooks, Peter. "Godlike Science/Unhallowed Arts: Language and Monstrosity in *Frankenstein.*" *New Literary History* 9 (1978): 591–605.

Ellis, Kate. "Monsters in the Garden: Mary Shelley and the Bourgeois Family." Pp. 123–42 in Levine and Knoepflmacher, eds., *The Endurance of "Frankenstein": Essays on Mary Shelley's Novel* (see below).

The European Magazine, and London Review, Containing the Literature, History, Politics, Arts, Manners & Amusements of the Age 33 (1978): 246–51.

Friedman, Michael H. *The Making of a Tory Humanist: William Wordsworth and the Idea of Community.* New York: Columbia University Press, 1979.

Grylls, R. Glynn. *Mary Shelley: A Biography.* London: Oxford University Press, 1938.

Homans, Margaret. "Dreaming of Children: Literalization in *Jane Eyre* and *Wuthering Heights.*" Unpublished essay, Yale University, 1979.

————.*Women Writers and Poetic Identity: Dorothy Wordsworth, Emily Brontë, and Emily Dickinson.* Princeton: Princeton University Press, 1980.

Knoepflmacher, U. C. "Thoughts on the Aggression of Daughters." Pp. 88–119 in Levine and Knoepflmacher, eds., *The Endurance of "Frankenstein,"* (see below).

The Lady's Monthly Museum, or Polite Repository of Amusement and Instruction 3 (1799): 433–35.

Levine, George, and Knoepflmacher, U.C., eds. *The Endurance of "Frankenstein": Essays on Mary Shelley's Novel.* Berkeley: University of California Press, 1979.

Marshall, Mrs. Julian. *The Life & Letters of Mary Wollstonecraft Shelley.* 2 vols. London: Richard Bentley & Son, 1889.

Moers, Ellen. *Literary Women: The Great Writers.* Garden City, N.Y.: Doubleday, 1977.

Nitchie, Elizabeth. *Mary Shelley: Author of "Frankenstein."* New Brunswick, N.J.: Rutgers University Press, 1953.

Scott, Peter Dale. "Vital Artifice: Mary, Percy, and the Psychopolitical Integrity of *Frankenstein.*" Pp. 172–202 in Levine and Knoepflmacher, eds., *The Endurance of "Frankenstein."*

Snyder, Robert Lance. "Apocalypse and Indeterminacy in Mary Shelley's *The Last Man.*" *Studies in Romanticism* 17 (1978): 435–52.

Spark, Muriel. *Child of Light: A Reassessment of Mary Wollstonecraft Shelley.* Hadleigh, Eng.: Tower Bridge, 1951.

Sterrenburg, Lee. "*The Last Man*: Anatomy of Failed Revolutions." *Nineteenth-Century Fiction* 33 (1978): 324–47.

————."Mary Shelley's Monster: Politics and Psyche in *Frankenstein.*" Pp. 143–71 in Levine and Knoepflmacher, eds., *The Endurance of "Frankenstein."*

Chapters 6 and 7. Jane Austen

Primary Sources

Austen, Jane. *Jane Austen's Letters to Her Sister Cassandra and Others.* 2 vols. Edited by
R. W. Chapman. Oxford: Clarendon Press, 1932.

———.*The Works of Jane Austen.* Edited by R. W. Chapman. 6 vols. London: Oxford
University Press, 1926 (vols. 1–5), 1954 (vol. 6).

Secondary Sources

Auerbach, Nina. "Austen and Alcott on Matriarchy: New Women or New Wives?"
Novel 10 (1976): 6–26.

———."O Brave New World: Evolution and Revolution in *Persuasion.*" *ELH* 39
(1972):112–28.

Austen-Leigh, J. E. *A Memoir of Jane Austen.* 2d ed. London: Macmillan, 1906.

Austen-Leigh, William, and Austen-Leigh, Richard Arthur. *Jane Austen: Her Life and
Letters: A Family Record.* 2d ed. New York: Russell & Russell, 1965.

Booth, Wayne C. *A Rhetoric of Irony.* Chicago: University of Chicago Press, 1974.

———.*The Rhetoric of Fiction.* Chicago: University of Chicago Press, 1961. 2d rev. ed.,
1983.

Bradbrook, Frank W. *Jane Austen and Her Predecessors.* Cambridge, Eng.: At the University Press, 1967.

Brissenden, R. F. "*Mansfield Park*: Freedom and the Family." Pp. 156–71 in Halperin,
ed., *Jane Austen: Bicentenary Essays* (see below).

———."*La Philosophie dans le Boudoir*; Or, A Young Lady's Entrance into the World."
Pp. 113–42 in *Irrationalism in the Eighteenth Century,* edited by Harold E. Pagliaro.
Studies in Eighteenth-Century Culture, no. 3. Cleveland: The Press of Case Western
Reserve University, 1972.

Brower, Reuben A. *The Fields of Light: An Experiment in Critical Reading.* London:
Oxford University Press, 1951.

Brown, Julia Prewitt. *Jane Austen's Novels: Social Change and Literary Form.* Cambridge,
Mass.: Harvard University Press, 1979.

Brown, Lloyd W. *Bits of Ivory: Narrative Techniques in Jane Austen's Fiction.* Baton Rouge:
Louisiana State University Press, 1973.

———."The Business of Marrying and Mothering." Pp. 27–43 in McMaster, ed., *Jane
Austen's Achievement* (see below).

———."Jane Austen and the Feminist Tradition." *Nineteenth-Century Fiction* 28 (1973):
321–338.

Burgan, Mary A. "Mr. Bennet and the Failures of Fatherhood in Jane Austen's
Novels." *Journal of English and German Philology* 74 (1975): 536–52.

Burlin, Katrin Ristkok. " 'The Pen of the Contriver': The Four Fictions of *Northanger
Abbey.*" Pp. 89–111 in Halperin, ed., *Jane Austen: Bicentenary Essays* (see below).

Butler, Marilyn. *Jane Austen and the War of Ideas.* Oxford: Clarendon Press, 1975.

Chapman, R. W. *Jane Austen: Facts and Problems.* Oxford: Clarendon Press, 1948.

Corsa, Helen Storm. "A Fair but Frozen Maid: A Study of Jane Austen's *Emma.*"
Literature and Psychology 19 (1969): 101–23.

Duckworth, Alistair M. *The Improvement of the Estate: A Study of Jane Austen's Novels.*
Baltimore: Johns Hopkins University Press, 1971.

Fergus, Jan. "Sex and Social Life in Jane Austen." Pp. 66–85 in Monaghan, ed., *Jane
Austen in a Social Context* (see below).

Fleishman, Avrom. *A Reading of "Mansfield Park": An Essay in Critical Synthesis.* Minneapolis: University of Minnesota Press, 1967.

Gonrall, J. F. G. "Marriage and Property in Jane Austen's Novels." *History Today* 17
(1967): 805–11.

Greene, Donald J. "Jane Austen and the Peerage." *PMLA* 68 (1953): 1017–31.

Halperin, John, ed. *Jane Austen: Bicentenary Essays.* Cambridge, Eng.: At the University Press, 1975.

Hodge, Jane Aiken. "Jane Austen and Her Publishers." Pp. 75–85 in Halperin, ed., *Jane Austen: Bicentenary Essays.*

————.*Only a Novel: The Double Life of Jane Austen.* New York: Coward, McCann & Geoghegan, 1972.

Hogan, Charles Beecher. "Jane Austen and Her Early Public." *Review of English Studies* n.s. 1 (1950): 39–54.

Lascelles, Mary. *Jane Austen and Her Art.* Oxford: Clarendon Press, 1939.

Lenta, Margaret. "Jane Austen's Feminism." *Critical Inquiry* 23 (1981): 27–35.

Levine, George. "Translating the Monstrous: *Northanger Abbey.*" *Nineteenth-Century Fiction* 30 (1975): 335–50.

Litz, A. Walton. " 'A Development of Self': Character and Personality in Jane Austen's Fiction." Pp. 64–78 in McMaster, ed., *Jane Austen's Achievement* (see below).

————."The Achievement of Jane Austen." *Key Reporter* 44 (1979): 2–4, 8.

————.*Jane Austen: A Study of Her Artistic Development.* New York: Oxford University Press, 1965.

————."*Persuasion*: Forms of Estrangement." Pp. 221–32 in Halperin, ed., *Jane Austen: Bicentenary Essays.*

Lovell, Terry. "Jane Austen and the Gentry: A Study in Literature and Ideology." Pp. 15–37 in *The Sociology of Literature: Applied Studies,* edited by Diana Laurenson. Hanley, Eng.: Wood Mitchell & Co., 1978.

McMaster, Juliet, ed. *Jane Austen's Achievement.* London: Macmillan, 1976.

Moler, Kenneth L. "The Two Voices of Fanny Price." Pp. 172–73 in Halperin, ed., *Jane Austen: Bicentenary Essays.*

Monaghan, David, ed. *Jane Austen in a Social Context.* Totowa, N.J.: Barnes & Noble, 1981.

Moore, E. Margaret. "Emma and Miss Bates: Early Experiences in Separation and the Theme of Dependency in Jane Austen's Novels." *Studies in English Literature* 9 (1969): 573–85.

Mudrick, Marvin. *Jane Austen, Irony as Defense and Discovery.* Berkeley: University of California Press, 1968.

Nardin, Jane. "Jane Austen and the Problem of Leisure." Pp. 122–42 in Monaghan, ed., *Jane Austen in a Social Context.*

————.*Those Elegant Decorums: The Concept of Propriety in Jane Austen's Novels.* Albany: State University of New York Press, 1973.

Page, Norman. *The Language of Jane Austen.* New York: Barnes & Noble, 1972.

Paris, Bernard J. *Character and Conflict in Jane Austen's Novels: A Psychological Approach.* Detroit: Wayne State University Press, 1978.

Price, Martin. "Manners, Morals, and Jane Austen." *Nineteenth-Century Fiction* 30 (1975): 261–80.

Roberts, Warren. *Jane Austen and the French Revolution.* New York: St. Martin's Press, 1979.

Schorer, Mark. "Fiction and the 'Matrix of Analogy.' " *Kenyon Review* 11 (1949): 541–60.

————."The Humiliation of Emma Woodhouse." Pp. 76–97 in *Jane Austen: A Collection of Critical Essays,* edited by Ian Watt. Englewood Cliffs, N.J.: Prentice-Hall, 1963.

Simpson, David. *Irony and Authority in Romantic Poetry.* Totowa, N.J.: Rowman & Littlefield, 1979.

Smith, Leroy W. "*Mansfield Park*: The Revolt of the 'Feminine' Woman." Pp. 143–58 in Monaghan, ed., *Jane Austen in a Social Context.*

Southam, Brian C. *Jane Austen's Literary Manuscripts: A Study of the Novelist's Development through the Surviving Papers.* London: Oxford University Press, 1964.

————."*Sanditon*: the Seventh Novel." Pp. 1–26 in McMaster, ed., *Jane Austen's Achievement.*

Spacks, Patricia Meyer. "Muted Discord: Generational Conflict in Jane Austen." Pp. 159–79 in Monaghan, ed., *Jane Austen in a Social Context.*

Swingle, L. J. "The Poets, the Novelists, and the English Romantic Situation." *Wordsworth Circle* 3 (1979): 218–28.

Tanner, Tony. "In Between—Anne Elliot Marries a Sailor and Charlotte Heywood Goes to the Seaside." Pp. 180–94 in Monaghan, ed., *Jane Austen in a Social Context.*

————.Introduction to Jane Austen, *Mansfield Park,* edited by Tony Tanner. Harmondsworth, Eng.: Penguin Books, 1966.

————.Introduction to Jane Austen, *Sense and Sensibility,* edited by Tony Tanner. Harmondsworth, Eng.: Penguin Books, 1969.

Trilling, Lionel. "*Mansfield Park.*" In Lionel Trilling, *The Opposing Self: Nine Essays in Criticism.* New York: Viking Press, 1955.

————.*Sincerity and Authenticity.* London: Oxford University Press, 1972.

Webb, Igor. *From Custom to Capital: The English Novel and the Industrial Revolution.* Ithaca and London: Cornell University Press, 1981.

Index